John Sherren Brewer

English studies: Essays in English history and literature

Edited with a prefatory memoir by Henry Wace

John Sherren Brewer

English studies: Essays in English history and literature
Edited with a prefatory memoir by Henry Wace

ISBN/EAN: 9783744715416

Printed in Europe, USA, Canada, Australia, Japan

Cover: Foto ©Paul-Georg Meister /pixelio.de

More available books at **www.hansebooks.com**

ENGLISH STUDIES

OR

ESSAYS

IN

ENGLISH HISTORY AND LITERATURE

BY THE LATE J. S. BREWER M.A.

PREACHER AT THE ROLLS
PROFESSOR OF ENGLISH LITERATURE AND MODERN HISTORY
IN KING'S COLLEGE LONDON

EDITED WITH A PREFATORY MEMOIR

By HENRY WACE M.A.

PREACHER OF LINCOLN'S INN
PROFESSOR OF ECCLESIASTICAL HISTORY IN KING'S COLLEGE LONDON

LONDON
JOHN MURRAY, ALBEMARLE STREET
1881

All rights reserved

LONDON: PRINTED BY
SPOTTISWOODE AND CO., NEW-STREET SQUARE
AND PARLIAMENT STREET

CONTENTS.

	PAGE
PREFATORY MEMOIR	vii
LIST OF MR. BREWER'S PUBLICATIONS	xl
A SERMON ON *The Psalmist of Israel*	xli

ESSAYS.

ON NEW SOURCES OF ENGLISH HISTORY	1
ON GREEN'S SHORT HISTORY OF THE ENGLISH PEOPLE	50
ON HATFIELD HOUSE	104
ON THE STUARTS	162
ON SHAKSPEARE	208
ON THE STUDY OF SHAKSPEARE	273
ON THE ROYAL SUPREMACY	297
PASSAGES FROM THE LIFE OF ERASMUS	344
ON THE STUDY OF HISTORY	379
ON THE STUDY OF ENGLISH HISTORY	400
ON ANCIENT LONDON	424

PREFATORY MEMOIR.

THE intrinsic interest of the essays contained in this volume, together with the high reputation of their author as a historian, a scholar, and a divine, might seem to render it unnecessary to recommend them to the attention of the reader by any prefatory observations. But, in addition to the value they will otherwise possess, it is hoped they will serve as some memorial of a character and a career which ought to be better known, and which deserve to be permanently remembered. The circumstances, indeed, of the author's life which concern other than private friends are few and simple. But they are connected with some of the chief movements of thought during the last half-century; they add a peculiar value to all he wrote, and a knowledge of them will enhance the interest of this volume. He had also a very large number of friends and pupils—among whom the present writer had the privilege of being numbered—who will be grateful for a brief record of his life and work.

John Sherren Brewer was born in the year 1810,

and was descended from an old Kentish family. His father, who had the same Christian names, was born in the communion of the Church of England, but joined that of the Baptists. He was a learned Biblical scholar, and devoted himself during his spare hours to the study of Hebrew. He naturally held a high position among the Dissenters, and for many years conducted with great success a school at Norwich. Out of a very large family, only four sons arrived at man's estate, of whom the eldest is the subject of this memoir. Notwithstanding his father's dissenting predilections he was sent to Oxford, and after a short time joined the Church of England. But the years he had passed in a dissenting communion were probably the origin of one branch of his extensive reading. He possessed a most intimate and most rare knowledge of the writings of the Puritans; and this circumstance adds a special value to the views he subsequently held respecting the history of the Stuart times. At Oxford he took a First Class *In Litteris Humanioribus* in one of the most distinguished years of a period when the class lists in that school contained a remarkable number of names which have since become eminent. There were only two other members of the same First Class in Easter term, 1832, one the present Lord Blachford, then Mr. Frederick Rogers, the other Sir Francis Doyle. Traditions are still current at Oxford of the unusual range of reading in which Mr. Brewer offered to be examined. He became a singular master of the most characteristic scholarship of that university, and his whole mind was imbued with its classical and philosophical influences.

His subsequent career at Oxford was, however, but brief. He married very early, and was thus precluded from obtaining a Fellowship. He resided, however, at the university for a while, giving instruction as a private tutor; and an edition of Aristotle's 'Ethics' which he prepared during this period, though long out of print, still maintains a place among the text-books on that subject, and is valued for some peculiar excellences. But his wife's father lost his fortune soon after their marriage; death and infirmity befell his children; and amidst domestic troubles and afflictions he removed to London. Here the whole of his subsequent career was passed. It was a laborious and anxious, and often a troubled one; but it brought into full activity his various energies and capacities, and called into play for the purposes of an active professional life all the culture and learning with which he left the university. He ceased to be only a scholar; but the influences of a very refined scholarship added, to the last, an unusual grace and delicacy to all his literary work.

It was by another of the influences of the Oxford life of those days that the commencement of his career in London would seem to have been determined. He had heartily joined the movement of religious thought into which so large a proportion of the younger members of the university were then drawn, and he was admitted to some intimacy with its leader, the present Cardinal Newman. He conceived for Dr. Newman a deep admiration and a warm attachment; in spite of their subsequent separation in thought and life, he retained to the last that attachment and admiration; and friendly letters from time to time passed between them with reference to Mr. Brewer's publications. Under the religious convictions thus fostered he resolved to enter the ministry of the Church, and he was ordained deacon on December 17, 1837. The choice of his sphere of work was eminently characteristic of him, and marks, perhaps, his sympathy with one of the noblest aspects of the Oxford movement. On the day of his ordination he became chaplain of the workhouse of the joint parishes of St. Giles's in the Fields and St. George's, Bloomsbury.

It might seem at first a very strange duty for a man of such training and such capacities to undertake. It is probably difficult in the present day to realise the circumstances amidst which he had to work. A new workhouse has now been built in Endell Street, and some of the worst parts of St. Giles's parish have been cleared away by the reconstruction of neighbouring streets. Great changes have been introduced into workhouse management; it was then simpler and less formal than at present; and the chaplain would naturally be brought more closely in contact with the ordinary circumstances of the suffering poor. In this workhouse, and amongst these poor people, Mr. Brewer worked for nearly eight years, until July 1845. About the same time as he undertook this duty he obtained some employment at the British Museum, and in 1839 he was appointed Lecturer in Classical Literature at King's College, London, when the present Archdeacon of Bath, the Venerable R. W. Browne, was Professor in the same department. But in none of his work was he more deeply interested than in that of the chaplaincy of the St. Giles's workhouse; and he delighted in bestowing upon it all the time he could spare from his work at the college. The religious services used to be held in the dining hall, as there was no chapel, and they must have offered but meagre opportunities for any development of ceremonial. But one of Mr. Brewer's first acts was to get together the boys and some of the men and women, and teach them to sing the Psalms to the Gregorian chants. The present chaplain to the workhouse, the Rev. John Swayne, states that Mr. Brewer is still remembered with pleasure and gratitude by some poor people whom he had under his charge forty years ago. The other day, says Mr. Swayne, the face and voice of one of them, whom Mr. Brewer prepared for confirmation, quite brightened up when asked if she remembered him; and she went on to tell how on alternate Sundays the school boys and girls went to his house during the preparation, and how kindly they were received. Another, who is now a servant in the church in Endell Street, recalled at once some little kindnesses he had shown her in an illness; and speaking of another suffering woman, now dead, on whom he bestowed great care, she said:—'Mr.

Brewer thought a great deal of her, I believe,' and then added spontaneously : ' In fact, I think he did think a great deal of all his people.' By ' a great deal ' Mr. Swayne understood this witness to mean ' very highly,' as though he saw the best in them, with eyes of sympathy, and not the worst. Such reminiscences, suddenly recalled after so long a time, afford a striking testimony to the devotion which Mr. Brewer must have bestowed upon this simple and often painful work. Perhaps his experience at this time deepened in his mind a sense, which was very characteristic of him, of the sacredness of common humanity, and gave a depth and solidity to his subsequent work as a scholar and man of letters.[1]

A scheme, however, was set on foot for erecting the church now adjoining the workhouse in Endell Street, its incumbency being united with the chaplaincy, and it was proposed that Mr. Brewer should be the first incumbent. He took great interest in the scheme, and it led him to the acquisition of one of his many accomplishments—that of a most remarkable knowledge of architecture. No doubt in this study he was partly influenced by his sympathy with the revival of ecclesiastical art and ceremonial; and he pursued it with a thoroughness characteristic of all his work. For some few years a good deal of his spare time was bestowed in measuring churches and other old buildings, and making careful models of them to scale. These models were made of card-

[1] In a volume published in 1855, entitled *Lectures to Ladies on Practical Subjects*, will be found a Lecture by Mr. Brewer on *Workhouse Visiting*.

board and the bark of the fir-tree, and were wonderfully accurate. But in the immediate purpose of his new study he was disappointed; a difference of opinion with the Rector of St. Giles's led to his declining the incumbency; and this involved his abandonment of the chaplaincy. His withdrawal from the workhouse marked the close for a while of his ministerial work. He had assisted Mr. Dodsworth, who was one of the leading clergymen of the High Church party, in his church in Albany Street, and he also officiated for a while at Ely Chapel, in Ely Place. But for some years he held no cure.

These years, however, were a period of great importance in the growth of his thoughts. About this time several leading members of the High Church party, and among them some of his best friends, joined the communion of the Church of Rome, and his mind deeply felt the strain which this defection occasioned. Like many others among the High Churchmen, he became attracted by a strong personal influence which had been making itself felt in opposition, though not in antagonism, to the Oxford school. He became warmly attached to the late Mr. Maurice, and entered with ardent sympathy into his general way of thought. He afterwards differed from him much in particulars; but he always had a high admiration of his genius; and he appreciated the aspect of truth which Mr. Maurice represented no less heartily than that which he had learned from Dr. Newman. Mr. Maurice became Professor of English Literature and Modern History at King's College in 1840, the year after Mr. Brewer became Classical Lecturer, and for some twelve years they were in every sense colleagues. Mr. Brewer co-operated very earnestly and generously with Mr. Maurice in his labours on behalf of the artisan class, and ultimately succeeded him as head of the Working Men's College, in Great Ormond Street, after having bestowed invaluable labour in lecturing there for many years.

It was characteristic of him, throughout his life, thus to appreciate the various elements of truth by which the great movements of his age were animated; and there was a very generous feature in his mind which was exhibited on such occasions. His sympathy was always strongly evoked for causes or for men when they were struggling against misconception and were unpopular, while he seemed to be put upon his guard towards them as soon as they became successful. As long, for instance, as it was somewhat of a reproach, and rather against a man's interests, to be regarded as a Tractarian, Mr. Brewer held firmly to the party; but as soon as they became fashionable he began to be interested in the new Broad Church party, which was struggling into influence through obloquy. This seemed to be an inveterate habit in his mind; and he was consistently on the side of Cato against the divinities of the hour. No matter whether it was the Tractarians, or Mr. Maurice, or Bishop Colenso, or the Athanasian Creed, or the Irish Church, some warm sympathy was sure to be given by him to the truth or the party which was being overridden under the predominant popular impulse. This temper of mind deserves the more to be dwelt upon, because it was probably connected with his power as an historian. It was peculiarly his gift to be able to enter—not so much with impartiality as with equal sympathy—into the views and feelings of the opposing parties whose struggles were worked out in history, and he was thus able to depict such struggles with their due lights and shades, and to exhibit reaction ever side by side with action. This was, indeed, a characteristic feature of Mr. Maurice's teaching; but the historical genius with which it was applied by Mr. Brewer was peculiarly his own.

At length a new sphere was opened to him, at once in his historical studies and in the Church. In 1857 he was appointed by the late Lord Romilly to the office of Reader at the Rolls Chapel, and he afterwards succeeded to the Preachership. The pulpit in which Bishop Butler's Sermons on Human Nature had been delivered was eminently suited to him. The movement of life towards the west had diminished the congregation of the chapel; but the select audience who attended were peculiarly capable of appreciating his thoughtful and scholarly sermons. They were for the most part meditative expositions of Scripture, characterised at once by the inductive method of interpretation which was most congenial to him, and frequently illuminated by his historical genius. It seemed to be always his main aim to penetrate into the true original meaning of the text he was considering, and he was never content with merely making a useful application of the current apprehension of it. His predecessor, Bishop Butler, said[1] he had often wished 'that it had been the custom to lay before people nothing in matters of argument but premises, and leave them to draw conclusions themselves; which, though it could not be done in all cases, might in many.' Mr. Brewer's modesty rendered this method very congenial to him; and his sermons not unfrequently seemed unconsciously constructed on some such plan. Discourses of this nature could not well be popular, but they were often deeply instructive. Sometimes, however, he would surrender himself to that current of sympathy with the struggles of human life which was ever flowing strongly within him, and would draw some vivid and touching picture of one of the great characters of the sacred history. It would not have been in accordance with the design of this volume to include any selection from his sermons, but a notice of his life and character would be wholly incomplete which did not afford some illustration of his deeper thoughts and feelings as a Christian preacher. At the end of this memoir, therefore, a sermon is printed[2] on 'The Character of David,' which exhibits a singularly beautiful combination of pious feeling, historic penetration, and almost poetic power of description.

But from about the time of his appointment to

[1] Preface to the Sermons.
[2] It appeared in the *People's Magazine* of the Society for Promoting Christian Knowledge in 1871, and is reprinted by permission.

this office at the Rolls Chapel the principal work of his life was divided between original historical studies at the Rolls Office, and lectures on history and literature at King's College, London. He was entrusted by the Master of the Rolls with the task of calendaring the papers in the Public Records relating to the reign of Henry VIII., and during the whole remainder of his life he devoted himself to this duty with an energy and a generosity to which justice can be done only by those who, from their own experience, are able to understand the immense labour as well as learning which it needed. A general description of the great national undertaking in which he bore this important part is given by Mr. Brewer himself in the first of the essays reprinted in this volume. But of his own work the best account which can be given in this brief memoir will be furnished by the following extract from the preface which Mr. James Gairdner has prefixed to the volume of Henry VIII.'s Papers just published. Mr. Gairdner succeeded him in the work, and was for many years his constant coadjutor and friend. He says:—

'Since the appearance of the last volume of this Calendar the work has been carried on under peculiar disadvantages, owing to the death of its original editor, the Rev. J. S. Brewer, which occurred when the materials of the present volume had been nearly got ready for the press. The loss, under any circumstances, must have been a great one; but, differing as this Calendar does from all the others of the same series, and requiring very special conditions for its successful execution, only those who are particularly interested in the work can appreciate the drawback to its future progress. To Mr. Brewer its whole plan was due—a design of considerable originality in its conception; and it was by his unflagging energy that the publication had been thus far completed in the face of obstacles which would certainly have cooled the ardour and worn out the spirit of any man less thoroughly intent on doing a good work entirely for its own sake. Historical students will not require to be informed of the remarkable and unique qualifications he possessed for a task which has now unavoidably fallen to less able hands. A man of extensive and varied reading, of careful and accurate thought, of altogether unusual breadth of view and fulness of information on every period of history and literature, especially the history and literature of his own country—he had been long familiar with historical MSS., both in the Public Record Office and elsewhere, when he was invited by the late Lord Romilly to take part in the work of cataloguing the National archives. The period assigned to him—the reign of Henry VIII.—was one which he at once perceived could only be treated satisfactorily on a larger and more comprehensive plan than that of the other Calendars; and, having submitted his scheme to the Master of the Rolls, he obtained authority to proceed with the work on the lines laid down by himself for its execution.

'Of this scheme and the reasons which led to its

adoption, a detailed explanation is given by Mr. Brewer himself in the Preface to the first volume of the work. But it may not be unadvisable in this place to remind the reader of its principal features, and relate briefly the process by which it was carried out. The papers of the reign of Henry VIII., which were deposited in the Public Record Office at the time when Mr. Brewer began his labours, formed only a minute portion of a large collection, of which the greater part was divided between the British Museum and the State Paper Office. Originally, there cannot be a doubt, the whole of that collection was deposited in the Treasury of the Exchequer. But early in the seventeenth century a large portion of it was abstracted by Sir Robert Cotton, and went towards the formation of his celebrated library now in the British Museum. In more recent times other portions had been transferred from the Chapter House at Westminster to the Rolls House, and to the State Paper Office. Thus parts of the same correspondence were scattered in four different repositories, and sometimes even parts of the same letter were to be found in different localities. Soon after the commencement of Mr. Brewer's labours, it is true, the contents of the State Paper Office, the Chapter House at Westminster, and the Rolls House, were brought together in the new repository in Fetter Lane; but the task of reuniting a series which had been so dispersed, and introducing order where confusion had reigned so long, was attended with difficulties which can only be appreciated by those who have attempted any similar labour.

'Under the most favourable circumstances it would have been an exceedingly laborious matter; but as the majority of the letters written in Henry VIII.'s time bore no date of year, the chronology could only be ascertained from internal evidence by an elaborate and comprehensive study of the whole correspondence, long before any attempt was made to summarise their contents in a Calendar. Some years were accordingly spent in a preliminary arrangement of the documents in the Public Record Office; after which pretty full abstracts were taken of all those in the British Museum which appeared at all likely to belong to the early years of Henry VIII. We then proceeded to make similar abstracts of the arranged documents in the Record Office; and finally, after carefully weighing the evidences of chronological sequence in the case of undated letters, we arranged the whole of our abstracts in the order in which they were sent to press.

'In this process of determining the chronology, however, it was found impossible to restrict ourselves even to the original letters and State papers in the Public Record Office and the British Museum. Contemporary letters of historical interest, derived from other and even from printed sources, supplied evidences which it would have been wrong to overlook, and notices of all such correspondence were accordingly included in the Calendar. For similar reasons it was likewise determined to include a far less interesting series of documents—the grants from the Crown, enrolled on the Patent Rolls, or recorded by the Signed Bills and Privy Seals. No progress could possibly have been made with this Calendar without very frequent reference to this class of documents, and brief notices of the whole series, chronologised along with the letters, were accordingly incorporated in the work. The contents of the French Rolls and of the Rolls of Parliament were treated in the same manner. In short, it was Mr. Brewer's design to include in this Calendar every known source of contemporary information regarding the reign of Henry VIII.; and upon this plan the work has been hitherto pursued from the commencement.'

But even this, though the most laborious and learned, was not the most remarkable result of Mr. Brewer's labours at the Record Office. It is the custom of the editors of the successive volumes to prefix introductions giving some account of their contents. These, as a rule, cannot well be long, nor can they enter into much detail. But Mr. Brewer was sensible that the subject assigned him possessed a unique and independent interest. He had before him, as described by Mr. Gairdner, the whole of the existing materials for the reign of Henry VIII., and he was therefore in a position such as no one had yet enjoyed for writing a complete history of that reign. It was a subject pre-eminently suited to him; for it needed, in greater measure perhaps than any other portion of English history, his remarkable knowledge of both the old and the new periods of European life.

At the time of Henry VIII.'s reign, the old and the new influences are seen in mortal struggle for the mastery, and to do justice to the drama it is essential for the historian to be in sympathy with both sides. Nothing was more remarkable in Mr. Brewer's mind than its capacity in this respect. He was a distinguished Aristotelian scholar, and thoroughly appreciated the grandeur of the vast logical structures which were raised by the theologians of the Middle Ages; but at the same time he was a devoted disciple of Lord Bacon, read his chief works incessantly, and endeavoured to follow the Baconian methods in all his studies and thoughts. Similarly, although deeply read in patristic theology, and, in accordance with his Oxford training, an appreciative disciple of the Caroline divines, he became an enthusiastic admirer of Luther, and, as is proved by the notes in his copy of the Jena edition of Luther's works, had studied him minutely. He regarded him as holding in theology a somewhat similar position to that of Bacon in philosophy—equally the author of an *Instauratio Magna*.[1] Add to this that he was a thorough Englishman in all his sympathies and tastes, and it will be seen what rare qualifications he possessed for the task he undertook.

His labours over the materials of his work gave him, moreover, one other advantage which, in all probability, will never be enjoyed by any one again.

---

[1] His admiration for Bacon as a philosopher and for Luther as a divine seemed to increase year by year. He prepared a very useful edition of Bacon's *Novum Organum* for the use of students at King's College, with a most interesting introduction. It was not published, but can still be obtained in the Secretary's Office at King's College.

The Calendars he edited contain an analysis, in chronological order, of every known document relating to Henry VIII.'s reign; and for this purpose he himself read them all through. Now that they have been analysed, it is most unlikely that any one else will go through the same labour. Yet the actual perusal of such documents is like the personal examination of witnesses, and must afford a more vivid, living, and accurate perception of their purport than can possibly be obtained at second hand. For years Mr. Brewer lived in daily intercourse, as it were, with the chief actors in the reign of Henry VIII. He read their private letters, and followed them into numberless details of their daily lives. He had a special gift for reading character; and the impressions of the men and of the events of the reign which such a man received amidst such exceptional opportunities must needs possess an unique value.

These impressions he communicated to the public in a series of prefaces to the Calendars, which constitute, when combined, a complete history of the reign to the death of Wolsey. He entered with too much enthusiasm into the work to be content with a mere prefatory sketch of the contents of each volume. He cast into the form of a finished historical narrative the results of his tedious research, and upon the composition of this narrative he bestowed an immense amount of time and labour which were in no way required of him in the discharge of his official duty. The preface to the first volume of the Calendar contains 122 pages, that to the second volume 279 pages, that to the third 435 pages, and that to the fourth 666 pages. Other volumes which he edited in the series of Record Office publications have introductions of considerable interest prefixed to them, particularly the volume entitled 'Monumenta Franciscana.' But the prefaces to Henry VIII.'s papers rise in all respects to the dignity of an historical work of the first order. They are written, like the essays which are here reprinted, in a singularly graceful and scholarly English style. They are full of animation and dramatic power; and they have been justly described as at once the most faithful and the most interesting account yet produced of the momentous period they treat. For the reasons already mentioned, they are never likely to be superseded. Unfortunately, they are attached to ponderous and expensive quarto volumes, so as to be practically inaccessible to the public. Mr. Murray, however, has offered to reprint them in convenient form at his own risk, and although some official difficulties have hitherto stood in the way, it is to be hoped that the consent of the Treasury to the production in a popular form of literary works of such unique character will not be finally withheld. Meanwhile, the most valuable and finished of Mr. Brewer's works, possessing a permanent and general interest, remain buried on the shelves of a few great libraries.[1]

[1] A very interesting review of the fourth volume of these Calendars and Prefaces will be found in the *Quarterly Review* for October 1877, and the following judgment of their value ought to be quoted:—'If,' says the writer, 'the Calendar does not utterly supersede all previous collections,

But, as has been mentioned, in addition to his work at the Rolls Office, Mr. Brewer was for the long period of thirty-eight years, from 1839 till 1877, engaged as a lecturer and professor at King's College, London. In 1839 he was appointed Lecturer in Classical Literature. In 1855 he became Professor of the English Language and Literature, and Lecturer in Modern History; and the latter two subjects being for a time combined, he became, in 1865, Professor of English Literature and Modern History. It illustrates the wide range and versatility of his mind, that he should thus have passed from Classics to Modern History and English Literature, and that he should have been equally successful in giving instruction in each subject. The transition corresponded very much with a change in his own intellectual interests, and with the increasing concentration of his attention on modern history and modern literature. He retained, indeed, to the last his affection for the classics, always maintaining that as a means of training for the mind English was not equal to Latin and Greek. When

the introduction in which Mr. Brewer has gathered up the innumerable threads, and has woven them into a consistent picture, so far surpasses all former narratives of the same events as to cause regret that he has not chosen rather to write a life of Wolsey, which everybody would have read, than to bury the fruit of so much study in prefaces to bulky and not very accessible volumes. With little additional labour he would have enjoyed greater freedom in the management of materials and in the use of colour, and literature would have been endowed with a popular masterpiece. Mr. Brewer has thought it a duty to devote the whole of his accumulated knowledge and power to the public work which has occupied so large a portion of his life. So few men are capable of extracting for themselves and digesting all the information his Calendar contains, that the elaborate introductions by the editor add immeasurably to its permanent utility and value. But it is impossible not to feel and to regret the generosity of so great a sacrifice.

students at King's College asked to be excused classical lectures that they might give more attention to Mr. Brewer's lectures in English, the classical teacher would send them to Mr. Brewer, well knowing what he would say to such an application. But his main characteristics as a teacher were the same, whatever the subject in hand. The most remarkable of these was his habit of placing himself side by side, as it were, with his pupils, and teaching them as a fellow-learner of superior knowledge and power, rather than as a master with a right to dictate to them. In his classical lectures, for instance, in which the present writer first made his acquaintance, he would go through very little of his author at a time— some ten or twenty lines perhaps of Horace in a lecture; and he would discuss every word with us, eliciting our own knowledge or lack of knowledge respecting it, and, with the dictionary before him, leading us step by step through the process which we ought to have gone through for ourselves. He checked at once those facile off-hand approximations to the meaning of a word or sentence with which beginners are too apt to be content; and thus from the first he made every thoughtful student realise in some measure the depth and complexity of the language of a great writer. He treated words with just the same laborious, patient, and penetrating observation which a man of science bestows upon the simple facts of nature; and in his company we learned one of the first great lessons of study—not merely our own ignorance as individuals, but the comparative ignorance even of those who know most. Though he knew so much more than we did, he always spoke and acted as if he were as much a learner as we were. The consequence of this modest thoroughness in his way of teaching was, that a term or two under him in such a subject as classics placed a capable student in a position in which he could study successfully by himself. Instead of merely acquiring a store of opinions and facts, he had got hold of the true method of working, and had been shown how to thread his way through the labyrinth. Mr. Brewer wrote Latin prose with singular elegance, and was a most severe critic of translations both from and into Latin and Greek. But the pupil whose work was being criticised, or rewritten, saw his master's mind at work in all the details of the process, and learned not merely what the result ought to be, but what were the reasons for it, and the means of producing it.

One other source of his influence over his pupils should be mentioned. The instrument he employed to urge and control them was praise and not blame. Many a young man left the lecture-room with better hopes for himself and the future because Mr. Brewer had detected and praised in his work some merit of which he was himself unconscious. 'The young men,' he would sometimes say, 'see visions; the old men dream dreams.' Perhaps such a discipline ran some risk of giving undue encouragement to youthful vanity. But his vigilant and critical judgment was ever at hand to check this danger; and the more frequent influence of such training was to induce young men to put forth for adventure in thought and action who would otherwise have stayed with folded hands at home.

Of his method in teaching history two of the essays in this volume will afford the best conception—those on the Study of History in general, and on the Study of English History in particular.[1] What is most conspicuous in them is the characteristic just noticed in his classical teaching. Instead of giving accounts of historical events or of their bearings on his own authority, he seemed to take his pupils by the hand, leading them to the best points of view from which to survey the historical drama, and then to make them feel that it told its own tale to careful and thoughtful observation. He would begin by fixing their attention on the main facts and outlines of a period or a reign, and would draw out of those leading facts, by a kind of historic induction, the great influences which were at work. He was still the companion of his pupils, pointing out to them, at every turn, not so much what he himself saw, as what they could see themselves if they were patient and thoughtful. In history, moreover, above all other subjects, he made them feel more and more, as he grew older, the vastness and mystery of the course of human life and action. His sense of the immense difficulty of unravelling the threads

[1] Much may also be learned respecting his method from a very useful book he published, under the title, *An Elementary Atlas of History and Geography*. The first edition contained a most interesting and characteristic introduction; but this was omitted in subsequent editions.

of history increased as he learned more of them in his studies at the Rolls Office. 'Ah,' he said once to a former pupil, 'when I lectured to you twenty-five years ago, I used to think I knew something about history; but I have found out now I know very little indeed about it.' But he held with unabated confidence to his conviction that the main facts of history and the lessons to be drawn from them are independent of conflicting interpretations of its details; and nothing was more characteristic of his teaching than the clearness with which he brought out these leading facts, and made his pupils feel that they were independent of his own opinion, or of the partial views of any historian. The great outlines of history in his hands assumed forms as clear and distinct as the leading facts of any natural science, and he made it felt that they could be accepted with similar confidence.

His researches, indeed, into the reign of Henry VIII. led him to one conclusion, which seems particularly worth mention, and which affords a very remarkable and instructive illustration of these views of the true method of interpreting history. He had penetrated, as we have said, into all the details of Henry VIII.'s reign with a completeness which had never before been possible; and the result, contrary to his own anticipation, was to confirm the general truth of the view of that reign presented by the two writers who had up to a recent date been the most popular authorities respecting it. The best sketch, he said, of Henry VIII.'s reign anywhere to be found is afforded by Shakespeare's play; and next in value to this he reckoned the narrative of Hume. Before he had thoroughly investigated the subject for himself, he distrusted Hume, but he was more and more struck by the sagacity with which that historian had penetrated to the true causes of events, and to the true characters of the chief actors of the time. Such a conclusion is not a little consoling to that large class of readers who must always depend on the great classical writers for their knowledge of history.

There was, however, one other subject on which Mr. Brewer was perhaps even more interesting and instructive than as an historian and historical lecturer. That subject was English Literature, which, as has been mentioned, was combined for some time with the other work of his chair at King's College. It offered scope for the exercise of all his capacities—as a scholar, an historian, a philosopher, a theologian, a man of letters, and one who had seen a good deal of the world. There was not a single writer of any consequence with whom he did not feel some native sympathy, and he loved to interpret them all, in their various bearings, in that patient inductive style which characterised him in all his work. Here, again, he adhered to his general method in teaching. He selected the great authors of the successive periods of our history, and their leading works; and concentrated the attention of his pupils upon them. When these were known and understood, the rest, he knew, would fall into their right places and find their level.[1]

[1] On this plan, at the instance of the Clarendon Press, Oxford, he pro-

He was fond of Lord Bacon's saying, that literature is the eye of history, enabling us, as nothing else can, to penetrate into the depths of its life; and to study a great author with him was to live again amidst all the influences of a former age.

One of the most valuable points, accordingly, in his method of teaching English literature was that he was never content with lecturing about authors. He would read in class portions of their greatest works with the same minute thoroughness as he used to bestow, when a classical teacher, upon the great writers of Greece and Rome; he would take his class into fellowship with himself, invite opinions from them, enter into discussion with them, and thus introduce them, with all the pleasure of conscious companionship, into the very heart and life of the book before them. Looking back on his lectures twenty-five years ago upon such authors as Shakespeare, Lord Bacon, Milton, Dryden, Pope, or Coleridge, it is difficult, notwithstanding his own belief already mentioned in the essential superiority of classical training, to doubt that English literature might be so treated as to become almost as powerful an instrument of education as the literature of Greece and Rome—that it might exert an almost equal influence in giving accuracy, thoroughness, and depth to the mind, while it would often lay a more powerful

jected 'A Series of English Classics, designed to meet the Wants of Students in English Literature.' Several volumes of the series have been published, under the editorship of writers of distinction. Mr. Brewer was to have written 'A General Introduction to the Series;' but unhappily this part of the design was never carried into effect.

grasp upon the heart. Mr. Brewer used it with singular success in the education of women. He taught for a while at Queen's College, London, and gave private lessons to a few privileged acquaintances. Some illustration of his method may be found in the paper read at King's College on the 'Study of Shakespeare,' which will be found in this volume; though it can convey but an imperfect impression of the personal life and sympathy by which, in this subject more especially, his instruction was animated.

Such were his public occupations. But in addition to these he accomplished an immense amount of private literary work. During a portion of his struggling life in London he wrote leading articles for the daily press, and for a brief interval acted as editor of the 'Standard' newspaper. But though he felt a strong interest in politics, some of his best qualities unfitted him for political controversy; and except that he took a warm part in opposition to the disestablishment of the Church in Ireland, his energies were happily diverted from this field of action. He continued, however, to write articles for quarterly periodicals, and the majority of the essays contained in this volume are, with the kind permission of the proprietors, reprinted from two of such publications, the 'Quarterly Review' and 'National Review.' He wrote many others, as is proved by some of the letters he preserved; but it has been found impracticable to trace them. He was always extremely reserved respecting such contributions, and placed far too little value upon them. For the

University Press at Oxford he edited Fuller's 'Church History,' and he bestowed a similar labour upon other old writers. A list of the works he wrote or edited, so far as can be ascertained from the catalogue of the British Museum, will be found at the end of this memoir.

Strange to say, with all this work upon his hands, he was ever at leisure to a favourite friend or pupil, and would spare an hour at almost any time for an interchange of thought with them. On each visit his conversation would be like one of his old friendly lectures, delivered, as the Oxford Statutes have it, *sine ulla solennitate*. No matter how young his visitor might be, he would talk to him as if he were on an equality with himself, and while pouring out his stores of learning and reflection would be ever endeavouring to elicit thought and information from his hearer. His modesty in this respect was one of his most remarkable characteristics. Genuine modesty is rare, and is very different from the quality, however laudable, of sincerely endeavouring to be modest. Mr. Brewer, in all his conversation and intercourse with others, acted and spoke as if he were learning from them, when in point of fact, as they might accidentally discover at a later time, he had an acquaintance with the subject under discussion in comparison with which their own was insignificant. There was nothing whatever artificial in this attitude. By that respect for other minds and other natures which made him treat his pupils as if they were fellow-students with himself, he was led to treat all genuine students and all thoughtful companions as capable of teaching him something even in the subjects he knew best. He would be vigorous and sometimes amusingly positive in stating his own views, but he was none the less eager to learn from even the rawest and least instructed companion; and one would often be surprised to find at the next interview that he had really been pondering over some suggestion which, at the time it was thrown out, he had summarily over-ridden. As a further illustration of this habit of mind, the following testimony from Mr. Gairdner, who was for twenty years his colleague in the Record Office, will be read with interest, and will confirm and supplement this sketch of Mr. Brewer's work and character:—

'I think if I were asked to name in a single word the point which distinguished him most from all other able men of my acquaintance, I should say it was his thoroughness, and his consequent eagerness to be informed of every aspect of a question or a fact. No man, indeed, was ever so condescending in argument—if condescending is not, in fact, an altogether inappropriate word to describe one whose modesty in tone and unassuming courtesy always welcomed what an antagonist could say in reply as a thing by which he himself might profit. For the truth is, however thoroughly he had mastered a subject, he invariably put himself in the position of one anxious to learn something more about it. I used to say sometimes that when I had a question to ask of him it was very hard, for he would ask me half a dozen before I got mine put to him; yet, after all, mine were easily disposed of, while his went to the very bottom of things, and required very careful consideration.

'Indeed, this questioning habit of mind was what constituted his peculiar strength. He did not place much reliance on mere logical deductions: he was a student of Bacon, and considered logic as a thing that went comparatively little way; yet no man appreciated the force of logic more than he did, and could discriminate with greater nicety how much a logical argument proved and how much it did not prove. But without entering into dialectics, one pregnant question from him would suffice to turn the point of an argument, and exhibit the subject in a very different light.

'His natural field of thought, however, was not mental science or philosophy. His favourite studies were history and literature; and it was particularly with relation to the former that I had most to do with him. Here it was that his questioning habit was of particular use to me, and I had occasion sometimes to mark its influence upon other men who had bestowed much more attention on particular subjects than myself. It is needless to say that in such a very large domain as history even the best of general scholars cannot be so much at home upon any one subject as the specialist. Yet I believe no one was ever so thoroughly acquainted with any one particular epoch but he would find, in the course of ten minutes' conversation, that Mr. Brewer had a grasp of the whole subject scarcely inferior to his own, knew all the important authorities, and could suggest inquiries likely to lead to very valuable results.

'No wonder that his advice was much appreciated in matters relating to historical publications. By the late Master of the Rolls, Lord Romilly, I know that it was greatly esteemed ; and the late Deputy Keeper of the Public Records, Sir Thomas Hardy, used to consult him almost daily on matters relating to the publication of the Chronicles and Calendars printed by authority of the Government. In the same way his advice was sought by the deputies of the Clarendon Press at Oxford in their scheme for printing editions of the English classics ; and the scheme as it stands, I believe, was drawn up almost entirely by him. I may add that in all these services he was not only thoroughly disinterested, but to a great extent self-sacrificing. Whether consulted by public bodies or by private individuals in matters relating to literature and education, he never, I think, received the slightest remuneration for all the good advice that he so freely imparted, but, on the contrary, put himself at times to not a little expense, and sacrificed much valuable time, for the establishment of what he conceived to be sound principles of action.'

Such was Mr. Brewer's work in London for some forty years. He had received no adequate recognition of his labours—indeed, nothing that could be called recognition—in money or position in the Church. He was a man of the most independent character, with few wants, utterly unworldly in spirit, and had been content to remain in comparative retirement. For his indefatigable and generous work at the Record Office he was paid only 400*l.* a year; and the remuneration for his duties at King's College and as Preacher at the Rolls was even more modest. At length, in the year 1877, he was offered the Crown living of Toppesfield, in Essex. It is a valuable preferment, being estimated to be worth nearly 1,000*l.* a year. But the parish is a purely agricultural one, situated in a bleak part of Essex, and difficult of access. Mr. Brewer was then sixty-seven years of age, and had lived in London ever since he left Oxford, more than forty years previously. The offer was kindly meant, and Mr. Brewer accepted it with gratification. But the result of such an inappropriate appointment was only too natural. Mr. Brewer threw himself with his characteristic energy into his new duties. He loved nature, he was particularly fond of gardening, and he had many points of sympathy with country life. His very complexion had more the air of a countryman than of a student, and there was something in his appearance that answered to the freshness of his mind. In this respect he was one of those who never become old. He entered with interest into the occupations of his parishioners; and at his funeral one of his churchwardens, who was a farmer, was recalling with pleasure a recent conversation with him on the merits of blackfaced sheep. He liked the simple ways of country people, and soon established a thoroughly friendly understanding with them. The manuscript sermons he has left behind bear striking testimony to the pains he took to accommodate himself to their thoughts, and to bring home to them the truths he preached. But the duties of a country parson in a bleak parish are a severe strain upon a man of sixty-seven, then undertaking them, for the first time, at the close of a laborious life. His old love for visiting the poor and infirm revived, and he overtaxed a constitution which required rest and quiet. One day in the depth of winter, in February of 1879, Mr. Brewer had to take a long walk to visit a sick man. On his return he complained of cold; he took to his bed; the illness affected his heart, and in three days he died. At his funeral, the demonstrations of respect and sorrow by his parishioners of all ranks proved that in the course of a few months he had won the hearts of the people of this Essex village. But it was a grievous waste of precious energies to impose such work upon him; and it is lamentable to think of his capacities being thus misdirected at the moment of their highest maturity, and of their being lost to the world before their work was accomplished. It is sad, too, to reflect that he had no time to enjoy such advantages as his preferment might in time have brought to him. The expenses of entering upon it were very great, and he died too soon to repay himself. He was just beginning to feel at home in his new sphere; he had resigned his Professorship at King's College, and had reduced his attendance at the Record Office; and he might have looked forward to some comparative rest. Not that he could have ceased working. He had undertaken, for instance, in addition to his historical work on Henry VIII.'s reign, to edit a reprint of Hume's History for Mr. Murray, and he did finish a revision of an abridgment of Hume, for the same publisher. He might, however, have welcomed leisure for pursuing the studies most congenial to him, and for indulging his favourite tastes. But this was denied him; and though he passed away in calmness and resignation, it is impossible for his friends not to lament that such a career never received in this world its natural close or its fitting reward.

He has left, however, monuments of his genius and labour which will hold a permanent place among the historical productions of our generation, as well as compositions which, like the essays in this volume, will always retain a high literary value. He possesses, moreover, a living memorial in the hearts and thoughts of a long succession of pupils, who were animated and guided by his teaching, and who will do their best to transmit its wisdom to others. Among them are to be reckoned not a few of the distinguished men of the present day; but many more who are less distinguished can never forget their gratitude to him, and will help to carry on his work to another generation. He was the unobtrusive and unselfish centre of a circle of generous thought and of Christian energy; and his memory will long be cherished with affectionate and grateful respect.

HENRY WACE.

March 1881.

A list of Mr. Brewer's publications recorded in the catalogue of the Library of the British Museum.

1. Aristotle's *Nicomachean Ethics*, with English notes, 8vo. 1836.
2. *The Court of King James I.*, by C. Goodman, Bishop of Gloucester, now first published, 8vo.1839.
3. Fuller's *Church History*; new edition, 8vo. 1845.
4. *The History of Popish Transubstantiation*, by J. Cosin, Bishop of Durham; a new edition, revised, with a memoir of the author, 12mo. 1850.
5. Bacon's *Novum Organum*; with introduction and notes, 1856.
6. *An Elementary Atlas of History and Geography*; new edition, 1871.
7. *What is Establishment?* or *Letters on the Church in Ireland;* with a preface, 8vo. 1868.
8. *The Endowments and Establishment of the Church of England,* 1873.
9. *The Athanasian Creed vindicated,* 1871.
10. *The Athanasian origin of the Athanasian Creed,* 1872.
11. *The Student's Hume;* new edition, 1880.
12. *Record Office Publications.*
    1. *Letters and Papers of the reign of Henry VIII.;* several vols.
    2. *Report to the Master of the Rolls upon the Carte and Carew Papers.*
    3. *Calendar of the Carew MSS.;* by Mr. Brewer and Mr. Bullen.
    4. Fr. Rogeri Bacon, *opera quædam hactenus inedita.*
    5. *Giraldi Cambrensis opera.*
    6. *Monumenta Franciscana.*
    7. *Registrum Malmburiense.*

A SERMON

ON

THE PSALMIST OF ISRAEL.

OF the value of the Psalms as the noblest and purest expression of devotiona feeling, there can be no better and no stronger proof than the extensive use of them among all classes. That book must be a Divine book which can touch the sympathies of all men in all times, and be equally acceptable to all, as the truest expression of joy and grief, of hope and despondency, of victory and resignation. The Psalms of David have been, from the time they were first written, the chosen vehicles of the various feelings which find a place in the heart of man. If the Jew rejoiced in the conquest over his national enemies, some Psalm of David offered the best and readiest mode of expressing his thanksgiving. If he was carried into captivity, ' Sing us one of the songs of Sion' indicated that his griefs found vent in a similar channel. At his birth, his marriage, or his grave, a Psalm of David was equally applicable, equally common. So it has since been among Christians. No occasion can befall the life of a Christian man or that of his nation for which he does not find in the Psalms of David some suitable exponent of his feelings.

But these Psalms have another and a narrower use, one

not less interesting if not so important; one also from which they ought not to be severed. Nowhere else can we gain so clear and satisfactory an insight into the innermost life of David. Such a character as David is rare enough among the rulers of this world. It is not common for kings to be poets and musicians, least of all to commit to verse their most secret thoughts and aspirations; to find and feel that love which David felt towards the Ruler of all men—a love which kings need above all other men, and seek in vain among their subjects.

The Psalms in fact may be considered as a series of autobiographical poems, in which the most momentous events of David's life are recorded. No man's life could be more varied than that life. A keeper of a few sheep in the wilderness; then suddenly taken from a task of obscurity to be the darling hero of his nation; then made the son-in-law of Saul; then the leader of a political party, persecuted by his sovereign; then the successor to his throne; then established there with greater security than fell to the lot of any other king; then driven from it by his own son; then brought back by the unanimous voice of the people, whose hearts he bowed as that of one man. What varied experience! What vast temptations! How fragmentary and disconnected this life appears, when viewed merely by the light of external occurrences! How striking the contrast to this aspect when compared with that life as viewed in the Psalms! There, with all its changes of joy and sorrow, of triumph and defeat, of humiliation and glory, a substantial unity lies beneath it, binding all these apparently heterogeneous elements into one grand, harmonious whole.

Putting aside for the present the religious faith and loyalty so conspicuous in all David's character, one great constitutive element of that unity is to be found in his shepherd life. He is the only King of Israel whose early training had been in the fields and the wilderness; not in the boisterous occupation of a huntsman or a herdsman, but in the more simple, meditative calling of a keeper of sheep. That is not precisely the quarter in which men look for kings, or from which they fetch their champions to fight against the Goliaths of this world. And though the occupation of David demanded the exercise of patience, courage, and forbearance; though there were wolves and robbers and lions from whom he must protect his flock; yet doubtless his brothers expressed the popular feeling as well as their own when they despised him as a simple uncouth rustic, when they rebuked him in those noted words expressive of their contempt for David and his calling: 'Why camest thou down hither, and with whom hast thou left those few sheep in the wilderness?'

Now it is this life with a few sheep in the wilderness that forms the basis and substantial unity of David's life and character. It never forsakes him; it is never forgotten. It continues as a golden thread throughout the various chequered scenes of his existence, from his boyhood to his grave. I do not say that it was essential to the development of his poetical character, for poets have been bred and brought up in cities; but it certainly was essential to that poetry of which David is the author. The frankness, the freshness the tenderness of his heart, the strong contrast afforded by David in these and other respects, not only to Oriental despots, but to Saul and his successors, plainly indicate that the shepherd life of David and the virtues developed by it are intimately linked together. Often in the weariness of rule and amidst the cares of royalty he must have reverted to those calm pleasures of his pastoral days—to the aloes by the river side, to the broad rock in the hot and thirsty land, to the valleys and green pastures, to the cedars of Libanus, to the fir-tree and the dwelling of the stork; to the handful of corn on the top of the mountains, to the pastures clothed with flocks, to the trumpet song of one deep calling unto another. Often must the remembrance of these sights and sounds have rushed into his soul with all the perfume of pure and holy joys, not the less potent and enduring because they were fraught with remembrances of early boyhood; when, with the deep reverence of that age still upon him, this earth was full of wonders, and he walked with God as a friend. With the gladness that thus rushed through his heart came mingled visions of the Almighty. And if a pure, happy, and even poetical childhood be needful to the formation of true greatness of character, of all that is truly heroical, we may be sure that to David his days with his father's sheep in the wilderness were not the least valuable or least important. Thus the pure and ennobling delights of Nature grew with his growth and entwined themselves with the fibres of his being. Nor was Nature to David, as to many poets, a mere vision of delight—no more; nor was it, as to others, a dark enigma of metaphysical conceits to delude and betray; still less, as to his son Solomon, a subject for scientific speculation. Nature did not give back to him, as to others, the mere reflex of his own thoughts and imaginations, only tenfold more dark and portentous; but Nature was to David the mirror of God. He saw in her, not, as men do now, a wonderful order, an overruling Providence, a moral government of the world, but the marks and indications, the very voice of a personal God, revealing Himself to man, speaking to him in a language of love which could not be mistaken. Nature was the robe in which God apparelled Himself, and drew near to His creatures: 'His voice breaketh the cedar-trees; His voice shaketh the wilderness. The heavens declare His glory; the firmament showeth His handiwork. He stilleth the raging of the sea, the noise of its waves, and the madness of the people. He sitteth in the heavens over all from the beginning; lo! He doth send out His voice, yea, and that a mighty voice.'

Whilst other men, therefore, seek friends among their fellows to whom they may unbosom their joys or communicate their sorrows, David turned to God—turned to Him as a warm, present, personal friend, in all the occurrences of life. His language is so much governed by this feeling of Divine endearance, that it might be considered as too familiar, and even unorthodox, had not the present generation broken down all the strong meaning of His words into the devotional dust of vague generalities: 'Go not far from me, O God; my God, haste Thee to help me.' 'Will the Lord absent Himself for ever, and will He be no more entreated?' 'Among the gods there is none like unto Thee, O Lord; there is not one that can do as Thou doest.' And still more strongly than all: 'Hold not Thy tongue, O God of my praise; for the mouth of the ungodly is opened upon me.' In these (and how many more passages might be quoted!) God is presented in a light which must have seemed passing strange and familiar to David's contemporaries, as it would be to many at this day—passing strange, as compared with the general scope of prophetic vision revealed in the Old Testament, where God is made known in thunders and lightnings, as an avenger of evil, rather than in this endearing light, in which He presents Himself to the heart of David. What human love can express itself in terms more passionate and real than those employed by David? 'Thou, O Lord God, art the thing that I long for; Thou art my hope, even from my youth.' 'Cast me not away in the time of age; forsake me not when my strength faileth me.' 'Whom have I in heaven but Thee? and there is none upon earth that I desire in comparison of Thee.' 'My flesh and my heart faileth; but God is the strength of my heart and my portion for ever.' 'O God, Thou art my God, early will

I seek Thee: my soul thirsteth for Thee, my flesh also longeth after Thee in a barren and dry land where no water is.' Words cannot express a stronger love than this. It is not the love of one—if it deserves the name—who gazes with admiration on this marvellous frame of nature, or breaks out into admiration at the works and wisdom of God manifested in His providence. It is not the resignation of the saint willing to exchange this world for another. It is not the ecstatic joy of the martyr stretching forth his hand to lay hold of an incorruptible crown. It is, if I may use the term, more human, more personal than these—an ardent passionate longing, which cannot rest satisfied with regarding the beloved object in any other light than in reference to itself; which must bind its personality with that of its own being. For love like this cannot exist except towards a person. And thus, as I have said before, throughout David's Psalms, God is addressed, not merely as a righteous judge, as a protector of them who put their trust in Him, as a refuge for those who are in distress, but as a personal friend, far more personal than any human friend can be. God is a friend to whom David turns spontaneously, finding in the thought and presence of God that joy, rest, and refreshment which only true personal love can bestow—turns with an ardour which nothing but his own words can express. 'The Lord is my strength and my shield; my heart hath trusted in Him, and I am helped; therefore my heart danceth for joy, and in my song will I praise Him.'

And this is the feeling which gives so delightful a poise, a unity so substantial to his whole life. This it is which like a holy flame devours up the dross, and turns all to precious purity. Poets have been fond of representing the effects of human love in exalting, purifying, and ennobling the souls and even the bodies of men. They have looked upon it as the groundwork of all heroism; as that which first gives true depth of character, true dignity of feeling to man or woman. And rightly so. But how much more deep and ennobling was the love of such a man as David to Him who is the source of all love—yea, who is love itself; for 'God is love,' says the Apostle, 'and every one that loveth is born of God and knoweth God!' David, indeed, had great failings—they were perhaps almost inseparable from such a nature. But this Divine love was ever burning brightly within him. This habitual recognition, not of God's presence only, to which men of religious minds may attain, but of that presence as the presence of a friend, more lovable, more near, more precious than any human friend can ever be, was a constant renewal of David's nature. His strength, his joy, as he calls it, it wrought out in David what human friendships work out in an inferior degree—a likeness and approximation to the person beloved; so that of David alone it is said, with all his great imperfections, 'He was a man after God's own heart.' That abiding sense of God's presence mingling in his earlier days with the simple joys of childhood and the fresh scenes of nature, linking the boy to the child in the first dawnings of enthusiasm, and the first essays of youthful strength, shedding its benign light over the thoughtful experience and meditations of his manhood, descended with him into the vale of years, connecting together every stage of his chequered life. And as he looked back upon the vision of past years, it was this that enabled him to exclaim in the familiar words, 'Though I walk through the valley of the shadow of death, I will fear no evil: for Thou art with me; Thy rod and Thy staff they comfort me.'

Could men now attain to this love of God, how would manhood grow in faith and hope as it grew in strength, instead of that unbelief and despair which spring up when they have outlived the simple creed of childhood! How might old age, like David's, glow with intenser love and more beatific vision, instead of burying beforehand all its nobler affections—without charity, therefore without faith or hope!

NEW SOURCES OF ENGLISH HISTORY.[1]

IT IS POSSIBLE that our readers may have seen near Temple Bar, close to the proposed site of the New Law Courts, a large stone building of unusual proportions and not less unusual style. Its lancet windows and portly tower surmounted with pinnacles cannot be mistaken among the forest of dingy chimney-pots and rickety tenements of Fetter Lane and the neighbouring alleys. This is the new Public Record Office, still in progress, and slowly advancing towards completion. Although one portion of the building has now been erected for several years, another generation will, in all probability, pass away before the whole is finished, according to the original designs of its architect. The neighbourhood around is classic ground. Like all things else, it has seen the ups and downs of life, it has experienced the caprices of fashion and gentility. Here fluttered in happier days poor Oliver Goldsmith and his peach-coloured coat. Here met, at Dr. Johnson's residence in Bolt Court, the greatest of artists and the greatest of politicians; and here the prying, bustling James Boswell, most assiduous of hero-worshippers, gathered leaf by leaf his immortal crown. In Fetter Lane still stands the house of Dryden the poet, now converted into the base uses of a beer-shop, once commanding an extensive view of

[1] From the *Quarterly Review* for April, 1871; under the following heading:—*Calendars of State Papers, published under the direction of the Master of the Rolls*, London, 1856–70. *Chronicles and Memorials of Great Britain and Ireland during the Middle Ages*, London, 1858–70. *Libraries and Founders of Libraries*. By Edward Edwards, London, 1865.

the Master of the Rolls' garden, with its flowers and fruit-trees. Here also, at a still earlier period, was 'the quiet retreat' of Gilbert Burnet the historian, and of his patron, Sir Harbottle Grimstone, not more famous for his law than for his marriage with Lord Bacon's niece, the last of her family. Now poets, painters, and historians have taken wing. The 'quiet retreat' has been invaded by the shrill whistle of the steam-press and the rattle of manufactories. Except a dingy chrysanthemum here and there, or a patch of grass in some forgotten and neglected corner, nothing remains of the Master's garden. Part of it is occupied by the Judge's chambers, part by the huge block of the National Record Office.

Externally, the new building has not much to recommend it on the score of artistic beauty. To which of the recognised styles of architecture it ought to be referred would puzzle Mr. Ruskin himself to determine. Its pinched buttresses, squared and gradiated with the undeviating precision of rule and compass, its quadrangular windows glazed with talc, the absence of all ease and freedom in its meagre ornaments and narrow proportions, reveal the mechanical graces of official Gothic. Evidently, it is intended to be more solid than beautiful, more useful than elegant. The interior is even less attractive than the exterior. A square vestibule, badly lighted, conducts the visitor to a number of narrow passages flagged with brick; iron doors to the right and left, marked with cabalistic numerals and furnished with small circular ventilators, divide these passages with geometrical exactness. Here are preserved in iron gratings, furnished with shelves of slate, the national records and State papers. Story succeeds to story, with imperturbable uniformity, from roof to basement. No thought of beauty or general effect has entered the mind of the architect, or, rather, has been permitted to enter it. There is none of that gracefulness of outline or grandeur of design which strikes the beholder in the galleries and Reading Room of the British Museum or the Houses of Parliament. The light and cheerful proportions, the polished floors, the oak and the mahogany of the French Foreign Archives, even the sombre ecclesiastical dignity of Simancas, find no place here. One thought, that of security, has absorbed all other considerations; and except the edifice were shelled by an invading army, or stormed in a civil insurrection, it is impossible to conceive what evil accident could ever befall it or its contents. Here, at all events, it may be supposed that, after escaping numerous perils of fire, water, and official neglect, the national records had found, like Æneas, a safe resting-place at last.

The collection is enormous. Into this vast receptacle the Law Courts, the Treasury, the Admiralty, the War Office, the Home, Foreign, and Colonial Departments, have disgorged their voluminous contents. The public acts of this nation, from the Doomsday of William the Conqueror to the Coronation Oath of Queen Victoria, the pulsations of the great machine of government, with all its complex operations, are here chronicled and recorded in all their immense variety from day to day and from hour to hour. Here is to be traced the open and the secret history of the nation; its transactions at home and abroad; its most subtle and mysterious negotiations; the employment of its treasures; the number and disposition of its forces; the musters of its population; the distribution of its land, its forests, and its manors; the rise and progress of its nobility and great families; its proceedings in Parliament; its charters, its patents, its civil and criminal judicature. Whatever, in short, this kingdom has for eight centuries done or proposed to do by the complicated functions of its Government and Administration, restless as the sea and multitudinous as the sands upon its shore, is here committed to safe, silent, and impartial witnesses. Stored up in iron gratings, classified and arranged, preserved, as far as human skill can preserve them, from innumerable perils, the public records of this kingdom now slumber in their new repository of stone and iron undisturbed, except when removed from their shelves to gratify the curiosity of the antiquarian or assist the researches of the historian.

With materials so vast, yet so important, two questions have perpetually arisen from early times : first, how are they to be most efficiently preserved ? and next, how turned to the best account ? Happily the nation has suffered little fron foreign invasions. Such misfortunes as have overtaken Strassburg, and destroyed its libraries and its manuscripts, are comparatively unknown here. Even in the Civil Wars of the fifteenth century, and in the Great Rebellion of the seventeenth, though the rage of party might dismantle or destroy mansions, monasteries, and cathedrals, it left uninjured the national muniments. Whether Romanist or Protestant, Cavalier or Roundhead, gained the ascendency, all alike in turn respected the archives of the kingdom, and preserved them from sacrilegious violence. Their worst enemies have been of an ignobler kind—rats and mice, fire, damp, and mildew: the negligence in some instances, the misplaced confidence in others, of those who were appointed to preserve them. Dispersed in various quarters of the metropolis, some at the Tower, some at Carlton Ride, some in the Chapter House at Westminster, others at the Rolls House; exposed to weather, dust, and smoke; stowed away in sacks, boxes, and hampers; unmanageable from their vastness and unwieldiness; little known, and therefore attracting little attention—successive Governments were contented to believe that these muniments were in some sense preserved, and equally contented that they should be of no use to any one. Careless and ignorant of their value so long as no inquiries were made, every obstacle was multiplied and all access was sedulously barred, whenever such access was desired, except in the case of a few favoured inquirers. History in this country has always found devotees and admirers in one guise or another. Even from the time of the Reformation some few, chiefly among the clergy, have busied themselves with historical or biographical or topographical investigations. At no period, not even in the fanatical ascendency of the gloomiest Puritanism, have the people of England been wholly indifferent to their national antiquities. The love of the past, the appeal to precedent, feudal castles and monastic ruins, parochial and cathedral churches, the visible memorials of former greatness, taste, genius, and faith, have helped to foster this historical spirit. Then, again, the general stability of our English aristocracy and gentry, undisturbed by violent political convulsions, rooted mainly on the same soil, and surrounded for ages by the same tenantry, has handed down the historical traditions of great families from generation to generation, and associated them with the sympathies of the living. We need not the statues of the Howards, the Stanleys, and the Cecils; we have their breathing representatives amongst us.

To those who fostered and gratified these national tastes and inclinations, generally at their own cost, and rarely with any expectation of remuneration, a liberal use of the national archives would have been a great boon; as, in truth, the freest access to these papers ought to be considered the best justification for the cost bestowed upon their preservation. But their appointed guardians, whose official emoluments depended for the most part on fees levied from inquirers, were not forward in promoting the wishes of antiquarians, nor were Ministers of State much inclined to listen to the applications of students. For any but historical and archæological purposes, nine-tenths of these papers had long ceased to be of any importance. Modern diplomacy was not liable to be compromised by the revelation of any secrets they contained. All the precautions that prudence required might have been easily secured by laying a prohibition upon such papers only as referred to events subsequent to the Peace of Versailles. But the formalities of office would admit of no such commonplace distinctions. A mysterious belief prevailed that Secretaries of State drank wisdom and inspiration from the despatches of Cardinal Wolsey, or solved the Gordian knot of policy by profound studies of the diplomatic correspondence of the sixteenth and seventeenth centuries. Who could tell whether, in the debates of the House of Commons, ministerial policy might not be assailed, or some question asked, which could not be conveniently parried without a reference to the State papers of the Tudors or the Stuarts? So those who would have turned these papers to the best account were jealously excluded from the use of them. And even when the rule was relaxed by Secretaries of State, like Lord Russell, combining literary taste with statesmanship, when a more liberal spirit was willing to make a partial concession to historians and biographers, the necessity was imposed upon the applicant of strictly defining the nature of his inquiry, the class of papers he proposed to examine, and the exact limits of his search. The interpretation of these conditions was left to the discretion of the keepers or the clerks of the office. It was at their option to produce or keep back whatever documents they pleased, and the inquirer had no remedy. Official catalogues, in many instances, did not exist; in no instance could they be consulted. The system of arrangement varied with the office: not uncommonly in the same office under different keepers. What could an inquirer do, hampered as he was by these restrictions? He might complain; but he had no means of substantiating his complaints. He might suspect; but his suspicions necessarily recoiled upon himself. In defence of a policy so vexatious and so frivolous, nothing could be urged except the old immemorial argument of tyrannical custom. And as, whenever any modification or reform was proposed, they alone were consulted who were most concerned in maintaining abuses, these restrictions bade fair to continue immovable, like the laws of the Medes and Persians. How they were swept away, and a wiser and more gracious system introduced, we shall have to tell hereafter.

But in spite of all these precautions for excluding the public, it was discovered that the great purpose, on which that exclusion was founded, had not been secured. Idle and ignorant curiosity, exposure to the avarice of collectors, the thumbs and fingers of careless readers, may inflict injury and loss on valuable books and papers; but public indifference has always been incomparably more prejudicial. Keepers of libraries and museums grow careless of treasures nobody cares to inspect, and no one inquires after. The true worth of these things is in the eyes and ears of the public, and no precaution is so effectual, no supervision so sure or so searching, as publicity. Statesmen in general are too much absorbed in the pressing duties of the day to trouble themselves with the griefs of scholars or the cares of historians. Yet occasionally they have been compelled to rouse themselves from their apathy. As late as the year 1836 a select Committee of the House of Commons was appointed, on the motion of Mr. Charles Buller, to inquire 'into the present state of the Records of the United Kingdom.' The result of their labours is preserved in a portly Blue-book extending to 946 pages. Among the witnesses examined on that occasion was Mr. Henry Cole, and this is the description he then gave of the condition of one class of the public muniments, under the old system of exclusion: ' Some (he says) were in a state of inseparable adhesion to the stone walls; there were numerous fragments which had only just escaped entire consumption by vermin, and many were in the last stage of putrefaction. Decay and damp had rendered a large quantity so fragile as hardly to admit of being touched; others, particularly those in the form of rolls, were so coagulated together that they could not be uncoiled. Six or seven perfect skeletons of rats (exhibited by the witness to the Committee) were found imbedded, and bones of these vermin were generally distributed throughout the mass' (Report, p. 427). After so racy a description, our readers will be prepared to hear of the minor evils of dirt, soot, neglect, and disorder. 'Sackfuls of records' are described by one witness as tumbling on the floor, others 'literally covered with filth.' Another witness produces a mass of documents ' in a state of actual fusion.' The doors and cases were insecure, the depositories ' dirty as a chimney-sweeper's room.' Large quantities of parchments 'were purloined and sold to the glue manufacturers.'

Such were the results of a system when the public were jealously excluded from the use of the national records, and the custodians of them were answerable to no regulations except to those of their own devising. Nor were these isolated instances confined to the last generation. Century after century reveals the same story of dirt, waste, and destruction, of inefficient keepers, of careless and penurious governments, of spasmodic attempts at reform, followed by long intervals of inactivity and neglect. Complaints of the disorderly condition of the public records and the want of proper Calendars date as far back as the Chancellorship of Bishop Stapleton, in the reign of Edward II. In the days of Elizabeth numerous documents had disappeared for years, until they were accidentally discovered by Master Hobby ' searching for a place to put gunpowder in.' When Charles II., in a fit of politic good humour, appointed Prynne, whose ears had been cropped for the freedom of his satire in the days of Charles I., Keeper of his Majesty's Records in the

Tower, the following pungent account was rendered by the
new Custodian to his royal benefactor : ' No sooner received
I your royal patent for the custody of your ancient Records
in your Tower of London . .'. but I designed and endeavoured to rescue the greatest part of them from that desolation and corruption in which . . . they had for many years,
for a large part, lain bound together in one confused chaos,
under corroding putrefying cobwebs, dust and filth, in the
darkest corner of Cæsar's Chapel in the White Tower, as mere
useless relics not worthy to be calendared or brought down
thence into the office amongst other Records of use. In order
thereunto I employed many soldiers and women to remove
and cleanse them from their filthiness, who, soon growing
weary of this noisome work, left them almost as foul as they
found them.' ' In raking up this dunghill,' continues Prynne,
' according to my expectation I found many rare, ancient,
precious pearls and golden Records . . . with many original
Bulls of Popes (some of them under seal), letters to and from
Popes, Cardinals, and the Court of Rome, besides sundry rare
antiquities, specially relating to the Parliaments of England.'[2] Even as late as the reign of George III. large
masses of public papers had so effectually disappeared that
their very existence was forgotten. In 1763, Mr. Edwards
tells us,[3] an officer of the Board of Trade had occasion to
refer to certain documents of the age of Charles I., and applied for that purpose to the Privy Council office. Nothing
was known there of the papers or even of the office to which
they belonged ; 'but a venerable clerk had a dim recollec-
tion that he had heard, in his youth, of the existence of some
old books in the room near the gateway of Whitehall, and
suggested a search, which, after many adventures with decayed staircases, locksmiths, flocks of pigeons, and accumula-
tions of filth, proved eventually to be successful.'

[2] Edwards, p. 261. [3] Ibid. p. 201.

So much for the way in which our Governments had settled to their own satisfaction, until very recently, one question of paramount importance, the preservation of our national papers, or, to adopt the euphuistic phraseology of Mr. Charles Buller's Committee, 'had manifested their solicitude for the safety of the Public Records.'

But it is time to turn to another branch of our inquiry, and examine what attempts have been made by the Government of this country to render its imperial muniments more generally accessible. Towards this result a most important preliminary step has been taken within the last few years. Formerly dispersed in twenty or thirty different localities, all the public papers of the nation have now been happily concentrated in one spot. They are no longer exposed to the perils of decay or mildew; neither 'rats nor mice' find harbour now among royal letters or accounts of the wardrobe; efficient precautions have been taken against theft, negligence, and disorder. Another reform not less important and beneficial to literary inquirers has been recently introduced. Under the old system, the public property of the nation, by some extraordinary delusion, had come to be regarded as the private property of its custodians, and as held by them for their exclusive emolument. Indexes and Calendars, made in official hours, were considered as the 'private and marketable property' of the clerks and keepers. It was their object, naturally enough, to sell their services at the highest possible rate; to exclude the public from consulting the Records except through the one accredited channel; to keep all information to themselves, or so overlay it with extraneous matter that their own emoluments might experience no diminution. 'The fees for searches,' says Mr. Edwards,[*] 'ranged in amount from two guineas to ten. The Calendars were usually worded in an equivocal and misleading way,

[*] P. 299.

expressly to whet the searcher's appetite. Fresh searches brought new fees. If a paragraph of a few words only in the long-sought document would fully answer the patient searcher's purpose, he could not have it. To the essential line or two were united, with Mezentian rigour, hundreds or perhaps thousands of dreary lines, that brought no information to the searcher, but brought in some cases a hundred guineas or so to the officer. It is still remembered that on one such occasion, when, after payment of multitudinous fees, caused by the ingenious construction of the Calendars, and by other cognate circumstances, the precious paragraph was at length disinterred and the weary and well-nigh disheartened fee-payer asked, finally, how much a copy of that paragraph would cost, the obliging functionary turned over the membranes, made his mental calculation, and in a gravely official tone replied, " *One hundred and forty-five pounds, Sir!* " '

These extortionate and vexatious regulations have now been swept away. Access to the State Papers and public muniments is as free and unfettered as to the manuscripts of the British Museum. Every inquirer may inspect whatever papers or parchments he pleases. He may take whatever copies he requires without restriction. On presenting his card to the Deputy Keeper, the treasures of the Record Office are thrown open to his use and inspection. In all these respects the liberal regulations at the new repository present a striking contrast to those of any other country. In France, the papers of the Foreign Office (*Archives des Affaires Étrangères*) cannot be approached, except through the medium of numerous rigid formalities. No copies are allowed, not even pencil memoranda, of any documents, however remote, or however disconnected with modern politics. The visitor might as well request permission to examine the sacred volumes of the Imperial correspondence, in its green velvet and gold bindings, as extort permission from the rigid archivist to take an extract from the despatches of Marillac or Chatillon, whose ambassadorial functions date from the Reformation. At Brussels it is not much better. At Vienna, at least until a recent period, the correspondence relating to Wallenstein and the Thirty Years' War was jealously withheld. At Madrid the chance of pursuing historical inquiries is precarious and capricious. Nowhere is the privilege of reading or copying the national State Papers and correspondence so full and unreserved as in England. Nowhere is the reader more at his ease, less fettered by restrictions, or made less painfully sensible of the obligations conferred upon him. In all these respects Lord Romilly has left nothing to be desired.

Here, then, it must be admitted that a great advance has been made, with the sanction of the Government, in the direction pointed out by Mr. Buller's committee; far greater, perhaps, than the most sanguine member of that committee could ever have anticipated. For the preservation of the public records all has been done that was required. For making those records useful and accessible to the nation, we have something more than a beginning. And yet not more than a good beginning. For imagine a reader turned adrift without handbook, catalogue, or index of any kind, into a library of half a million of manuscripts of which he knows neither the titles nor the contents. By what intuition, by what prophetical insight, can he expect to discover what he wants? How is he to select from the vast and heterogeneous masses such papers as immediately bear upon his own researches? Without guide or index it is impossible for him to know whether further inquiry will be rewarded with success, or further examination will confirm or contradict his previous impressions. Catalogues are therefore indispensable, were it for no other reason than that of giving efficiency to the privilege of consulting these collections,

ESSAY I. NEW SOURCES OF ENGLISH HISTORY. 13

conceded by the Government and sanctioned by the nation.
It is absurd to collect and preserve our national muniments, at a great cost, and then suffer them to fall a prey
to neglect and vermin. It is absurder still, if possible, to
build a National Record Office at a vast cost [5] for storing
these muniments, and yet exclude the public from consulting and using them. But absurdest of all is it to concede
this right, to incur all these expenses, and then neutralise
them all by withholding the only means that are required
for rendering the privilege real and effectual. The preparation of indexes and catalogues may be the last step in the
process; it is the first in the convenience of the reader, and
it is more indispensable to him than any other. It is of less
consequence to him how papers are arranged or where they
are placed, provided only he can obtain a correct knowledge
of their contents. Without this knowledge, the most exquisite order, the most perfect arrangement, are no better than
a sealed fountain. It might have been right for the Committee of the House of Commons to direct, as a first and
principal requirement, that the public muniments should be
methodised and arranged. As a preliminary step to their
due preservation, as a foundation for future operations, no
advice could be sounder. But to arrange and methodise
with no intention to ulterior proceedings, to arrange and
methodise with no view to use, is both wasteful and preposterous. To erect a vast and cumbrous machine, of many
parts, at a heavy cost, and then withhold the only thing
requisite to make it work, is neither wise nor economical.
Two courses were open to the Government: either to have
left the records in their original state, abandoning all idea
of a General Record Office, or by a wise and judicious liberality to justify the expenditure incurred in its erection by

[5] The first block of the New Record Office cost 88,490*l*., and there are four more blocks to come, according to the designs of the architect.

making these records available for the studies of historians and biographers; of all, in short, who are interested in the use of them. The Government has adopted the latter alternative: we think not only wisely, but with the full sanction of the nation. It has incurred no inconsiderable expense in building a general Record Repository. It has appointed officers to superintend and carry on the necessary operations. To give effect to these measures, to justify what has been done, indexes and catalogues are indispensable.

But here is the difficulty. If previous keepers had framed catalogues of these papers and parchments in the first instance; if their successors, as their stores accumulated, had done what is now doing under the Master of the Rolls, the task would have been comparatively easy. On the other hand, the neglect of centuries has now to be repaired. Documents of the greatest value and interest have increased from year to year, until the new building, spacious as it is, has grown already too narrow for its accumulating hoards. Hundreds of busy heads and hands at the Home, the Foreign and Colonial Offices, at the Treasury, the War Office and the Admiralty, in the Chancery, the King's Bench, and the various Law Courts, are daily and hourly engaged with Cyclopean activity in copying or ingrossing innumerable sheets of paper and parchment, doomed eventually to find their last resting-place in the new Record Office. How to grapple with the enormous mass, how to select from such multifarious collections, what catalogues to make and how to make them, are grave and puzzling questions. Equally puzzling is it to know how to satisfy the wants and requirements of all, or of the greatest number of readers. One man is exclusively interested in the problems of history, another is wholly indifferent to such speculations. This man is investigating the genealogy or ramifications of some great family; another is inquiring into the variations of prices;

a third wishes to discover the relations of land and capital, the improvement or deterioration of labour, the social development or decline of this class of the population or of that. The materials required by one set of readers are of no interest to another. Who shall decide upon such conflicting claims? Each has something to urge in his own behalf, and all may light upon discoveries of great moment to the present or future welfare of this country.

Then with what class of record shall the work of indexing commence, supposing that competent hands can be found to undertake the task of making Catalogues or Calendars? For, commonplace as such labour may appear to be, it demands qualifications of a peculiar kind not readily met with; extreme accuracy, unwearied diligence, a thorough knowledge of the subject, tact and judgment to discriminate what is important and essential from what is not. If the funds for such a work were unlimited, it might be easy to satisfy all demands. But that is not to be expected. All that can be done is to apply the annual grant voted by Parliament in the most economical and judicious manner. Whether this has been done or not we now propose to inquire.

Of the vast multitude of papers deposited at the Rolls, some are exclusively legal and technical; others historical and diplomatic, like the 'State Papers' proper; others miscellaneous relating to the Exchequer—an ample category embracing in its comprehensive range all that relates to the treasures, revenues, finances of the Crown and the country; issues and receipts; subsidies, mint, wardrobe and household accounts; works and public buildings; blood-money, secret service, forest accounts, and the like. To these must be added the papers of the Admiralty, the War Office, the old court of the Star Chamber, and others of minor importance.

Even for an uninitiated reader, it would scarcely be difficult to judge of the relative value and attractiveness of these various classes of documents, numerous and perplexing as they seem; and if he had any doubts, they might be removed by turning over the pages of any popular living historian. The correspondence of kings, of statesmen, of ambassadors, takes precedence of all others; for without them the great drama of history, the intrigues of Cabinets, the moving incidents of flood and field, are nothing better than an unmeaning panorama and dumb show. Historians have sometimes been laughed at for their almost exclusive affection for heroes, kings, and demi-gods. It has become a fashion of late to insist upon social and economical questions, the rate of wages, the prices of food, the distribution of wealth, the laws that determine the development of humanity, as more suited to the functions of philosophic history, as if kings were of less importance to us than 'their tax-gatherers.' But so long as the world will persist in thinking that, in the history of the Tudor times, it cannot dispense with Henry VIII., his wives and his ministers, or in that of Mary and Elizabeth, with the fires of Smithfield and the Spanish Armada, or in that of the Stuarts, with Charles I. and Oliver Cromwell—so long as history will gather round the actions and lives of individual men events of the greatest interest to all, and send its readers to sleep when it assumes the garb of philosophy, so long will the historian stick to the concrete elements of flesh and blood, and value mainly, if not exclusively, those materials which are in this way best suited to his purpose.

Perhaps it was out of deference to some such feeling as this that the Master of the Rolls was guided in selecting the papers and correspondence of the State Paper Office for commencing his operations. On the 7th of December, 1855, Sir John Romilly addressed a letter to the Lords of the Treasury, stating 'That although the Records, State Papers, and documents in his charge constituted the most complete and perfect series of their kind in the civilised world, and were of the greatest value in a historical and constitutional point of view, they were comparatively useless to the public from the want of proper Calendars and Indexes.' He added that, in order to effect this object, it would be necessary for him to employ a few persons fully qualified to perform the work which he contemplated. The Treasury assented to the proposal, and from that period is to be dated the commencement of that class of the Rolls publications known by the somewhat vague and unattractive appellation of 'Calendars of State Papers.' Of the editors employed by the Master of the Rolls four were already in the service of the Government, Mr. Lemon, Mr. Thorpe, Mr. Hamilton, and Mr. Sainsbury. To Mr. Lemon were entrusted the Domestic papers of the reign of Elizabeth, to Mr. Thorpe the Scottish papers from 1509 to 1603, to Mr. Hamilton the Irish, and to Mr. Sainsbury the Colonial Series.[6] Of the editors taken from out of doors, the Domestic papers of the reign of James I. were committed to Mrs. Green, those of Charles I. to the late Mr. Bruce, the Foreign papers of the reign of Elizabeth to Mr. Stevenson, who has since resigned, and the entire correspondence of the reign of Henry VIII. (which could not be divided, like the others, into separate series) to Mr. Brewer. On the death of Mr. Lemon the papers of Elizabeth were transferred to Mrs. Green, who had already completed her 'Calendar of the State Papers of James I.'

Of these Calendars forty-five volumes have already appeared; eight of them edited by official and thirty-seven by unofficial editors. This disparity is not to be attributed to any deficiency of zeal and ability on the part of the former, but to the fact of their being employed on official duties from which the non-official editors are exempt. It must, however, be considered as a complete justification of the Master of the Rolls in asking, and of the Lords of the

* See *Calendars of State Papers*, p. 1.

Treasury in granting, the supplementary assistance required by Lord Romilly. If the work had been left to official editors alone, it is clear from the rate of progress that a century must have elapsed before any one series of these Calendars could have been completed.

For the prosecution of this work the Treasury grants an annual sum of 1,500*l*. Two editors, in addition to those already mentioned, are employed abroad; Señor Gayangos, in the place of the late Mr. Bergenroth, and Mr. Rawdon Brown at Venice.

On the manner in which the several editors have executed their tasks we do not propose to enter. After selecting men of ability and known experience, the Master of the Rolls did wisely in prescribing the fewest general rules, sufficient to ensure a certain degree of uniformity, but leaving to each editor a discretion and freedom as to details. It must be satisfactory to the nation and to Lord Romilly to find that his judgment in this respect has been justified by the result; and the use already made of these works by the public journals and the approbation bestowed on them afford the best proof of his sound discretion. Already they have furnished new details and more correct views, not only to the grave historian, but to writers catering, like the Messrs. Chambers, wholesome instruction or amusement for the passing hour. Popular they are never likely to be, in the full meaning of the word, for a 'Calendar of State Papers' conveys to many readers no other idea than that of a dry and colourless abstract of formal diplomatic papers. As Acts of Parliament and international treaties are papers of State, all State Papers, in ordinary estimation, must be something like Acts of Parliament or antiquated diplomacy. It never seems to have occurred to those who think thus, that as Kings and Queens, at least in earlier times, could have no individual existence apart from the State, the knowledge of their personal history is mainly to be derived from their correspondence, that is, from their State Papers.

But the popular notion of the dryness and repulsiveness of diplomatic documents is founded on the common misapprehension that they are exclusively concerned with grave affairs of State, whereas, in fact, they descend to the minutest details of social life and domestic manners; and for this sufficient reason. In the sixteenth and seventeenth centuries it was the custom of the Government of this country to confiscate all the letters and papers of attainted persons, without distinction. Thus it was that the diaries, the household accounts, the private correspondence of the accused were transferred to the Exchequer, and there they remain to the present day. Imagine such a process as this suddenly put in force against a nobleman or statesman in this century. Imagine the correspondence of the husband and the wife, their household bills, their rent-books, their private journals, seized unexpectedly and religiously preserved in some Government office. Could any personal history be more various or more minute? Such was the process not once but frequently repeated in the reigns of the Tudors; in such a reign especially as that of Henry VIII., when every individual of the nation was violently tossed from side to side, and every foremost leader was brought in succession to the block. Whether they were nobles, like Buckingham or Henry Howard Earl of Surrey—whether ministers of the highest station, like Wolsey and Cromwell, trusted with State secrets —whether criminals of lofty rank, or inferior agents, their private papers and correspondence, with the rest of their property, escheated to the State; and though their lands might be restored, much of their correspondence was detained, and remains to this day in the national archives. Thus it is that all kinds of miscellaneous information, familiar letters, tutors', tailors', shoemakers', and even milliners' bills; the daily, personal, and household accounts, the passing gossip and speculations of the time, have joined company with instructions to ambassadors, projects of alliance, the deep mysteries of State, the fall of princes and the death-warrants of nobles. So the tragedy and comedy of the world has been blended together strangely and grotesquely enough by the natural operation of the law, and not from any system or contrivance.

And even in regard to the purely diplomatic correspondence of the sixteenth and seventeenth centuries, of which lively and ignorant critics affect to speak with so much disdain, it must be remembered that ambassadors and statesmen in these earlier ages condescended to the humbler functions of 'Special Correspondents.' Newspapers at this day hold a part, and not the least essential, in diplomacy. A correspondent at the seat of war is a lay ambassador, who sends home, for the benefit of the ministry, information as precise, as trustworthy, as secret, as expeditious, as any that is received at the Foreign Office. Probably more so; probably a wise and sagacious minister is enabled to test more accurately the pulse of the times, to fathom more precisely the tide of public opinion, by these unofficial than by the gravest official reports. But when no such means of information existed in the days of the Tudors and the first Stuarts, ambassadors themselves acted as caterers of news; they were 'Special Correspondents' for their own Courts. What plenipotentiary, nowadays, would not think it beneath the dignity of his vocation to transmit a description of the personal appearance of the Sovereign to whom he was accredited; of the shape of his leg or the colour of his beard, the dress he wore at church or on horseback, how he rode or how he walked, what were his pastimes and the manners of his court, the age and features of his wife and children, the fashions, the foibles, the ceremonies, the banquets, the gossip in and out of doors, the thousand little personal traits of character, the innumerable small details which give life and animation to history? Such topics are too trivial for the purple and fine linen of modern diplomatists. It would fall wholly beneath its dignity to record how Henry VIII. gave 4*d*. to a boy to throw up his cap for a snow-balling ; how Anne Boleyn was mobbed by a crowd of angry women as she sate in a bower with her royal paramour; how her daughter, Queen Elizabeth, with her *beaux yeux* and her Latin, terrified the outlandish ambassador; how her successor James I. hated cold water; or how his son Charles I. demeaned himself with Henrietta Maria! The liveliest materials of history have been banished nowadays to newspaper paragraphs and special correspondents; but it was not so then. For then it was as much a part of an ambassador's function to cater news for his royal master as to worm out the secrets of government, to send home as faithful an account of the ordinary doings and talk of the times as of the combinations of kings and statesmen. In illustration of these remarks we submit the following extracts, taken from Mr. Brown's 'Venetian Calendar,' not because they are more exclusively interesting than many others, but because readers of Shakespere, who may not be readers of history, may more easily judge what sort of information is to be found in these Calendars. The writer refers to an entertainment given in 1527 by Cardinal Wolsey :—

'I wrote to you on the first, transmitting the King's reply to Luther's letter. Last evening I was present at a very sumptuous supper, given by Cardinal Wolsey, there being amongst the guests the Papal, French, and Venetian ambassadors, and the chief nobility of the English Court. I considered myself out of place beside a very beautiful damsel, each of the guests having one to his share. During the supper the King arrived, with a very gallant company of masqueraders, and his Majesty, after presenting himself to the Cardinal, threw a main at dice, and then unmasked, as did all his companions; whereupon he withdrew to sup in one of the Cardinal's chambers, the rest of the guests continuing their repast, with such variety of the choicest viands and wines as to be marvellous.

'Supper being ended, they proceeded to the first hall, with which you are well acquainted, and where a very well-designed stage had been prepared on which the Cardinal's gentlemen recited Plautus' Latin comedy, entitled the "Menæchmei." On its conclusion, all the actors, one after the other, presented themselves to the King, and on their knees recited to him, some more and some less, Latin verses in his praise. Having listened to them all, the King betook himself with the rest of the guests to the hall where they had all supped, the tables (at which they seated themselves in the same order as before) being spread with every sort of confection, whereof they partook.

'After the marvellous collation a stage was displayed, on which sat Venus, at whose feet were six damsels, forming so graceful a group for her footstool, that it looked as if she and they had really come down in person from heaven. And whilst everybody was intently gazing upon so agreeable a sight, the trumpets flourished, and a car appeared drawn by three boys stark naked, on which was Cupid, dragging after him, bound by a silver rope, six old men, clad in the pastoral fashion, but the material was cloth of silver and white satin. Cupid presented them to his mother, delivering a most elegant Latin oration to their praise, saying they had been cruelly wounded: whereupon Venus compassionately replied in equally choice language, and caused the six nymphs, the sweethearts of the six old men, to descend, commanding them to afford their lovers all solace, and requite them for past pangs. Each of the nymphs was then taken by the hand by her lover, and to the sound of trumpets they performed a very beautiful dance. On its termination the King and his favourites commenced another with the ladies there present, and with this the entertainment and the night ended, for it was already daybreak. I then went home sated with so much revelry, and am despatching a public letter for the Signory, to be given to Sir John Russell, now on the eve of departing for France on his way to the Pope.

'London, 4th January, 1527.'

The second extract refers to the same Cardinal after his fall.

'On the 11th ultimo, I wrote account of current events here, and most especially of the recent arrest of Cardinal Wolsey. Subsequently the King, having determined on his removal to this castle of London (*i.e.* from York), sent Captain Kingston with his guard to effect it. On arriving at a place sixty miles hence (*sic*) he found the Cardinal very ill, and in bed, so that the day before he had confessed and communicated; and although the captain exhorted him to hope for the best from the King's clemency, declaring that he was to convey him at his entire convenience, and that he might remain where he was so long as he pleased, yet at the end of two days he departed this life, at the close of which he drew a deep and loud sigh; and some six hours afterwards there was put into the earth that personage who had prepared for his remains a more costly mausoleum than any royal or papal monument in the world, so that the King intends it to serve for himself, *post multos et felices annos*, having caused the Cardinal's arms to be erased from it.

'It is said that his right reverend lordship's indisposition was preceded by two very bad symptoms. When first arrested, owing to mental depression, he would take no food, *nisi coactus*, and then came flux, and he could not retain anything in his stomach. According to report, his mind never wandered at the last, and on seeing Captain Kingston, he made his attendants raise him in his bed, where he knelt; and whenever he heard the King's name he bowed his head, putting his face downwards. He then asked Captain Kingston where his guards were, and being answered that lodging was provided for them in several chambers on the ground floor of the palace (*palaccio*), he requested they might all be sent for into his presence. So as many having entered as the place would hold, he raised himself as much as he could, saying that on the day before he had taken the Sacrament, and expected soon to find himself before the supreme Judgment seat, so that at such an extremity, he ought not to fail speaking the truth, or leave any other opinion of him than such as was veracious; adding, "I pray God that Sacrament may be to the damnation of my soul, if ever I thought to do disservice to my King," and so on.'

But besides the circumstantiality and vividness of detail, the documents contained in these Calendars have the advantage of being contemporary with the events they record. They reproduce not only the facts but the very atmosphere of the past, with a fidelity no imagination can realise, however powerful. The ablest of modern histories are necessarily tinged with the passions and prejudices of the historian, with the spirit and thoughts of his own times. The more strongly he sympathises with his own age, the more dramatic his faculties, the more creative his fancy, the stronger is his propensity, the more irresistible his temptation to invest the past with the colours and drapery of the present. The best are liable to this weakness, whilst inferior writers rather glory in it than attempt to avoid it. They falsify and exaggerate from design, as the readiest means of attracting popularity. But these Calendars furnish the best corrective for this tendency. Occupied solely with the passing current of events, steeped exclusively in the passions ns and prejudices of the past, and with the thoughts and emotions awakened by them, contemporary letters reproduce for modern readers not only the acts but the agents, as they lived and felt, as they trod this earth, with their schemes and devices, their hopes, their ambition and their fears. Theirs is the glistening of 'real eyes,' the aches of real hearts, but of eyes and hearts as they glistened and ached in days long gone by. These are the advantages of contemporaneous letters and journals—of papers such as these Calendars contain. They may not be history, but they are the truest and most authentic materials for history. They are the sources to which the historian must resort for the clearest, the most correct, the most satisfactory information.

If, then, the Master of the Rolls and the Government had done no more to make such materials accessible they would have deserved the gratitude of the nation. Something they were bound to do. They could not allow the public free access to these papers without providing a catalogue of some sort, for the due use as well as for the needful security of such invaluable collections. One Committee of the House of Commons after another had insisted upon this as a chief and primary obligation. 'Public indexes and calendars should be completed forthwith, either by the ordinary diligence of the persons usually employed for the purpose, in each office, or, if necessary, by extra assistance provided by public expense,' is the recommendation of the Select Committee of the House of Commons, appointed as far back as 1800, reinforced and reiterated by the Select Committee of 1836. Yet, towards this necessary and indeed imperative measure, no steps were taken until within a recent period. The necessity was urgent; for without catalogues and indexes these national documents might as well be buried in the tombs of the Capulets, and, until catalogues are completed, all other means for diffusing a knowledge of these papers must be not only incomplete but unsatisfactory.

This raises a question whether it would not have been more acceptable to the public, as some have thought, if the money now expended on Calendars had been devoted to printing the documents themselves, or, at least, a selection from them. In determining this question, it must be remembered that no selection would have answered the primary purpose of the Calendars. The necessity would still have remained of compiling indexes of the public papers, sufficiently copious to satisfy the purposes of literary inquirers, and save the needless wear and tear of delicate documents, many of which are in a frail and perishable condition, catalogues sufficiently distinct to identify the papers when needed, and produce them when required; and, lastly, to prevent loss and embezzlement. It was not absolutely necessary for these purposes that such Calendars should be printed; but then it would have been requisite to multiply copies of them in manuscript; and no manuscript Calendar can ever be so handy or so complete, or so useful to the public as a printed one. The main object of making the records of the kingdom and their contents better known would have been in great measure overlooked. Readers in foreign lands, or at a distance from the metropolis—and they are generally those who have most leisure and inclination for historical studies—would have been virtually excluded from the benefit. How great is the disadvantage of a manuscript Calendar as compared with a printed one, is evident from the spare and meagre use of those papers in the British Museum, of which only a manuscript calendar exists. Even in point of economy it is very doubtful whether in the end a manuscript catalogue has any advantage over a printed one, whereas, in all other respects, its inferiority is too manifest to admit of dispute.

But a stronger argument on this head remains, and one which appears to us conclusive. During the last five centuries and a half the history of our State Papers and our national Records is a series of prodigious efforts made at long intervals by energetic keepers and enlightened Governments to rescue them from gross neglect, disorder, and embezzlement, followed by most unfortunate relapses. The labours of men like the Master of the Rolls, alive to the value of the collections committed to their charge, and desirous of consulting the truest interests of the nation, have collapsed more than once under less enlightened and less active successors. Their reforms have fallen into abeyance, and old abuses have regained their former supremacy. We do not anticipate such a destiny for Lord Romilly's labours. We do not anticipate that some future Record historian will have to say of them what he has to say now of the reforms of Chancellor Stapleton, of Lambarde, of Prynne, of George Grenville, of Lord Colchester, of everyone, in short, who ever grappled manfully with the abuses of our Record Offices, that their efforts were transient and fruitless. It is not to be imagined that, some thirty years hence, a Committee of the House of Commons will produce a Report of documents consigned to disorder and oblivion, of manuscripts stowed away in forgotten pigeonholes and neglected corners; but this we will say—or rather Mr. Edwards shall say it for us—that 'the systematic preparation of Calendars for the public use, and for the public use alone, is obviously the sufficient and only remedy against such fatal contingencies. It is only by printed Calendars of our national papers, which men can take home and con over in the leisure of their studies, that the value of these papers can be fully appreciated. It is only by such Calendars and the researches suggested by them that the almost inevitable tendency of these papers to get mislaid or forgotten can be effectually counteracted. And as there are no manuscripts at home; or even abroad, in public or in private, at all comparable to our own in historic importance, and none so intimately connected with our national credit, so there are none which have a stronger claim on the attention and liberality of the Government.

There must then be Official Calendars of the whole collection for office purposes, and no selection of documents will satisfy these requirements. If they can be made besides generally useful to the public, that is a gain, and that utility has been one object of the Master of the Rolls. As Keeper of these Records, as bound by the repeated recommendations of the House of Commons, calendars and inventories for the better use and safer custody of the Records under his charge were with Lord Romilly a primary obligation. Nor until such calendars have been completed is it easy to see how any satisfactory selection can be made. Supposing, what is hardly probable, that all who were interested in consulting these papers could agree upon a principle of selection, long before such a selection had approached its completion new papers would have turned up, additions and alterations would have had to be made, a new series would be required to supplement the first, whilst the varying tastes, pursuits, and requirements of many readers would have remained unsatisfied. Hardly any two judges would be found to agree why this document should be selected and that rejected. Nor indeed is it possible for the most skilful to lay down abstract rules as to the relative importance of any class of historical papers. Their real importance cannot always be measured until they are viewed in their connection with others. Their true meaning and value are not patent at first sight, nor perhaps until subsequent researches have long after flashed an alien light upon them, and invested with an unexpected gravity what by itself seemed trivial and unimportant. In all researches of this kind no editor can be trusted to select for another. He may methodise, index, and catalogue, leaving the inquirer to sift his materials and push his investigations further, if needful; but the task of selection each man must undertake for himself. With a thoughtful historian that selection will vary at every stage of his investigation—at every hour when fresh light dawns upon him. What at first filled him with rapture, he will upon maturer inquiry reject; what seemed insignificant at first sight, tedious and even repulsive, will often commend itself to his riper judgment; for of history it is true what Bacon said of physical causes: 'It cometh often to pass that mean and small things discover great, better than great can discover the small.' As to the other alternative of publishing all documents indiscriminately at full length, we prefer to quote the able remarks of Mr. Tytler, the Historian of Scotland:—

'To print all the records and muniments. . . . would require an enormous sum; so it comes to a choice or balance between having a correct knowledge of the contents of all the records and letters illustrating English history, and having a small corner of our history, perhaps extending to twenty or thirty years, illustrated by the Records themselves. No historians familiar with the use of original materials would hesitate, I think, to use the Catalogues. By them he would be enabled to collect all the scattered lights which might illustrate the general History of England from a large mass of original documents. In the other way he would acquire a minute knowledge of a very curtailed portion; but the lights thrown upon important points of history within this portion would be proportionably scanty. Besides this, it is evident that were the whole, or even the greater portion of the records to be printed, it would only be the substitution of an unfathomable sea of " print " for an unfathomable sea of " manuscript." In the end, to render such a mass available to the historian, catalogues and indexes, with a brief analysis of the documents, would be found necessary. Thus, at last, you must have *Catalogues raisonnés*. Would it not be easier and far less expensive to have them at first ? Again, when any serious difficulty or obscure point occurs, a historian, in his anxiety for truth, must inspect the original. Hence he may in many instances dispense with printing the record or letter itself, but without the catalogue he remains ignorant of its existence. The advantages of first making catalogues are also great when viewed in connection with the plan of afterwards printing a selection of the records themselves. Being once acquainted with the whole mass of records, letters, State Papers, &c., in short, all the materials illustrating the civil, ecclesiastical, or constitutional history of the country, this selection will be made under the most favourable circumstances. The most valuable for the purpose of history will be chosen, and there will be the greatest chance of all being printed from originals. Lastly, the benefits resulting from this plan of forming catalogues will be most important in checking the progress of historical error.'[7]

These arguments appear to us unanswerable. But whilst there is one class of critics who set such an inordinate value on our public muniments that nothing will satisfy them short of printing all at full length, there is an opposite class who reject them all as equally unworthy of credit. They are possessed by a strange notion that of all historical evidences State Papers are the least trustworthy. It is the fixed creed of these objectors that statesmen and ambassadors indulged in a perpetual masquerade, and joined in a general combination to hide the truth, not only from the public—which might appear plausible—but from each other—which must appear absurd. Without, then, insisting on the fact that State Papers were secret papers, never intended for the public eye, and therefore not likely to offer any temptation or ad-

[7] *Report of Select Committee*, p. 715.

vantage for disguise, what possible motive, it may be asked, could there be for a foreign ambassador in a foreign Court to pervert the facts which fell under his own observation? Why should the Spanish, the French, or the Venetian envoys residing in England transmit to their respective governments studious misrepresentations of what was passing around them? That would have been to neutralise the very purpose of their mission, and unquestionably have exposed them at once to disgrace and dismissal. Or, if such had been the practice of any one of them, can it be imagined that all were embarked in the same ridiculous plot? Did all combine in the same tale of misrepresentation, and were all their despatches written by consent in a sort of ambassadorial conclave? If not, the inconsistency displayed in their separate reports and despatches would certainly have betrayed them. It is hardly needful to expose seriously so transparent a sophism—so transparent indeed and so absurd, that it could never have been entertained for a moment by any one who possessed any real knowledge of the subject, or had taken the trouble to verify his suspicions. Ambassadors, like other men, have their national and individual prejudices. They are liable to be misled by those about them. They are exposed to the temptation of sending home their own views of the facts, and of selecting those facts which are most in accordance with their own prepossessions and their own interests. Statesmen have objects to be gained by diplomacy and statecraft, the free use of which they consider legitimate; and no one in reading their reports would accept them all implicitly as simple, unbiassed representations of the truth. But the same objection will apply to every kind of correspondence, oral or verbal. Dr. Johnson's conversation is no more to be received for a faithful representation of Whiggery than the journal of Whitelock or the Presbyterian Dr. Baillie is to be regarded as an accurate description of Charles I. and the

Cavaliers. The thoughts and the writings of politicians, like those of other men, are variously coloured by passion, by prejudice, by employment, by party, by the desire of success or the fear of discomfiture. Are they for this reason absolutely and entirely false? If the historian is to reject them on this ground he must equally reject all testimony; and all history, whether of his own or of any other time, becomes impossible. But the correspondence of statesmen is not more distorted by prejudice and falsehood than that of ordinary men, not even when engaged in some diplomatic intrigue they may have wished to deceive the outside world; for though they might hide their real intentions from others, they could have no object in deceiving their own agents and ambassadors. Outside the charmed circle the world is deluded and deceived, but once within it and all things appear in their true colours. This is the advantage of such publications as these Calendars. They take the reader behind the scenes; they lay bare before him the puppets and the real men, the phantasies and the facts, the true and ostensible motives. If there be deceit, they furnish him with the means of detecting it. They enable him to divide the false from the true. Moreover, they supply him with the cross lines of evidence; they furnish the means of comparing statement with statement, of confronting one witness with another. Testimony may be false, events in history may be perverted, mathematical accuracy is nowhere attainable; but society stands on no better testimony than this. Its contracts, its laws, its dealings, and its obligations rest on no surer foundation. Does any man question its sufficiency in the actual business of life? Then why should he doubt its sufficiency for the past?

So long indeed as the old and exclusive system prevailed, there was a tendency among historians, in their triumphant possession of a few diplomatic papers, to rear specious and paradoxical theories on the slender and barren foundation of a very small number of original discoveries. Some inquirer, more careful or more fortunate than others, had the good fortune to enrich his pages with extracts from the national archives. Through their help he has been enabled to discover new facts, to remove antiquated prejudices, to place past events in a clearer and more certain light. Confident in their support, it was natural that he should overrate their importance in their novelty. The tendency to convert history into a panorama of brilliant and disconnected pictures, often exaggerated in themselves, still more exaggerated from the disproportionate prominence assigned to them, was naturally fostered by the possession of a few contemporaneous documents in which the authenticity and minuteness of the facts, or the unexpected revelations afforded by them, contrasted strangely with the cold, meagre, and uncertain outlines of the accepted and traditional belief; and thus, naturally, comprehensiveness of view and justness of conception were too often sacrificed to brilliancy of detail and richness of matter. But whereas formerly, in consequence of strict official restrictions, a few ears only could be gleaned, now a whole harvest is offered to the world; where access to a few papers and liberty to print them was fettered by vexatious regulations, thousands are now thrown open to view.

Were there, then, no other advantage to be gained from these Calendars of the Master of the Rolls, it is no slight one that in placing before the reader the whole facts, so far as they can be known, they set before him the order in which these facts occurred, their connection, and their relative proportions. For history generally a more just and equitable treatment is thus secured; a more careful and considerate adjustment of all its parts. Hasty and imaginative writers are thus deterred from imposing their own conceptions upon their readers, and careless ones from wandering too far from the plain truth without control or fear of detection. Till now readers had no alternative except to surrender themselves implicitly to the guidance of the historian who could move their feelings and enlist their sympathies most strongly, if not always by the most just and legitimate means. No means were at hand for testing the fidelity of their guide or the certainty of the path through which he was leading them. It could not be expected that they should submit to the same laborious process, or prosecute researches amidst obscure and confused documents, or reconcile contradictory statements, or determine the weight of conflicting evidence. It was not possible for them to ascertain when the historian had abandoned the calm impartiality of the judge for the partial province of the advocate. So not only modern history, but English history in particular, has continually presented the strange and unedifying spectacle of different writers, possessing apparently the same opportunities, and drawing their information equally from the same original documents, arriving at opposite and irreconcilable conclusions; thus lending plausibility to the notion that truth is unattainable, at least in all that pertains to the history of this country, whatever may be said for that of Greece or Rome.

Happily a better era is at hand, not merely in the superior authenticity, accuracy, and minuteness of the information supplied by these Calendars, but in the facility for testing and applying it. Here, at all events, the reader possesses an infallible means of verifying history, of counteracting partial or exaggerated statements. He is enabled to trace the real progress and development of events, to ascertain their order, their proportions, and their natural significance.

To the value of the materials thus carefully tabulated and digested the chronological arrangement adopted in these Calendars has contributed not a little. Merely as a matter of arrangement a chronological order, for all historical purposes, is superior to any other. It is the simplest and the most intelligible in principle, the most practicable in execution. If disarranged—and to accidents of this kind all papers are liable—it is most easily replaced. But a classified arrangement, whether of books or historical documents, specious as it may appear to some, is illusory, and sooner or later ends in inextricable confusion. Hardly any two persons can agree on the classification in the first instance; still less on the manner in which it ought to be carried out. If it be too minute it defeats itself, if too narrow it fails to meet all requirements. The other principle—if principle it can be called —of allowing all manuscripts and papers to remain in their original disorder, as in the Bodleian Library and Bibliothèque Impériale at Paris, is wholly indefensible. What is the consequence? No student, however laborious or persevering, can be sure of mastering the documentary evidence relating to any one period or any one subject on which he is employed. His search is baffled at every point; his most careful investigation ends in disappointment. Hours are wasted in searching indexes or examining collections without result for want of a little preliminary arrangement, the total absence of which can scarcely be considered as otherwise than discreditable. Until the recent efforts of Mr. Bond, it was not much better at the British Museum. Even to discover there the number of the Catalogues was evidence of no small proficiency; and when that was done, what a scene of disorder presented itself to view! Theology, classics, history, philosophy, were jumbled together in the most chaotic confusion. Here, a paper of the reign of Henry VIII. is wedged in by some extraordinary accident among those of Charles I. or Elizabeth; there, another of Charles V., or Ferdinand the Catholic, finds a place among topographical collections or county histories.

Life is not long enough to grapple with so many obstacles. The best years and freshest energies of a writer are exhausted long before he has arrived at the end of his preliminary researches. He must go far a-field not merely to collect the straw and the bricks, but in this case straw, bricks, clay, and mud, are all tumbled indiscriminately in disorder before him, and he has patiently to turn over the immense heaps, to cull here and there, with vast labour and waste of time, the materials he requires. So wearisome is the toil, so little has been done in our great libraries to lighten or remove it, that few are willing to undertake it. Much easier is it, and much more remunerative, to reproduce ancient fallacies, or refurbish popular errors, than to extend the limits of inquiry and tempt new regions in the face of so many discouragements. In all these respects the Calendars of the Master of the Rolls show as great a superiority over their confused and confusing predecessors, as the chronological arrangement of which they are the index is preferable to the non-arrangement of the Bodleian, the Bibliothèque Impériale at Paris, the British Museum, or the absurd classifications adopted at Simancas and the Old State Paper Office. If disorder reigns supreme in the former, system and subdivisions in the latter are carried to excess. In Simancas no one can tell, as no one could tell in the old days of the State Paper Office, where his inquiry is to begin or where it is to end. Documents relating to the same events, the same person, and the same period, appear and reappear under every conceivable disguise. They so wind and double in and out, first under one classification and then under another, that it is hard if the plainest story does not elude the most zealous pursuit at last. Home Papers, Foreign Papers, War Papers, Navy Papers—then a faithful progeny of such prolific parents—Border Papers, Rebellion Papers, Calais Papers, Scotch Papers, Irish Papers; and of Foreign as many divisions as there were states or people with whom the mother country cultivated relations; France, Germany, Spain, Portugal, Italy, Switzerland, and so on—all the non-essential and non-natural divisions of an artificial system torment the patience of the most devoted and most conscientious reader. For purely diplomatic purposes it may be admitted that such divisions and subdivisions were, at one time, not without their use; and if it were important for the Foreign Minister of this day to be thoroughly acquainted with the policy of this country in reference to Italy and the Pope in the 16th century, or if it were requisite for him to be intimately acquainted with all the despatches connected with the descent on the Isle of Rhé, or the negotiations for the marriage of Charles II., it might still be prudent to retain these formal and tedious classifications. Archivists, impenetrable to the wishes of the world outside, might still set common sense at defiance, and brave the anger and impatience of those who only value these muniments for their historical importance. But such a principle of arrangement leads to endless subdivisions and lands the reader in a practical absurdity. Suppose, for instance, that an ambassador has been sent to the Pope. As a matter of course he lands at Calais; from Dover he despatches a letter to the King or his minister announcing his arrival. He has something to say at every Court he visits in succession, some secret negotiation to reveal, or some anecdote to tell. Now, then, patient and ingenious reader, under what series is his correspondence to be arranged? Under Home, Calais, Flanders, France, Sardinia, Italy, or Papal States? Under one or under all? Under all, by the rules of diplomatic arrangement; and through all must the inquirer hunt for the dislocated members of his subject. The simplification of these endless divisions, and their reduction to a few, clear, and intelligible classifications, is not the smallest service conferred by the Master of the Rolls on historical science. Arranging the papers under the fewest possible heads, he has made the basis of his Calendars Chronological.

On that subject we might be tempted to enlarge, did not our space forbid us. We have only room for one or two observations. First, by a chronological arrangement, all the materials relating to any given period of time are brought within a reasonable and a readable compass. In the next place, the worth of the evidence is more easily sifted, and contradictory statements more readily compared. Whether history should be written in the form of annals, or whether it should assume a freer and more philosophical form, may be doubted; but it can be no question whether the materials to be used by the historian should be chronologically arranged or not. The essential order of events is only to be discovered, in the first instance, from the natural order, the true development from the apparent. In no other way is it possible to detect the minute movements of history, the gradations of action and reaction, the ceaseless complications of antagonistic forces, the rise and fall of opposing influences. It may be that the last age was too fond of insisting on the grandeur and philosophy of history, and so exhausted it of all real dramatic and human interest; but are we not in danger of falling into the opposite error? Are we not beginning, both in art and literature, to imitate the Chinese fashion of sacrificing to minute and obtrusive detail the higher and more spiritual graces of both?

In selecting, therefore, the State Papers, and adopting a chronological arrangement for his Calendars, the Master of the Rolls occupied an untrodden path and inaugurated a new method for the study of history. Whatever other nations may have done for the advancement of historical literature, none has ever yet ventured to publish chronological abstracts of its official papers. Not only France and Germany, but minor States like Italy, far surpass us in their grand collections of annalists and historians. We had nothing to show that can bear comparison with the labours of Dom Bouquet, of Pertz, or even of Muratori. Whilst their works have given a new stimulus to historical studies on the Continent, and raised up a host of consummate historians, like Thierry, Michelet, Guizot, and Sismondi, the history of England has remained, until lately, a barren field, scarcely better explored than it was in the days of Carte or Hume. But in these Calendars of State Papers we stand wholly unrivalled as a nation. Nothing like them has yet been produced; nothing to which future historians, whether of this country or of Europe generally, are likely to owe so many obligations. Henceforth, the historian, here or abroad, who undertakes to treat of any questions connected with the period traversed by these Calendars must turn to them as his surest guides and most unerring authorities. From their pages he will have to learn the true history of events by which the politics of Europe were moulded during the 16th and 17th centuries. They can never be dispensed with; they will never be superseded.

We have devoted a considerable portion of this review to these Calendars of State Papers, not only because they are prior in date, but, in our judgment, superior in importance, to all the other Rolls' publications. It was not until two years after, and probably in consequence of the success of his first effort, that the Master of the Rolls was induced to apply to the Treasury for an additional grant to enable him to publish the 'Chronicles and Memorials' of the United Kingdom. On this, as on the previous occasion, his application was based on an Address presented by the House of Commons to the Crown,[8] representing that a 'uniform and convenient edition of our ancient historians would be an undertaking honourable to his Majesty's reign, and conducive to the

[8] July 25, 1822.

advancement of historical and constitutional knowledge. His Majesty was therefore prayed that the necessary steps might be taken for the furtherance of such a publication.

As the monastic chronicles already in print were often defective, and generally scarce and costly, whilst others of equal value existed only in manuscript, the Master of the Rolls announced his intention of giving preference, in the first instance, to those works 'of which the manuscripts were unique or the materials of which would help to fill up the blanks in English history.' He stated also that he had in view the formation of a *Corpus Historicum*, within reasonable limits, and which should be as complete as possible. The plan thus judiciously marked out has, upon the whole, been faithfully observed, as faithfully, perhaps, as could be expected from the nature of the work. Of the eighty and odd volumes given to the world, sixty at least contain new and original matter: the rest present more perfect and complete editions of authors found only in a fragmentary form before, or they supply more accurate and convenient texts. Considering how precarious is the preservation of manuscripts, how numerous the accidents of fire, damp, neglect, and spoliation to which they are liable, the determination of the Master of the Rolls to give preference to those works 'of which the manuscripts are unique' will command general satisfaction. Science is independent of early discoveries, poetry owes little to mediæval authors; but to history the loss of contemporary documents and original records is the mutilation of a limb, the extinction of a planet from its hemisphere. The loss of a single manuscript is often a sort of literary homicide; it is the utter and irremediable destruction of an author. By such misfortunes, a mist settles down on certain periods of history, never to be cleared away; great events in the lives of men and of nations become involved in impenetrable obscurity; *opinio manet opinio, et quæstio quæstio*. It is, moreover, a curious and humiliating paradox in bibliography that manuscripts of worthless authors may often be counted by hundreds, whilst of great authors there is only one. In selecting, therefore, unique manuscripts, in the first instance, for publication, the Master of the Rolls was doing his best to place the materials of history beyond the reach of accident, and in so doing he was filling up the blanks neglected or overlooked by previous editors.

But in so doing, these Chronicles and Memorials necessarily assumed a place subordinate to that of the Calendars of State Papers. They were in their nature supplementary to other collections antecedent in date, and in some cases more intrinsically valuable. For in this portion of his task the Master of the Rolls had been preceded by editors and collectors of great ability; by Archbishop Parker and Sir Henry Saville (the celebrated Provost of Eton), by Twysden, by Gale, by Hearne, and many others. The field had been occupied, though somewhat in a desultory and ineffectual manner, by various historical societies; and not the least by Mr. Petrie. All these, single editors and societies, sedulous and industrious in their different degrees, had the advantage of a first choice. Naturally they selected for publication such authors as they deemed most valuable; not always with sound judgment and discrimination, not always with equal regard to accuracy: still a vast body of important and valuable materials had by their labours been given to the world. It only remained for Lord Romilly to supply the omissions of previous editors, to rescue from oblivion what still remained worth preserving; and, if the munificence of the Government would extend so far, to set forth more accurate and convenient editions of such authors as had been published already.[9]

[9] For this purpose the 'Descriptive Catalogue' of Sir Thomas Hardy furnishes invaluable information. The conscientious labour and care bestowed on that work by its author is beyond all praise.

But that which seemed to render the task easy made it more difficult. The earlier gleaners in the vineyard could scarcely do amiss. They had but to stretch forth their hands, certain that whatever they grasped and presented to their readers could not fail of being acceptable, and equally certain that their labours had not been anticipated. But when, after the continued toil and research of three centuries, it was necessary for the last comer to determine the value of what his predecessors had overlooked or hastily rejected, a much greater amount of caution, skill, and knowledge was necessarily required. It was indispensable to know not only what was worth publishing, but what had not been published before under the numerous aliases and disguises so common in mediæval annalists, so puzzling to the modern historian.[1]

If unlimited time had been allowed for such researches, or if the House of Commons and its economists could have been content to wait ten or a dozen years, the task might have been comparatively easy. But that was not to be expected; nor was the example of the late Record Commission or its historical doings by any means encouraging. It would have been in vain to point to the historical productions of France and Germany, to the grand collection of

[1] Many of the larger religious houses had an historiographer attached to the establishment, whose duty it was to keep the records of the house and post up its annals from year to year. The mere events connected with his own peculiar establishment would have afforded the annalist but meagre and unsatisfactory topics; and therefore the main body of his work was taken, in the first instance, *verbatim* from some popular chronicle of the day. Into this substratum the local chronicler interpolated notices relating his own monastery; such as the death, election, and character of the abbots; records of benefactions, and the like. It is owing to this practice that a chronicle substantially the same appears again and again under a dozen different titles—as many titles in fact as there were religious houses in which it was adopted -but with local additions and variations. Hence the common blunder of Hume, and even of more recent writers, in quoting th same work under different names as independent and distinct authori-

Dom Bouquet, commenced before the first French Revolution and not yet finished, or to the equally superb *Monumenta Germaniæ* of Pertz, now steadily advancing to its grand climacteric. As little would it have sufficed to show how these works had given a new stimulus to historical studies on the Continent. What economist in the House of Commons would have listened to such arguments? So much money for so much work; be it a seventy-four, an Armstrong gun, a fresco, or an ancient historian. No tangible result, no measurable work, no money. Other nations may dispute and discuss what form of publication is abstractedly the best. They may dig deep their foundations; they may spend years in preparation, and satisfy their respective Governments by annual reports. But that is not possible in England. So, in addition to his other difficulties, the Master of the Rolls had to determine on a mode of publication, which, if some might regard as not absolutely the best, was most feasible under all circumstances. He departed from the Continental plan of committing the work to one or two editors, and restricted the use of notes. He discarded the idea of a *Corpus Historicum*, such as Bouquet's and Pertz's, and resolved on publishing each history and chronicle complete and by itself. Though some may condemn this arrangement as not so scientific or philosophical as that of the great Continental editors, we are inclined to think that the plan forced upon Lord Romilly by the necessity of the case was, in fact, the most judicious he could have adopted, even had he been free to choose. It is true that these ancient historians repeat themselves and perpetually reproduce the very same matter in the very same words. It is true that they sometimes borrow or steal from each other without misgiving or mercy. True also that a great number of them think it necessary to commence their narrative with Adam and the fall of man—a fashion we have abandoned as uninstructive and unnecessary, and somewhat tiresome to boot. But, then, what mode of publication is to be adopted? Shall these repetitions and superfluities be retrenched? Shall each author make his appearance stripped of these accessories, and reduced to his native and essential proportions? That might be a process which more persons than one would think advisable. The idea is not a new one. It has many attractions. It would have its advantages in saving the reader's time and temper. The facts of history would be brought within a more convenient and reasonable compass. Considering the dislocation of historical materials, their confusion and dispersion in all sorts of byways and corners, nothing looks more attractive than such a plan as this, nothing seems more orderly or more sensible. It is precisely the same as any writer of history would adopt for himself in some form or another. But, attractive as it seems, it is more specious than real. The advantages it offers are dearly purchased by serious evils. If adopted, it becomes necessary to divide each author into segments; to place one portion of his work in one volume, another in a second, and the rest in a third. The unity of his work is, in a great measure, destroyed. The means of comparing one part of it with another is embarrassed with numerous difficulties. Questions connected with the general character or the individuality of the author are obscured, and still more so if some portions are suppressed as either foreign to the period embraced or anticipated already. The student of one period of history is under the necessity of purchasing the whole collection, or he must encumber his shelves with a number of odd and unnecessary volumes. On these grounds the Master of the Rolls, though intending, as he says, to form 'as complete a collection' as was possible of our national mediæval historians, rejected the Continental system. 'It is important,' he remarks, 'that the historical student should be able to select such volumes as conform with his own peculiar taste and studies, and not be put to the expense of purchasing the whole collection: an inconvenience inseparable from any other plan than that which has been in this instance adopted.' If the facts of history were as passionless as those of science; if they admitted precisely of the same rectification; if they were wholly independent, like the facts of science, of the character of the *testis,* then a mere dry chronicle of facts would constitute the perfection of history. It would have attained that highest of all intellectual conditions—the dry light, the *lumen siccum* desired by Lord Bacon. On the contrary, the driest history is not only the dullest, in all senses of the word, but it is often the narrowest and the least instructive. The historian who treats his subject *ab extra* misses continually its finest and subtlest essence. He fails to master it, except in its mere formal and superficial phenomena. His spirit must be in conformity with the actions he narrates, or he cannot understand them; still less can he present them to others. At the great drama of human happiness and misery, of human passions, virtues, and failings, no man is suffered to remain an indifferent and yet an intelligent spectator. Precisely as the artist endeavours to translate into lines and colours the emotions and impressions nature has made upon him, the historian endeavours to interpret for posterity an image of the times as those times have stamped themselves on his brain and his affections. Even in the choice of his materials, even in his omissions, there is something significant of the man, of the weakness or the strength of his judgment, the poverty of his imagination, or the meagreness of his sympathies. Therefore it is not only his work, but his manner of working that must be taken into account; not the facts only which he registers, but his own moral and intellectual habitudes and those of his age. We can no longer be satisfied with that passionless interpretation of history which, professing to be literal, extinguishes its living significance, any more than we can allow the historian to substitute his individual fancies for true historical data. A larger criticism demands that we shall draw from the historian himself the true method of interpreting his narrative. For this process the plan adopted by the Master of the Rolls of publishing each author by himself, instead of the French and German method, is infinitely preferable, if not indispensable.

The correctness of Lord Romilly's judgment has been confirmed by the popular verdict. The notice attracted by his publications forms a striking contrast to the general apathy and indifference with which the productions of former Record Commissions were universally regarded. They were not, indeed, without their value—very far from it—but they were interesting only to a few. Reviewers naturally fought shy of books printed in uncouth type, unwieldy in form, and not unfrequently ushered into the world without a word of comment or a line of prefatory matter. If any body of scholars and gentlemen ever industriously resolved on the most wrong-headed way of insuring failure, none were ever more ingeniously successful in this respect than these Commissioners. Among the number are to be found the names of Mr. Hobhouse, Lord Dover, Sir James Mackintosh, Henry Hallam, and John Allen, all men of ability and eminence, all deeply interested in historical studies. Yet it is hard to say whether their want of judgment or of ordinary prudence was the more conspicuous. They could scarcely have gone astray without premeditated malice, for no country in the world is so rich in historical materials as our own; nowhere are those materials more varied, more copious, or more complete. It would be hard to hit upon any subject connected with the progress of society, the growth of our institutions, the development of our commerce, of our army, or our navy, or our colonies, the rise and fall of this class or of that in the community, to the accurate comprehension of which our national muniments do not contribute the most attractive and most momentous illustrations. But, from some strange obliquity of judgment, the Commissioners selected for publication such records as were of the least interest to the general reader; made them still more repulsive by printing them with all their original manuscript contractions, adopted the most cumbrous folio, proceeded without system, began what they could not complete, and entrusted the most difficult tasks, in more than one instance, to the most incompetent editors. What wonder that their labours were treated with neglect and contempt? These errors the Master of the Rolls has prudently avoided. He has confined his attention to the two grand sources of history—the State Papers and the Chronicles. He has selected for editors the most experienced scholars. In the form, the type, the text of his works, he has consulted the convenience of the ordinary reader; and by the prefatory matter prefixed to each volume has enabled both learned and unlearned to judge of its contents.

It is not to be presumed that all these works are equally interesting and equally important, yet of all it may be said that they have either contributed to a more accurate knowledge of English history, or brought to light fresh information, or replaced doubt by certainty. Future historians will have much better materials for their investigations than fell to the lot of their predecessors; but their labours and responsibilities will be increased in proportion. They will be no longer permitted to rest satisfied, as in the days of Hume, with a superficial examination of the truth, or with clever but inadequate theories. They will no longer be allowed to take up history as a whim or a holiday task in an idle moment, or as a mere relaxation from the severer pursuits of science or philosophy. Whatever else these works of the Master of the Rolls may have accomplished, they have made our demands on the historian more rigid and more exacting. Precisely in proportion as they have drawn more general attention to the subject, as they have shown how ample and various are the authentic materials, how many and divergent the lines of investigation, in proportion as they have brought the whole subject within the penetrating glance of a more critical, and it may be said of a more captious age, in the same proportion will the historian find himself under the necessity of satisfying requirements that never entered the imagination of former generations. Such is the necessary consequence whenever fresh materials are brought into the field of any definite region of study, be it theology, philosophy, or history. Men are compelled to consider the relation of the new matter to the old—to institute contrasts, to discover similitudes, to advance their views, to change the customary posture of their minds. This increased activity creates of itself new powers and new intellectual demands. It enforces more concentrated observation, more critical sagacity—not merely because the new is better understood in its connection with the old, but because the old itself grows into bolder relief and clearer forms from its juxtaposition with the new. It is doubtful whether the advancement of science and learning in all directions is not due much more to these causes than to any superior method of inquiry—whether the matter does not in this, as in other cases, determine the method. But, however this may be, we are persuaded that these works must eventually produce a great revolution in history —perhaps in history generally, certainly in the history of this country—as great as this generation has witnessed in the histories of Greece and Rome. Nor shall we be far wrong in anticipating for historical studies in general a much profounder interest and a more philosophic appreciation than have hitherto fallen to their share. Strange would it be if it were otherwise. The current of events shifts and winds with such amazing and breathless rapidity—the present so eludes our grasp, that the past seems to offer to many the only safe standing-ground for their imaginations and affections. Contentment with the present, and the somewhat contracted sympathy which such contentment brings with it, is certainly not the failing of this century whatever it may have been of the last. Whether in the apprehension of great changes and in the sense of political insecurity are to be found the most powerful incentives to the cultivation of history, as in the great historical era of Rome, and of France within our own remembrance, it is not needful to determine. That such changes have been pre-eminently favourable to it is unquestionable; that at no time has the past been studied with such passionate earnestness, and consequently with such fulness of appreciation, as when it seemed to be drifting furthest from the present, will scarcely be denied. But whatever may be the cause, the appetite for history is a great and increasing one. To its healthy development the Rolls' Publications will contribute not a little, as they have already given to its growth a new and energetic impulse.

A SHORT HISTORY OF THE ENGLISH PEOPLE.[1]

THE extraordinary popularity of Mr. Green's 'Short History' must be regarded as one of the most curious literary phenomena of the day. Within the space of a brief twelvemonth, or a little more, it has reached the unprecedented sale of 32,000 copies, according to the announcement of its publisher. The fact is noticeable. Had Mr. Green suddenly dawned upon the world as a delightful poet or fascinating novelist of the latest stamp, his success could not have been more remarkable. The reading public are not so indulgent to historians in general. A second or third edition moves off languidly enough. The sale of a few thousand copies satisfies the most ambitious expectations of author and publisher. But here is an author comparatively unknown, or known only to a small circle of friends, who distances at once all competitors—not in some new field of inquiry, not in the pathways of scientific discovery, but in the well-trodden arena of English history. Those who have little acquaintance with the subject, and those who are, or at least profess to have been, familiar with it from their childhood, who are fully persuaded that there are no fresh facts to be elicited, and no further discoveries to be made, are equally loud in Mr. Green's praises. Hostile criticism in every quarter is fascinated and disarmed.

The secret of this extraordinary success it is not difficult to divine. Mr. Green's style is eminently readable and

[1] From the *Quarterly Review* for April, 1876; under the following heading:—*A Short History of the English People.* By J. R. Green M.A. With Maps and Tables. London. 1874.

attractive. A lively imagination, not always under the most rigid control, imparts its own colours to the dry details of history, where a more scrupulous or conscientious writer would have wearied himself, and fatigued his readers, unwilling to venture beyond the arid region of facts. Every one nowadays demands that whatever else history may be it shall be made interesting. It must trench as closely as possible on the borders of fiction. The influence of a great writer amongst us, who has poured such unmeasured contempt on the Dryasdusts of this and a past generation, has created the belief that the unimaginative historian must also be an incompetent historian. So the demand for history—lively, attractive, and sparkling at all hazards—has produced the required supply. The temptation is great, and Mr. Green has not always been able to resist it. It was not in his nature to do so. For him, the animated, the poetical, and the picturesque exercise an irresistible fascination. He has a natural tendency to supply from his own fertile and fervid imagination the dramatic details that are wanting in his cold and colourless originals.

It is true that in this respect he does not stand alone. It is also true that from the days of Lord Macaulay historians have justified themselves by his example in the use of rhetorical exaggeration, on the supposition that in no other way is it possible to represent to the dull and jaded perceptions of modern times the stirring incidents and emotions of the past. Mr. Green may think that he has sufficient warrant for following a precedent sanctioned by such eminent authority. We think otherwise. Not even in histories written for readers whose judgment and knowledge may be mature enough to prevent them from being misled, and whose skill may be sufficient to distinguish between truth and error, ought the baseless suggestions of the imagination to intrude upon the strict province of fact—of facts resting on unquestionable evidence. But in histories for the young—if Mr. Green's book be intended for the young —for the inexperienced and uninitiated, who are sure to take upon trust all that their teacher tells them, and are likely to be more impressed by the fictitious than the true, this licence is even less justifiable. Many readers of English history will never go beyond Mr. Green's book. They will place implicit confidence in a writer whose style and whose genius they cannot fail to admire. Their conceptions of social progress, their judgment of past events, of the great personages that have moulded or modified our national destiny, will be determined exclusively by a perusal of Mr. Green's pages. In his case, therefore, strict accuracy is more important than in works which make no pretensions to speak with authority.

That such a caution is by no means unnecessary in this case may be inferred from the careless and indiscriminate applause lavished on the labours of Mr. Green by the journals and periodicals of the day. We will do him the credit to believe that no one is more conscious than himself of his own defects and imperfections. No one knows better than he the vastness of the task he has undertaken, and the impossibility, in the present state of historical literature, of doing justice to all portions of the subject alike. On some it is clear he has bestowed greater care and attention than on others. If in some parts of his work we trace the conscientious study and examination of original authorities, in others he has trusted exclusively to secondary sources, attempting little more than a reproduction, after his own fashion, without exercising much independent judgment, and not always with rigid accuracy, of the opinions and conclusions of his predecessors. What else could he do? Mr. Green, we presume, has not yet attained to the age of Methuselah. He has not the 'brazen entrails' or iron frame of the celebrated Greek Father, for he distinctly announces in his Preface that his work was 'written in hours of weakness and ill-health,' and he urges this as an apology 'for the faults and oversights,' of which he is 'only too conscious;' an apology which all who know anything of the immensity of his task will be ready enough to accept.

But such being the case, it is not easy to understand the extraordinary assertion of the leading journal of the day, 'that this history of Mr. Green will be found an able guide to every student of history through the latest as well as the earliest portions of the political and social life of England.' To those who have taken the trouble to examine the book with the slightest attention such praise must appear extravagant and ridiculous. In 'the latest portions' of his history, Mr. Green has been satisfied with producing a meagre outline of the main facts of the time, bestowing very little attention on the political or social condition of the country. Whilst his history of England to the death of Queen Anne occupies 700 pages, the narrative from the House of Hanover to the year 1873, including the political complications under George III., the American War of Independence, the French Revolution, the rise and fall of Napoleon, the Peninsular War, the Battle of Waterloo—not to mention the religious reforms of the Wesleyans, the attempts of the Pretender in 1715 and 1745, the victories of Clive in India, the impeachment of Warren Hastings, the financial schemes of Pitt—is despatched in little more than a hundred pages. To 'the battles of the crows and kites,' as Milton stigmatises somewhat contemptuously the pre-Norman history of this country, Mr. Green has devoted more than twice the space he has allotted to the whole of the nineteenth century and the Victorian era. We do not quarrel with him for this want of proportion in his work; but it must be obvious how little historical criticism can be trusted when it can discern no difference in the study, thought, and treatment bestowed on the earlier, as compared with the later, portions of Mr. Green's labours.

The objects which Mr. Green proposed to himself are stated with tolerable precision in his Preface. 'It is a history,' as he informs us, ' not of English kings, or English conquests, but of the English people.'

' At the risk of sacrificing *much that was interesting* '— the italics are our own—' and attractive in itself, and which the constant usage of our historians has made familiar to English readers, I have preferred to pass lightly and briefly over the details of foreign wars and diplomacies, the personal adventures of kings and nobles, the pomp of courts or the intrigues of favourites, and to dwell at length on the incidents of that constitutional, intellectual, and social advance in which we read the history of the nation itself. . . . If I have said little of the glories of Cressy, it is because I have dwelt much upon the wrong and misery which prompted the verse of Longland and the preaching of Ball. But, on the other hand, I have never shrunk from telling at length the triumphs of peace. I have restored to their place among the achievements of Englishmen the "Faërie Queene" and the "Novum Organum." I have set Shakspere among the heroes of the Elizabethan age, and placed the scientific inquiries of the Royal Society side by side with the victories of the New Model. If some of the conventional figures of military and political history occupy in my pages less than the space usually given them, it is because I have had to find a place for figures little heeded in common history—the figures of the missionary, the poet, the painter, the merchant, and the philosopher.'

Well and good. We dispute no man's right to illustrate any phase that he pleases of English history. Nor do we stay to inquire what sort of mastery any student would acquire of so important a subject, who should know little or nothing of the actions of kings and nobles; should be wholly unacquainted with the foreign relations of this country, or the wars in which it had been engaged, or should attempt to disentangle—if disentangle he could—its internal from its external policy. Mr. Green regards war as mere 'butchery.' He thinks that it 'plays a small part in the real story of European nations, and in that of England its part is smaller than in any.' We ask what this country would have been without war, morally as well as politically? We should be glad to learn how, without war, it would have obtained its colonies, its Indian Empire, its internal consolidation ; without war, its national strength and unity ; its proud and vigorous independence ; its moderation, promptitude, courage, and endurance. To precedence among the nations it never could have made the slightest pretensions, regarded in itself, in the extent of its natural territory, in its insulated and distant position. So far is Mr. Green's assertion from being correct that there is no nation to whom war has been more beneficial, from first to last, than to England. There is no nation liable to lose more, to sink more rapidly into apathy, selfishness, and corruption, than England, when, satisfied with its own security and exclusiveness, it shuts itself up from the rest of Christendom. Unjust wars—wars for simple aggression—no one will uphold ; and, fortunately, they have been rare in the history of this country. But war in a righteous cause, war in defence of the just rights, whether of ourselves or of others ; war for national and religious independence—for resistance of arrogant pretensions—such war is not only justifiable, but the nation that steadily declines it must forfeit its claim to respect. So far as England is concerned, the most brilliant periods, not only of its political strength and development, but of its intellectual greatness and social progress, have followed in the train of war.

But allowing Mr. Green the full benefit of his own

opinions on this subject, what are we to think of the judgment of his reviewers who so enthusiastically characterise his work 'as the one *general* history of the country, for the sake of which *all* others, if young and old be wise, will be speedily and surely set aside?' We have Mr. Green's own admission that he was not attempting 'a general history;' that he has passed lightly over details of foreign wars and diplomacies, of adventures hitherto regarded as important by the students of English history. No one can doubt, who has examined his pages, that he has not only passed lightly over them, but in some instances omitted them entirely. Mr. Green then, on his own showing, had no intention of writing a complete or general history of England. He was not contemplating the extinction or displacement of all previous manuals. He has composed a very lively and attractive, but very partial account of certain phases only of English history, of certain incidents which he considers are more important than others, more suited to his special purpose of illustrating 'the constitutional, intellectual, and social advance of the nation.' So far, then, from dispensing with plainer and less pretending manuals, Mr. Green's work has made the study of such manuals more indispensable than ever. If they were not necessary before, they have become absolutely necessary now, in order to guard Mr. Green's readers against certain errors into which he has been betrayed either by the liveliness of his temperament, or his overweening predilection for certain favourite political and religious theories. They are absolutely necessary in order to supplement details neglected and omitted by Mr. Green, without which no history of England can be complete.

For though popular progress, and the advancement of the masses in intellectual and social development, as distinguished from the actions of kings and nobles, may be a very important part, it is not the whole of history, still less the whole of the history of this nation. The influence of kings and nobles, at all events until recent times, has been so marked and continuous, so intimately blended with every national effort, political, social, or intellectual, that 'their personal adventures,' as Mr. Green somewhat contemptuously styles them, cannot be disintegrated from the general body of our history without blurring its lineaments and mangling its due proportions. In no other country have all classes been more completely interfused; nowhere else have royalty and nobility been less confined to isolated and exclusive channels. Among no other people have kings and nobles stood so little aloof from the political and religious struggles and controversies of the times; or passed, as it were, from one camp to another, as deeply engaged, as profoundly interested in the great questions of the day as the people themselves. From Magna Charta to the last Reform Bill it is not the people alone, in the restricted sense applied to that word by Mr. Green, that have engaged in the fight for political, intellectual, or religious liberty. The battle on more than one occasion has been fought and won for the people by their kings and their nobles, when they themselves were careless or apathetic, engrossed only by their merchandise and their oxen. If kings and nobles had borne so small a part in popular progress, as Mr. Green seems to imagine, if they had been exclusively occupied with their own 'personal adventures' and 'personal interests,' considering the intense loyalty of Englishmen in general, their respect for aristocracy, and their love of law, this nation would have presented to the world a very different spectacle from that which it now presents. Constitutional and religious liberty, a firm and temperate government, combined with unrestricted individual freedom of thought and action, would have been as far off from us as they are from others we need not name.

But Mr. Green is not favourable to monarchy under any

form. He cannot distinguish it from tyranny, or regard it in any other light than as an obstruction to popular progress and inimical to popular liberties. Monarchy and nobility are *spuria vitulamina*, they are a noxious parasitical vegetation destroying that which gives them nourishment. So for neither, for kings especially, has he a needless good word to throw away. He cannot regard with equanimity, much less with complacency, the conduct and character of any Sovereign who, in the conscientious conviction that the maintenance of his own authority was a trust committed to him for the good of his people, has failed to show entire willingness to surrender it, however onerous, at the first summons. Between the assertion of a right and the mistakes and excesses into which mankind are liable to fall in asserting their right, when roughly called in question, Mr. Green can draw no distinction. To such errors he can extend no toleration. Therefore kings and queens fare badly at his hands. They are tyrants and oppressors, existing apparently for no better purpose than that of satisfying their own lust of power and sacrificing their subjects to their own selfishness. It is not merely that James I. is a coarse buffoon, a drunkard, a pedant, a contemptible coward;[2] that Charles I. is a compound of avarice and baseness, with 'neither the grander nor the meaner instincts of the born tyrant;'[3] that George III. 'had a weaker mind than any English king before him save James II.,' with no 'capacity for using greater minds than his own;'[4] but even Sovereigns generally associated in the memories of Englishmen with the greatness and prosperity of their nation escape no better. Elizabeth is a voluptuous and indelicate coquette, whose 'levity carried her gaily over moments of detection and embarrassment where better women would have died of

[2] 'Short History,' p. 464.　　[3] Ibid. p. 5 0.
[4] Ibid, p. 741. Is the second Pitt included in this proscription?

shame.' 'Nothing,' continues Mr. Green, 'is more revolting in the Queen, but nothing is more characteristic, than her shameless mendacity. It was an age of political lying, but in the profusion and recklessness of her lies Elizabeth stood without a peer in Christendom.'⁵ 'No woman ever lived,' he adds, in his habitual tone of exaggeration, 'who was so totally destitute of the sentiment of religion.'⁶ Even Alfred the Great, or Ælfred, as it is now the fashion to call him, hardly satisfies Mr. Green. He has the inherent vice of kings. Under him monarchy is disguised with a mysterious dignity; 'treason,' as Mr. Green pathetically laments, 'is punished with death;' the freeman is degraded, and 'the old English democracy'—a favourite dream of modern constitutional historians—' passed into an oligarchy of the closest kind.'⁷

No wonder, then, that Mr. Green declines to march with such a ragged company, and unceremoniously dispenses with nobility and royalty. Kings enter his pages, and disappear from them in most erratic fashion. Who they are, by what right they reign, whence they come, and whither they go, when they were born, and when they die, are trifles too insignificant for Mr. Green's consideration. Rejecting the old and familiar divisions of English history into reigns and dynasties, Mr. Green adopts arbitrary divisions of his own, more congenial to his own conceptions of popular progress. Thus to pass over his first chapter, which takes the reader through the Anglo-Saxon, or, as he prefers to call it, by a misnomer, the 'English Kingdoms,' from 607 to 1013, the Norman Conquest figures under the general heading of 'England under Foreign Kings.' It is placed in the same category as the Danish predatory invasions, and the peaceful legitimate accession of the Angevin House in the person of Henry II. It might have been supposed that the Conquest

⁵ 'Short History,' p. 365.   ⁶ Ibid. p. 369.   ⁷ Ibid. pp. 56, 57.

of England by William, with all its tremendous results, the new relationships into which the country was thus brought with the Continent of France—its re-organisation consequent on the policy of the Conqueror—would have appeared sufficiently important to have merited a distinct recognition from Mr. Green. With the single exception that William was a foreigner, he had nothing in common with the Danish or Plantagenet chieftains or kings with whom he is confounded by Mr. Green.

Again, his fourth chapter is entitled ' The Three Edwards,' for Mr. Green cannot entirely divest himself of these regnal divisions. It might be expected from the title that the contents of the chapter would correspond to the description annexed to it. But of the fifty years and more of Edward III. the author brings his reader down to the fifteenth only. Then, beginning *de novo*, he treats of the whole reign, not under ' The Three Edwards,' but under a fresh title of the ' Hundred Years' War,' from 1336 to 1431, landing his readers at the close in the tenth year of Henry VI. How this ' Hundred Years ' is made out, or what the last years of Edward III., or the reigns of Richard II. and of Henry IV., had to do with war, we fail to comprehend. Even Mr. Green himself is hardly satisfied with his own ingenuity : for the divisions he has laid down in the text of his book he has judiciously abandoned in the ' Chronological Annals ' prefixed to it.

We cannot spare time to criticise in detail these strange vagaries—we can hardly call them by any better name—nor can we sufficiently express our astonishment how a sensible man of unquestionable genius like Mr. Green should from thoughtlessness or singularity be tempted into such violations of common sense. He commences his division of ' The New Monarchy ' with Joan of Arc in 1422, and brings it to a close with the death of Thomas Cromwell in 1540. By this arrangement the Reformation begins with the fall of that active and unscrupulous Minister, and closes with the final settlement and conquest of Ireland in 1610. With the same singular perverseness, he strings together, under the phrase of 'The Second Stuart Tyranny,' the last four years of Charles II. and the reign of James II., as if there had been no difference between the one and the other. And here, again, as if the termination of the Stuart dynasty had not been sufficiently marked or sufficiently characteristic to form of itself a distinct epoch, the Hanoverian succession is grouped with the reigns of Charles II. and James II., under the general title of 'The Revolution,' ending with the Ministry of Walpole. Could any arrangement be more absurd, confused, or incongruous?

Bene dividit qui bene docet, is the old school maxim; and in no subject of human inquiry is it more essential than in history, especially for the young. But such divisions as these only perplex instead of assisting the learner. They are too arbitrary, too wide, and too indeterminate to be of any real service; what is worse, they give to the whole work a fantastic appearance, as if it were a series of clever and somewhat paradoxical essays on English history rather than the history itself. And as in essays of this kind the author selects and arranges the facts without strict regard to their true sequence and development, and is much more concerned with exhibiting his own conception of events than the events themselves, so is it here. To our mind, the old divisions by reigns and dynasties are not only more precise and convenient, but in reality more sound and philosophical—if that is to be the great object of historical manuals,—if the young, and we might add, those of maturer age, are not to theorise first and learn the facts afterwards. The old divisions by reigns are at least certain and positive. There can be no mistake when this or that monarch lived and died, what events took place, what measures were passed, and what was the condition of the nation at the time. By such an arrangement the student is enabled to compare one king with another, one dynasty with that which precedes or follows it, and to grasp the principles and characteristics of each. But to map out with precision the rise and gradations of political tendencies or of social development is impossible. The commencement and the close of the Tudor or the Stuart epochs are confined within definite limits. Not so 'The Hundred Years' War' and 'The New Monarchy.' But beyond all this, for younger students no clearer and no better method can be devised than the old-fashioned divisions of earlier manuals. None afford such facilities for grouping the facts of history in their natural chronological order, without needlessly burdening the memory. None suffice so well to cluster them round the central figure, of whose life, character, and conduct more is known than others, and more information has been preserved. History thus gains both in unity and clearness, which is more than can be said for disquisitions on political constitutions or social progress. Much as the modern philosophical historian may despise 'a drum-and-trumpet history,' or 'the personal adventures of kings and nobles,' there cannot be a question that the personal influence of the Sovereign in this nation has always been too great to be overlooked; it has always been most intimately blended with the social, political, and religious progress of the people. With the lives, actions, and characters of our monarchs we associate certain distinct and leading impressions of their times.

But before we turn to Mr. Green's special treatment of English history, we have a few words to say of a minor but not unimportant matter. In the use of proper names before the Conquest, Mr. Green has followed the recent fashion of adopting the ancient forms. Thus Alfred appears as Ælfred,

Olave as Anlaf, Egbert as Ecgberht, Aldhelm as Ealdhelm, Edward as Eadward, Edmund as Eadmund, Elgiva as Ælgifu. Happily for his readers, but not so happily for himself, this rusty and antiquated armour does not sit easily on Mr. Green, and he drops it occasionally to appear in a more natural and sensible guise. So, for the strictly orthodox spelling of Cuthberht he gives Cuthbert (p. 33), not known in Anglo-Saxondom; for Gunnilde, Gunhild (p. 57); for Hæstin or Hæsting, Hasting; for Godrum or Guthram, Guthrum; for Eadburge or Eadburhge, Eadburh; for Ceolwulf, Cenwulf (p. 41); all due to his own ingenuity, and unsupported by the authority of Anglo-Saxon history. For Ina or Ine, he writes Ini; for Ludecan, Ludeca (p. 41); for Swithun, Swithhun (p. 43); for Liofa, Leofa (p. 53); and so of many others. Do we condemn him for this? Not in the least. We only wish he had broken from these ridiculous trammels a little more freely, and blundered—if blundering it must be considered—into the light of common sense and familiar usage. How far, we ask, is this absurd masquerading of antiquity to proceed? What advantage is the student of history expected to derive from it? Do those who adopt it propose to extend it, as in consistency they ought, to the names of Norman and Angevin kings? For William, William the Red, Henry, and Matilda, are as much accommodations to modern usage as Alfred, Edgar, Edwy, and the rest. If the names of men, why not the names of places? Rochester, Nottingham, Norwich, Middlesex, Essex, Worcester, Strathclyde, and Pucklechurch, all freely employed by Mr. Green, were just as much unknown to Anglo-Saxon ears and eyes as any other modern conventional spelling.

On other objections, more cogent than these, but well known to the Anglo-Saxon philologist, we forbear to insist. But our readers may take it for granted that this philological puritanism is not free from impurity itself. It assumes as a standard of orthodox spelling what never was a standard. It affects to represent in modern letters characters found in the Anglo-Saxon alphabet, for which we have no modern equivalents. It professes to escape from modern conventional forms, and submits to what it denounces.

Not more reasonable is the recent outcry against the use of the term 'Anglo-Saxon.' For this epithet Mr. Green employs the term 'English,' with manifest disadvantage to precision and clearness. 'English Chronicle' does not convey to modern ears any other notion than that of a chronicle written in the English language, as that word is generally understood. For the word 'Anglo-Saxon' we have the best authority—that, namely, of the people themselves and their rulers. Here are a few instances from Anglo-Saxon times. '*Angul-Saxonum* basileus,' King Edwy (Kemble's 'Anglo-Saxon Charters,' ii. 318). '*Angulsaxna* imperator' (Ib. 325). '*Angol-Saxonum* rex,' King Edward (Ib. 141). '*Angul-Saxonum* rex'(Ib. 143). *Angul-Saxonum* rex,' King Edward, A.D. 1044 (Ib. iv. 79). '*Angol-Saxonum* rex,' in 1049 (Ib. 115). '*Anglo-Saxonum* basileus,' in 1050 (Ib. 123).

But, leaving these matters, we turn to Mr. Green's general conception of English history and its constitutional development. Avoiding the beaten path of his predecessors, Mr. Green treats us at the outset to a view of our English forefathers as they ' wandered over the sand flats of Holstein and along the marshes of Friesland.' He dismisses in a couple of pages the Celtic and Roman occupation of the island as comparatively of no importance, as certainly it is of no importance to those who accept his theory, without modification, that English history begins with the landing of Hengest, and all that the Romans had done four centuries before was swept away and destroyed. This theory, first broached by a writer of boundless ingenuity and conjecture, has been more authoritatively presented to our acceptance by Professor Stubbs, who finds in Mr. Green a most docile disciple : 'They '—the Angles, Jutes and Saxons—' entered upon a land whose defenders had forsaken it, and had carried away with them most of the adventitious civilisation which they (the Britons) had maintained for four hundred years ; whose inhabitants were enervated and demoralised by long dependence, wasted by successive pestilences, worn out by the attacks of half-savage neighbours and by their own suicidal wars ; whose vast forests and unreclaimed marsh-lands afforded to the new-comers a comparatively easy conquest.' He adds : ' The Teutonic occupation of Britain was a migration, and not a mere conquest. The nations so migrating came from a settled country, and must be credited with the same amount of organisation here which they had possessed at home.' ' The new-comers have but to divide the land, and then, for peace or war, justice or politics, simply to reproduce their old condition.⁸

Notwithstanding the great authority of Professor Stubbs, we think it impossible to accept such a theory as this without modification. It is at variance alike with history and probability. It requires the sacrifice of all the original records of the Teutonic Conquest. That sacrifice Mr. Kemble was prepared to make, and by the free application of the modern critical solvent, by which myths and sagas are turned into history, and history into myths and sagas, Mr. Kemble boldly asserted that Hengest and Horsa, and all their battles with the Britons, were no better than poetical figments, unworthy of credit. If the land was not forsaken, when these mythical chiefs found a settlement in it, at least they exterminated its inhabitants, slaying man, woman, and child, and converting their dwellings into ruins. It is true that a British writer, living within a century after the Teutonic invasion, confirms the accepted account in its main outlines, mentions not only the arrival of the three tribes in three

⁸ Stubbs's *Select Charters*, pp. 1, 6.

F

keels (*cyulis*), which appears so like a mythical number, but describes the struggle between the Britons and the new comers as still undecided in his own days. So far from the land being 'forsaken,' he speaks in rapture of its twenty-eight strongly fortified cities [9]—its adornments, like a bride —its alternations of upland and pastures—its shining fields and productive rivers. But Mr. Kemble eluded this difficulty, as he eluded others, by boldly challenging the authenticity of the British historian. He set Gildas aside, as he set aside all other facts which stood in his way, with the grim imperturbability of a Regulus.

Mr. Green unfortunately has cut himself off from this resource. He admits not only the authenticity of Gildas, but of 'the prescientific' account of the 'Anglo-Saxon Chronicle,' or rather of Bede, from whom that account is mainly derived.[1] That account describes the obstinate struggle, maintained by the natives for three-quarters of a century, with continual alternations of success, before the Saxon invader could establish himself on so much of the island as is comprised in the counties south of the Thames, not including Cornwall and part of Somersetshire. Do these facts countenance the supposition that these Teutonic conquerors took possession of a land whose inhabitants 'were enervated and demoralised by long dependence?' Do they show that theirs was 'a comparatively easy conquest,' considering that the Norman made himself master in little less than a year? Is it likely that, in the face of these difficulties, the new comers would proceed to reproduce on new ground, without any adventitious admixture of race or institutions, precisely the same usages and the same constitutional forms as they possessed in their original settlements in the days of Tacitus?

[9] 'Bis denis bisque quaternis fulget civitatibus.'—Gildas, § 3.

[1] 'They (the brief jottings which compose the English (Anglo-Saxon) Chronicle) are undoubtedly historic, though with a slight mythical intermixture.'—*Short History*, p. 7.

But if the occupation of the south coast, though cut off from the rest of the island by vast forests—by the Thames running at that date in a much broader channel than it runs now—was so slow and so laborious a task ; if the Anglian settlements on the East coast, naturally protected by great fens and estuaries, constituted for so many years the only acquisitions of the Anglo-Saxon invaders, we must conclude that the work of havoc and desolation could not have been so great or so complete as it has now become the fashion to assume. The statement of Mr. Pearson, whose conscientious inquiries have been most unjustly depreciated, has probability, at least, in its favour :—

'Popular belief,' he says, ' supposes that the Saxon conquest was one great event, consummated like the Norman in a few years, and that it exterminated the native races and destroyed the traditions of Roman art and law, covering England with a people more purely Germanic than can be found in Germany itself. We cannot construct a true history of the times, but we can prove this hypothesis to be false.'[2]

Elsewhere :—

'The common belief that the Keltic population of Britain was exterminated or driven into Wales and Brittany by the Saxons, has absolutely no foundation in history. . . . We hear of great slaughters by the Saxons on their bloody battlefields, but no massacres after the fight are recorded, except in the single case of Anderida. . . . We know by the complaints of Welsh poets that a race of Romanised Britons, whom they call Loegrians, took part with the invaders against their Keltic kinsmen ; and we cannot suppose that the Saxons would cut the throats of their allies after the war. The object of the races who broke up the Roman empire was not to settle in a desert, but to live at ease as an aristocracy of soldiers, deriving rent from a peaceful population of tenants.

[2] Pearson's *History of England,* i. 83, 2nd edition.

Moreover, coming in small and narrow skiffs, the conquerors could not bring their families with them, and must in most cases have taken wives from the women of the country. That the Saxon language was not, like the Norman and Frank, exchanged for a Latin dialect is probably due to the long duration of the struggle. During four generations of men fresh recruits were perpetually swarming in from the shores of the German Ocean to take part in the subjugation of the island.'

Then, pointing out the permanence of the Latin culture and the intermixture of Latin words in the language of the country long after the conquest was established, Mr. Pearson concludes :—

'The days of the great Roman feasts were still celebrated under Christian titles; the Roman colleges of trade were continued as guilds; Roman local names were preserved by the conquerors as they found them; Roman titles, duke and count, were assumed by the Saxon chiefs; Roman law has formed the basis of the Saxon family system and of the laws of property. The Saxon Conquest was a change of the highest moment, no doubt, but it did not break up society; it only added a new element to what it found. The Saxon State was built upon the ruins of the past.'[3]

These statements commend themselves to common sense and historic probability. The island had flourished under Roman rule. There had been nothing, after the close of the first century, to interrupt its prosperity. The South, especially, freed from all danger, enjoying undisturbed tranquillity, had devoted itself to agriculture and the exportation of corn —a fact which alone would be sufficient to show a state of things very different from that of vast uncultivated forests and unreclaimed marshes, and incompatible with any great civil dissensions, which are fatal to trade and agricultural industry. The whole land was covered with Roman villas,

[3] *History of England*, i. 103

granaries, fortresses, and aqueducts. It was intersected by Roman roads, in direct communication with the great cities. Roman troops, garrisoned on the northern frontier, kept at bay the invasions of Picts and Scots. Roman walls and forts, still standing after the desolating effects of sixteen centuries, attest the strength and greatness of their original design, and equally attest the impossibility that walls and fortresses could have been swept away by the Northern races; for whatever else these races possessed, they did not possess either the skill or the means, if they had even the desire, of levelling to the ground these stubborn memorials of Roman civilisation. The history of the Anglo-Saxon Conquest is an abridgment of the history of the conquest of the Roman empire by the Northern tribes. It is the story of barbarians taught the use of arms and the value of discipline in the Roman camp; of mercenary soldiers taking Roman pay, while the Roman abandoned himself to luxury; of wandering hordes driven out of their homes, or incited to plunder by Alaric and by Attila; of settlers seizing upon the defenceless outposts of the great and unwieldy empire, giving shelter and protection to runaway slaves, to political and religious refugees during the disputes of Arian and orthodox, of emperors and their rivals. Driven into fenced cities for protection, the natives were decimated by plague and famine. The communications, intercepted by barbarous soldiers and marauders, increased and hastened the evil; discontented slaves betrayed their masters, and acted as guides to the stranger. But the process was naturally slow, and attended by many variations of fortune. It barbarised the original inhabitants, it civilised the barbarian, thus bringing both closer together. The Teuton became less Teutonic after the second and the third generation; the Celt, free or Romanised, found that he had only exchanged one master for another. He adopted the Anglo-Saxon tongue and institutions with the same ease or indifference as he had formerly adopted those of the Roman—with the same ease, in fact, as the Irish of the pale have adopted the tongue, the dress, the fashions, and the customs of the English colonists.[4]

But, however this may be, we cannot think that Mr. Green was justified in passing over with such a meagre and hasty notice the Roman occupation. The Celt is still amongst us, neither extinguished nor obliterated, notwithstanding the pressure and successful domination of a stronger race. We are still surrounded by memorials of the Roman occupation. Stories borrowed from the Celtic times hold their place in the most popular forms of our English literature. It was the Celt that fired the poetical imagination of the Saxon. It was from the Celt he borrowed his Arthurian Legends, and heroic stories telling of human aspirations ending in discomfiture; of human prowess, in spite of superhuman efforts, struggling in vain against a mysterious and overwhelming evil. His long and ineffectual wrestlings with his Saxon foe died down to rise up again in legends symbolising in tender and pathetic strains his own unhappy history—

[4] We doubt much whether even the Christian faith had so completely disappeared as is sometimes assumed. It is certain that churches were still in the land at the arrival of St. Augustine and his companions: as St. Martin's in Kent (Bede, i. 26); and the original edifice of Christ Church, Canterbury, which Ethelbert gave to the new missionary. If these existed in Kent, exposed to the earliest ravages of the Northern invaders, it is a fair presumption that other churches existed in other parts of England; another proof, if another were needed, that Roman arts and buildings were not entirely swept away. Moreover, Ethelbert's queen, Bertha, was a Christian; he had married her with the express stipulation that she should be allowed the free exercise of her religion (Bede, i. 25), and for this purpose St. Martin's Church had been assigned to her use. But this presupposes that it was still used as a Christian church. Ethelbert could not, therefore, be so ignorant of the Christian faith as has been supposed from the poetical account of his interview with St. Augustine (Bede, i. 35). Celtic slaves and drudges, still holding more or less of the Christian faith, would not fail to communicate it, however imperfectly, to Anglo-Saxon women and children, thus preparing the soil for the fuller preaching of St. Augustine, whose teaching would appear to Bede, with his ultramontane prejudices, the only true teaching of Christianity.

the wrecks of kingdoms and families, the unnatural divisions of brothers, the stain and dishonour of the domestic hearth, the temporal triumph of the wicked, the untimely death of the defenceless and the innocent. Whilst his sturdy and plodding conqueror, with infinite common sense, but no real poetic inspiration, was devising problems of self-government, securing justice by a clumsy and complicated system of police, and fencing his house and his pocket against all comers, the Celt was finding consolation for his own sufferings in reflections on the sadness of nature and the mysteries of human destiny. The truth is, that the Celtic influence has been marked and permanent throughout our national life, only Mr. Stubbs and Mr. Green have looked for it, where it is essentially weakest, in constitutional order and progress. For the history of the Celt, his social and political condition, his religion, his conversion to the Christian faith, his efforts in resisting the Roman and Anglo-Saxon yoke, the student will search Mr. Green's pages in vain.

This new fashion of ignoring the Roman occupation of Great Britain, and starting at once from the Anglo-Saxon invasion, is due to the desire of tracing our constitution to the days of Tacitus.[5] Our English Constitution, it is contended, with all its attributes of popular representation, or the right of the people to take part in the legislative assemblies of the nation, existed already in perfection—in greater perfection if we follow Mr. Green—among our untamed forefathers in their 'black-timbered homesteads of Holstein.' So, in spite of the improbabilities already detailed, it is

[5] Mr. Stubbs even traces to Tacitus our parochial system. 'The mark,' he says, 'becomes the sphere of a single priest, and is called his parish; the kingdom becomes the diocese of a bishop.'—*Select Charters*, p. 8. Mr. Green goes further. 'The holding of the English noble became the parish, and his chaplain the parish-priest, as the king's chaplain had become the bishop, and the kingdom his diocese,' p. 30. Whatever may be the origin of our parochial system, we are convinced that neither the one nor the other here given suggests the true explanation.

assumed (1) that the Teutonic occupation of Britain was a migration and not a mere conquest ; and (2) that the nations so migrating 'must be credited *with the same amount of organisation here which they had possessed at home.*'⁶ Nothing more remained for the due evolution of this theory than to postulate that this organisation must be identical with that which Tacitus described as existing four centuries before. There stands in the way of this theory the awkward fact that the language, the institutions, the general characteristics of the Teutonic races on the Continent differ widely from those among ourselves ; and this necessitates a further assumption not complimentary to our German allies, that we are the true Teutons, not they ; that 'The Teutonic System,' whatever that system may be, has been developed in its native strength and purity only on the shores of Britain in the face of a Celtic foe, and theirs is a bastard growth. These diversities are accounted for, in the words of Mr. Stubbs, by 'the variations of physical and mental characteristics, which in the progress of fourteen hundred years have been developed between the English and North German types;' by 'natural ones, their food and water . . . by the workings of the land on its inhabitants;' by 'political ones, the total difference of histoy, and mental and moral discipline.'⁷ But if these influences have affected the North German types on the one hand, are they not likely to have modified the English on the other ?

Since, however, these Teutons transplanted their whole system of organisation into Britain, as it existed on the Continent, and Tacitus must be accepted as a correct exponent of that organisation, writers like Mr. Green find consolation in the thought that in the primordia of our English Constitution kings were elective, and the great council of the nation was a popular assemblage of the free. 'The King,' says Mr. Stubbs, ' is chosen on the ground of noble descent;

⁶ The italics are ours.   ⁷ *Select Charters*, p. 2.

but his royalty does not, if we take the simple words of Tacitus, imply much authority. . . . The whole business of the nation is transacted by the councils of the nation' (p. 4). But, however these things may have been in the 'black-timbered homesteads of Holstein,' Mr. Stubbs, whose judgment and knowledge are far superior to Mr. Green's, warns us against supposing that monarchy was ever elective here, or that government was democratical. He is careful to exclude the popular element from the great deliberative council or Witenagemot, in whom the powers of legislation and taxation were exclusively vested. ' It is not a folk-mote' (a popular assembly), he says; 'although it represents the people; it is not a collection of representatives; its members are the *principes*, the *sapientes*, the *comites*, and counsellors of royalty, the bishops, the ealdermen, and the king's thegns' (p. 11). Not so Mr. Green, boldly departing from his more cautious and sagacious guide. '*Every* freeman,' he says, 'was his own legislator, in the meeting of the mark, or of the shire, *or of the kingdom*. In each the preliminary discussion rested with the nobler sort. . . . He (the freeman) was by right a member of the " great meeting," as of the smaller; and in "that assembly of the wise " (the Witenagemot) lay the rule of the realm. It could elect or depose the King'— Mr. Stubbs says, with a judicious reservation, ' when it was able.' ' The higher justice, the imposition of taxes, the making of laws, the conclusion of treaties . . . belonged to the Great Assembly. But with this power the freeman had less and less to do. The larger the kingdom the greater grew the distance from his home. . . . Practically '—it was never otherwise, according to Mr. Stubbs—'the National Council shrank into a gathering of the great officers of Church and State, with the royal thegns, *and the old English democracy* passed into an oligarchy of the closest kind.'[8]

[8] *Short History*, p. 56.

There is not the slightest warrant whatever for this assumption. There is no reason for supposing that the freeman ever enjoyed the political rights here claimed for him by Mr. Green, or that kings were elective here. Directly royalty touched English soil it ceased to be elective, and became hereditary. The language of our early historians admits of no other interpretation. Occasional variations from the rule, caused by internal anarchy, or by pressing political necessity, cannot be considered as constituting any solid objection to this statement. Much as Mr. Stubbs supports the belief that the German tribes transplanted into England their political system, without modification or admixture, he is constrained to admit in his more cautious moments that, from the very first, the authority of royalty was augmented by the necessities of war; and, further, that royalty was hereditary. 'The new kings,' he says, 'are kings of the nations which they had led to conquest (i.e. of their own people), not of those they had conquered. In each case the son is named with his father, as sharing, in the first assumption of the title, a recognition of the hereditary character, which is almost the only mark distinguishing the German kingship from the elective chieftainship.'[9]

But Mr. Green's assumption of a democratical element in our earliest constitution colours his whole history, and affects his treatment of it throughout. It is to this we owe the disproportionate length occupied in his pages by the Anglo-Saxon period, as compared with others. To the same fundamental conception is due that division of his work, to which we have referred already, 'The New Monarchy,' commencing with the reign of Henry VI. and ending with the death of Thomas Cromwell.[1] At that epoch, he assures us

[9] *Constitutional History*, i. 67.
[1] 'If we use the name of the New Monarchy to express the character of

'The Parliament was fast dying down into a mere representation of the baronage and the great landowners. The Commons, indeed, retained the right of granting and controlling subsidies, of joining in all statutory enactments, and of impeaching ministers. But the lower House was ceasing to be a real representative of the "Commons," whose name it bore. The borough franchise was suffering from the general tendency to restriction and privilege which, in the bulk of the towns, was soon to reduce it to a farce. Up to this time all freemen settling in a borough, and paying their dues to it, became, by the mere settlement, its burgesses; but during the reign of Henry VI. the largeness of borough life was roughly curtailed.' 'It tended,' he continues, 'to become a narrow oligarchy. The internal government of the boroughs . . . passed from the citizens—freely gathered in boroughmote—into the hands of Common Councils, either self-elected, or elected by the wealthier. . . . It was to these "select men" that clauses in the new charters generally confined the right of choosing their representatives in Parliament. The restriction of the county franchise, on the other hand, was the direct work of the aristocracy.'

To these tendencies Mr. Green attributes the restrictions of the franchise to the forty-shilling freeholders, the virtual disfranchisement of leaseholders and copyholders, and corruption in the management of elections.[2]

We do not deny the accuracy of the picture; but Mr.

the English Sovereignty from the time of Edward IV. to the time of Elizabeth, it is because the character of the monarchy during this period was something wholly new in our history. There is no kind of similarity between the kingship of the old English (Anglo-Saxon), of the Norman, the Angevin, or the Plantagenet Sovereigns, and the kingship of the Tudors. The difference between them was the result, not of any gradual development, but of a simple revolution; and it was only by a revolution that the despotism of the New Monarchy was again done away.'—*Short History*, p. 284. These last words are remarkable as a frank confession of the revolutionary character of the Long Parliament.

[2] *Short History*, pp. 265, 266.

Green is mistaken when he attributes this 'revolutionary change,' as he calls it, to the King or the nobles. It took place precisely at the time when, on his own showing, the Lower House had attained its highest and most perfect development; for he assures us it was 'to the reign of the House of Lancaster,' or to a period before the New Monarchy that the lawyers of the Long Parliament referred, 'for their precedents of constitutional liberty,' and, he might have added, of parliamentary rights and privileges.[3] The violation of constitutional liberty, the creation of a novel despotism of which he complains, followed immediately upon the time when, according to Mr Stubbs, ' the great lords were content to act as leaders and allies of the Commons;' when kings and lords alike ' looked to the Commons for help;' and the Commons had gained 'a consolidation, a permanence, and a coherence which the baronage no longer possessed.'

This, then, was the use they made of their power, to introduce a revolution subversive of constitutional liberty, according to Mr. Green, for every one of the disfranchising acts of which he bitterly complains was the work of the Commons, not of the King or the aristocracy. If it were ' a New Monarchy,' then it was new in the sense contended for by Mr. Stubbs, that never before had kings or barons deferred so much to the will of the Lower House—never had its power been more consolidated. It is not the barons but the Commons who petition the Crown, 'That whereas knights of the shire had of late been chosen by outrageous and excessive numbers of people of small substance, for the future the said knights shall be elected in every county by people resident and dwelling in the said counties, whereof every one shall have in free tenements to the value of 40s. by the year at least, above all charges; and that they which shall be so chosen shall be dwelling and resident within the said coun-

[3] *Short History*, p. 284.

ties' (8 Hen. VI.). It is the Parliament, not the King, which prefers the request sixteen years after that this enactment may be strictly observed. In fact, if these regulations with regard to elections must be deemed revolutionary and significant of arbitrary and irresponsible power, the guilt rests upon the Commons and not upon the Crown. There is no period in our history down to the middle of the seventeenth century when more exaggerated notions prevailed of the supremacy of Parliament, than in this reign of Henry VI., the time, that is, when, as Mr. Green thinks, we are entering 'on an epoch of constitutional retrogression,' and 'Parliamentary life is almost suspended, or is turned into a form by the overpowering influence of the Crown,' and 'the legislative powers of the two Houses are usurped by the Royal Council.'[4] Why, this is the very period when, upon an appeal of the Upper House to the judges on a matter of privilege, the latter declared that ' they ought not to answer that question, for it hath not been used that the justices shall in anywise determine the privileges of the High Court of Parliament; for it is so high and mighty in its nature, that it may make law, and that is law it may make no law' (32 Hen. VI.). But Mr. Green, not content with the plain and simple fact that the lawyers of the Long Parliament referred for precedents to the days of the Plantagenets and Lancastrians, imagines that they ignored all continuity, and ' silently regarded the whole period,' from the year 1471 to 1640, ' as a blank.' This he thinks, was ' not merely a legal truth but a historical one;' for ' what the Great Rebellion, in its final result, actually did, was to wipe away every trace of the New Monarchy, and to take up again the thread of our political development, just where it had been snapt by the Wars of the Roses.'[5]

With Mr Green's leave, the parliamentary lawyers of the Civil Wars knew no such figment. They admitted no such

[4] *Short History*, p. 283.   [5] Ibid. p 284.

fracture in the chain of our political existence. They appealed to the Act of Richard III. in their arguments against Benevolences. In their proceedings against the Duke of Buckingham (2 Char. I.) they asserted that 'it hath been the ancient, *constant*, and undoubted right and *usage* of Parliament to question and complain of all persons found grievous to the Commonwealth.' Even of the two judges who opposed the levying of ship-money in Hampden's case, so far from ignoring 'The New Monarchy' of Mr. Green, Judge Hutton appeals to the Acts of Henry VIII. and of Elizabeth, in confirmation of his sentence in Hampden's favour.

But Mr. Green as much underrates the importance of Parliament, or rather of the Lower House too often confounded with Parliament, in the period of 'The New Monarchy,' as he overrates it before that epoch. He adopts too literally the assertions of Coke and others, who, in their anxiety to justify their opposition to the royal prerogative, and magnify the rights and privileges of the House of Commons, made use of language which will not endure the test of strict historical criticism. It was Coke who solemnly assured the House 'that King Alfred made an Act, with the advice of his wise men, to have two Parliaments every year,' and was as solemnly believed! It was Coke who persuaded the House that the Statute, 1 Henry V., declaring that the knights of counties shall not be elected unless they are resident in the county at the time of election, meant no such thing, but only that they should 'know the state of the county and the grievances thereof!' Whilst Judge Hutton improves upon Coke's statement respecting King Alfred, 'that it was then conceived it was necessary to have Parliaments often to redress inconvenience'![6]

---

[6] Rushworth, iii. App. p. 193. The Long Parliament lawyers never could, or never would, disabuse their minds of the notion that Parliament before the Tudors and after was identical. Parliament in the earlier

In these views Mr. Green is influenced by the modern notion that popular representation in the literal sense lies at the root of our Constitution; and, he thinks, whenever obstacles are thrown in the way of its free development, our constitutional existence is in abeyance. We, too, believe that representation lies at the root of our national life, and that our kings, from the days they set foot on these shores, were not arbitrary but constitutional monarchs; *reges politici*, as the ancient lawyers loved to remind them. But then that representative body was not the Commons but the great Council of the nation, the *principes* and *optimates* (the Witenagemot) in the Anglo-Saxon, the *magnates* or *proceres* of a later period; and these as representing in the temporal and spiritual lords the two great and permanent elements of a Christian nation, its worldly and eternal interests, were the supporters and advisers of the Crown—the head and impersonation of the people. In them, under the Crown, all the functions of Government, whether legislative or judicial, were originally vested, as the King's advisers and ministers. As in the exercise of their judicial powers it was natural that they should consult the judges, not as associates, but as assistants, so it was equally natural that in demanding aids for the service of the nation they should consult the wishes and convenience of those by whom such aids were to be furnished. For no considerate reader will now suppose that in the constitution of his Parliament (A.D. 1265) De Montfort had any serious intention of establishing popular representation, as that phrase is now understood, or, in the words of Mr. Green, 'the right of the whole nation to deliberate and decide on its own affairs, and to have a voice in the selection of the

period meant the Great Council, to which the Commons were assistant but were not necessary. Parliament in the Stuart time meant, in the minds of the Commons, the exact reverse. As late even as the 6 Edward III., Parliament remained sitting when the Commons had left.

administrators of Government.'[7] If this had been his object, he would not have been so careful for the orderly summoning of the knights from every shire—a class whose interests and intimate connection in various ways with the great nobility he could not have overlooked—and have shown so little consideration for the borough members.[8] It was his real object to strengthen the powers of the barons and restrict those of the Crown. For the *Communitas baronum* was still considered as forming properly the whole Legislative Assembly of the nation—and the Commons were summoned only 'to give their assent to what should be ordained in the great Council of the nation, viz. the lords temporal and spiritual.'[9] From the first they were mere 'assistants,' not assessors of equal rank and privilege; sitting on lower benches in the same House;[1] attending on the Lords as they are summoned now to attend them on certain occasions. Their immediate business done—that is, the amount of aids in money to be levied and the mode of levying it—they leave to the Great Council of the Lords to determine all questions connected with the internal and external policy of the nation—war, peace, and judicature. 'Whatever pleases the King and the nobles will be agreeable to them' (28 Edward III.). 'It does not beseem the poor Commons to give advice' (7 Richard II.). 'Right as to judgment does not belong to them' (1 Henry IV.). 'The King's Council is to decide all Bills and petitions left unfinished by Parliament' (15 Henry VI.).

Other considerations point to the same conclusion. The

[7] *Short History*, p. 153.
[8] This would be still more evident if, as has been thought, the tenants in chief of the Crown were the sole or principal electors of the knights of the shire. The late decision that peers have no right to vote at Parliamentary elections was entirely at variance with constitutional usage.
[9] 'Ad consentiendum hiis quæ de communi consilio regni, prælatorum, magnatum et procerum, contigerit ordinari.'
[1] Until the reign of Edward III. they had neither separate house nor Speaker.

Lower House neither aimed nor could aim at such an ambitious task as Mr. Green in his enthusiasm would impose upon it. Certain qualifications were from the first required in the knights, citizens, and burgesses, which in the temper of those times, the scantiness of education, the absence of political knowledge, were sure to constitute a select class both of electors and representatives. *Ex discretioribus et probatioribus*—'the most honest (or of the best blood), lawful and discreet freemen '—*homines valentes*, the 'most worshipful' of the Commons; these are the distinctions accorded to the knights of the shire and the borough members;[2] and when by changes in the state of society men of inferior rank and position crept in, the Commons themselves petitioned that the qualifications, sufficiency, and abilities of the knights should be so restricted as to prevent the election of persons of mean qualities and estates (23 Hen. VI.); not as if this were a novel practice introduced by the great baronage, as Mr. Green asserts, but conformable with all previous usage. For acts regulating the abuses of elections were common long before 'The New Monarchy;' whilst for the borough members, who were required to be resident in the borough, and were not taken from men of the same rank as the knights, the necessities of trade—although members were allowed a certain sum for their expenses—would prevent them from accepting an onerous and costly office, drawing them from their occupations, when travelling was slow, distant, and dangerous. In fact, it was to this aristocratic, and not to its popular element, that the House of Commons owed its importance: a consideration very necessary for those who wish to understand its subsequent disputes with the Stuarts.

[2] In the 47 Edward III., in the election for knights, the rule prescribed is *armigeri digniores et probiores, in actibus armorum magis expertes*. Such a one is the Knight in Chaucer's pilgrimage.

But not until the reign of Elizabeth; in spite of the endeavours of constitutional critics, who would twist the concessions of Edward II. and his son into greater importance than they deserve. Constitutions on paper are one thing, in practice another; and Mr. Green is quite right in thinking that 'our political history is the outcome of social changes,' and must be interpreted by the state of society. It is the neglect of this truth that makes the study of constitutional history, as it is called, so utterly dry, barren, and repulsive. The history of this country stands high above the level of its statutes and its Rolls of Parliament. It is not what the Commons in those days might or might not do, according to the pedantical interpretation of their privileges by the lawyers of the Long Parliament, but what, considering their relations to the Crown, their position and influence among the people, and still more their recorded acts, was their own conception of their duties, their own interpretation of their legislative functions. It was certainly not that which Coke or Eliot or Pym, or later exponents of constitutional history, have asserted in their behalf. It was certainly not the right of erecting themselves into inquisitorial tribunals to extinguish liberty of conscience, as when, in later years of James I., they expelled from the House Mr. Sheperd 'for his speech on the Bill for keeping the Sabaoth (*sic*), otherwise called Sunday' (18 Jas. I.). It was not when, setting important business apart, they fined Dr. Manwaring 1,000*l.* for a foolish and extravagant sermon upon monarchy, and rendered him incapable of holding any civil or ecclesiastical office. Nor yet again when in the bitterness of their Calvinism they insisted on imposing their own interpretation of creeds and articles upon Mountagu and Sibthorp. The Commons in the fourteenth or fifteenth century never imagined for a moment that it was for them to decide the exact limits of the royal prerogative. Frequent as were their sittings under Edward III., and complete as was their constitution as the third estate of the realm, not a hint escapes them that it is their privilege to select 'the administrators of Government,' to promote statesmen and divines who fall in with their humours, and displace and silence those who do not. They have not the remotest thought that ' their will was to be the rule' (as claimed in 1628) 'by which all that was to be taught, and all that was to be done in England, was henceforward to be gauged.' They fell not into the inconsistency of disputing the right of the Crown to dispense with the law, and then claiming the right for themselves of pronouncing that to be illegal which the judges had declared to be legal. They might, by regulating their supplies, desire to remove grievances, but those grievances were mainly fiscal, not the grievances of the Commons under James I. or Charles I.; not a fixed design to concentrate within themselves unlimited control over all functions of the State; in other words, to transfer the supremacy of the Crown to the Commons, and degrade the King, in the favourite language of Milton and his admirers, to the condition of an elective chief magistrate. Some may think it desirable that it should be so. But when they contend, as Mr. Green contends, that the leaders of the Great Rebellion took up 'the thread of our political development just where it had been snapt by the Wars of the Roses,' less prejudiced observers will be inclined to challenge his assertion. They will think that the Long Parliament and its advisers, notwithstanding their appeals to ancient precedents, were taking up a position as strange to the earlier House of Commons, before the Reformation, as it was foreign to the practice, if not to the theory, of the Constitution; at least so far as that Constitution had been interpreted by practice from the reign of Edward I. to the reign of Elizabeth. The real

innovators were the lawyers and Parliaments of the Great
Rebellion. The real Conservative of the old lines of the
Constitution was the King himself. It was the Commons
of 1640 who were establishing a New Monarchy.[3]

Our readers must not, therefore, expect to find in Mr.
Green a safe or impartial guide in that most intricate and
difficult portion of our history—the reigns of the Stuarts.
It is not merely that this division of his work has been less
carefully studied, or that he has trusted too implicitly to
second-hand authorities; but his own strong prejudices incapacitate him from seeing any but one side of the question,
and that a very narrow and erroneous one. What is still
more strange, he cannot always do justice to those authorities
he recommends to his readers. He singles out Mr. Gardiner's 'History of England, from the Accession of James I.,'
as 'invaluable for its fulness and good sense, as well as for
the amount of fresh information collected in it;' but he
departs from it as widely as possible.[4] He stigmatises
Clarendon at one time as perverting 'almost every fact' in his
account of the Long Parliament, 'by deliberate and malignant
falsehood;' yet within two years after (1642) pronounces
him to be of great value. Either Mr. Green has been
carried away by the impetuosity of his feelings, or he has
been drawn by stress of time to complete this portion of his
task without due preparation—pardonable enough, it must
be admitted, considering the gravity and immensity of the

[3] Here is Mr. Green's own statement: 'Pym was the first English
statesman who discovered and applied to the political circumstances
around him what may be called the doctrine of constitutional proportion.
He saw that as an element of constitutional life Parliament was of higher
value than the Crown; he saw, too, that in Parliament itself the one
essential part was the House of Commons. . . . When Charles refused to
act with the Parliament, Pym treated the refusal as a temporary abdication
on the part of the Sovereign.'—*Short History*, p. 519. No question. But
where does Mr. Green find this notion in the 'old lines' of the Constitution?

[4] *Short History*, p. 461.

attempt. For, whatever may be Mr. Green's defects, his History is no mere compilation. It has all the characteristics of original thought, of rapid generalisation, of warm personal feeling—too much to be implicitly trusted. To Mr. Green, James I. appears as a drivelling and cowardly pedant, who had formulated a theory of absolute monarchy, and converted it into a system of government.[5] We are asked to believe that already, before his accession to the English throne, he entertained opinions subversive of 'national liberty.' There is something inexpressibly ludicrous in this imputation. A shambling, good-natured monarch, resolved 'to take his ease' in his new kingdom, far from the rugged soil of Scotland, and its equally rugged Presbyterianism, James had no higher object than to keep things as he found them. His theory of 'absolute royalty,' resting, as Mr. Green will have it, on 'the inviolable bases' of 'the divine right of bishops' and 'the divine right of kings,' was expressed in his famous axiom, 'No Bishop, no King,' and implied nothing more than his admiration for the easy-going rule of an English Sovereign, as compared with his own experience. The peace and plenty of his Tudor predecessors were attributed by James to the preference they had shown for Episcopacy, and the support they had given it. The deference paid by the clergy to the Sovereign—a habit established by long usage from the days of Henry VIII.—the superior social position and culture of the English bishops, as compared with 'Jack and Tom, and Will and Dick,' of the Scottish Presbytery, recommended the English hierarchy to James. Deeper than this his theories went not, whether of Church or of State. He must be acquitted of all the perilous designs, as well as of the gross immoralities ascribed to him by Mr. Green, who has drawn a portrait more like that of Tiberius than James I. 'Good-humoured

[5] *Short History*, p. 465.

and good-natured,' says Mr. Gardiner—a good-nature too easily abused—' he was honestly desirous of increasing the prosperity of his subjects. . . . From his earliest youth not a syllable was ever whispered by the foulest slanderer against the morality of his life; and though he was certainly not abstemious, he was known to be perfectly free from the vice of drunkenness.'[6]

But Mr. Green has either failed to realise the new position and feelings of the Commons at the time, or failed in enabling his readers to realise them. If the footing was a new one, as Mr. Green thinks, on which the king now stood in reference to Parliament, it was not to the attitude of the Sovereign, but of the Commons, to which that novelty is chargeable. It is not he but they who are the aggressors. It is the King who is compelled to act on the defensive in behalf of that prerogative which had been hitherto regarded ' as the ancient and undoubted birthright and inheritance ' of the Sovereign. It is the Commons who desire to establish their new 'liberties, franchises, and privileges ' on the ruins of that prerogative. We are not discussing the moral right, but the facts, which are not to be judged by the Constitution as remodelled at the Revolution of 1688, but as that Constitution was interpreted, and had been interpreted, for two centuries and more at the accession of James I.[7] The

[6] *History of James I.*, i. 55.
[7] 'That the position which the Commons now claimed,' says Mr. Gardiner—who will not be accused of leaning too much to the royal side —' was in some respects new it is impossible to deny. They and not the Lords stepped forth as the representatives and leaders of the English nation . . . It was nothing to them that their predecessors in the Plantagenet reigns had sometimes spoken with bated breath, and had been often reluctant to meddle with affairs of State. It was for them to take up the part which had been played by the barons who had resisted John, and by the earls who had resisted Edward. Here and there, it might be, their case was not without a flaw; but the spirit of the old Constitution was upon their side.'—*Spanish Marriage*, ii. 151. Briefly, that is, the letter of the law was in favour of James and Charles, the

pedantry of which Mr. Green complains is not due exclusively to James. If any lawyer or statesman at the present day should insist upon ignoring all later precedents and custom, and insist, as the Constitutionalists of the Long Parliament insisted, with the approbation of Mr. Green, upon taking up the thread of the Constitution from the point where it had been snapped two centuries ago, on whom would the imputation of pedantry rest? In law the practice determines the theory. It is the reversal of this obvious rule that constitutes pedantry; and that was precisely what the legal advisers of the Long Parliament—using that expression in its extended sense—were doing. But their pedantry was, after all, a mere mask. It had nothing to do with the determination of the Commons. That determination rested on very different grounds.

Mr. Green is alive to the fact that 'our political history is the outcome of social changes;' but he has failed to explain satisfactorily the great enigma, how it was that 480 country-gentlemen, of the best blood of England, belonging to a class of strongly Conservative instincts, and remarkable for their attachment to the Crown, should either have become the tools of subtle lawyers and Republican theorists, or have adopted a line of conduct so much at variance with their general moderation and loyalty. If it be said that the army and not the Parliament must be held accountable for the subsequent excesses which ended in the subversion of the Constitution, there still remains the puzzle how these 480 gentlemen could have been so deficient in ordinary prudence and moral courage as to submit without a struggle to a faction they despised. The truth is, that the House of Lords had become a mere shadow. It simply reflected the decisions of the Commons, and was therefore voted down as

spirit of the law with the Parliament. Yet it must be remembered that both parties appealed not to the spirit but to the letter.

useless. But the House of Lords is the mainstay and bulwark of the House of Commons, and when it ceases to be powerful and efficient the Commons become a rope of sand. If they are the motive, the Peers are the regulating and restraining power. 'To depress the nobles,' says Lord Bacon, 'may make a king (or a House of Commons) more absolute, but less safe, and less able to perform anything that he desires. I have noted it in my "History of King Henry VII. of England," who depressed his nobility; whereupon it came to pass that his times were full of difficulties and troubles; for the nobility, though they continued loyal unto him, yet did they not co-operate with him in his business. So that in effect he was fain to do all things himself.'[8] This is the true reason of that supremacy of the Tudors, and the necessity on their part of personal exertion and rule, for which Mr. Green endeavours to find a different explanation. But in this desire of theirs to humble the nobles, the Tudors transferred fresh powers to the Commons. The suppression of the monastic houses, and the distribution of their lands among the gentry, or 'the second nobles'—to use Bacon's expressive phrase—for the ancient nobility were too diminished and too little in favour to share in the plunder,—gave them a vast increase of wealth and influence. They now took the place of the older baronage in the struggle with the Crown; and were formidable assailants, from their wealth, their numbers, and 'their immediate authority with the common people.' The older nobility, excluded from all share of authority under Henry VIII. and Elizabeth, and reduced below fifty, were doubled in number by James I., who saw the necessity of some protection against the aggressions of the Commons, as Cromwell afterwards saw. But the result was unfortunate. The old Lords did not agree with the new; and the House of Commons found in the Upper House,

[8] Essay XIX., *On Empire.*

among the older aristocracy, men as much opposed to the Crown as themselves.

'Queen Elizabeth,' says Carte, 'a princess of great wisdom and spirit, equally zealous of the rights of the Crown and tender of the welfare of her subjects, preserved the prerogative very well, to the end of her reign, by never suffering it to be touched upon or to come into debate in the House of Commons. . . . King James, conceited of his own wisdom, and fond of displaying his learning and eloquence in long speeches, took a different method from his predecessor, and talked himself out of the prerogative. He fancied that he could reason his Parliament into an allowance of it, not considering that they might naturally have as good an opinion of their own wisdom as he had of his, and that the very debate of a matter in an assembly of men, whose rule of acting is founded on precedents, gives them a right to dispute it for ever. . . . He was guilty of as great an error in laying aside the forms of Majesty and the ceremonial of a Court. . . . Coming from a country where they used to make very free with their kings, James did not care for the trouble of ceremony, to which he had not been reconciled by custom; and laid aside the State and forms of a Court to consult his own ease, and to allow all the world promiscuously the pleasure of hearing the learning which flowed from his mouth.'

His successor took an opposite course. Proud and reserved, the undignified bearing of his father, always lavish and necessitous, always exposed to contempt for his foolish good-nature, shocked Charles' sense of decorum. Resenting the least impeachment of the honesty of his own intentions, demanding rather than courting the confidence of his subjects, 'he did not consider them enough to think it worth his while, or consistent with his dignity, to gain them by the ordinary methods used for that purpose. He had very high notions of the majesty and rights of princes, and thought the distance between them and their subjects so vastly great, that he would not condescend to humour his Parliaments, and could so ill-brook any contradiction from them, that as soon as they entered upon any measures disagreeable to his inclinations, or less respectful . . . to his authority, he chose to part with them abruptly in anger, rather than try to bring them to a better and more complaisant temper by the arts of persuasion and management. He was truly zealous for the honour of the nation, and the good of his subjects, an excellent economist, and had no expensive vice to maintain. . . . He thought he had as good a right in every part of his prerogative as he had in those chief rents, aids, and services which his subjects were by ancient tenure obliged to pay him out of their estates; and therefore, when his Parliaments'—on whose advice and assurance of support he had undertaken the war of the Palatinate—' refused to relieve his necessities and those of his kingdom, he, in order to provide for both, had recourse to methods of raising money which had been frequently taken by his predecessors in former times, but which seemed new and extraordinary by having been long disused.'⁹

⁹ Carte's *Life of Ormond*, i. 354. This writer adds—a fact unknown to most readers—that in order to maintain the dignity of the Court neglected by James I., the King caused different rooms in the palace to be allotted to the different orders of nobility; so that none of inferior rank were allowed to enter those set apart for persons of superior quality. For this reason written orders were hung in the different rooms warning persons of lower grade from entering. It happened that Sir Henry Vane, who had entered one of the forbidden rooms, was surprised at the announcement of the King's approach, and finding no way to escape, hid himself in a cupboard, concealed by a long carpet. The King observing that the carpet moved, pushed it with his cane, and discovering Sir Henry, held his cane over him with a very angry gesture. There was, however, some reason for this attempt to maintain decorum at Court. 'In Queen Elizabeth's time,' says Selden, 'gravity and state were kept up. In King James' time, things were pretty well. But in King Charles' time, there has been nothing . . but *omnium gatherum, hoite-come-toite.*'

But into the reign of Charles I. we have neither time nor inclination to follow Mr. Green. He has not only taken too partial a view of the subject, and all his sympathies are one-sided, but in the very outset of the reign he has fallen into such strange errors and confusion that it is almost impossible to follow him. He ascribes the dissatisfaction of the Commons in the first Parliament of Charles I. to the circumstance that 'Bishop Laud was put practically at the head of ecclesiastical affairs,' although this did not happen till afterwards. As Charles succeeded to the Crown on March 1, and Parliament met in the summer following, it is not easy to see how Laud, however zealous he might be, could have found any sufficient opportunity for interfering 'in ecclesiastical affairs,' and thus incurring the suspicions of the Commons. History at least mentions no such act. The only justification for this remark offered by Mr. Green is the assurance that Laud drew up, 'at once, a list of ministers marked O. and P.—orthodox and Puritan.'[1] But he omits to tell his readers that this was a private paper drawn up at the desire of Buckingham, and what use, if any, Laud made of it Mr. Green leaves us to conjecture. 'The most notorious among the High Church divines,' he adds, 'Dr. Montagu'—his right name was Mountagu—'advocated in his sermons the divine right of kings, and the Real Presence, besides slighting the Protestant Churches of the Continent in favour of the Church of Rome. The first act of the Commons was to summon Montagu to their bar, and to commit him to the Tower.'[2] To those who are acquainted with Mountagu's writings and history, it will be hard to determine which of the two has been the more strangely misrepresented by Mr. Green. The prosecution of Mountagu was not the first act of the Commons, nor was his treatment at all such as Mr. Green describes it. The first Parliament

[1] p. 481. [2] p. 481.

of Charles I. met at Westminster on June 18. The
Commons fell at once, tooth-and-nail, upon the unhappy
recusants, insisting that the penal laws against Catholics
should be rigidly enforced. And though by the marriage
articles of Henrietta Maria it had been provided that the
Queen should have the free exercise of her religion, the
Commons prayed the King, 'that none of his subjects
not possessing the true religion by law established should be
admitted into the service of his most royal consort.' This
is a tolerably clear indication of the spirit with which they
were animated. It was not until July 6 that they sent
for Mountagu; not because he had 'advocated in his sermons
the divine right of kings and the Real Presence,' still less
for 'slighting Protestant Churches of the Continent;' for
no such sermons are ever mentioned, if indeed they ever
existed. His offence consisted in writing a book called
'A Gag for an old Goose,' in answer to a *Roman Catholic*
attack called 'A Gag for the new Gospel (of Protestantism).'
In defending the Church of England Mountagu took the same
line as was taken by Hooker, by Andrews, and by Overall,
and is held to this day by nine-tenths of the clergy and
laity of the Church of England, even by Mr. Green himself.
In so doing he distinguished the position and doctrine of
the Church of England, from Romanism on one side, from
extreme Calvinism on the other. This, and this only, was
his offence. Attacked by two Puritan ministers, named
Yates and Ward, for what they stigmatised as Arminianism,
Mountagu published a crushing reply, entitled, 'Appello
Cæsarem.' The Commons now took the initiative; though
strictly it was not their concern, but that of the Upper
House. They appointed a committee to extract such
passages from the two books, or rather from the latter, as
tended to disturb the Church and State. The charges were
arranged under three heads, but not one of them such as

Mr. Green describes. First, they found 'The Appeal' was derogatory to the late King; because, as James had expressed himself unfavourable to Arminianism, and declared that the Pope was Anti-Christ, it was dishonourable to maintain the reverse—a strange method, it must be admitted, of upholding religious liberty! Secondly, the book, they affirmed, tended to disturb the Church and State as putting 'a jealousy betwixt the King and his well-affected subjects . . . . These he (Mountagu) calls Puritans, but does not define a Puritan;' . . . and 'the encouragement he gives to Popery, by affirming Rome to be a true Church.' The third charge was, that he had printed his book before it was examined by My Lord of Canterbury, and so infringed the privileges of Parliament, knowing that there was a complaint in the House against him! For these notable offences he was not sent to the Tower, as Mr. Green states, but was committed to the Serjeant-at-Arms, with an intimation that he would be released on giving a recognisance for 2,000*l*.

In consequence of the plague and the scanty attendance, the House was adjourned to Oxford, on August 1, but not until the Commons had given a further indication of their new disposition by restricting the grant of tonnage and poundage to *one* year. What Mr. Green means by saying that while 'voting a subsidy, the Commons restricted the grant of certain customs duties,' we do not understand, for *two* subsidies had been granted already, and it was not until afterwards that the Commons insisted on restraining tonnage and poundage to a single year. From the days of Edward IV. the right of levying these dues had been granted to the Sovereign for life. They had become, in fact, part of the royal prerogative, for the assent of the Commons was regarded as merely formal. 'Charles refused to accept the grant,' says Mr. Green; but the opportunity was never afforded him of refusing. The Bill was thrown out by the Lords in consequence of this unusual restriction. This decision left the matter unsolved, and Charles levied tonnage and poundage, waiting until the two Houses could agree between themselves whether to grant or deny it.

What follows is equally puzzling. Mr. Green makes Buckingham resolve 'to break with the Parliament' before it met at Oxford. 'He suddenly demanded a new subsidy'— but this was afterwards—'a demand made merely to be denied. . . . But the denial increased the King's irritation, and he marked it by drawing Mountagu from the Tower, and promoting him to a Royal chaplaincy.' As Mountagu was never sent to the Tower, it is needless to say he was not taken from it. Besides, Mountagu had been Royal Chaplain already some months before. So Mr. Green's chronology and all his deductions fall together.[3]

In his more generous moments, Mr. Green is candid enough to admit that Charles had no design at the outset 'of establishing a tyranny, or of changing what he conceived to be the older constitution of the realm.' He had no settled purpose of abolishing Parliament; 'but his belief was that England'—rather the Commons—'would in time recover its senses, and that then Parliament might reassemble without inconvenience to the Crown.'[4] But these moods are rare; and Charles stands forth in his pages as one whom the victories of Protestantism abroad had no power to draw 'out of the petty circle of politics at home;' as one who had given his assent to the Petition of Right, bidding Parliament rely on his royal word, but paltered with his pledge—quite a mistake, as Mr. Gardiner has shown—as one who was unworthy of the loyalty of those who supported

[3] At p. 482, Mr. Green adds, 'Sir Thomas Wentworth, Cope, and four other leading patriots were made sheriffs.' We suppose for Cope is meant Coke.

[4] *Short History*, p. 499.

him; perfidious alike in his negotiations with the Parliament and the army, 'jangling with Bradshaw and the Judges' at his trial, and only gracing his life by his manner of leaving it.⁵ A most harsh and ungenerous judgment.

Mr. Green has much to learn, and no little to unlearn. There cannot be a greater mistake than to suppose that Charles was indifferent to the victories of Protestantism abroad, as Mr. Green states, if by that is meant the support of his sister's cause. But that support was impossible so long as the Commons refused the necessary supplies. It was not the King, but the Commons, who could not be drawn out of the circle of domestic politics to consider the dignity of the nation in its foreign relations, or take a just and true view of international policy. Much as he is maligned, there was, perhaps, only one man at the time who saw that a period had arrived when this nation must remodel its diplomacy. In their narrow puritanism the Commons determined their policy by their religious prejudices. Spain had been the nation of priests and Jesuits, therefore every true Protestant must insist upon war with Spain; and peace with Spain was rank Popery. But Spain had for some time ceased to be formidable. France, under Louis XIII., was laying up stores for the ambition and aggrandisement of Louis XIV. Holland, whilst England was exclusively engrossed in 'the petty circle of politics at home,' was covering the seas with its fleets, and was prepared to dispute the naval supremacy of England. A war of England with Spain was exactly what Richelieu and what the Dutch wanted; and if the King and his advisers had been driven into such a war, as the Commons professed to desire, the naval greatness of this country would have been in great danger of being eclipsed for ever.

If Mr. Green does not imagine that the tax on ship-

⁵ *Short History*, pp. 500, 502, 554.

money was a mere pretext for raising revenue, his language is at least incautious on that head.⁶ So far from being of any pecuniary advantage to the Crown, and 'without cost to the Exchequer,' the reverse was the case, for not only every shilling of the tax was expended on the navy, but, in his desire to furnish an efficient fleet, the King spent large sums of his own.⁷ Ship-money was, in fact, a much heavier impost upon the Crown than upon the subject; for, like all the Stuarts, Charles took special pride in the navy, and to the Stuarts this arm of the service is greatly indebted. More than this, it was this very navy, built by ship-money, which protected England from the insults and aggressions of the Dutch in the time of the Commonwealth, and was turned by the Parliament against the King. How else does Mr. Green suppose that Tromp could have been driven out of the Channel? Did Cromwell or the Commons give their thoughts to the navy? Did they employ their revenues in ship-building?

We have scarcely space to notice Mr. Green's extraordinary defence of the execution of Strafford, on the ground that the nation 'in the last resort retains the right of self-defence,' and that the Bill of Attainder was 'the assertion of such a right.' No doubt in 'the last resort.'⁸ But before such a plea can be fairly urged, it is necessary to show that the

---

⁶ 'Shifts of this kind,' he says, 'did little to fill the Treasury,' p. 502.

⁷ 'I shall remove a scandal that hath been put upon the King, how that his Majesty hath meant to make a private, personal, and annual profit by it [ship-money]. What he hath done is well known, and I dare confidently say all hath been spent without any account to himself, and that his Majesty hath been at great charge besides towards the same purpose; and I heard it from his own royal mouth . . . that it never entered into his heart to make such use of it, and said he was bound in conscience to convert it to that use it was received for, and none other; and that he would sooner eat the money than convert it to his own private use.'— Chief Justice Finch, in Rushworth, iii. App. 233. The correctness of this statement is fully borne out by original Records.

⁸ *Short History*, p. 523.

accused has become so dangerous an enemy to his country as to justify it in proceeding to such extremities. That was not shown in Strafford's case. If it had been, there would have been no need for the Commons to abandon his impeachment and resort to a Bill of Attainder. This looks, as in truth it was, a determination on the part of the Commons to crush him at all hazards; to assert the dangerous doctrine advocated by St. John, their representative, that they had the same right of taking his life without legal process, as they had ' to knock wolves and foxes on the head.' But Mr. Green indulges strange notions of law and equity. He thinks that for 'the first six months of the Long Parliament' the changes it had wrought, of which this impeachment and execution of Strafford was one, 'had been based strictly on precedent, and had in fact been simply a restoration of the older English Constitution as it existed at the close of the Wars of the Roses.'[1] Yet within those six months Parliament had violated its own ' Petition of Right;' in the letter, by committing Laud to the Tower without specific charges to which 'he might answer according to law;' in the spirit, by its arbitrary proceedings against Strafford. In those six months it had incapacitated the bishops from sitting in the House of Lords; it had sent commissioners to deface and desecrate the churches; it had impeached the Judges for giving sentence at the King's request in the case of shipmoney—an unheard-of punishment for bad logic or bad law (if it was bad law), and a penalty, if impartially administered, sufficient to have exterminated all parliaments. It had expelled from the House all projectors and monopolists, except such as favoured its own proceedings. In its hatred of illegal subsidies, it had borrowed of the City 100,000*l*. to bribe the Scotch, and yet condemned the subsidies legally granted to the King by Convocation. Finally, to show its

[1] *Short History*, p. 523.

tender regard for the Constitution, and how much it was concerned in taking up the thread of it 'where it was snapped at the Wars of the Roses,' it extorted from the King's necessities, and his desire of saving Strafford, an Act to provide that neither House 'should be adjourned except at their own order, or Parliament be dissolved except by Act of Parliament.'

On its subsequent proceedings we need not insist. There was not a single arbitrary act which it had condemned in the King that it did not imitate and outdo. It may be questioned whether if Charles had gained the victory he would have overthrown the Constitution; unfortunately there is no room for that doubt in the history of the Long Parliament. Charles met the close of his unfortunate career with dignity, and has rooted in the minds of Englishmen a feeling of personal loyalty to the Sovereign which all Englishmen acknowledge, whatever be their politics. The Long Parliament, unable to maintain its own dignity and the freedom of the people, sunk in a universal hiss of ignominy and contempt.

But the culminating injustice of Mr. Green's book will be found in his treatment of George III. He cannot find words strong enough to express his fixed and rooted aversion for a Sovereign, whose main fault it was, in the eyes of his political enemies, that he wished to restore something like the equilibrium of parties, set aside by his predecessors, and to rescue the nation from a narrow and permanent oligarchy. Mr. Green admits that even the best of the Whigs, with Rockingham and Burke at their head, were unfavourable to all schemes of Reform.[2] They shrunk, he asserts, from all sympathy with public opinion. 'At a time when it had become all-powerful in the State, when Government hung simply on its will, the House of Commons had ceased in any real and

[2] *Short History*, p. 751.

effective sense to represent the Commons at all.'³ We stay not to inquire under what party or by whose agency this country had been reduced to a condition so disastrous. For nearly half a century the Whigs had monopolised place and power; and never in the history of England, not even in the reign of Charles II., had the arts of corruption been more actively or unscrupulously plied. Never had it been more unblushingly avowed that honesty and patriotism were mere names for venality. Under any circumstances it was not desirable that such a state of things should continue; nor would they have existed at all, or certainly not in such excess, had there been an Opposition to criticise and resist the 'hoary jobbers' represented by Newcastle, or the haughty intimidations of a ruling oligarchy. If then George III. had had no higher object in view than that 'of airing himself in the character which Bolingbroke had invented of a Patriotic King,' as Mr. Green contemptuously declares—even if he had had no higher purpose than to break up a vicious system which had led to such fatal results, George III. would have deserved the thanks of his people.

But Mr. Green cannot see or acknowledge any good in any act or motive whatever of George III. 'For the first and last time,' he observes, 'since the accession of the House of Hanover, England saw a King who was resolved to play a part in English politics; and the part which George III. succeeded in playing was undoubtedly a memorable one. In ten years he reduced government to a shadow, and turned the loyalty of his subjects into disaffection. In twenty he had forced the colonies of America into revolt and independence, and brought England to the brink of ruin.'⁴ And further on, in reference to the accession of Lord North to office, Mr. Green does not scruple to say: 'George was, in fact, sole minister during the eight years which followed; *and the*

³ *Short History*, p. 743.   ⁴ *Ibid.* p. 740.

shame of the darkest hour of English history lies wholly at his door.'[5]

Is this the language, we ask, which a thoughtful historian, writing for young readers, would feel that he was justified in employing? Is it such as can be with safety commended to inexperienced judgments? To our sense nothing can be more extravagant, or unbecoming. Mr. Green writes not like a grave historian, but as a partisan of Wilkes, Beckford, and Junius—as if he had been poaching on their preserves for the choicest flowers of violent and vulgar rhetoric. To answer these and other accusations in detail would be quite beyond the question. If George III. was the vain, selfish, unscrupulous tyrant he is described by Mr. Green, how is it that the longer he reigned the more was he beloved by his subjects? How is it that when dynasties were falling, and revolutions were subverting all other thrones, the throne of George III. stood safer and securer every hour? How is it that, in spite of his youth and inexperience, in spite of the numerous difficulties he had to encounter at the outset, his government became at every decade more firm, more steady, and more acceptable to his subjects? How is it that he lived down the bitter, factious, and unscrupulous opposition of a party who had resolved to dictate to him what ministers he should choose and what measures he should follow, until, not merely the House of Commons, as Mr. Green insinuates, but the people at large rallied round the King and withdrew all confidence from his opponents? Every fresh historical investigation has lightened the load of malignant aspersions once resting on his memory. Nobody now, except Mr. Green, believes in Burke's 'Thoughts on the present Discontents,' or accepts, as an accurate statement of facts, his theory of an interior cabinet of 'the King's friends.' No one now thinks that this clever but unscrupulous calumny was anything

[5] *Short History*, p. 749.

better than a party invention to conceal the incapacity of the Whigs and their mutual recriminations. It is not true that George III. in ten years reduced government to a shadow, even on Mr. Green's own showing; for with all the array of talent against him, with the Stamp Act and other measures hostile to the American colonists bequeathed to him by the Whigs, Lord North's administration, though not free from mistakes, defied all attempts to shake it. Equally untrue is it that the King forced the American colonists into revolt. That revolt was the result of causes over which the King had no control. It would have come under any circumstances. Was the King to allow the claim of Independence? Was he to submit without a struggle to the dismemberment of the Empire—for America was as much a part of the Empire as Scotland or as Ireland? That, at all events, was not the opinion of the nation, not of Chatham, not of Burke, not of Rockingham, not of Bedford. What would Mr. Green have? The *right* of the mother country to tax the colonies had always been insisted on, though not enforced. It was asserted by all parties alike, however divergent their political opinions. In deference to the will of the nation the King was bound to assert that right when it was called in question on the other side of the Atlantic. Whatever might be his private opinions he could do no otherwise; for that he acted from a sense of duty and not wholly from inclination is now very well known. Burke might argue that it was inexpedient to press the right, but the clearer judgment of men in general saw that the question could not be so decided. It was a right that we claimed, and as a right it was denied; and it was nobler for this country, and for America itself, that it should be so, and that by Lord North's reduction of the tax to a nominal sum the baser motives of gain should not demoralise or confuse the question. As to Mr. Green's remark that by this tax the nation was brought to the brink of ruin, he is only airing himself as a poet or epigrammatist. The statement is mere nonsense. The War of Independence, measured even by its material results, was not less advantageous to us than it was to our colonists. Instead of diminishing it augmented our prosperity.

We cannot spare room for further criticism, or we should be inclined to protest against Mr. Green's tirade that, 'it is touching even now to listen to such an appeal of reason and of culture against the tide of dogmatism which was soon to flood Christendom with Augsburg Confessions, and Creeds of Pope Pius, and Westminster Confessions, and *Thirty-nine Articles*.'[6] Nor can we dwell, as we had intended, upon his singular hostility to the Church of England. But we cannot forbear noticing his strange assertion that the Church of England alone, among all the religious bodies of Western Christendom, has failed 'through two hundred years to devise a single new service of prayer or praise.'[7] If that remark be intended to apply to the public services of the Church of England, we are not inclined to accept it as any condemnation. But if it is to be taken in its largest sense, if Mr. Green includes in it devotional services for the use of families or individuals, or of praise in the sense of hymnology, he has forgotten Ken, Wilson, Keble, and a score of others.

Upon inaccuracies in detail we have not insisted, prejudicial as such inaccuracies must be in a manual intended for schools, for it is not to be expected that in so wide a subject they could be altogether avoided. Our objections are of a graver and more general kind. It is against the whole tone and teaching of the book that we feel ourselves called upon most emphatically to protest. Under the disguise of a school history, Mr. Green has disseminated some very violent opinions in politics and religion. His design is not

[6] *Short History*, p. 307. [7] *Ibid*. p. 610.

the less subtle and dangerous because, in accomplishing this object, he has been misled into ingenious perversions of facts, and in the ardour of his temperament has misrepresented the conduct and motives of men—of those especially who have upheld the Church and the Monarchy. His sympathies seem not with order, but with disorder; not with established Government, but with those who have attempted to overthrow it. In the most ardent and furious of the leaders of the French Revolution he finds 'a real nobleness of aim and temper,'[a] which he denies to the champions of good government, or the peaceful upholders of religion and morality. To him the aristocracy, in conjunction with the Monarchy, seem the plagues of mankind, united in a dire conspiracy against popular freedom, progress, and development. Is this a history, we ask, to be put into the hands of the young and incautious? Is it from this they are to learn wisdom and moderation, to form just and equitable judgments of past events, or of the great actors of times that are gone? Is this the teaching by which they are to estimate rightly the deeds of kings, the worth of an aristocracy, the beneficial effects of order and religion? We think not. We have warned our readers against the errors and tendencies of Mr. Green's book. It is for them to exercise the necessary precautions, both for themselves and for those who are committed to their care and guidance.

[a] *Short History*, p. 778.

HATFIELD HOUSE.[1]

TWENTY miles from London, according to the evidence of its ancient milestone—nineteen, if we speak with the precision of modern topographers—stands the town of Hatfield, on the great northern road. As the traveller, glad to escape, if only for a few hours, from 'the sooty forge' of this huge metropolis, turns the gate of the railway yard and reaches a gentle dip in the road, the town lies straight before him. It occupies a hollow on the right and left, and these are evidently its most ancient quarters. The picturesque white-washed houses—never, we may hope, to be improved away—with their gable-ends facing the street, and their one overhanging solar or sunny chamber, might without much effort on his part carry back the visitor's imagination to the days of the Tudors, when stone was still confined to churches and baronial residences, and red-brick marked the luxurious and degenerate. At a later period in its history the town crept along a steep ascent at its back, appropriately called the High Street, until its further progress in that direction was barred by the ancient palace of the bishops of Ely and the park of the Earl of Salisbury. At the top stands the parish church on one side, founded before the Conquest, and 'The Salisbury Arms' on the other, having supplanted, or at least absorbed, its ancient rival, 'The George,' according to

[1] From the *Quarterly Review* for January, 1876; under the following heading :—Royal Commission, Historical Manuscripts ; Reports III. and IV. Manuscripts of the Most Honourable the Marquis of Salisbury, at Hatfield House, pp. 147 and 199.

the Darwinian principle of the survival of the fittest—whether of the absolute fittest is quite another question.[2]

With these exceptions there is not much in Hatfield to attract the artist or the antiquary. Its chief importance consists in its connection with the ancient palace and the present residence of the Marquis of Salisbury. Yet without any vanity it may boast a more respectable parentage than most towns of its size in England. Long before the days of the Conqueror it had risen into importance. Under the name of Hetfelle, belonging to the monks of Ely, to whom it was given by Edgar in the days of St. Dunstan, it figures in the pages of Doomsday. 'Here is a parish priest,' says the record, 'with 18 *villani* (or inhabitants); 18 *bordarii* (rustic labourers of a better class) drive 20 ploughs, and there might be 5 more: there are also 12 cottiers, 6 serfs, and 4 mills.' But for riches of riches in those days—there was wood enough to fatten 2000 porkers. The whole extent of the manor was computed at 40 hides, or between 3000 and 4000 acres.[3] It was distributed in varying proportions into arable, wood, meadow, and pasture; but its lard and its bacon were undoubtedly the chief jewels in its crown—at least to the monks of Ely.

Here, then, a small colony of Benedictines, draughted from the great abbey, divided their meditations between earth and heaven; for the property was too valuable to be entrusted exclusively to a lay bailiff, and the monks were too good economists not to look after their own estates.

---

[2] Readers of Shakespeare well remember that St. George was a favourite sign in the days of the Tudors.

'St. George that swinged the dragon, and e'er since
Sits on his horseback at mine hostess' door.'

[3] In a survey made by Hugh Norwold, Bishop of Ely, in the reign of Henry III., Hatfield was estimated to contain 2260 acres of wood, pasture and arable. Episcopal and monastic property, then as always, was apt to be disestablished and curtailed by unscrupulous lords.

They had no regular cell or established dependency; but they must have had some residence on the site of the ancient palace, for when the abbey of Ely was erected into a bishopric in the year 1108, Hatfield became an episcopal residence, and at Hatfield several of the bishops of Ely died, though none seem to have been buried there, with the exception of Louis de Luxemburgh, Cardinal-Archbishop of Rouen, who bequeathed his bowels to Hatfield church, and the rest of his remains, according to the strange fancy of the age, to other places. Here, then, under the shadows of its umbrageous and aged oaks—yearly diminishing in number, but still the great ornament of Hatfield Park—or wandering in its glades and grassy slopes, did the monks and the bishops of Ely—for the most part monks—recreate themselves from their spiritual labours. Basking on the sunny side of an eminence in the south-western sun, sheltered from the north by thick woods, Hatfield and its park are to this day one of the last spots in our metropolitan counties to experience 'the touch of churlish winter.' In the late autumn the leaves are green and the turf soft and spongy, either from these causes or the undulating nature of the ground, when other parts of England, and especially the eastern counties, are chill, bare, and dreary; still more in the undrained flats of Cambridgeshire and the fens of Ely.

There was little to disturb their meditations. The town, with its various occupations, kept a respectful distance at the foot of the hill. If, like Tennyson's monk, any one of them felt inclined to

'go forth and pass
Down to the little thorp that lies so close,'

there was not much more to occupy his thoughts and attention than the small talk and small doings which, from the days of Sir Percivale, have formed the staple amusement of such 'little thorps,' with little alteration until now. Along the great northern road, which then passed through the town, might be seen the troops of Henry IV. despatched against the insurrection of the Percies; while, in the civil wars, when Warwick, the King-maker, launched the forces of the Lancastrians against Edward IV. at the battle of Barnet, the monks found more congenial occupation in attending the wounded and dying fugitives that poured into Hatfield and the surrounding villages on the disastrous defeat of that day.

The social effects of the civil wars were remarkable. Even before they had come to an end, taste, literature, and art had begun to develop themselves with a splendour and magnificence amongst us they had never exhibited before. It is not merely the time when Caxton was devoting his new printing press to the production of the best English authors, poets or historians, under the shelter of Westminster Abbey, but architecture, with all its appliances of the noblest type, eclipsed its previous efforts. These were the days of Morton and Alcock, Bishops of Ely; of Islip, Abbot of Westminster; of Wheathampstead and Wallingford, Abbots of St. Albans; of many other ecclesiastics, whose taste and whose genius are still manifested in the exquisite tracery of their screens and shrine-work—in the free, flowing, and delicate proportions of chapels and church-towers, still supreme in their beauty in spite of the rigid iconoclasm of the sixteenth century, or the puritanic bigotry of the seventeenth.

It was under these new influences, so very different from what we should have been led to expect, that Morton, afterwards the favourite minister of Henry VII., rebuilt and beautified the bishop's palace at Hatfield. It was a new era in the art of building; it forms no less a remarkable comment on the times that he should have abandoned the older materials and neglected all those precautions for defence and safety which occupied the attention of earlier architects. Whether it was that the use of artillery had convinced men of the inutility of embattled houses, with their moats and their outworks, or whether a greater sense of security had come over the nation when the fury of the civil wars was exhausted, houses of red-brick now came into vogue, and a more general regard to comfort and convenience is observable. Of Bishop Morton's palace, which must have been erected between the years 1479 and 1486, a charming fragment remains attached to Lord Salisbury's mansion at Hatfield. It formed the rear of the ancient building, which consisted of four sides, the front of which, with its grand entrance, faced the old London road, and stood on a line with the north-western corner of the present mansion. The quadrangle was divided, as in many colleges of the two Universities, by a broad walk leading from the great gate in a straight line to the present tower of red brick, erected by Bishop Morton. The two wings flanking the tower formed the old banqueting hall, covered with an open and ornamental timber-roof, still in excellent preservation. At one end of the hall was a chapel, at the other stands an archway of red-brick, by which access was gained to the various apartments of the palace from the rear. Nothing can surpass the fineness and rich colour of the old material, in which no stone has been used, or the skill and judgment shown in adapting it to the mouldings and mullions of the windows. As this portion of the palace stood nearest the town of Hatfield, in the rear of the ancient building, it is fair to infer that greater labour was bestowed upon the front. Of this, however, and of the two flanks, nothing remains except, perhaps, the gatehouse, which now forms the northern and usual entrance to Hatfield House, since railways have extinguished the glories of posting and the still more glorious family coach, with its six white horses, the favourite equipage of the first Earl.

We have stayed a little longer on this description of Hatfield Palace, because of its historical associations. It was the favourite residence at various times of four English Sovereigns—Henry VIII., Edward VI., Elizabeth, and James I. Within its walls Edward VI., then a child of nine years old, began his first lessons in French, under the tuition of Richard Coxe, afterwards Bishop of Ely. Here Parker, afterwards Archbishop of Canterbury, chaplain to Anne Boleyn, preached to Elizabeth, then a towardly child, seven years old. It was at Hatfield that Elizabeth herself resided during the reign of her sister Mary; and at Hatfield undoubtedly, and under the celebrated oak which tradition has associated with her name, it is more than probable that she learned the news of her sister's death and her own accession to the throne. It may be thought strange that a young lady should be found sitting under an oak in the damp and dark days of November, especially a princess, on whose life so much depended. But, with the leave of our modern historians, Elizabeth was no ordinary woman: she was remarkable alike for vigour of body and for strength of mind. The open air was her delight. In advancing age, when exercise was painful and she was not able to stand without assistance on dismounting from her horse, she still continued to ride—brave Englishwoman as she was, and fit to rule over Englishmen. Six months before her death, when she was in her seventieth year, solitary and unwell, she continued her walks in the park, and actually rode ten miles at a hunting party.[4] She almost died in the open air, in a garden, although her last sickness fell in the late autumn of 1602 and the early winter of 1603. In the open air, under a tree, it was her custom to give audience. It was

[4] Calendar of State Papers, Dom. Eliz. 1602, p. 232.

under her favourite oak at Hatfield, in this very same month of November, and near the same day, that she received Fytton, the Vice-Treasurer of Ireland in 1575. It was at Hatfield that the Spanish Ambassador, De Feria, hastening from the dying chamber of Mary to pay his respects to the rising sun, announced to Elizabeth the expected dissolution of her sister; and at Hatfield, before she had taken one step towards London, Elizabeth arranged with the celebrated Sir Thomas Gresham, three days after Mary's death, for a loan of 25,000*l.* to pay the expenses of her coronation, and for another 25,000*l.* to recruit her exhausted exchequer.[5]

But other than crowned heads, and scarcely less than crowned heads, have rendered Hatfield memorable. It was here that the Lady Frances Brandon was born, on the 17th of July, 1517, the eldest child of the romantic marriage of Charles Brandon, Duke of Suffolk, and Mary, the French Queen, between two and three in the morning. It must have appeared a strange sight in those days, when neither bishops nor their chaplains were permitted to marry, to see nurses and midwives, in all the bustle incident to such occasions, crowding the passages and brushing the skirts of grave clerks and ecclesiastical celibates. Such a scandal would not have been tolerated in earlier times; and it serves to show how completely the more rigid notions and discipline of the Middle Ages had been broken down before the advancing spirit of the times. West, who had succeeded Alcock as Bishop of Ely, had been sent with Suffolk in his embassy to France. He was doubtlessly of council with the Duke 'in his whole course of wooing,' and probably for old acquaintance' sake had lent him his palace at Hatfield on this memorable occasion. The christening which followed on Saturday

[5] For these loans she paid 12 per cent. Her predecessors, according to Gresham, had paid 14 per cent. for similar loans.

morning, in Hatfield Church, may serve as a hint to admirers of magnificent ceremonial.

'The road to the church,' says the record, 'was strewed with rushes, the church-porch hung with rich cloth of gold and needle-work; the church itself with arras [tapestry] representing the story of Holofernes and of Hercules'—the juxtaposition of these worthies we do not profess to understand—' the chancel with arras of silk and gold; and the altar with rich cloth of tissue, covered with images, relics, and jewels. In the said chancel were, as deputies for the Queen [Katharine] and the Princess [Mary], Lady Boleyn' —not Anne, but Elizabeth, wife of Sir Thomas Boleyn—' and Lady Elizabeth Grey. The Abbot of St. Albans was godfather. The font was hung with a canopy of crimson satin powdered with roses, half red and half white'—the York and Lancaster badges—' with the sun shining, and gold fleurs-de-lys, with the French Queen's arms [Mary's] in four places, all of needlework. On the way to church were eighty torches borne by yeomen, and eight by gentlemen. The basin, covered, was borne by Mr. Sturton [son of William Lord Stourton?], the taper by Mr. Richard Long, the salt by Mr. Humphrey Barnes [Berners?], the chrism by Lady Chelton [Shelton]. Mrs. Dorothy Verney [Mistress or Miss, that is, and not Mrs.] carried the young lady, assisted by the Lord Powis and Sir Roger Pelston, accompanied by sixty ladies and gentlemen, and the prelates Sir Oliver Poole and Sir Christopher, and other of my Lord's [Suffolk's] chaplains. She was named Frances, being born on St. Francis's day.'[6]

Here, indeed, was a grand ceremonial, which labouring chamberlains and modern masters of ceremonies might long toil after in vain to imitate. But it is not for her gorgeous christening that this lady was remarkable. Though not born to a throne, she was declared heir to a throne by an Act of

* Calendar of State Papers, Henry VIII., vol. ii. p. 1108.

Parliament, and her claim was only set aside by the imperious intrigues of Dudley, Earl of Northumberland, in favour of her unfortunate daughter, Lady Jane Grey. Lady Frances, who thus made her *début* into the world in the hospitable precincts of Hatfield, was the very type of severe and appropriate English motherhood, at a time when young gentlemen still 'carved before their fathers at the table,' and young ladies in formal array stood beside the cupboard, occasionally reminded of their good behaviour by a tap from one of those formidable fans which the ladies in Tudor times carried at their girdles.[7] This is that mother whom Lady Jane Grey described to Roger Ascham, when he inquired how she came to take so much pleasure in reading Plato instead of amusing herself in the park, like other young ladies of her age. 'One of the greatest benefits that ever God gave me,' she replied, 'is that He sent me so sharp and severe parents, and so gentle a schoolmaster. For when I am in presence either of father or mother, whether I speak, keep silent, sit, stand, or go; eat, drink, be merry or sad; be sewing, playing, dancing, or doing anything else, I must do it, as it were, in such weight, measure, and number, even so perfectly as God made the world; or else I am so sharply taunted, so cruelly threatened, yea, presently sometimes with pinches, nips and bobs, and other ways (which I will not name for the honour I bear them)—so without measure disordered, that I think myself in Hell, till the time come that I must go to Mr. Aylmer'—her schoolmaster. It may be thought that this was not exactly the best way of educating daughters, and that it would have been better if Lady Jane, like her relative, Elizabeth, had varied her study of Plato with outdoor exercise and pastime in the park. Yet nothing

---

[7] It was no empty threat of Hotspur: 'Zounds! I could brain him [knock his brains out] with his lady's fan.' Whether ladies ever did administer this discipline to their sons and husbands, history does not record. Perhaps heads were harder in those days.

can show more convincingly the great progress which had been made in the education of women during the reigns of Elizabeth and James I., than a comparison of their letters in the Hatfield Collection with any of an earlier period. In clearness of expression and in beauty of penmanship they beat their male rivals out of the field. The letters of Elizabeth herself, of Lady Winchester, Lady Russell, Lady Rich, Lady Essex, the Countesses of Northumberland and Southampton, Lady Lovell, Lady Tresham, and others, may fairly stand comparison with those of any age.

On the death of Bishop West, in 1534, Hatfield Palace changed owners. It was made a condition, on the appointment of Bishop Goodrich, that he should resign the manor and palace into the hands of the King. By what right the Bishop alienated the property of his see was not a question that troubled the conscience of bishop or king : it was not one that Tudor sovereigns suffered to stand in their way when they had a mind to Church property. Henry had already possessed himself of York House, belonging to the see of York, on Wolsey's attainder. He had laid his hands upon Tittenhanger, belonging to the Abbey of St. Albans. To take Hatfield from the bishops of Ely was only another step in the same direction. It is true there was a talk of compensation; but such compensation consisted in exchanging poor and inconvenient manors without habitation for rich and convenient ones with habitation, or lands encumbered with spiritual obligations for lands that had none—a policy understood by Elizabeth. Much in the same way Henry discharged Wolsey's obligations, when he seized the Cardinal's property, paying off the unfortunate debtors 'by desperate tales:' that is, by bonds due to the Crown, but long since abandoned as hopeless—a method of paying good debts by bad ones; a stroke of finance more to be admired than imitated. Thus Hatfield came into the possession of the Crown, and there it remained until 1607. James I. preferred Theobalds, a more magnificent house, belonging to Lord Salisbury, and offered him Hatfield in exchange. On the 15th April, in that year, Cecil took his last leave of his patrimonial mansion.

'Being very desirous,' he writes to Sir Thomas Lake, 'to see the house of Theobalds and parks, now drawing near the delivery into a hand which, I pray God, may keep it in his posterity, until there be neither trees nor stone standing, I must confess unto you that I have borrowed one day's retreat from London, whither now I am returning this morning, having looked upon Hatfield also, where it pleased my Lord Chamberlain (Thomas Howard, Earl of Suffolk), my Lord of Worcester (Edward Somerset), and my Lord of Southampton (Shakespeare's patron), to be contented to take the pains to view upon what part of ground I should place my habitation.'[8]

The transfer was not completed till some months after. Meanwhile, the summer and autumn were spent in providing materials for the Earl's new habitation. They consisted chiefly of Caen stone, to the amount of 500*l*., for which he had a warrant from the King of France. Tattenhall, in Staffordshire, Worksop, in Nottinghamshire, and the quarries of Northamptonshire were laid under contribution. Whether to these must be added 'a newly-discovered material' found upon the estates of the Earl of Northumberland, which had 'a rich agate colour' when polished, would be hazardous to affirm; for the Earl, in addition to his other occupations, had the 'architectonic tastes' of his father, and at this very time was ornamenting and altering Salisbury House, in the Strand, and erecting a vast Exchange, called 'Britain's Burse,' on the site of the present Adelphi, much to the

[8] State Papers, James I., MSS. xxvii. No. 7. The bill for the transfer was read a first time in the House of Commons, 29th May.

chagrin of the citizens of London. The bricks and flints of the old palace—though by what means it could have fallen into decay is hard to imagine—furnished materials for the new. Late in the autumn of 1607, the ground was cleared for the foundations. Of the progress of the work in 1608 no account has been preserved; but in May 1609, carefully deposited among the papers of Her Majesty's Record Office, we come upon 'An Abstract of all the Charges that his Lordship is to be at more than he hath disbursed for the full finishing of his building at Hatfield, except joining, plate-locks, painting, and gardening.' The sum total is set down at 8,146*l*., with an estimate for deductions amounting to 710*l*., if certain ornaments were omitted. By the summer of the same year the new house had reached the roof of the present hall, and the floor of the great chamber, now the library. In the following November half the long gallery, facing the south, had attained the first storey, 'to the height of the pedestals on the upper range.' At the commencement of 1610, notwithstanding the hindrance caused by the wet autumn of the previous year, the building was so far advanced that Janivere, the joiner, residing in London, a Fleming or Frenchman, as it would appear from the name, had gone down to Hatfield to take the measurement for the wainscot and the oak chimney-pieces, the designs of which were to be submitted for his Lordship's approval. Of the estimate made in July 1609, which was finally fixed at 8,500*l*., the Earl had paid at Michaelmas 4,000*l*. In April 1610, the amount expended was 5,424*l*., and 3,779*l*. more were required to finish the work. Part of this increase was due to alterations made in the chapel, amounting to 150*l*., and to 50*l*. besides, for a new chapel window.[9] By the 23rd

[9] This window is filled with stained glass, representing different subjects from Scripture in different compartments, with Latin inscriptions below. As each of these designs and inscriptions exactly fills the compartment of the window allotted to it, they must have been coeval with the

of November, the joiner had completed the wainscot and panelling. We spare our readers the technical details, valuable as they are, for illustrating the history of an art now nearly lost. Of the specimens that remain, in its application to domestic architecture, few that we know of are equal in richness, freedom, and beauty, to those still preserved in their primitive freshness at Hatfield. No decoration of plain surfaces, no gaudy and costly gilding, no mediæval papering, no colouring—for fresco is out of the question in this damp and variable climate—can be compared in our estimation to the old oak wainscot of our ancient houses, with its rich friezes and bold architraves, its festoons and its pilasters, its free and vigorous projections, its panels with their simple and severe mouldings, or enriched with delicate arabesques, as they are in parts of Hatfield House; and certainly none are so refreshing to the eye. Besides the feeling of massiveness, strength, and comfort thus gained; besides the contrast of rich brown walls with the delicate white ceiling, interlaced with fretwork, these oak decorations have the advantage of harmonising with the rougher materials of our rough and vigorous climate. Neither France, Italy, nor Wardour Street can surpass our unstained English oak in the delicacy of its graining or the variety and warmth of its tints. In this respect the staircases, galleries, lobbies, doors, and doorways of Hatfield House are a delightful study to those who can open their eyes and use them. For this species of decoration the Earl wisely spared no expense. He spread it over all parts of his mansion with extraordinary profusion, from the Doric and Ionic columns with their friezes and 'swelling panels,' their triglyphs, cartouches, watercress and ogives,

framework. The glass itself is of the same date with that of the chapel of Archbishop Abbot's Hospital at Guildford. Both are probably Flemish.

in the King's and the Queen's bed-chambers—for the Earl built his house with the view of entertaining royalty—down to the plainer work in the chapel, with its cipher and square, or the mitre and square of the hall.¹

By the 17th of May 1611 the new mansion was rapidly approaching completion. The great hall was filled with tables and forms; the upper part of the screen, framed and carved, was ready for fixing. The masons had finished the walls of the great east chamber (the drawing-room). The scaffolding erected for 'whiting' the fret ceiling of the long gallery 'was to be cleared upon Tuesday.' The jambs for the windows in the great chamber (the library), framed in London, had been promised by Janivere, with a foot-pace, to be laid, 'which is a-working, and then that room will be fully finished.' The withdrawing-chamber, the closet of the chapel, and the rooms adjoining were 'ready to be lodged in within three weeks.' In July the work was still going on: 'the great chamber' was hanged and ready, the foot-pace and wainscot completed; and 'Dallam (how names fall into oblivion!) was to be sent down to tune the pipes of the wind instrument' (probably an organ). The king's chamber and the rooms adjoining were matted and hanged. The chimney-pieces of plain wainscot had been set up in the gallery. 'The closet, chimney-piece and hangings, chairs and stools,' for the chapel, 'were suitable ready.' The frieze, and the pulpit, indispensable in great households, were 'to to be done upon Thursday;' the andirons only were wanting. On the 15th January 1612 the masons were still engaged in paving the chapel with black and white marble, of which not more than one-third was completed; and the whole was to be finished in Mid-Lent or thereabouts. But before

---

¹ According to the original design, there were no marble chimney-pieces. The first was introduced by the second Earl in 1612, for which he paid 50*l*. His father had a keener artistic instinct.

Mid-Lent Death had laid his cold hand on the noble owner and architect. He was never destined to reside at Hatfield, or Cecil-Hatfield, as he proposed to call it. Visions of kings and queens passing through these spacious and magnificent apartments; audiences held in the great west chamber with its foot-pace; masques, revels, and music in the east chamber, were not to be realized in his time. But if ever any man had a grand conception of what such a house ought to be, where royalty might defile in full panoply, through its various apartments, without crowd or confusion, not shorn of its dignity like a provincial magistrate, that conception was realized at Hatfield. Two great chambers, each 60 feet long and 27 wide, on the east and west sides respectively, connected with a gallery 160 feet long, occupying the whole of the southern front, offer far greater advantages for grand entertainments, and enable a house full of guests to pass more freely from one end to the other, descending to the hall or the chapel by either of the opposite staircases, than rooms ranged in the same straight line, frigidly reproducing the same proportions, like the joints of a telescope or a nest of square boxes. Bedrooms in those days were not so numerous as modern usage requires. The more graceful sex formed a minority at festal gatherings. My lady's lady and my gentleman's gentleman were left behind; or if the one attended her mistress and the other his master, the lady's maid generally slept with her mistress, and my lord's gentleman occupied a pallet by the side of his master. Where the accommodation was scanty, two men of rank made no scruple of sharing the same chamber. The personal attendants of the great in those days were gentle by birth, and not unfrequently noble. So far from the truth is Lord Macaulay's flirt at the English clergy, whom he mistakes for the Dominie Sampsons of the novelist, and their wives for the menial waiting-women of his own time. Even Locke,

Whig and philosopher as he was, did not sit at the same table with his aristocratic and liberal patron. He ate with the chaplain, at the side table. But neither one nor the other thought themselves degraded, or were degraded in the estimation of their contemporaries, by this rigid distinction of rank.

Sir Robert Cecil was his own architect. Two workmen on his estate—a mason named Conn, and a carpenter named Lyminge—were his builders and surveyors, whilst his steward, Thomas Wilson, acted as general superintendent, paid the wages, and exercised a general supervision over the buildings and the gardens. The mansion, open to the south, occupies three sides of a hollow square, of which the north is 228 feet long, the two sides, east and west, $137\frac{1}{2}$ feet respectively, and the south front 133 feet 4 inches. Were it only for its architectural details Hatfield House is remarkable, more especially considering the means and instruments employed in its erection. In apartments so vast and so numerous no blunders were committed. No gigantic staircase—obtruding its vastness, like Behemoth, into a diminutive hall—thrusts the sleeping apartments out of windows; no long narrow passages, pierced with doors exactly of the same shape and dimensions, and at the same intervals, puzzle the sensitive guest with a superfluous feeling of responsibility. Even in that difficulty of all difficulties, for which neither Greece nor Rome, nor Gothic pinnacle, to the dismay of modern architects, affords any solution—we mean the modern chimney-stack—the Earl, with his uneducated workmen, has afforded lessons modern builders might do well to study if not to imitate. Boldly grouping his chimneys, slightly enriched with interlacement, he made them subservient to the general effect of the whole design. At every distance they stand out against the sky, adding variety and effect to the outline

It is probable that the house was never entirely completed according to the Earl's intentions. We miss the full complement of the twenty gables, with their twenty lions, and their twenty vanes. We miss the grand quadrilateral esplanade, enclosing the house with its architectural *enceinte*, and cutting it off from the definite bay outline surrounding country. We miss the great gates at its northern and southern extremities, with their long level line of Purbeck marble, from end to end, flanked with myrtles or formal orange-trees. Time, also, has laid its hand here and there on turret and stone-work. The clock-tower has been shorn of its full proportions. Still, the marvel is how so grand a work could have been carried out with such hands, and in so short a space; how, to this moment, not an opening large enough to admit the blade of a penknife is to be found in the parquetry floor of its long gallery, nor a panel has started from the walls. These were the workmanship of obscure English hands before technical education was invented. Could they, we will not say be surpassed, but be equalled by English carpenters and masons now?

Of the books, pictures, and antiquities, we propose not to speak; we must turn to less familiar subjects. Whilst the Earl was thus occupied in building, a new era of gardening and picturesque horticulture had sprung up in England. The readers of Bacon will call to mind his essay on this subject; the readers of Milton will remember his association of study and contemplation with 'trim gardens.' By a policy fatal to his successor, James I. had sent the English gentry to reside on their estates in the country; there to study law, like Hampden, or divinity, like Falkland, or chemistry, like Digby. Country houses showed the result in their greater air of refinement, in their libraries, in their fountains and terrace walks. The Earl was not indifferent to these things, immersed, as he seemed to be, in politics, with his abstracted

air, and his large lustrous eyes apparently gazing on vacancy.
His grounds absorbed as much of his attention as his house.
The garden on the west side belonged to the ancient palace.
The garden on the east side, with its great flight of steps
from the terrace, dates from the new house. It consisted of
an upper and a lower level. It was to have been enriched
with fountains, 'two in the quarters of the upper part and
one in the midst of the lower part, each receiving their
water from that next above it.' In addition to these was a
pleasaunce, called in the papers of the times 'The Dell,'
since better known as 'The Vineyard,' occupying the two
opposite banks of the Lea. Nothing can be more picturesque
or more delightful on a hot summer's day. Its steep slope
of the greenest turf descending to the river, its primly-cut
methodical yews, with their parallel alleys, carry the imagination back, without an effort, to the days of Donne, Burton,
and Herbert. Such poetry and such prose, so fresh, so
scholarly, so contemplative, solemn as these yews, quaint
and as fantastic as they, could never have been meditated
except in retreats like this, and only in such retreats can
they be fully appreciated. Delightful in itself, it is still
more delightful from the contrast of its geometrical primness
with the unclipped limes and oaks growing in untamed
strength and majesty in the dark avenue which abuts upon
it. 'Went to see my Lord of Salisbury's palace at Hatfield,'
writes Evelyn, no bad judge of houses and gardens, 'where
the most considerable rarity, besides the house, inferior to
few then in England for its architecture, were the garden
and vineyard, rarely well watered and planted. They also
showed us the picture of Secretary Cecil, in mosaic work,
very well done by some Italian hand.'[2] This retreat was

[2] Procured in 1608 by the celebrated Sir Henry Wotton, then ambas-
sador at Venice. Contemporary letters speak of it as a very good likeness.
Probably it was copied from Hilliard's picture of the Earl, now at
Hatfield.

designed by a Frenchman, as we learn from a letter of the
Earl's factotum, addressed to the Earl himself; and at the
visit of Evelyn, who prided himself on his *jets d'eau*, seems
to have possessed more of its original features than it retains
at present, for he says, 'it was rarely well watered.' 'At
the river (Lea),' says the letter just mentioned, 'the Frenchman meaneth to make a force (a forcing machine) at the
going out of the water from the island, which by the current
of the water shall drive up water to the top of the bank above
the dell, and so descend into two fountains.' For this purpose
the bank on the other side of the Lea had to be levelled and
the earth transported to the east garden. These water-
works are explained by a rude sketch, with which we will
not trouble our readers. For this vineyard and his other
grounds the Earl received from France, through the care of
Madame La Boderie, wife of the French Ambassador, 20,000
vines at the cost of 50*l*., and 10,000 more were expected.
'This evening came to me,' says the steward, 'the French
queen's gardener, that hath brought over the fruit-trees for
the King and your Lordship; 2,000 for the King, and above
500 for your Lordship. . . There are two other gardeners
besides this man, sent over by the French queen, to see the
setting and bestowing of these trees.' From Lady Tresham,
at Lyndon, whose husband had bestowed great care on horticulture, he received the offer of fifty cherry-trees; vines and
nectarines from Sir Edward Sulyard; liquorice, with explana-
tions for its culture, from the Earl of Shrewsbury; and a
Norfolk tumbler for his warren, from Sir Edward Coke. His
two gardeners were Montague Jennings and John Tradescant,
afterwards horticulturist to Charles I., and father of the still
more celebrated John Tradescant, founder of the Tradescant
Museum, now better known as the Ashmolean Museum, at
Oxford.

But it is not for its bricks and mortar, or the skill

exhibited by its architect, or its curious gardens, or even its ancient surroundings, that Hatfield House is famous. Its greatest treasure consists in its collection of original papers, from Edward III. to the House of Hanover, embracing the correspondence of Lord Burghley and his son, from the reign of Henry VIII to the middle of the reign of James I. No period in our annals is more full of 'moving accidents;' in none certainly was the spirit of the nation more profoundly stirred, or the chief actors on the stage of its history cast in a mightier mould—

'Sad, high, and working, full of state and woe.'

It embraces the two most fiery ordeals through which any nation can be doomed to pass. The conflict of opposite elements equally strong, their alternate preponderance, their eventual fusion, invest the whole of this epoch with a dramatic interest and grandeur never surpassed. Within its limits there is scarcely any event of moment, scarcely any personage that 'frets his hour' on the stage of history, that is not set in a clearer light, or brought more vividly home to the reader, by the Cecil manuscripts. Bequeathed by Lord Burghley to his son, Sir Robert, the first Earl of Salisbury, containing a more complete and voluminous collection of the papers of the son than even of the father, the correspondence preserves, as might be expected, important information for the life and ministry of both. The settlement of the kingdom on the accession of Elizabeth; her correspondence with Mary Queen of Scots; two of the celebrated Casket letters in French, numbered by Burghley's own hand—one a clumsy imitation of Mary's hand, and suspiciously manipulated; the various intrigues carried on by noble and ignoble agents on both sides; the hopes and disappointments of the Howards; the Anjou and Alençon marriages; the preparations for the Armada; the brilliant and impetuous career of Essex; the disputes, intrigues, and jealousies fomented by the succession and the reign of James I.; the Rye Plot, the Gunpowder Plot, the designs of Garnet, the divided counsels of the seminary priests and the Jesuits, the marriage and escape of Arabella Stuart:—these, and many more, are presented in unbroken succession to the reader. With these guides he may thread his way securely through the dark shadows of the past. Theirs are the freshness and vivacity of contemporaneous narrative, the vividness of eye-witnesses and actors in the scene before him. Here are the letters traced by the hands of men like Wolsey, hurled from the height of greatness to dishonour; or of others like Essex, penning his last lines, as the moments fast ebbed away, the night before his execution. Here are the sighs and tears of despairing wives and relatives, watching intently for the least ray of mercy. The pangs, the hopes, the anxieties, the disappointments, the anguish of poor humanity, the intrigues of the great, the necessities of the fallen, are here consigned to minute and perpetual memory,—the only living and tangible element that remains of those who have long since crumbled into dust. All else has perished. These poor sheets of paper, once warm beneath the hands of those who traced the characters inscribed upon them, of kings, queens, princes, statesmen, the prosperous and the miserable, the triumphant and the dying, the noble and the ignoble,—these form a visible and material bond, that brings the present, by undying sympathy, into close proximity with the past. Over these pages has passed the breath of other centuries. The eyes of distant generations have wandered over their contents. The spirit which once animated them is before us, not as in the imagination of the poet, or in the narrative of the historian, but in its native sincerity unalloyed and undisguised.

The collection at Hatfield is enriched by the letters of

Edward VI., Katharine Parr, Donna Maria, Elizabeth as Princess and Queen, Mary Queen of Scots, James I., Ann of Denmark, Francis II., Henry IV., Philip II. and Philip III., Catherine de' Medici, Arabella Stuart, Princess Elizabeth the daughter, Henry and Charles the sons, of James I. With these is a host of brilliant but inferior satellites: the Emperor of Russia, Philip and Maurice of Nassau, William Elector Palatine of the Rhine, the dukes and princes of Anhalt, Holstein, Saxony, Brandenburg, and Würtemberg, *omnia magna loquentes*. But more interesting to the English reader is the correspondence of men whose names are famous in the annals of his country. Of these scarcely one is absent. Among them are to be found the Duke of Norfolk and others who bore the name of Howard; Sir Nicholas Bacon and his two sons, Anthony and Francis the philosopher; the Dudleys, including among them the celebrated Earl of Leicester and his countess; the Somersets, the Montagues, the Greys, the Hattons, the Clintons, the Throckmortons, the Cobhams, the Hunsdons, the Wentworths, the Harringtons, the Percies, the Talbots, the Sidneys, the Lumleys, the Poulets, the Parkers, the Stanleys, the Mildmays, the Dorsets, the Petres, the Egertons, and others—the *dii minores* of the collection—too many to enumerate. For the mature and declining years of Elizabeth and the earlier years of James I., we have Sir Thomas Bodley, the founder of the Bodleian Library; the brilliant Earl of Essex; his intimate friend Southampton; Sir Walter Raleigh, Carr, and the Duke of Buckingham; Sir Fulke Greville, the most thoughtful poet of that or any age, the great dramatist only excepted; Sir John Davis, excellent alike as historian, lawyer, and poet; Sir Edward Dyer; Secretary Davison; Coryate, dear to the lovers of quaint books; Hilliard, the portrait-painter, carver, and gilder, who decorated Elizabeth's tomb in Westminster Abbey; Overbury, the victim of a lady's revenge; Sir Henry

Savile, the editor of St. Chrysostom, and many others. Nor must we altogether omit the Churchmen, were it only for the curious information afforded by their letters as to the state of their different dioceses [3] and the condition of the clergy, or the uncompromising zeal with which those of the northern province especially persecuted the unhappy recusants. Among these are the archbishops, Parker, Grindal, Whitgift, Bancroft, and Abbot; the bishops, Jewell, Barlow, Sandys, Horne, Pilkington, Coxe, and others; all of whose names are associated with the work of the Reformation in England. Nor must we forget to add to the list two pathetic letters, written in his misery and disgrace, by Cardinal Wolsey to his quondam servant and secretary Gardiner, and a grand des-

[3] These letters are of much deeper interest than might be expected from episcopal correspondence in general. They afford clear information as to the religious faith of the gentlemen and noblemen in different parts of England. Thus, in a report of the Bishop of Worcester, which embraced the county of Warwickshire, we find that the Combes, associated by tradition with Shakespeare, had become recusants, like many others in the same county, and were distrusted by the Government. To 'Mr. Thomas Combe' the poet bequeathed his *sword*; a clear indication—not the only one—of Shakespeare's regard for gentility. This may help to explain something of that sense of humiliation betrayed in the Sonnets, at his profession as an actor and tragedian; and the sorrowful tone in which he vindicates his dramatic writings from 'the fools and fightings,' the bear-bating and Bartlemy shows, with which an indiscriminating public was too apt to confound them. There is scarcely any notice in this or similar collections relating to the drama—itself an evidence of the slight regard in which it was held, —with the exception of a letter of Lady Southampton, written to her husband, in which she refers to Falstaff and Dame Quickly as household names. Some sort of dramatic representation was considered indispensable at royal entertainments, and on one such occasion we find Cecil securing the services of Ben Jonson and his clever but somewhat conceited associate, 'Niny-go' Jones as Jonson in his wrath was accustomed to call him. In a letter from Sir Walter Cope to Lord Cranborne, written in 1604, the following passage will be interesting to readers of Shakespeare; 'Babage is come, and says there is no new play that the Queen (Ann) hath not seen; but they have revived an old one, called 'Love's Labour's Lost,' which for wit and mirth, he says, will please her exceedingly. And this is appointed to be played to-morrow night at my Lord of Southampton's.' See Mr. Brewer's report to the Historical Commission.

patch, of sixty pages long, to the same Gardiner and his associate Foxe respecting Henry's divorce, and the excellent qualities of Anne Boleyn.

But we must resist the temptation to discursiveness, and we do so the more readily as we are anxious to say something of the career and character of the great statesman to whose care his descendants are mainly indebted for this remarkable correspondence. Father and son were alike eminent, though in different ways. If the one, amidst the storms of religious controversy—a subject on which Englishmen feel strongly, and at this period of their history found martyrs on both sides ready to slay and be slain, in maintenance of their convictions—tided this nation innocuously into comparatively still water, the other displayed no less skill, moderation, and judgment, in handing over peacefully to a new and strange succession that supreme authority which had hitherto continued for so many years in a purely English race. We question whether any two statesmen ever had more grave or knotty problems to solve, compared with which our Chinese or Indian perplexities, and our difficulties with indigenous races, are little better than child's play. We doubt if any skill, moderation, or discretion less than theirs could have brought into tolerable fusion the conflicting dualism of this nation with less sacrifice of life, less tumult, and less insurrection. But, whatever may be the opinion of others on this head, of this we feel quite certain, that none would ever have accomplished such great objects with less fuss, observation, or pretentiousness; with less boastfulness of what they had done, perhaps with less national gratitude for doing it. The very ease and noiselessness with which, through their management, this nation took up its new position, in both instances, and passed safely through two of the most critical phases of its existence, have blinded men to the difficulty of the problems these ministers had to solve, and have equally blinded them to the industry, prudence, forethought, and moderation which provided for all contingencies and anticipated every difficulty. But on this we must insist no further. We turn to Sir Robert Cecil.

Lord Burghley was twice married; in the first instance, when he was twenty years old, and a student at St. John's College, Cambridge, to Mary, sister of Sir John Cheek, tutor to Edward VI. From this union the Exeter branch of the present family is descended. About two years after, and, according to some authorities, in the year 1545, two years before the death of Henry VIII., he married Mildred, the eldest daughter of Sir Anthony Cook, sister to Ann, the mother of Sir Francis Bacon, and to Elizabeth, the wife of John Lord Russell.[4] He had by her one son, Robert, and one daughter named Ann, married to the Earl of Oxford. Lady Mildred died in 1589. Like her sisters, Lady Russell and Lady Bacon, she had been well educated; and the letters of these ladies at Hatfield House show that their learning had not disqualified them for the active duties of life. Lord Burghley was absorbed in politics. Sir Nicholas Bacon was gouty and corpulent: he had reached the age when bodily exertion ceases to be agreeable. And though we will not do Lord Bacon the injustice to suppose that he had his mother in his mind when he wrote that curt passage in his Essays, 'Wives are young men's mistresses, companions for middle age, and old men's nurses;' Lady Bacon, like her sisters, was a notable nurse and a strict housewife. She was by no means inclined to lay aside the rod long after her sons, Anthony and Francis, had attained the age of discretion. All three sisters—for of Lady Killigrew little is known—were strongly tinctured with Puritanism. They were great frequenters of sermons, preferring Travers to Hooker.

[4] There is an original portrait of Lady Mildred at Hatfield House.

Under these influences Robert Cecil was trained,[5] and had for his playmate Robert, the celebrated Earl of Essex, whose father was so much enchanted with Lady Mildred's good management, that he desired 'his son's education should be in Burghley's household.' In 1581, Robert Cecil was sent to St. John's College, Cambridge; in 1584, according to the prevailing fashion of the time, he visited Paris to learn the French language, which he acquired to perfection, and attend the disputations at the Sorbonne. In the famous year of 1588, he was in the train of Lord Derby at Ostend. Even at this early stage of his career, Elizabeth, whose penetration and skill in judging the characters of men few will dispute, had distinguished him by marks of her favour. 'I received,' he writes to his father, 'a gracious message from her Majesty, under her sporting name of *pigmy*, bidding me take care of my health, and looking to hear from me.' Such personal allusions, even from royal lips, are scarcely agreeable; certainly were not agreeable to Sir Robert, who was then contemplating a marriage with Miss Brooke, sister to the notorious Lord Cobham, to whom he was united the year after. But he was too good a courtier to resent such reflections on his diminutive stature, and is yet a little too sensitive not to remonstrate. He tells his father that he had not presumed to answer her Majesty, but he had sent a letter to Mr. Stanhope, his cousin, 'which I know he will show her. I show I mislike not the name she gives me only because she gives it. It was interlaced with fairer words than I am worthy of.'

The tact and temper displayed on this occasion were admirable, but both were unavailing. Not only in her playful moments, but on grave occasions of State, Elizabeth

[5] The date of Sir Robert's birth is unknown. Nor do the papers at Hatfield throw any light on the subject. It is assumed with some probability to be about 1563; that is, some years after Elizabeth's accession.

K

continued to address him as 'the little man,' 'the pigmy,' 'the elf,' or ἐλφε, as she sometimes wrote it. He bore these sallies with admirable good temper and wonderful self-command. With the Queen herself it did him no harm; rather, it tended to augment his influence with her, of which she might have been jealous, had he possessed an exterior as commanding as Hatton, Leicester, or Raleigh, or to 'his head and head-piece of vast content,' had added those personal attractions which might have tempted him, like others, to presume too much upon her favours.[6] From his youth to the close of her reign he was never subjected to those mortifications which fell so often to the lot of others. He rose rapidly in her good graces without ever experiencing a single reverse. Such unusual success was partly owing, no doubt, to his own tact, temper, and abilities, in which he was surpassed by none of his rivals; partly because Elizabeth felt somewhat piqued in defending him against his more brilliant opponents, and in justifying a preference so little in harmony with her supposed predilections. For though she never advanced a mere simpleton for his good looks, yet, like her father, if she is not belied, she valued handsome features and gallant bearing. 'She loved a soldier,' says Naunton, 'and had a propension in her nature to regard and always to grace them.'[7] Unlike James I., she had no objection to see swords flash out among the fiery courtiers who surrounded her throne and competed for her smiles; for she lived in times when the nation was menaced on all sides, and nothing but the indomitable pluck of Englishmen could have surmounted the dangers that threatened her. But, besides all this, noble blood and ancient descent were always a passport to her good graces, provided that the pos-

[6] According to the recumbent figure in Hatfield Church, his height was five feet and two or three inches.
[7] *Frag. Regal.* p. 215, ed. 1808.

sessor of them did not come too near to her sceptre. In these respects, Sir Robert Cecil had nothing to mar his advancement. He was not allied by birth to the ancient aristocracy of the realm, though he came of a good family. He was sickly from his youth; and with the exception of a handsome but pale face, and dark, melancholy eyes, he was not qualified by the graces of his person to shine in the gay throng that crowded round the Queen, or take part in the amusements of a Court, where every lady was expected to dance, and every gentleman to wear a sword and seek occasions for using it. A head, squarely set on rounded and disproportioned shoulders, gave him the appearance of being deformed; and the effect was exaggerated by the dress and fashion of the times. The large ruff, the trunkhose gartered above the knee, the scarlet or yellow stockings drawn tightly over the legs, and the lightest shoes of Spanish leather, made the men, especially those of small stature, look top-heavy — a very unfair advantage for tall, slim, and graceful men, over their less favoured brethren. Unlike Essex, the idol of both sexes; unlike Raleigh with his handsome and 'well compacted person,' his ready wit, his pleasing and plausible tongue, Cecil needed the powerful ægis of the Queen's protection to shelter him from contempt.

And to need that protection, what greater recommendation to a woman's graces? Or even to be thought to need it? Never did his enemies make a greater mistake than when they attempted to undermine his influence by maligning his motives, his person, or his actions. It served only to create a stronger prejudice in his favour, a more fixed determination on her part to appear in his vindication. He had too much good sense, too much self-control and moderation, to be moved by the perpetual calumnies to which he was exposed, wisely remarking, 'He that will not be patient of slander must procure himself a chair out of this world's circle.' But if he was unwilling to justify himself or vindicate his own conduct, that task was much more effectually undertaken for him by the Queen. Here is one proof among many.

In 1601, Sir Robert Sidney, governor of the cautionary towns of Flushing, had occasion to send over to England a confidential messenger, named Browne. Elizabeth gave him audience the next morning after his arrival. 'I had no sooner kissed her sacred hand,' says he, 'but that she presently made me stand up, and spoke somewhat loud, and said, "Come hither, Browne," and pronounced that she held me for an old faithful servant of hers, and said : "I must give content to Browne," or some such speeches. Then, as the train followed her, she said : "Stand back, stand back; will you not let us speak but you will be hearers ?" Then she walked a turn or two '—it was in the open air—' protesting her most gracious opinion of myself. "And before God, Browne," said she, "they do me wrong, that will make so honest a servant be jealous that I should mistrust him," meaning Sidney. I forgot to tell your lordship that when I first kneeled I delivered your lordship's letter, which she received, but read it not till I was gone. Then, assuring him of her "affiance to my lord," and taking a turn or two, she asked for a stool, which was set under a tree, and I,' says Browne, ' began to kneel, but she would not suffer me ; insomuch that after two or three denials which I made to kneel still, she was pleased to say that she would not speak with me unless I stood up. Whereupon I stood up.' She then discussed many topics with the messenger, showing her complete mastery, notwithstanding her advanced age, of the minutest points of foreign policy. As the conversation turned upon the perils of the Zealanders, she said, ' " Alas ! poor Zealanders, I know that they love me with all their hearts."' 'I added,' continues Browne, 'that they prayed continually for her. "Yea, Browne," said she, "I know it well enough, and I will tell thee one thing. Faith, there is a Church of their countrymen in London"—meaning the Dutch church in Austinfriars—"I protest, next after the Divine Providence that governs all my well-doing, I attribute much of the happiness that befals me, to be given me of God by those men's effectual and zealous prayers, who, I know, pray with that fervency for me as none of my subjects can do more."' Mr. Secretary Cecil came in, 'who was pleased to grace me,' says Mr. Browne, 'still more and more, and talk was ministered again of the army.' After some remarks on this subject, ' her Majesty presently said unto me, "Dost thou see that little fellow that kneels there?" (meaning Cecil); "it hath been told you that he hath been an enemy to soldiers. On my faith, Browne, he is the best friend the soldiers have." Cecil answered, "that it was from her Majesty alone from whom flowed all soldiers' good." I shall think of it during my life,' says the narrator; and well he might, for Elizabeth possessed in perfection that rarest of all royal virtues, the art of being gracious. She knew how to reach at once the hearts of her subjects, because, rigid as she was in exacting implicit obedience, praise from her fell with double effect, because it was never given except when she felt it was deserved.

If complete devotion to her service, which none appreciated better than Elizabeth, could win her approbation, none did more than Sir Robert to deserve it. His time, his thoughts, and his abilities were given up to his royal mistress. It has been cast in his teeth that he had no friends; and if by that it be meant that he had no powerful political associates, that he headed no party, sought no friends and no allies, the reproach is just. But if it be meant that he was cold and insensible to affection, there never was a greater mistake. The correspondence at Hatfield furnishes a continual disproof of such an assumption. He was the last man to wear his heart upon his sleeve; but beneath that cold and reserved exterior lay hid a force of character, a depth of passion, an energy of affection, which nothing but repeated acts of ingratitude or unworthiness could alienate. *Sero sed serio* was the motto he adopted in preference to the old motto of his house, and nothing could better express his character.[8] He was slow to give his confidence, but where he had once given it he was slow to change it. He was cautious in bestowing his affections, and bore much and long before he withdrew them. Slow to take offence, when once offended he was not hasty in relenting. Cool, calm, moderate in his judgment, when once his determination was fixed he was not easily shaken from it. In all these respects he formed the most striking contrast to the headstrong, impetuous, rash, and passionate Earl of Essex —now quarrelling with his best friends for some trifle, light as air; now opening his heart to his most dangerous enemies. Now 'the saddest soul on earth,' sighing, sorrowing, languishing, wishing to die because he had offended his Sovereign, and the next moment guilty of the most unpardonable rudeness. Now all for Puritan sermons, exercises, and devotions, then indulging in the profanest oaths or intriguing with Lady Derby, Miss Southwell, or Miss Brydges;—the gayest Lothario at the Court.[9]

[8] At the same time, probably, as he altered his crest. 'Cecil is labouring for peace. . . . He has found a new pedigree by his grandmother from the Walpoles, and altered his crest from a sheaf of wheat between two lions to two sheaves of arrows crossed and covered with a helmet, to distinguish his retinue from his brother's.'—*Fran. Cordale*, 21, *July*, 1599.

[9] See the letter addressed to him by Lady Bacon on his carnal backsliding in Birch's *Mem. of Eliz.* ii. 218. From a letter of the same lady to the Earl, in the Hatfield Papers, never before published, we take the following curious extract:—

'I crave leave and also pardon, my special good Lord, for uttering my unfeigned Christian affection to your honour in this simple manner, which much rather I would have done by humble speech, if my health and access to your own person might conveniently have concurred. Therefore, now, thus upon it is, my good Lord, I was made to be thus bold. Lately

In one respect it was no disadvantage to Cecil that he had
no friends, in the sense that a powerful minister has friends
for whose advancement the world expects, as they themselves
expect, that he is to exert his influence in high quarters.
In this he was the reverse of Essex; for Essex, unhappily, was
a man of many friends, who measured his importance by his
ability to procure for them office and emoluments. Flattered
by this persuasion, he pressed their suits with passionate zeal
and indiscretion, with utter contempt for the claims of others
and bitter hostility towards all whose opposition he suspected.
Because the Queen would not suffer him to speak insolently
of Raleigh in her presence, he burst out into torrents of abuse,
raking up his private history, and telling her that he disdained
'his competition of love,' and could have no comfort to give
himself 'to the service of a mistress that was in awe of such

in a place of a preaching minister, in the city, frequented as I may,
the lecture finished, I said to a Court friend of mine apart, one I am
sure must and doth love you well, and then was there; 'I wish many
time,' quoth I, 'that her Majesty's self did hear such wholesome and fruitful doctrine, as we do hear and enjoy under her. 'That were,' quoth he,
'happiest for her and comfortable to us all.' 'Surely,' quoth I, 'her want
thereof and also of catechising in that high place causeth great want of
the right knowledge of sin, and thereby great carelessness for sin; yet is
there one nobleman that in his youth doth remember his Creator, and
loveth both the Word of God and the good preacher, and goeth beyond
his ancients in avoiding swearing and gaming, with such common corruption there.' 'Whom mean you?' *inquit.* 'Even one,' *inquam*, 'to whom
I am so much bound, that I owe to wish him daily increase of godliness
with blessed success in his worldly state;' and named indeed the Earl of
Essex. 'Is it he you mean?' *inquit*, 'would to God he did so, but he
sweareth as mighty oaths, woe am I for it!' 'Sorry,' *inquam*, 'I am to hear
it, but yet I trust not ordinarily with great grievous oaths.' 'Alas!'
inquit, 'he is a terrible swearer,' which words methought struck my heart
in respect of the Earl. 'Lo,' *inquam*, 'the hurt of no catechising in
Court! for by expounding well the law and commandments of God, sin is
laid open and disclosed to the hearers, and worketh in them by God's
spirit more hatred of evil, and checketh our proneness natural to all sin,
by lack whereof even our councellors, both old and young, are pitifully
infected with that contagion to their own danger and lamentable example
of others what degree soever;' and so we parted.—*Hatfield MSS.*, cxxvii.
68.

a man!' To add to the unmanliness of this attack, wholly unprovoked except by his own jealous and suspicious temper, he avows, and even glories in the avowal, that he spoke as loud as he could, that Raleigh, who was Captain of the Guard, and stood near the door, 'might very well hear the worst that I spoke of him.' The editor of his letters thinks this an indication how little 'he owed to the wiles of the courtier.' We think it an indication how little he owed to good manners, or regard for others whenever he suspected them, rightly or wrongly, of crossing his path.

In 1596, after the death of Walsingham, when the duties of the Secretary's place were executed by Sir Robert in consequence of his father's sickness, Essex was anxious to secure the appointment for Sir Thomas Bodley. He had already endeavoured to detach Bodley from the Cecils for no other reason than to make Bodley dependent on himself. His conduct on this occasion was disgraced with the same arrogance, the same jealousy, the same imperiousness as he had displayed on the former. Sir Thomas confesses that Essex 'sought by all devices to divert the liking and love of the Queen, both from the father and the son [Burghley and Sir Robert], but from the son in special. And to draw my affection from the one to the other, and to win me altogether to depend upon himself, did so often take occasion to entertain the Queen with some prodigal speeches of my sufficiency for a secretary, which were ever accompanied with words of disgrace against the present Lord Treasurer (Sir Robert) . . . that both my Lord Burghley and his son waxed jealous of my courses.' On talking over the subject with Cecil afterwards, the latter freely confessed to him that the Earl's daily provocations were so bitter and sharp, and his comparisons so odious, when he professed to balance the claims of the two, that naturally enough the Cecils had no great desire to further the promotion of one who was thus pushed forward to their disparagement.¹

It was the same on all occasions, whether he wished to advance Bacon, or Southampton, or Blount, or Sir Gilly Merrick. He could endure no rival, he could allow no merit in others who differed from him, and he always sought to disparage it. He scrupled at no means in supplanting those who seemed to enjoy any share of the Queen's favour; and he resented every honour she bestowed upon others as an injury to himself. Such men are neither sagacious nor discreet; and it is not surprising that Essex should never have understood the character and temper of the Queen; still more that he should have fallen into the fatal mistake of imagining that force would avail where persuasion failed. He might as well have attempted to hold a lion by the paw as overawe a Tudor. Strong and determined always, never were they more strong and more determined than in the face of opposition; never so calm and courageous as in the presence of danger. Strong monarchs all, they sometimes suffered their ministers and servants to run great lengths, because they knew no fear. But woe to the man who, forgetting he was a servant, or presuming on his importance, advanced himself as a rival, or allowed so much as his shadow to fall upon the throne. He was as remorselessly and effectually crushed, and with as little consideration and afterthought, as the king of the forest might tread upon an insect. With a little temper and a small modicum of discretion, Essex might have carried all before him. He was of noble descent; he had powerful kinsfolk; his father had done good service in Ireland; what was more, Burghley and his father were intimate friends. The stage was clear; there was no Hatton, no Leicester, no Sir Philip Sidney to compete with him for the palm. Frank, liberal, chivalrous, intrepid, possessed of

¹ Birch, ii. 62.

all those qualities of mind and person which help to make men popular, he could scarcely fail of success. 'There was in this young lord,' says Naunton, 'together with a most goodly person, a kind of urbanity and innate courtesy, which both won the Queen and too much took upon the people, to gaze upon the new adopted son of her favour.'[2] He was, besides, a new-comer in a Court from which the freshness and elasticity of youth had departed—a sort of spoiled child in an aged household, to whom much waywardness is forgiven for the sake of the future and the past. The Cecils would gladly have been friendly with him. Even in his last years, the aged Treasurer, in one of the Earl's sullen fits, because the Lord Admiral had a patent of nobility, sent kindly inquiries after him; gave him the best advice to come to Court and plead his own cause, 'whereto I will be as serviceable,' he says, 'as any friend you have to my power . . . able and ready with my heart to command my tongue to do you honour.'[3] Not a year passes, not a month scarcely, in which Sir Robert, the son, although he had not much reason to love Essex, does not exert himself in the Earl's behalf. Is it in the Cadiz voyage? Is it in the Earl's wish to intercept the Plate fleet? 'He desires only the keeping up of the journey's reputation [the expedition of Essex], and that he should lie off the islands to intercept the Indian fleet.'[4] Is it in providing for his Irish expedition? Cecil provides all that Essex desires. 'You heap coals of kindness,' is the acknowledgment of the Earl in a paroxysm of gratitude.[5] Was this all hypocrisy, was it deception? Was it a deep-laid plan to ruin Essex and bring him into disgrace? Is not Cecil's own explanation much more natural and probable? In his first letter to James of Scotland, after Essex, in his reckless habit of accusing others, had falsely charged Cecil

[2] P. 268.   [3] Devereux, *Essex*, i. 471.
[4] *Hatfield MSS.*, liv. 75.   [5] *Ibid.*, lx. 20.

with espousing the Spanish claim to the succession—a charge of all others most perilous for his reputation with Elizabeth or her successor—this is his calm statement:—

'If I could have contracted such a friendship with Essex, as could have given me security that his thoughts and mine should have been no further distant than the disproportion of our fortunes, I should condemn my judgment to have willingly intruded myself into such an opposition. For who know not that have lived in Israel, that such were the mutual affections in our tender years, and so many reciprocal benefits interchanged in our growing fortunes, as besides the rules of my own poor discretion, which taught me how perilous it was for Secretary Cecil to have a bitter feud with an Earl Marshal of England, a favourite, a nobleman of eminent parts, and a councillor, all things else in the composition of my mind did still concur on my part to make me desirous of his favour.'[6]

The statement is strictly true. His forbearance towards the Earl, after many provocations, was remarkable. Even after the close of his unfortunate Irish expedition, from which Essex had returned in direct violation of the Queen's command, Cecil continued to befriend him. Surprised for the moment by his unexpected appearance, and ignorant of the cause of it, Elizabeth had received him graciously, but her anger returned with double force upon reflection. Such flagrant violation of his duty and disobedience to her express commands could not be suffered for example's sake to remain unpunished. But she had stronger reasons even than these for her displeasure. She had learned from various quarters his designs in Ireland—designs wholly incompatible with his loyalty as a subject. Yet throughout this period of his disgrace until his traitorous attempt against her person,

[6] *Hatfield MSS.*, cxxxv. p. 55, published by Bruce for the Camden Society.

Cecil interposed his best offices in the Earl's favour. It was through his interposition that Essex was committed to the care of Lord Keeper Egerton, his friend, instead of being sent to the Tower. It was Cecil who conveyed to Essex his satisfaction that the Council appointed to examine him —of which number Cecil was one—were to report favourably of his conduct to the Queen, and ' I will do anything to further your contentment.' It was Cecil's speech in the Star Chamber, when the conduct of the Earl was called in question, that was marked with a greater tone of moderation than that of any other of the judges, though Egerton was of the number. When, to avoid being tried in the Star Chamber, the Earl, at his own earnest request,[7] was brought before a Commission, though Cecil condemned him for abandoning his post contrary to the Queen's command, he mitigated the severity of his remarks by giving Essex credit for his services in Ireland. His conduct on this and other occasions when the Earl was concerned, won for him general approbation. 'Sir Robert Cecil,' says a writer of the time, by no means his indiscriminate admirer, 'is highly commended for his wise and temperate proceeding in this matter, showing no gall, though perhaps he had been galled, if not by the Earl, by some of his dependants. By employing his credit with her Majesty in behalf of the Earl, he has gained great credit, both at home and abroad.'[8]

Exasperated at their own disappointments and their master's disgrace, the followers of Essex vented their vengeance against the supposed author of their misfortunes. They threatened Cecil with violence. They posted lampoons on his doors in Salisbury Street and elsewhere. 'Here

[7] He sent a letter to the Queen, begging that 'this bitter cup ' (appearing in the Star Chamber) 'might pass from him.'—*Chamberlain's Letter*, p. 77.

[8] J. B. (Petit) to Peter Halins. *State Papers, Domestic*, by Mrs. Green, 14th June, 1600.

lieth the toad at Court, and here lieth the toad at London.'[9] They attributed to him the injustice, as they were pleased to call it, of keeping Essex in prison. They vilified his person in taverns and eating-houses, observing, 'that it was an unwholesome thing to meet a man in the morning who had a wry neck, a crooked back, and a splay foot.'[1] So powerful was the influence of the Earl, or so audacious were his followers, that none dared to contradict them. But this animosity was not confined to the humbler dependants of the Earl. From Ireland Lord Grey had already written to Cobham to complain that Essex had resolved to shut out from advancement all who wished to maintain a good understanding with Cecil; and though many may doubt Grey's prudence, few will question his veracity. 'My Lord of Essex,' he says, 'doubting whereupon I should be so well favoured at Court, and especially by her Majesty, hath forced me to declare myself either his only, or friend to Mr. Secretary [Cecil] and his enemy; protesting that there could be no neutrality. I answered that no base dependency should ever fashion my love or hate to his Lordship's passions. As for Mr. Secretary, I had diversely tasted of his favour, and would never be dishonest or ungrateful. In conclusion, he holdeth me for a lost child, and in plain terms told me he loved not my person, neither should I be welcome to him, or expect advancement under him.'[2]

But our limits warn us to be brief. We cannot pursue the erratic career of this nobleman any further. Yet for one or two observations on the romantic incident connected with the close of it we must find a place. In the story of the ring and the Countess of Nottingham we place no credit; not merely for the reasons alleged by Ranke that this gossip came to light several generations after the event, embel-

[9] *Hatfield MSS.*, lxxxiii. p. 53. [1] *Ibid.*
[2] Dublin, July 21. *Hatfield MSS.*, lxii. 71.

lished as such anecdotes are with new colours and new incidents at every repetition, but because the details are in themselves inconsistent and improbable. To those who know how carefully all prisoners were guarded in the Tower when left for execution, it will appear incredible that the Earl 'suspicious of those about him '—for so the original story runs—'and not caring to trust any one of them with the ring, as he was looking out of his window one morning' —where did the narrator suppose he was confined?—' saw a boy, with whose appearance he was pleased; and engaging him with money and promises'—his keeper of course taking no notice—'directed him to carry a ring, which he took from his finger and threw down, to Lady Scroope, a sister of the Countess of Nottingham, with a request that she should present it to her Majesty.' These directions he must have given to a boy wandering about the Tower, whom he had never seen before, and must have furnished him with sufficient instructions how to find Lady Scroope, and what to say to her, without attracting the notice of the warders.[3] 'The boy carried the ring by mistake to Lady Nottingham, who showed it to her husband, and insisted upon her retaining it.' The story goes on to say, that when the fatal secret was revealed to the Queen, she burst into a furious passion, and shaking the dying Countess in her bed,

[3] Hume, whose shrewd good sense is shocked with the obvious absurdity of this portion of the story, conveniently omits it, and states that 'he [Essex] committed the ring to the Countess of Nottingham, whom he desired to deliver it to the Queen,' thus coolly departing from his authority, and falling into a greater absurdity than that which he avoids. Would Essex commit the ring to his known enemy, and desire her to deliver it to the Queen? It was not Lady Nottingham but Lady Scroope, who was a 'friend of his Lordship.' And then how does Hume suppose that Essex in the Tower communicated with Lady Nottingham at the Court? But sceptic as Hume was, he dearly loved a little sentimentalism; as credulous and indulgent a critic in history, as he was rigid and exacting where Christianity was concerned. But when was credulity ever severed from scepticism?

exclaimed, *that God might pardon her but she never would, and from that day resigned herself to the deepest melancholy.*' The reader is left to infer, or is plainly told, that Elizabeth— whose 'fond attachment' was shocked by the Earl's silence and obduracy in never applying to her for pardon—had consented to his death in a moment of resentment, and thus learned too late how much she had been deceived by those around her.

Of the death of Essex and the last illness of the Queen the most minute and authentic details have been preserved, not only by those who sedulously picked up the gossip of the day, like Chamberlain and like Carleton, for the amusement of distant friends, but like Cecil, Cary, Howard, Northumberland, Cobham, Raleigh, and others, who were about the Queen and at the very centre of information. Yet to all of them, judging by their correspondence at the time and afterwards, this story and its tragic ending were utterly unknown. Essex was tried and condemned on Thursday, the 19th of February; in due course of law he should have been executed on the Saturday following, but was reprieved till the next Wednesday (Ash-Wednesday). On the Friday after his condemnation he sent a message to the Queen, requesting that Egerton, Buckhurst, Nottingham, and Cecil might be sent to him, especially the last, whom he had wronged by asserting at the trial that Cecil had sold his country to Spain. The Queen ordered these four to visit him on the Saturday; when he requested their forgiveness, and made 'a very humble suit to her Majesty that he might have the favour to die privately in the Tower, which she granted, and for which he gave her most humble thanks.'[4] The day before his execution the Queen herself nominated seven or eight noblemen who were to be present on the occasion and take the

[4] See Cecil's letter to his intimate friend, Sir George Carew. *Carew MSS.*, iv. 35.

necessary warrants to the Tower.[5] Every step in the whole proceeding was marked with the greatest order and deliberation. It betrays nothing of the vacillation which romantic historians attribute to Elizabeth or of reviving tenderness and attachment. It is clear from Raleigh's letter to Cecil, printed by Murdin from the Hatfield MSS., that to the last Cecil was reluctant to shed blood. It is certain, also, that he was extremely anxious to save 'the poor Earl of Southampton,' as he calls him, who merely for the love of Essex had 'been drawn into this action;' but he felt how difficult the task would be to find arguments to persuade the Queen. 'And yet,' he says, 'when I consider how penitent he is, and how merciful the Queen is, as I cannot write in despair, so I dare not flatter myself with hope.'[6] If Elizabeth had wished to pardon Essex, such despondency on the part of Cecil would have been unintelligible. She could not with justice have condemned the subordinate agents and have allowed the principal culprit to escape. To us her conduct on this occasion seems exactly consistent with her actions throughout her reign, and with her treatment of the Earl in particular. Though her personal feelings might occasionally predominate, they were only transient. In the end, the Queen universally rose above the woman, as in Mary she invariably sank below. In Elizabeth the responsibility of a great ruler predominated over her weaker inclinations. To use her own language on another occasion, she could *in her own nature* dispense with severity as well 'as any power that liveth,' where error had been committed, 'not out of lack of duty but of circumspection;' but she could not 'allow her kingdom and the lives of her subjects to be dallied with, for God had given her these upon other con-

[5] State Paper Office, sub an., p. 591.
[6] Letter to Essex and the Irish Council, August 10, 1599. *Hatfield MSS.*, cxxxiii. 182.

ditions; and whilst He vouchsafeth to continue us over them we will not be accusable for anything within our power to perform.' *Passer solitarius,* as Cecil calls her, and as all great rulers and great thinkers must be, the melancholy observable at the close of her life had more or less taken possession of her long before the fall of Essex. How could it be otherwise? She had a great task before her—formidable enemies on every side—a kingdom of small dimensions, assailed by the Scotch and the Irish nearer home—by the Spaniard, the Pope, and the Jesuit, abroad. In her fearlessness, in her confidence in God and her people, she never fenced herself round with guards or ramparts. The most accessible person in her kingdom, her ears, like her palace, were open to all comers—she trusted her safety and her life to her subjects, reposing implicit confidence in their loyalty. If she reaped ingratitude where she had shown the greatest indulgence—if in the man the most boastful of devotion to herself and her service she had found treason and disloyalty—is it so surprising that the retrospect should sometimes have filled her with melancholy? But that to the very last she maintained her composure, her dignity, her strength of mind and sense of duty unimpaired, is clear from her interview with Sir W. Browne, to which we have already referred, and with Scaramelli, the Venetian Envoy, only one short month before she died—and no idle impure gossip of Spanish malignants or of other traducers of her memory can impair this evidence. If she exacted from those who served her the strict fulfilment of their obligations, if she was less tolerant to those who failed to make good what they had undertaken to perform, she set them an example in her own person of rigorous attention to the duties of her station. No melancholy, no plea of indisposition, no infirmities of advancing age were sufficient to withdraw her from the burdens of royalty, or could tempt her to sacrifice them to

L

personal ease and convenience. To the last she sat at the
Council table; to the last she was ready to receive every
foreign ambassador who visited these shores. To the last
she maintained the dignity, the splendour, and the majesty
of royalty; strong in the loftiness of her resolution, victorious over weakness and infirmity; a Queen to the end, associating monarchy in the minds of her subjects with national
greatness, magnanimity, and vigour, which no faults of
her own, no failings of succeeding ages, could diminish or
extinguish.

We have come to the closing scenes of her reign, and to
that event in it with which the name of Sir Robert Cecil has
been often intermingled, and his love of intrigue is supposed
to have had full scope for its development. Whatever
judgment men may be inclined to pass on his secret correspondence with the Scotch King, his own statement cannot
be questioned, that nothing tended more than the course he
adopted 'to quiet the expectation of a successor,' and save
the nation from the disturbances incidental to a disputed succession. It secured the failing years of Elizabeth from
numerous mortifications; for among so many claimants the
declaration of a successor involved greater inconveniences
than is sometimes imagined. It removed needless jealousies
between the Queen and her successor, fomented by the interested adherents of both. It prevented James from entering upon foolish intrigues to secure his right, which might
have plunged him into insuperable difficulties at the outset
of his reign. If Sir Robert, in thus consulting the truest
interest of the nation, advanced his own; if he employed
the opportunity thus offered him in repressing the designs
of Cobham and Raleigh, it must be remembered that the
first advances did not proceed from himself, but from James.
Never once did he ' imagine a thought which could amount
to a grain of error towards' his Sovereign, or vary from his

duty and affection. With one single exception, no allusion to Raleigh is found in Cecil's portion of the correspondence; for he cannot, in justice, be held accountable for the contemptuous expressions in the letters of Lord Henry Howard.[7] Of Raleigh it is hard to speak with justice and moderation, and his unhappy end makes the task still harder. Sailor, poet, historian, statesman—qualified to shine alike in the arts of peace and in the perils of war—to a spirit of adventure he added a tinge of romance, a fervour of imagination, a passionate valour which no dangers could daunt, no disasters extinguish. The charm of his conversation was acknowledged by all from the highest to the lowest; by Elizabeth, 'who took him for a kind of oracle;' by the poet Spenser; by evidence more unexceptionable still. Among the papers at Hatfield there is an invitation addressed to him from the little Lord Cranborne, then quite a child, begging Raleigh to come, for without him they were like soldiers deprived of their General. 'Come, do come,' he says, with the pardonable impertinence of childhood, 'and lay aside your idle occupations.' Yet with all these claims on the love and admiration of his contemporaries, Raleigh had few friends, and of those few his most intimate associate was, of all men, the Lord Cobham. His quarrel with Essex, which terminated in such bitter and implacable hatred, is well known. His friendship with Cobham ended in mutual recriminations equally bitter. He was not always scrupulous

[7] Cecil's own correspondence with James was first published by Mr. Bruce from the originals at Hatfield. But Sir David Dalrymple published in 1766 a small volume which he was pleased to entitle, 'The Secret Correspondence of Sir Robert Cecil with James VI. of Scotland,' though not a single letter from Cecil appears in the whole collection. Sir David states in his preface: 'By what arts it was that Cecil established himself in the favour of King James, and at the same time supplanted his rivals, will appear from the perusal of the following sheets.' This was not Sir David's only offence against accuracy. He was guilty of one more gross and unpardonable still in his Memorials for that reign.

in the means he employed for enriching himself, and securing his own advancement; and thus he alienated friends and created enemies. Conscious that, in consequence of his hostility to Essex, he was in ill odour with James, believing that James would espouse the dislikes and the friendships of Essex, Raleigh was anxious to secure himself against the change which must inevitably follow on the death of the Queen. To regain his credit with her, he complained that he was abandoned and his faithful services were left unrewarded.[8] To fathom the designs of Cecil and obtain some avowal of his intentions, which might turn to his own advantage as occasion served, Raleigh boasted that he would never consent to James's accession. Such professions, intended for the ears of Elizabeth, were not wholly disinterested; were, in fact, to be interpreted in an opposite sense to King James. But whatever secret intrigues Raleigh and Cobham engaged in were revealed by James to his new ally. Cecil shunned rather than courted such expressions of confidence. 'I would,' he writes to the King, 'most humbly crave it of your Majesty that I might rather be left to mine own discoveries of their greatest secrets, than to receive any light from you of their deepest mysteries.' James, in fact, was inclined to be too confidential. In the pride of his own wisdom, in the satisfaction he felt on gaining Cecil to his cause, he was beginning to be fussy and officious, little aware what eager, watchful eyes were fixed upon him, ready to take advantage

[8] See his letter to Elizabeth in Edwards's '*Life of Raleigh*,' ii. 258, from the Hatfield MSS. In this letter he evidently glances at Cecil as one of 'those seeming great friends,' from whose supposed amity he reaped only 'lean effects.' He afterwards confessed that he had acted ungratefully, and 'failed both in friendship and in judgment. . . . I must never forget what I find was in your Lordship's desire, what in your will, what in your words and works, so far as could become you as a Councillor, and far beyond all due to me.' (Letter to Cecil, printed by Edwards from the *Hatfield MSS.*, ii. 288.)

of the least incautiousness, and carry their revelations to the Queen.

Sir Robert wisely kept his own counsel, 'dropping a stone,' to use his own phrase, 'into the mouths of these gaping crabs,' who thought to betray him into a less reserved communication of his confidence by exaggerated professions of love and loyalty. He quietly reminded them that James had often asserted it was not possible for anyone to be a loyal subject to Elizabeth who paid court to himself; and when the season for action was come it would be time enough to declare his intentions.

He was amply rewarded for his peril and anxiety on the accession of James. Elizabeth was parsimonious in her distribution of rewards, and, notwithstanding his arduous services, conferred no distinctions on Cecil. In the reign of James honours fell rapidly upon him. He was created Baron of Essingdon in May 1603; Viscount Cranborne, 20th of August, 1604; Earl of Salisbury, 4th of May, 1605; was Lord Treasurer and Secretary in 1608. Meanwhile Raleigh —disappointed in his expectations, coldly received by James, as his wife was by Queen Anne—forgetful of the fate of Essex, if not actually following in his footsteps—was so far compromised in Cobham's proceedings as justly to fall under suspicion. He was still on the most intimate footing with Cobham, at that time making great efforts to leave England for Brussels, the great focus of intrigue for the Jesuits and their English adherents. Again and again he had importuned Cecil without success. In the meantime the Government had obtained intelligence of a plot called 'The Bye Plot,' probably from some of those who were engaged in it; —for in these plots the Roman Catholics proved false to each other—and in the examination of the prisoners the Council came upon traces of another conspiracy in which Cobham and Raleigh were implicated. Raleigh was brought before them, and after his examination was concluded, he wrote to Cecil, accusing his former friend Cobham of carrying on treasonable communications with Aremberg, the ambassador from the Archduke. It seems to us that in thus accusing his friend—an act by no means creditable to Raleigh—he imagined that Cobham had betrayed him. He was not aware that it was not Cobham, but his brother, George Brooke, who had played the traitor. To save himself or to obtain his brother's estate, Brooke had accused his associates to Cecil.[9] He made a merit of his discovery, urging Cecil to move the King for grace, and asserting that Cecil knew what he had done to redeem his offences.[10] Stung by the infidelity and ingratitude of Raleigh, Cobham recriminated. When he was shown the accusation under Raleigh's hand, 'Oh traitor! oh villain!' he exclaimed; and then added, that he had only entered on these courses at Raleigh's instigation, who would never let him alone.

An attempt has been made to get rid of this charge against Raleigh by assuming that Cobham, who varied in his statements, was 'such an impudent liar,' that his word could not be trusted. At the same time it must be remembered that Cobham and Raleigh had lived for many years upon the most intimate terms; and if the maxim *noscitur a sociis* be of any value, this is not a very satisfactory mode of exculpating Raleigh at Cobham's expense. The variations in his story were probably the effect of mortal terror. Moreover, Raleigh admitted his knowledge of Cobham's designs. 'Lost I am,' he says, in his letter to James, 'for hearing a vain man; for hearing only, but never believing or accepting.'[1] Evidently, then, he had listened, on his own ad-

[9] This is tolerably certain. Brooke and Gray had already confessed the plot before July 16. Raleigh was committed to the Tower the day after, and Cobham about the same time.

[10] Brooke to Cecil, July 22, among the Hatfield Papers.

[1] January 21, 1603-4. Printed by Edwards from the Hatfield Collection.

mission, to Cobham's suggestions. But though he had been so extremely intimate with Cobham, he never remonstrated with him for harbouring such dangerous designs; and if Cobham's account cannot be accepted, neither can we 'place implicit confidence in Raleigh's,' as Mr. Gardiner observes. We gladly conclude our remarks on this subject with the words of the same candid and able historian: 'Whatever may be the truth on this difficult subject, there is no reason to doubt that Cecil at least acted in perfect good faith.'[2]

We would gladly have found space for a few observations on the character of James I., whose councils for the first few years of his reign were directed by Cecil. More familiar and sociable, James was cast in a weaker mould than Elizabeth, and loved ease and hunting better than business. Coming from Scotland with exaggerated notions of the wealth of England, haunted by hungry followers who expected to be rewarded, he, like them, looked upon this kingdom as the Promised Land, of which the milk and honey were inexhaustible. He had the good sense to see that he could not remove from their offices the ministers of the late Queen, and fill their places with his Scotch adherents, who had no knowledge of business and were not accustomed to rule a great nation. Good-natured to a fault, unwilling to refuse, and anxious to avoid the importunities of those who waylaid him even in his bedchamber, he fled from his persecutors to the hunting-field, or bestowed grants of money without much consideration how they were to be paid. 'His Scotch tone, which he rather affected than declined,' says Fuller, 'seemed strange and uncouth to English ears.' His want of dignity and impatience at the tediousness of court ceremonial contrasted unfavourably with the splendour, dignity, grace, and majesty displayed by Elizabeth on these occasions. The plainness of his dress was not set off by the

[2] *History of England* i. 87.

graces of his person,[3] for, like his master, Buchanan, he had an antipathy to cold water, and his ablutions were rare. Slouching in his gait, an awkwardness partly occasioned by his perpetual exercise on horseback—partly from weakness in his legs—an infirmity he bequeathed to his successor— he had a habit at court audiences of leaning or lounging for support on Carr or Buckingham, a fashion, however, not confined to James. But, with these disadvantages, James was by no means the fool, or the coward, or the pedant, he is represented. Still less was he the sot, not to say worse, that he appears in the pages of Mr. Green.[4] We must protest against this clever writer serving up to his readers as authentic history a *réchauffé* of discreditable and discredited anecdotes, invented for party purposes in the time of the Great Rebellion, to make the Stuarts odious. The most virulent traducer of James, Anthony Weldon, the clerk of his kitchen, who waited at the King's table, distinctly states that he was temperate in his drinking, and he never saw the King overtaken with wine. Whatever he might be morally, there is no evidence whatever to show that James was physically a coward. He was an admirable horseman and a daring rider—qualities not generally thought to be the concomitants of cowardice. He was no more a pedant than was the fashion of his age, and certainly never appeared in that light to the eyes of his contemporaries. To the fouler accusation countenanced by Mr. Green, we reply with Bishop Hacket, who, from the time when he was two and twenty, stood at the King's table, that 'the Devil and the Jesuits durst not say so. The most venomous scorpion

[3] 'His clothes,' says Hacket, who stood at his table, 'were thrifty, and of better example than his courtiers would follow.' (*Life of Williams*, i. 225.)

[4] *History of the English People*, pp. 464, 473. Surely Mr. Green has not fallen into the common blunder of applying to James I. what Harrington relates of the King of Denmark.

did. never touch him with that sting.'[5] Strange is it that from the days of such impure and hireling scribblers as Weldon, Peyton, and Oldmixon, the vilest imputations on the memory of James, and the most ridiculous light in which he has been held up to posterity, should have been due to his own countrymen.

But we must draw these observations to a close. Of feeble frame from his youth, worn out by excessive labour, still more by herculean efforts to bring into better order the entangled finances of the Crown—for he had greatly reduced the debt, in spite of the King's inconsiderate liberality—Sir Robert was attacked by rheumatism in the right arm, on the 4th of December, 1611. He recovered only to fall into a worse relapse at the commencement of the next year. In January he was recommended by the Bishop of Durham to try the Bath waters. Soon after he was attacked by scurvy and dropsy, and towards the close of April visited Bath, attended by three physicians. His last letter to his son William, dated from Bath the 8th of May, is preserved at Hatfield. He complains that the swelling of his legs and knees had not been diminished by the use of the waters, and he evidently expected little relief. Preparing for death, he resolved to return to Hatfield, but was taken worse on the road, and died in the parsonage-house at Marlborough, on the 24th of May, between one and two in the afternoon. The corpse was carried to Hatfield and buried without any great pomp, 'by his special appointment,' on Tuesday, the 9th of June. His will, dated 3rd March, 1611 (1612), has a codicil added on the 17th of May, 1612, containing certain bequests to Richard Watson, his surgeon, among others, and to John Dacomb, 'the most diligent and discreet solicitor that ever served any man, protesting that in mine own estate I had been overthrown by large expense and lack of

[5] Hacket, *Life of Williams*, p. 226.

care, if he had not been.' In his will, after confessing himself 'a grievous sinner,' and relying only 'on the precious blood of Jesus Christ, shed upon the cross for me and all mankind,' he proceeds in the following strain :—

'Because I would be glad to leave behind me some such testimony of my particular opinion in point of faith and doctrine, as might confute all those who, judging others by themselves, are apt to censure all men to be of little or no religion, which by their calling are employed in matters of State and government, under great kings and princes, as if there was no Christian policy free from irreligion or impiety, I have resolved to express myself and my opinion in manner following. First, concerning the infinite and ineffable Trinity in Unity and Unity in Trinity, and the mystery of reconciliation in Christ Jesus, as it concerns the Church, the saints, their sins, their souls and bodies, and lastly, their retribution in heaven;—in all these points, and every of them, I do assuredly believe in my heart, as I have always made profession with my mouth, whatever is contained in the Apostles' Creed.'

Then proceeding to touch upon the Sacraments, he closes this portion of the will with the following solemn asseveration :—

'Therefore I do here in the sight of God make profession of that faith in which I have always lived, and hope to die in, and fear not to be judged at that great account of all flesh, and purpose to leave it behind me, as full of life and necessary fruit as I can, for the direction of my children, as their best patrimony, and for the satisfaction of the world as the truest account I can give for myself and my actions.'

He then directs his executors that his body shall be buried in Hatfield Church, 'without any extraordinary show or spectacle,' and that a fair monument shall be erected, 'the charge thereof not exceeding 200*l*.' The mourners were to be confined to his own servants and intimate friends, for he desires 'to go without noise and vanity out of this vale of misery, as a man that hath long been satiated with terrestrial glory, and now contemplates only heavenly joy.'

In conformity with these directions his son William, the second Earl, erected a chapel in 1618, which now stands on the north side of the chancel of the present church of Hatfield.[6] The Earl's monument, in black and white marble, consisting of a recumbent figure resting on a slab and supported by four emblematical figures, with a wasted corpse underneath, was the work of Symon Basyll, the predecessor of Inigo Jones as surveyor of the King's works. His bill is so exceedingly curious that we insert it here without abridgment, for the entertainment of those who are interested in these matters.

'*January* 4, 1613 (1614).—A note of such stone as is required for the finishing of the intended tomb, according to a model thereof made for the Right Hon. the late Lord Treasurer of England, with an estimate of the workmanship and setting up:—

	FEET
Of white marble for the 6 figures	140
Of touch for both the tables	70
Of Kaen for enrichment	3

'The charge of sawing and corving (carving) of the 6 figures, if they be done according to art and true proportion, are worth 60*l.* a piece	360*l.*
'The two tables of touch, with sawing, polishing, and the workmanship of the same	60*l.*
'The carriage of the said tomb to Hatfield, setting of it up, and finishing	40*l*
Sum. tot.	460*l.*

SY. BASYLL.

'It is very requisite that there should be models made of the figures first, to see whether they are according to proportion, which if they be made there must be consideration had of that charge.'

---

[6] The builder's estimate for this chapel, including all charges, amounted to 432*l.* 19*s.* 4*d.*, and is still preserved among the Hatfield Papers. It included a vault underground twelve feet square; and the dimensions of the chapel, which was commenced on February 26, 1618, and was completed by the end of the year, were 40 feet by 21 feet.

As the Earl intimates in his will, he had never been careful of money matters; and though he had parted with portions of his lands, and among the rest with Canterbury Park, he died 37,867*l*. in debt. As a set-off he had lent money to the amount of 16,437*l*. to various friends, and among the rest, 300*l*. to Sir Francis Bacon. To satisfy his creditors, his executors were directed to sell lands and woods to the required amount. Among those who insulted his memory, after the most fulsome professions of attachment while he was living, was Henry Howard, Earl of Northampton, author of the letters in the so-called 'Cecil Correspondence with James I.;' and with singular ingratitude Sir Francis Bacon, if it be true, as at the time was generally believed, that his Essay on Deformity was pointed at Cecil.[7]

At an early period in their career the two Bacons had attached themselves to the party of Essex, in opposition to their uncle and cousin, the Cecils. Dazzled like many others, by the brilliant and imperious qualities of the Earl, and totally misunderstanding the Queen's temper and disposition, the Bacons expected that the Cecils would be driven from their long tenure of office, and Essex be installed in their place. In the gross flattery addressed by Anthony Bacon to his patron, the Earl, it would appear as if he were carrying into practice the maxim commended by his more celebrated brother, that 'the ears of great men are in their feet,' such is its obsequiousness and extravagance. But Anthony had the credit of remaining faithful to the last. Francis, more cautious and more cold, withdrew himself in time from the fall in Siloam. That the suspicions of both against the Cecils were unfounded, especially in the greatest matter of all, the Solicitorship, is certain from the letters of

---

[7] 'Sir Francis Bacon hath set out new Essays, where, in a chapter of *Deformity*, the world takes notice that he paints out his little cousin to the life.' (Chamberlain to Carleton, December 17, 1612. Court of James I.)

Burghley and his son written in Bacon's favour.[8] It is confirmed by Bacon's own admission to Burghley. With singular want of good feeling and discretion, Bacon, on the authority of a 'wise friend,' had repeated a gross accusation of corruption against his cousin. Then finding that he was mistaken he retracted the imputation against his 'right honourable kinsman and good friend, Sir Robert Cecil,' confessing he was too credulous, almost with the same ease, not to say levity, with which he had repeated the calumny. But a keen moral sensibility was not an eminent characteristic of Bacon's conduct, as will appear by the following letter, preserved in the Hatfield Collection:—

Lady Dorothy Pakington to Lord Salisbury.

'MY VERY GOOD LORD,—Whereas I have understood of your Lordship's late favour and care had of two of my daughters, in taking them from the place of danger, and putting them into safe keeping, at what time one of their sisters was, by the practice of Sir Francis Bacon, in marriage with one Cunstabell, cast away, I thought it my duty, by some few lines, to testify my thankfulness to your Lordship for the same. And where I have also heard that your honor, together with some other Lords of his Majesty's Privy Council, examining the manner of his proceedings in contracting my daughter to Cunstabell, she being but twelve years of age, and finding her age abused, and how carelessly and slenderly she was provided for, without jointure or other provision for her, taking pity of her estate your Lordships were pleased to take some further care for her, which forasmuch as I have endea-

---

[8] See Spedding's *Life' &c. of Bacon*, i. 257, 296, 355; and Cecil's letter to Egerton, thanking him for his efforts in favour of Bacon. 'I have no kinsman,' he says, 'living, my brother excepted, whom I hold so dear;' and adds, 'that there was no likelier to deserve it' (the Solicitorship). (Birch, i. 165.) It is strange that this letter should have been so overlooked.

voured by sending unto the said Bacon to know what is done for her, and instead of satisfaction, have received an insolent letter of contempt, penned after his proud manner of writing, —my husband nor my brother knowing nothing, as being secluded and thrust out from all privity of dealing therein,— I am forced to beseech your Lordship to let me know what order is taken for her. And thus being sorry I have such cause to complain of his bad dealing, whom your Lordship heretofore recommended to me, and whose folly hath lately more abounded in procuring the said Cunstabell to be knighted, being of himself a man of very mean estate,—whereby he hath taken all ordinary means of thriving from him,— craving pardon for my boldness, I humbly take my leave. From Drury Lane, this 28th of November, 1607.

'Your Lordship's poor well willer to my best power,
 'DOROTHE PAKINGTON.'

In these remarks we have endeavoured to clear the fame of Lord Salisbury from the groundless imputations cast upon it by the biographers and admirers of Essex, Raleigh, and the Bacons. In the absence of all evidence to the contrary, it has been found an easy task to account for the failings and misfortunes of these eminent men by attributing them to the intrigues and the selfishness of Cecil. It has been presumed that, in the collection of his papers at Hatfield, proofs might be found to confirm these imputations, though Dr. Haynes, who edited a portion of them, had distinctly stated more than a century ago, that the noble Lord, who gave him free access to these manuscripts and leave to publish them, had never desired him to suppress unfavourable statements, and was 'as far from requiring any such management of the character of his great ancestor, as his ancestor was from standing in need of it.' The remark is strictly true, whether applied to the father or the son; and historians may disabuse themselves of the notion, so freely indulged in, that the papers at Hatfield contain evidence unfavourable to the first Earl. The correspondence is full, minute, and explicit. It reveals the whole life of the man, *velut in tabula*, from day to day and from year to year, without interruption. No portion of it has been suppressed or mutilated to conceal awkward facts, or make the worse appear the better cause. So far from confirming the imputation of selfishness, envy, and secret intrigue in preventing the advancement of his rivals, real or supposed, the whole evidence points the other way. The letters addressed to Sir Robert by those who required his good offices, even when they had done little to deserve his kindness, the continual appeals made to generosity by his political rivals, their friends, their relatives, and their associates, point him out as a man who was both gentle and forgiving, ready to interpose in behalf of those who needed his interposition, open and accessible to pity. Elizabeth, towards the close of her reign, did not grow less exacting of obedience; she was not more inclined to overlook political offences—a severity which might well be forgiven, considering the numerous plots against her life and her reputation, the ingratitude of many, the conspiracies of not a few. If the closing years of her reign were free from bloodshed; if out of those who joined in the treason of Essex—and among them were the Earls of Rutland, Bedford, and Southampton, Lord Sandys, Lord Monteagle, Lord Cromwell, and a hundred and fifty more of the best blood of England—none forfeited their lives except the Earl and a few inferior agents, that result was due to the wisdom and moderation of Cecil. It was the same in the Gunpowder and other plots, during the reign of her successor—plots in which more were implicated than the Government thought good to divulge. For it was the cha-

racter of this minister to discourage severity, and not drive
the guilty to desperation by excluding them from all hope of
repentance and forgiveness. If there is any exception to
this remark, it is to be found in his treatment of the Roman
Catholics, but even here his inclination to tolerance is remarkable. 'For the matter of priests,' he wrote to James, 'I condemn their doctrine, I detest their conversation, and I foresee
the peril which the exercise of their function may bring to
this island; only I confess that I shrink to see them die by
dozens, when at the last gasp they come so near loyalty;
only because I remember that mine own voice, amongst others
to the law [for their death] in Parliament was led by no
other principle, than that they were absolute seducers of the
people from temporal obedience.'[9]

The world knew him merely as a statesman, and his
abilities as a statesman few will deny. But he was not so
exclusively a politician or a statesman as his father. 'He
was a man,' as Dr. Birch justly remarks, 'of quicker parts, a
more spirited writer and speaker than his father.' His correspondence shows that he had more wit and liveliness, and
a more general and genial culture. Weighed down by the
cares of State, brought up in more terrible times, Lord
Burghley was seldom seen to smile. He never unbosomed
himself until the gates of Theobalds were closed upon him.
Then, in the companionship of his children, he found himself
a child again, entering into their romps and amusements
without a thought beyond them. But Robert, his son, though
equally attached to his children, unbent himself more freely
in the circle of his immediate friends; was warm, generous,
and constant in his attachments, and sociable in his companionship; now drinking a friendly glass with Sir George
Carew, now smoking with Sir Roger Ashton, the King's Cham-

---

[9] Bruce p. 34. From the Hatfield Papers.

berlain, a friendly pipe, in spite of 'The Counterblast against Tobacco.' But to do adequate justice to his merits, to set his character in its true light, is the province of the biographer and historian, not of the reviewer. What is here said, and much more might be said, may possibly contribute to a juster estimate of this great statesman.

THE STUARTS.[1]

For this splendid monument to the memory of the Stuarts we are indebted to the devotion of a lady. An Englishwoman by birth, an Italian by adoption, as she informs us in her preface, Madame la Marquise Campana de Cavelli combines in herself the opposite characteristics of the two races. To the passionate imagination and enthusiasm of the Italian she unites the conscientious labour and research we are accustomed to appropriate to the natives of our own country. Inspired with a strong and almost romantic sympathy for the Stuarts, or at all events for Mary d'Este, the unhappy consort of James II., as the sole Italian who had ever mounted an English throne, the Marquise has no intention of suffering her feelings to evaporate in useless enthusiasm. Like a thorough Englishwoman, she has set to work to justify her predilections; and we have the result in two magnificent volumes, the first instalment of six, containing letters, journals, portraits, engravings of rare prints and medals—everything, in short, that can throw any light on the manners, the reigns, the exile, the deaths of an unhappy race devoted to misfortune by a sort of inevitable fatality, like the Labdacidæ of old. Beginning at Saint-Germain-en-Laye, which the Marquise visited in 1864, and where she seems to have

[1] From the *Quarterly Review* for July, 1872, under the following heading: *Les derniers Stuarts à Saint-Germain-en-Laye ; Documents inédits et authentiques prisés aux Archives publiques et privées.* Par la Marquise Campana de Cavelli. Paris, 1871. Tomes i. ii. 4to.

caught the first idea of her work, she extended her inquiries to England, Germany, Spain, and Italy. She has disinterred from unknown or forgotten archives family papers, reports of Italian residents in England, confidential communications to foreign courts, hitherto concealed from the most diligent historians. If we were disposed to be hypercritical, we should say that many of these documents, especially the letters of Mary d'Este, have a value in the eyes of the Marquise which will scarcely be shared by less enthusiastic admirers. But where there is so much that is really excellent and really novel, so much laborious research that can never find its adequate return, it would be unjust to discover faults. The true and lasting reward of the fair authoress will be— and probably she desires no more—that to all future historians of the Stuart times her work will be indispensable. Even if posterity should not entirely reverse the verdict of history, it may, through her exertions, mitigate some of its severity.

Commencing with the year 1672, and the negotiations for the second marriage of James, Duke of York, these volumes bring us to the year 1689, and the unhappy attempts of James II. in Ireland. The main intention of the Marquise, in fact her sole object in the first instance, was to gather up the personal history of Mary d'Este. For this purpose she visited the old château of Saint-Germain. In the neighbouring church she found herself standing, as she tells us, before a humble monument, with as humble an inscription—JAMES II. After the most diligent inquiries, she was able to discover no traces of the tomb of his consort. She questioned the inhabitants of Saint-Germain : no one had ever heard of the life or sepulchre of Maria Beatrix. She visited the libraries and archives of Paris. After long search, she discovered that Mary's remains rested in the nunnery of Chaillot. She hastened to Chaillot ; nunnery, and all remembrance of it, had utterly perished. 'Disappointed, but not discouraged,' she continues, ' I redoubled my zeal, hoping at least to exhume the historical *souvenirs* of Maria Beatrix. I passed many years in the most celebrated archives of France, Italy, England, and other countries with a passionate ardour. The mortal remains of this Queen always escaped me ; but her memory grew beneath my gaze ; her career appeared to me every day more noble and more beautiful. I received from all quarters numbers of documents, packets of letters written by Maria Beatrix, in which she laid open the whole course of her private life and political doings from day to day. I was desirous of publishing this correspondence, for therein the world would see in all its brilliancy the charms of this touching figure, whom the indifference or hostility of so many historians had consigned too long to unmerited oblivion, or the attacks of calumny.'[2]

But the Marquise soon found, as others employed in similar researches have found before, that her materials increased more rapidly than she had anticipated ;

> ' They began to multiply,
> Like sparks that from the coals of fire do fly.'

Her industry, her researches, her perseverance, were rewarded by an overflowing harvest of materials not less valuable for the general history of the times than for the biography of Mary d'Este. This abundance compelled her to remodel her plan, and extend the limits of her work ; and thus, without losing sight of her original purpose, her attention was naturally turned to the great historical events in the age of the latter Stuarts—an age so full of magic interest to all readers, whatever their principles and their predilections. Consequently she has not only illustrated the personal history of James II., his queen, and his descendants, but she has collected and published a large mass of documents throwing

[2] Pp. 7, 8.

light upon the times which preceded and followed their downfall. The politics of William III., the fatal measures and infatuation of James II., the intrigues of foreign courts, the treachery of statesmen, the discords between the moderate Roman Catholics and the Jesuits, all find ample illustration in her pages. And though the Marquise disavows the character of a historian, though she is satisfied with confining herself to the humbler task of faithfully presenting to the public the historical treasures she has been fortunate enough to collect, she deserves great praise for her moderation and wise discretion. In the present condition of our historical materials, when so much that is necessary for an impartial and sound estimate of the most difficult epoch in our history remains buried in private collections, we hold that for some time to come the greatest service that can be rendered to this country is not a professed history, but the careful collection and arrangement of such materials as these. Violent religious and political prejudices have already sufficiently obscured the reigns of the Stuarts. What we now want are authentic papers by which we may correct the misrepresentations of party, and form a sounder and more impartial judgment.

Although, therefore, the Marquise makes no secret of her sympathies for the exiled house of the Stuarts, although she thinks that James II., in particular, has received scanty justice from the hands of our Protestant historians, she has prudently forborne all direct attempt to rescue his name from that odium under which it has laboured so long. She has not even ventured to remove any of the superfluous dust with which his memory has been artificially overcharged and blackened. She has been content to let her documents tell their own story, without putting a word into their mouths—without any attempt to extenuate or exaggerate their credit—whether they seemed to make for or against her cherished opinions. Her readers are left to form their own conclusions—a task very few, we are inclined to think, will be willing to undertake, unless the old Greek historian was mistaken in his estimate of human nature; and we are less inclined than were his contemporaries to rely on the opinions of others. The Marquise, therefore, must not be surprised if, though she find a ' fit audience,' it should prove a very select one; or if the chief return for her labour and self-sacrifice should be little more than the pleasure she has felt in the pursuit of an amiable object. Chivalry and enthusiasm have long been at a discount amongst us; and even if it were otherwise, they are not likely to be revived over the forgotten memories of James II. and his fallen house. Whigs and Tories, Conservatives and Radicals, have long since acquiesced in their verdict, and would scarcely feel grateful to any one who should attempt to disturb it. What does it matter whether the character of James be one shade or several shades less black than Macaulay has painted it? What will it signify whether, in his historical apotheosis of Whiggery, the Whig apologist has not always been as scrupulous as he ought to have been in the choice of his authorities, or uniformly careful in the examination of his facts? Even if our enthusiastic admirer of the Stuarts could convict him of gross partiality and numerous mistakes, the final resultant would remain much the same: it would still be disagreeable enough to our English notions. No amount of ingenious pleadings could get rid of the fact that James was not only a Roman Catholic, but a very bigoted Roman Catholic, that he carried into his religious convictions the untempered zeal of a convert, as well as a formality, stiffness, and opiniativeness that were native to him. We should still feel that he was as inflexible as his father, Charles I., without his father's attachment to the religion of his subjects, as indifferent to the good opinions of others as Charles II., without his brother's good nature.

In fact, their fatality, or destiny, let our authoress call it what she will, has pursued the Stuarts beyond the grave; their evils have not perished with them. Unlike other men who are rarely punished twice for their offences, and whose sufferings, like those of Charles I., or whose hopeless exile, like that of James II., have been regarded as some atonement for their faults, history has been unusually severe and bitter to their memories. It has looked exclusively at their failings; which were obvious enough and offensive enough; it has been far from indulgent to their better qualities; it has hardly allowed them any. The popular estimate of James I. has been derived in the main from libels, misnamed history, written in the time of the Commonwealth; of Charles II., and of James II., from writers like Kennet and Burnet, who must have condemned themselves had James II. appeared otherwise in their pages than a sanguinary bigot and despot, regardless of the lives and the liberties of his subjects. More modern historians have solaced their disappointment in actual by an ideal Whiggery, which has no place in nature or in history. They have been carried back in their brilliant imaginations to a time when in the triumph of William III. all the men (provided they were Whigs) were brave and honest, and all their women were lovely and virtuous. Setting out with such strong prepossessions, it was not to be expected that they should scrutinise too narrowly evidence unfavourable to James II., or suspect of partiality and exaggeration assertions so much in accordance with their expectations and their wishes. Even when, as in the case of Sir John Dalrymple, more accurate research had brought to light undoubted information unfavourable to the more active agents of the Revolution, Whig historians could not easily forego their prejudices, or reconstruct their theories. Though contradicted by unimpeachable evidence, the current impression was too powerful to be shaken; rather than relinquish it, they atoned for any admitted demerits in the main instruments of the Revolution by adding a few additional shades of darkness to the period that preceded it.

But this was not their only or their greatest error. Following the example of Fox, historians of the Revolution of 1688 have generally commenced their work with the reign of James II. If this was done with the notion of setting forth more vividly the evils from which William III. is supposed to have delivered us, those evils did not commence with James II., nor did they entirely vanish with him. If it were done with the view of showing how amazing was the contrast between James and his son-in-law, the contrast is no less mistaken than it is exaggerated William was a Stuart as well as James II. He was every whit as much determined as James that the royal power should suffer no diminution in his hands. He was as resolute in maintaining his prerogative as James. He exercised his dispensing power more frequently. If James maintained a standing army at Hounslow Heath, William had his Dutch Guards. If James was severe and stern in executing punishment, the torture in Scotland and the massacre at Glencoe exceeded in ferocity the executions at Taunton. If James countenanced Jeffreys, William took Kirke into favour, and pensioned the still more infamous Titus Oates. If James treated his Protestant advisers with disrespect, Schomberg and Ginkell dined at William's table whilst Marlborough and Godolphin stood behind his chair. The main difference consisted in this, that William was a Protestant and James a Roman Catholic; that William plunged this nation into a costly continental war with France, from which James kept aloof; that William fought the wars of the Dutch with

English money and English troops; that he utterly neglected our navy and our commerce, and burthened us with a heavy national debt. Whether the motives which determined the foreign policy of Charles II. and his brother were ignominious or otherwise, the material advantages of that policy to the nation cannot be denied. It enabled this country to recover itself from the exhaustion of the civil wars. When Charles II. ascended the throne, our navy had sunk to so low a condition that in all our magazines and stores there were not 'arms sufficient to put into the hands of five thousand men, nor provision enough to set out ten new ships to sea.'[3] Within less than ten years of that time Colbert had converted a few rotten hulks of the French marine into a navy, consisting of sixty ships of the line and forty frigates. If the policy of non-intervention be good statesmanship now, it was not only good but indispensable then. Was it for our advantage to fight the battles of other people? Was it for us to relieve the Dutch by engaging in a war with France, whilst they were pursuing their own commerce unmolested and we were neglecting ours? For a cause in which we were nowise concerned, were we to strain every nerve in grappling with a powerful and warlike adversary, when at best victory was dubious, whilst Holland, like the fox in the fable, looked on and ran off with the prey? That is exactly what William and the Dutch wanted us to do. That is precisely what he was always attempting to do when he became King of England. Happily, causes we have now to explain—causes too much overlooked by modern historians —kept us, in spite of ourselves, in spite of the frantic absurdities and fanaticism of the times, from falling into the snare. If to Charles II. and James II. we owe, as Whig historians are fond of asserting, our Protestant religion

[3] Echard's *History of the Revolution*, p. 10.

and civil liberties, we owe to them also the preservation of the monarchy, with all its attendant blessings.

To make this clear, we must trespass a little on the indulgence of our readers. The death of Charles I. was not the only instance, as Milton would have been delighted to inform his hearers, of English kings who had come to a violent end. But the death of Charles, though like that of other kings in its violence, was in its character wholly unique, a fact which Milton did not perceive. In this nation there had never been anything like it before, and we know not whether there has been in any nation or any age; for the fate of Louis XVI. was totally different, and the parallel sometimes insisted on by French historians and philosophers is wholly fallacious. In all rebellions against previous English Kings, it was the conspiracy of one branch or scion of the royal family against the other. The succession remained intact, though the right of succession might be disputed; though the monarch fell, the monarchy remained. By the death of Charles I., for the first time since our existence as a nation, monarchy and the monarch fell together; the nation was not only without a head for the first time, but all its functions ceased; its constitution was at an end. The Church had been already put down, and so far the spiritual authority of the Crown was extinguished. The House of Lords, the constitutional advisers of the Crown, was defunct; for what use was there of constitutional advisers when there was no one to advise with? But there remained the army and the House of Commons. The House of Commons could neither summon nor prorogue itself, least of all at the command of the army; and the army, which by the Constitution of this country knows no command but that of the King,[4] could not and would not obey the Commons. Here,

[4] See the Militia Act passed in the year 1662. 'Forasmuch as within all his Majesty's realms and dominions, the sole and supreme power,

then, were two concurrent and incompatible authorities.
Government was at a dead-lock: it fell, as it always must
fall, on such occasions, to the strongest; and the destruction
of monarchy ended in military despotism. The Church of
England was effectually disestablished, for its property was
taken from it and its worship proscribed. Had Cromwell
been less resolute, less large-minded than he was, the
spiritual despotism of this country would have been as complete as its civil anarchy. The Presbyterians could not
tolerate the Independents, nor the Independents the Presbyterians; and when both had got rid of the Church of England, they vented their wrath, their venom, and abuse,
against each other. In the name of liberty they had put
down the Church of England, and raised up the most bitter
and malignant forms of persecution. In the name of liberty
they had pulled down the monarchy, and with it all the
constitutional safeguards for civil and religious freedom.

Repentance came too late. Even Cromwell would have
restored, had it been possible, some of those constitutional
forms he had been instrumental in destroying.[5] For, how-

government, command, and disposition of the Militia, and of all forces by
sea and land, and of all forts and places of strength is, and by the laws of
England ever was, the undoubted right of his majesty.' &c., 'and that
both or either of the Houses of Parliament cannot, nor ought, to pretend
to the same,' &c.

It may be urged that Parliament did command the army in the wars
against Charles I., which is very true; but then it evaded the Constitution
by issuing its orders in the king's name, avowing by this act its own inability by the Constitution to command the army.

[5] So desperately did even Cromwell's own party cling to the old forms
of the Constitution, that it was this desire more than any other that urged
them, and no doubt Oliver himself, to revive the title of king in his person.
'That which inclined the most,' says Baillie, 'to further the Protector's
kingship, was their expectation of *a regular government* thereby, without
the perpetuating of a military rule by the sword, to which so vast and
arbitrary charges would always be necessary.' Cromwell was only diverted
from this design by being informed by Fleetwood of a strong combination in the army to oppose that motion. (See Baillie's Let. to Spang,
November, 1658.) As Lambert and other officers secretly cherished the

ever unconstitutionally men may rise to power, none are more anxious in fencing the power, thus gained, by constitutional securities. But that could not be. Rulers and ruled had fallen alike into a false position, from which it was impossible to extricate themselves. Their struggles only served to entangle them the more. Every year the usurper found it necessary to rivet more closely the chains of his authority; every year his attempts to restore the forms of the Constitution became more hopeless and desperate. To a mere tyrant this would have been a matter of indifference; in the case of Cromwell we are convinced that it did more than anything else to embitter his days and break his heart —far more than the pertinacious and malignant abuse of the Presbyterians, the dangerous and subtle designs of Sir Harry Vane, the ambition and dissensions of his Major-Generals, the plots of the Royalists, or a thousand pamphlets cloaking his assassination under the specious pretext of 'killing no murder.' Monarchs without one tithe of Cromwell's ability may with ordinary prudence be sure of the love and obedience of their subjects, because they rule by law, and the law is respected in their persons; but the bravest and most brilliant of fortunate usurpers are a perpetual memento and exemplification of the weakness of the law, and of the rewards to be obtained by trampling the Constitution under foot. How can they expect obedience who are in themselves flagrant and successful examples of disobedience? How can they preach reverence for law who have taught men, by their own transgression, the advantage of transgressing it? Nothing

hope of succeeding Cromwell and perpetuating a military despotism in England, they strenuously opposed all attempts on the Protector's part to render the crown hereditary. This was the great reason why he never dared to nominate his successor, and so suppress the agitation and intrigues that troubled his government, and kept the nation in perpetual ferment. Thurloe tells a curious story of the shifts to which they were driven to cover their hypocrisy.

remains but the rule of force and compulsion—a simple and
undisguised appeal to arbitrary power. All government,
except that of the stronger, is at an end. The freedom of
the people is the destruction of their ruler—their slavery
his only security and confidence. Of this there could be no
more evident proof than the solitude and silence at Cromwell's death. Men might admire then, as they have done
since, his genius, his prowess, his superiority to the common
run of usurpers; but we question whether a single tear of
affection or regret was shed upon his ashes. From the
Royalists, of course, he could expect no sympathy; the
Presbyterians regarded him as an apostate; the Vanists as
the rebel Absalom who kept out the true David; his own
soldiers and the Independents suspected and watched all his
movements; for many of them, expecting to be 'half-kings
themselves,' looked upon the augmentation or continuance
of his rule as worse than despotism. Order broken at the
head becomes orderless throughout; the current diverted at
the source returns not to its natural bed, but is lost in sand
and shallows. Had Richard possessed the energy and abilities
of his father, the result would not have been otherwise than
it was. When he succeeded to the throne the horizon was
perfectly clear, there was not a cloud to be seen in it as big as
a man's hand. Charles, with a few followers, wandered about
in exile, hopeless, helpless, and forlorn. The feeble attempt
of the Cavaliers in his favour had been completely and
rapidly suppressed; the whole nation was overawed by
the strongest military discipline; there was apparently
neither the wish nor the ability to rise. Nay, more; the
peaceable succession of Richard was insisted on as a proof of
God's approbation. He had had no hand in the King's death
—was rather inclined to deal kindly with the Royalists. He
had never sought the government, but it was thrust upon
him. He had been accepted and approved by the House of

Commons. The rightful King had been dead for twelve years, and there was no likelihood that his son would succeed him. The common good required that the land should not remain without a governor; whilst the numerous and bitter factions, political and religious, daily multiplying in numbers and malignancy, and ready at any moment to fly at each others' throats, made people ready to acquiesce in almost any form of government and any governor, without too narrowly scrutinising their precise legitimacy.

Yet with all these advantages in its favour, the Republic, from no ostensible cause, collapsed in an instant, in the utmost tranquillity at home and abroad. It fell so completely, that not a vestige of it remained; it fell among the execrations and outcries of those who, a few months only before, would have regarded its ruin as impossible. Not a hand was stretched out to support it. Of those who had bled and fought for it—whose interest and reputation were most deeply concerned in its continuance—though they were men of undoubted courage and experience—with swords in their hands—not a handful could be found to strike a single blow in its favour, or make the smallest sacrifice for that which they had hitherto identified with the cause of God. 'That an army,' says Baxter, 'that had conquered three such kingdoms, and brought so many armies to destruction, cut off the King, pulled down the Parliament, and set up and pulled down others at their pleasure; that had conquered so many cities and castles; that were so united by principles, and interest, and guilt, and so deeply engaged, as much as their estates, and honour, and lives, came to, to have stood it out to the very utmost; that had possessed so much of their wisdom and religiousness; and had declared such high resolutions against monarchy:—I say that such an army should have one commander (Monk) among themselves, whom they accounted not religious, that should march against them

ESSAY IV. THE STUARTS. 175

without resistance, and that they should all stand still, and
let him come on, and restore the Parliament, and bring in
the King, and disband themselves, and all this without one
bloody nose! Let any man, that hath the use of his understanding, judge whether this were not enough to prove that
there is a God that governeth the world, and disposeth of the
powers of the world according to His will!'

'That a nation,' says Milton, proudly moralising with aristocratic complacency on these events, 'should be so valorous
and courageous to win their liberty in the field, and when
they have won it, should be so heartless and unwise in their
counsels, as not to know how to use it, value it, what to do
with it themselves; but .... basely and besottedly to run
their necks again into the yoke which they have broken—
will be an ignominy if it befall us, that never yet befell any
nation possessed of their liberty.'[6]

In this absence of all serious resistance to the return of
Charles II., and the frantic delight of people in general
at the Restoration, it might be supposed that the old order
was not only entirely restored, but had in fact become
stronger than before. It is usual with historians to insist on
the unqualified submission exhibited by his subjects to their
new king, to paint in glowing colours the unanimity of his
welcome, as if the whole nation, forgetful of all prudent and
rational restraint, had hastened to throw itself at his feet,
ashamed of its past misconduct, and resolved to atone for its
disobedience to the father by unbounded servility to the son.

'So tears of joy for his returning spilt,
Work out and expiate their former guilt.'

No doubt that joy was great; no doubt it was the object
of loyal poets and Cavaliers to make the most of it. Those
who had been the main instruments in the King's restoration,
or who expected to profit by it, were not likely to underrate

[6] *Easy Way to Establish a Free Commonwealth*, p. 410.

the popularity of an event in the success of which they were so intimately concerned. But that joy was not so real, not so unanimous, not so profound, as careless or interested observers might have imagined. It was not unmixed delight at the restoration of royalty. Intenser, perhaps ignobler, feelings had their share in it. The great Presbyterian party hated Cromwell, hated his son, hated his Independent generals, who jeered at their classes and their synods, and turned their most reverend divines into ridicule. 'God keep the Presbyterians out of the hands of the Independents and Sectaries when they come to have power,'[7] is the exclamation of one, not the meanest among them, even before the supremacy had been confided to Cromwell. 'The Independents labour,' he says, 'to get all the power of the army they possibly can into their hands, and the command of all the great towns and cities; and by one way or other to turn out of place, keep out, obstruct, blast, all cordial, zealous Presbyterians, and which no doubt is done to give the Presbyterians liberty of conscience! And now they give the Presbyterians good words, viz., that they will send them packing to Rome; that it were a good deed they were hanged and knocked on the head; their guts gored out; that they are anti-Christian priests, cursed priests, damned priests, and such like.' The victory at Dunbar over their co-religionists—the Scotch—had not improved the temper of the Presbyterians; nor had the airs of insolent triumph, assumed by their implacable enemies—the Independents— on that occasion, reconciled them the more to Cromwell's government. They have been taunted by Milton for their hypocritical denunciation of the King's murder, still more for their sedulous praise of the 'Eikon Basiliké,' and their dishonest attempt to create a sympathy for royalty in its sufferings at the expense of their enemies—the Independents.

[7] *Edward's Gangrena*, part ii. p. 66.

All these now crowded to Dover at Charles's landing, and were not the least forward in their shouts of congratulation.

Nor were the Sectaries, as they were then called—that is, the interminable shoal of religious dissentients who were neither Presbyterians nor Churchmen—wholly indifferent to the King's return. For many years Cromwell had relied upon them implicitly, as men who detested monarchy, and were the vehement enemies of the Stuarts. He had preferred them wherever he could to all places of trust and authority. He had recruited his army mainly from their body; but in the latter years of his reign he had found it necessary to change his policy, and oust them from their employments.[8] They took their disgrace with much sorer anger and resentment; and though they did not change their principles, or become converts to monarchy, they readily swelled the throng of those who were the enemies to Cromwell and his family. If they were to have a king at all, or any settled authority, as well it should be in the person of a rightful king, as of one who had no right, and had besides deceived them.

And thus a variety of motives were working in the minds, if they were not patent in the faces, of those who crowded round the King at his return: jubilant Cavaliers, who had been unexpectedly restored to their country; Churchmen waiting for their incumbencies; Presbyterians, sponging out the memory of past offences by outrageous loyalty; time-servers, who had waited on events, and, like

[8] 'The sectarian party, in his army and elsewhere, he chiefly trusted to and pleased, till by the people's submission and quietness he thought himself well settled, and then he began to undermine them and work them out. And though he had so often spoken for the Anabaptists, now he findeth them so heady and so much against any settled government, and so set upon the promoting of their way and party, that he doth not only begin to blame their unruliness, but also designeth to settle himself in the people's favour by suppressing them.'—*Reliquiæ Baxterianæ*, by Silvester, p. 74.

Milton, though with none of his disinterestedness, had been Churchmen, Presbyterians, Independents, Seekers, as the wind veered and the seasons changed. There were king-killers, like Lenthall, prepared to swear that he 'who first drew his sword against the King committed as great an offence as he that cut off his head;' hoary old renegades, like Sir Harbottle Grimstone, ready to address the new comer as 'the glory of kings and the joy of his subjects;' poets, like Dryden, excusable for their flatteries and their fictions; multitudes who shed tears because others shed tears, or shouted the louder because others were shouting.

Was that swarthy man, then in the prime of his manhood —ever ready with a jest on his lips and a smile in those mysterious eyes, graceful, easy, and careless—in reality deceived by this hurricane of loyalty? As cheer rose upon cheer from the thousands of spectators that witnessed his landing, as men crowded to touch the hem of his garment and kiss the prints of his footsteps, and all the roads from Rochester to London swarmed with people, 'as if the whole kingdom had been gathered there;' when the two Houses of Parliament 'solemnly cast themselves at his feet, with all vows of affection and fidelity to the world's end,' was Charles deceived? Did he believe that all this demonstration was genuine? He knew mankind much too well. As a boy he had seen the same crowd, and the same Parliament, pursuing his father to destruction. Later in life he had been a reluctant actor in the farce at Scone, when Presbyterians pelted him with insults in the disguise of sermons, libelled his father and his mother before his face, and compelled him to sign the Solemn League and Covenant. A wanderer for ten years, surrounded by needy and disorderly followers, who pestered him with real or imaginary sufferings in the royal cause, he had learned to see the selfish side of professed loyalty. Proscribed first by one state and then by another, at the bidding of the usurper, never sure of protection from any, no sooner was it known that his restoration to the crown was probable, than he was overloaded with gifts and professions of service. 'The magistrates of the town of Breda took all imaginable care to express their devotion to the King, by using all civilities towards [him], and providing for the accommodation of the multitude of his subjects who resorted thither to express their duty to him. So that no man would have imagined, by the treatment he now received, that he had been so lately forbid to come into that place!'[9] Such a life, as he through untoward circumstances had been compelled to lead, is at no time favourable to the development of the nobler qualities and affections. But those of Charles were specially unfortunate. Driven from his home when a mere boy, before he had been trained in any steady principles; deprived of his father; left to the care of his mother, whom he could not highly respect; educated by Hobbes, so far as he was educated; inspired with a distaste of the Protestant religion, of which he knew little, 'except the ill-bred familiarity of the Scotch divines'—who can wonder if he entertained very questionable notions both of morality and religion? Who can wonder, considering the nature of his experience, if he were convinced that other men had as little of either as he himself possessed?

But with Charles the pursuit of pleasure, and an apparent indifference to any precise form of religion, was a part of his policy. It served him equally well with Episcopalian, Presbyterian, Independent, and Sectary. Some might hope that one so undetermined might eventually be won over to their views; all might expect tolerance; if not, the intolerance they suffered could not be imputed to the King. *Point de zèle* was the sagacious maxim of a diplomatist as far-sighted, as subtle as he; one who had lived through

[9] *Clarendon's Rebellion*, vii. 496, ed. 1826.

disastrous times as Charles had done. Besides, he knew well how opposition brings out opposition; how the ardent, romantic, obtrusive attachment of his father to certain principles in the Church and the State had involved him in trouble inextricable. He knew that enthusiasm brings enthusiasts about it. He had come to reign peaceably if he could; to enjoy, if it were allowed him, and as long as it was allowed him, the good things of peace and plenty, after long abstinence and forced self-denial. He wished needlessly to trouble no one; to alarm no one by appearing too serious, too earnest, or too difficult in any matter. In this nonchalance there was an object, beyond mere appetite in his pursuit of pleasure, though carried too often to excess. It sufficiently blinded men to his real character, and threw them off their guard. In the laxity of familiar and unrestrained conversation, those who were admitted to his confidence often dropped hints and indications of their real character and designs which were never afterwards forgotten. 'For,' says Halifax, who knew him well, 'when he thought fit to be angry, he had a very peevish [pertinacious] memory; there was hardly a blot that escaped him.' From his easy, compliant good humour he reaped this advantage—no small one in a nation so distempered and distracted as this was—that though no minister could confidently reckon on the continuance of his confidence, he knew that his displeasure, unlike that of Charles I., would be neither severe nor lasting; whilst those who opposed him flattered themselves that there was no permanent or insuperable obstacle against their being taken into favour. Though the nation, through the Speaker of the House of Commons, had complimented Charles 'as having not only Jacob's voice but Jacob's hands;' though they offered their daily petitions to the Throne of Grace that the King might be rewarded with the fatness of Jacob's blessing, they had taken the prudent precaution of not leaving him a guinea in his pocket. 'What troubles me most,' he said, in his agreeable, bantering way, ' is to see so many of you, gentlemen, come to me at Whitehall, and to think you must go somewhere else for your dinner!' Profuse as was their profession of loyalty, they had taken care to disband the army; the militia was commanded by men notoriously unfavourable to his pretensions; the navy, as we have stated already, was utterly inefficient. There stood he in the midst of the shouting and prostrate crowds, a king only in name, a possessor of his father's throne only so long as the *popularis aura* might continue to blow from the same favourable quarter.

He had been indebted for his return to the mysterious policy of one man, whose motives are even to this day an enigma to historians. In the brilliant throng of statesmen, generals, courtiers, and country gentlemen, there was not one, now that success had been achieved, that did not believe it was owing to his own individual advice and his own particular prowess. There was not one who did not equally expect a reward proportionate to his own estimate of his own services, and would have taken mortal offence if the royal ear had been deaf or indifferent to his claims or his counsel. Thousands of expectants started up in forgotten holes and corners; thousands flocked home from abroad to lounge at the stairs of Whitehall; to pursue him from gallery to gallery, and room to room, with suppliant looks and 'asking faces.' Never was a king more popular, more beloved, more persecuted, teased, and pestered.

He could not shut the doors, like any ordinary mortal, against this Egyptian swarm of respectable mendicants that found their way even into the King's bedchamber. He could not give out that he was 'sick or dead,' or even gone into the country. He was a rapid walker, and few men could keep pace with him—a habit he had probably acquired to avoid such incessant importunity. He had a trick, also, of pulling out his watch as a hint to long-winded suitors. But even these little artifices, never very effectual at any time, were scarcely available at his Restoration. Though the clouds were broken, the elements of confusion were still abroad; they might coalesce as easily and as unexpectedly as they had dispersed, and he was powerless to prevent it; therefore it was of the utmost importance to his safety, and the preservation of his throne, that he should offend and disappoint no one; and in this respect his policy harmonized with his natural temper. Hating the stiffness and formality of a court, unlike his brother James II., he was fond of unbending himself to those below him. He could exchange raillery with Halifax, Rochester, and Shaftesbury, without losing his temper, when they presumed on his familiarity; he could listen without impatience to the grave speeches of mediocrities, like Essex, Russell, and Temple. When petulant ministers threw up their appointments, with the honourable expectation of embarrassing his government, he received their resignations without betraying a spark of uneasiness or resentment. Nothing could throw him off his guard; no danger, no difficulty, no complication, could impair that affable, easy, nonchalant air which left him at leisure to see the faults and failings of other men and effectually conceal his own.

And if this was dissimulation—as they thought who were disappointed in finding him not so tractable as they had expected—he needed it all. He had returned a king upon sufferance. Though he was by inheritance the rightful king, he was in fact in no better condition than an elective monarch. He owed his crown to a party, and how far he might count upon the strength or stability of that party he had no means of ascertaining; it might be more their humour than their loyalty, as Dryden affirms, to which he was indebted. At all events, they would take effectual care to monopolise his favours, and make him dependent on themselves. It was impossible it should be otherwise. It was impossible that they or he should forget that he was indebted to them exclusively for his restoration, to which he himself had been able to contribute nothing. He had no Dutch army, like William III.; no merits or services of his own to plead; not a shred of power, authority, or influence beyond what they and the nation, at their bidding, chose to concede. He had only a barren title—and that, as we shall presently see, was far less valid, with many of his subjects, than is generally imagined—and his own good star to trust to. If by these counters he could play the game of monarchy, like a wary and experienced gambler, against such fearful odds, the greater praise was due to his ingenuity. And a very hazardous game it was, and one that demanded a wary and vigilant player. For twenty years had these men who now bowed the knee before him, though disgusted with Cromwell and the Commonwealth, set kings and kingship practically at defiance; for nearly ten of those years had they been the obstinate and successful opponents of his father. During ten of those years and more they had filled every place of honour or of profit with Roundheads and Presbyterians. They had driven out the loyalists from employment; they had ejected from their livings the Episcopal clergy; they had supplemented the different corporations with their own creatures. Then succeeded the rule of Cromwell; and wherever he had displaced their nominees or created new appointments, he had filled them with stern republicans and anti-monarchists. The loyal party was reduced to the lowest ebb. Nothing can show more completely their utter feebleness and inefficiency, even when the nation was sick of Richard Cromwell, than their inability to bring back the king, and leave his restoration to their political antagonists. Of the disbanded soldiers of Cromwell 25,000 are said to have been scattered chiefly about the metropolis. They were mortal foes to the very name of Stuart: they were almost republicans to a man. Their association in the same regiments, their attachment to The Cause, gave them unusual facilities for combination. The loss of their employment, their position, and their pay rendered them reckless. If a standing army had been allowed, they might have been drafted and dissipated in its ranks. As it was, they formed a continual and perilous nucleus for disaffection; and, either here or in Holland, they were the active and untiring agents in all the plots that disturbed the tranquillity of Charles II. For republicanism with them was an idol and a passion;—a passion that had grown strong in the abeyance of the monarchy, and had been fed by the remembrance of their former good fortune. As Dryden sings :—

> 'The good old cause revived a plot requires;
> Plots, true or false, are necessary things
> To raise up commonwealths and ruin kings.'

Nor were the embers of that fiery enthusiasm which had once burned fiercely in the land, dull and cold as they might seem to careless observers, utterly extinguished. The time was yet comparatively recent when Presbyterian and Independent had encouraged from their pulpits the doctrine of king-killing, under the example of Phinehas, and imprecated curses upon the people who did 'the work of the Lord deceitfully.' When the drum and the fife were silent, more inspiriting than drum and fife did these screaming ecclesiastics call upon their excitable audience to wash their garments in blood, and to come to the help of the Lord against the mighty. The most sacred occasions, the most solemn hours, brought no respite to their reiterated imprecations. Devotion itself was turned into a libel against the royal authority, and the precepts of the gospel were travestied into incitements to murder. 'Do justice upon the *greatest*; Saul's sons are not here spared, no nor may Agag, or Benhadad, though themselves KINGS. . . . Zimri and Cozbi, though Princes of their people, must be pursued into their tents. . . . This is the way to consecrate your hands to God.' (Herle's Sermon before the House of Commons, Nov. 5, 1644.) 'What soldier's heart would not start, deliberately to come into a subdued city and take the little ones upon the spear's point? To take them by the heels and beat out their brains against the wall? What inhumanity and barbarousness would this be thought? Yet if this work be to revenge God's Church against Babylon [Charles and the Cavaliers], he is a blessed man that takes and dashes the little ones against the stones.' (Marshal's Sermon before the Commons, Feb. 23, 1641.) 'Those mine enemies which would not that I should reign over them, bring hither and slay them before me. Let me see them executed, KINGS, Rulers, people conspiring rebellion against the Lord and against His Christ.' (Maynard to the Commons, Oct. 28, 1646.) Once more:—'There is no dallying with God now, much delay hath been used already, too much. God is angry, and He seems to say this once more: "Will you strike, will you execute judgment, or will ye not? Tell me; for if you will not, I will. I will have the enemy's blood and yours too, if you will not execute vengeance upon delinquents [the Cavaliers]. The day of vengeance is in my heart, and the year of my Redeemer is come."' (Case to the Commons, 1644.)

It would be easy to multiply hundreds of instances; more violent even and more bloodthirsty than these. But these, and such as these, were the addresses encouraged by the House of Commons, and suited to the taste of the greatest deliberative assembly in the nation. One may infer what sort of teaching echoed throughout all the pulpits of the land when this was the most approved fashion in the highest quarters; when the milder teaching and Christian moderation of the Church of England were put down, and the Church itself was disestablished. Nor in the progress of liberty, or rather licentiousness, which succeeded on the death of Charles I., had this spirit abated. Here are a few specimens of the bitter herbs of that rhetoric which greeted the return of his son. 'Charles Stewart, the son of that murderer, is proclaimed King of England; whose throne of iniquity is built on the blood of precious saints and martyrs.' ('Day of Hope,' p. 1, 1660). 'As for the title of this Prince [Charles II.], who would fain be accounted the right heir, let us remember from whence he had it and how 'tis now tainted. Were it never so just, the treason of the father hath cut off the son.' ('True Portraiture of the Kings of England,' p. 39.)

What could monarchy, stripped of all power, oppose to such principles and doctrines as these? Could it fall back upon the divinity of kings and the peril of touching the Lord's anointed? Could it set up its divine and indefeasible right? Could it entrench itself behind the Tudor notion of its divine supremacy? All these had been given to the winds. Presbyterianism, the irreconcilable enemy to civil supremacy, had claimed divine right exclusively for itself, and, under pretence of purity, had taught men to believe that no other authority than its own was divine. Presbyterianism, exactly suited to the temper of a people that had always depreciated monarchy, had led Englishmen into a fashion of thinking, talking, and writing about kings which had been hitherto alien to the nation. It had pressed rudely and irreverently into the charmed circle; it had stripped monarchy of its majesty; it had laid kingship bare, and trampled it under foot; it had encouraged the dregs of the people to draw nigh and put their heel upon the neck of royalty. The execution of Charles had been a practical proof, more convincing than any logic, that kings might be called to account by their people, or at least by those who professed to act in the name of the people; it had taught men to think that in their name and with them was the true source of all authority and power. A new era had dawned for monarchy, whether as noble, as grand, as true, as magnanimous, as that which it succeeded, is altogether another question; but a new era certainly, as dull, mean, business-like, and prosaic, as any Scotchman or Presbyterian could have desired.

Of course, in the usual and accepted style of loyal and complimentary addresses, the Commons might flatter themselves and Charles that monarchy was restored as before. They might congratulate him and themselves that he had by his return knocked off their shackles and turned their prison 'into a paradise of pleasure;' but Charles was far too sagacious to be deluded by such professions. If he had learned anything in his long exile, it was the worthlessness of such adulation. If there was any creed to which he was constant, it was a general disbelief in man or woman. How, with such flagrant, such oppressive examples as the scenes before him, could it be otherwise? Here was the whole House of Commons, who had listened to and encouraged rebellion, now professing that until he appeared, 'not many months since, England was but a great prison, where the worst of men were our governors, and their vilest hests the laws by which they governed.'[1] Here were zealous Presbyterian ministers ready to conform and accept of preferment on any or on no pretext. Here were anti-monarchists suddenly converted into the most zealous of loyalists; and those who had drawn their swords against his father were eager to

[1] See the Speaker's Address to the King in the name of the Commons, in the summer of 1660, in *Ralph's Hist.* i. 13.

consign to everlasting perdition the whole generation of regicides. Root and branch reformers made common cause with the Cavaliers, and were just as ready to exterminate their former friends as once they would have exterminated their new-found allies. A man of strong principles or of great resolution might perhaps have stood alone and uninjured in the general shock and confusion of honesty, faith, and patriotism. But Charles was not of that number; and it is at least due to him to say that he never professed to be. He had the ghost of his father's murder before his eyes— that murder which he must have felt to be in the highest degree cruel and unjust; that murder which he felt was inflicted for his father's maintenance of those rights of monarchy and that Church of England which these men now professed it was their greatest delight to see restored. It is easy to condemn him for caring little for parliaments—we conceive it hard how he should ever have respected them. It is easy to condemn him for studying too much his own pleasure, ease, and security: that was all for which he thought a throne valuable. It is easy to denounce his ignoble traffickings with Louis XIV., but he probably thought he was robbing the Egyptians, and doing his own nation no harm. His reign was not noble; how could it be? Monarchy had ceased to be considered as the highest trust —it had ceased to be regarded as the image of God's vicegerency on earth. He might write on his coins, 'King by the grace of God;' but he had been taught that he was king only by the breath of his people. 'Since the King or the magistrate' (says Milton) 'holds his authority of the people, both originally and naturally for their good, in the first place and not his own; then may the people, as oft as they shall judge it for the best, either choose him or reject him, retain him or depose him, *though no tyrant*, merely by the liberty and right of freeborn men to be governed as seems to them best.'[2] When subjects set up such a rule of selfishness, when they consider, as Milton would say, that the foundation of government is exclusively for their own profit, their own pleasure, and their own caprice, can they be surprised if rulers follow their example? When they falsely and foolishly assert that government is a contract between king and people, which the latter may break at the dictates of folly, whim, and injustice, can they wonder if rulers like Charles look upon government as a contract where all is fair and each party must look to his own interest? If nations wish to make their kings selfish, ignoble, and grasping, tell them they are subordinate to the people they rule; tell them they are not accountable to God but to His creatures; tell them that theirs is a mere human ordinance: and we know of no lesson that can more effectually degrade both rulers and people; none that can make obedience more slavish or dominion more selfish and more arbitrary.

We have no intention of pursuing the history of this reign into its minuter details. Nor need we; for the whole is a drama in which, after a few preliminary skirmishes, inferior actors give place, and the whole interest centres in two opposite and pre-eminent chiefs—Shaftesbury and the King. It is a game of chess, played by two masterly hands, to whom all the rest are no better than rooks and pawns. At first sight, indeed, nothing could appear more disproportionate than this encounter; nothing more certain than that the King would and must succumb. His easy, indolent, irresolute temper seemed but a feeble match for the restless, fiery, turbulent genius of Shaftesbury, with whom the excitement of political intrigue had become a second nature.

'Pleased with the danger when the storm ran high,'.

as Dryden says of him; pleased because it ministered to his

[2] *Tenure of Kings*, &c. p. 281, ed. 1806.

vanity, and found full occupation for his restlessness, nothing satisfied him better than when he was working on the passions of other men, and goading them to frenzy. A lover of mischief and a plotter from his youth, he had abandoned the cause of Charles I. to side with the Parliament; he abandoned the Commonwealth to take part in the Restoration; he abandoned the Court because Charles had recalled his declaration of Liberty of Conscience; and he now headed the popular party who had driven the King to take that step, to dabble in the infamous Popish plot, and become the most determined enemy of toleration. Indifferent to all religion, his Protestant zeal imposed upon the zealous Protestantism of other men; an unflinching champion for arbitrary measures when in power, he persuaded Russell, Essex, Stamford, and Salisbury, men of weaker minds and stronger prejudices than his own, that he was the champion of parliamentary rights and constitutional liberty. None could deny him the possession of wit, of eloquence, of versatility, of intrepidity, and audacity; and few will deny that whilst he had all the qualities to make a great, popular, and successful tribune, he had no superfluous spark of generosity, patriotism, virtue, or honour, to prevent him from becoming one.

Against an opponent at once so able, so bold, and so unscrupulous, it was not easy for Charles to make head. He was besides double-weighted. He had to fight under numerous disadvantages. There was not a minister admitted to his councils on whom he could thoroughly rely— some for their utter incapacity, others for their cowardice, some for their excessive selfishness. Arlington and Buckingham were not to be trusted; Sunderland notoriously betrayed him, and Halifax was a trimmer. Monmouth went over to the enemy; the Duke of York was an intolerable incubus. Never were two men more unlike than these brothers. The one, if not as his enemies said, wholly indifferent to religion, taking up with it as he found it, willing to please his people in this as in other things, if he could; the other, not satisfied with his conversion to the Roman Catholic faith, unless he flaunted his conversion in the face of all men. The one, even in the gravest affairs of state, hating formality—receiving deputations in his bed-chamber in his dressing-gown; the other, formal and ceremonious, even with his own brothers and most near relations. It is certainly much to the credit of Charles II. and his good breeding that he endured so long and so patiently such a respectable and insufferable bore as James, especially as it was utterly impossible that Charles can have loved him.

For ten years the battle gathered round the body of the Duke of York, to use an Homeric illustration, and raged with increasing violence. To exclude James from the succession, and separate the two brothers, according to the old maxim, *Divide et impera*, was the unceasing object of Shaftesbury and the Whigs. To this end they directed all their energies, careless of the honesty or justifiableness of the means, wholly indifferent who suffered so long as they were victorious. It is quite possible that Shaftesbury may have been innocent of the detestable Popish plot. It is to be hoped that he scorned association with such unmitigated scoundrels as Oates, and Tong, and Bedloe. It is to be hoped that he was innocent of the nefarious project for raising subscriptions to pay and encourage the mendacious trade of information, though appearances are grievously against him. It may be possible, though it is not very probable, that he was not cognisant of the acts of his agent, Stringer, or of others equally unscrupulous; but that he made use of the Popish plot to further his own designs, that he goaded the fanatic passions of the nation to madness that he did all in his power to render justice impossible, to sacrifice innocent blood, to obstruct and pervert the truth, is undeniable. No one now believes that the Popish plot was other than a gross delusion—that Lord Stafford, that Roman Catholic priests, lawyers, and gentlemen, who were condemned to death for a supposed participation in it, were not judicially murdered. There is not a blot in our annals more foul than this, none on which an Englishman can look with a greater sense of shame and humiliation. Yet that plot, but for Shaftesbury and the Whigs, would have fallen into the contempt that it deserved from the first—into the contempt in which Charles had been willing to leave it. They employed every method to inflame the angry passions of the mob, to delude the simple, to terrify the doubting, to intimidate honest witnesses; until even to venture a hint that Oates might not be altogether trustworthy, or point out contradictions and discrepancies in his evidence or that of his agents, exposed the audacious questioner to the peril of being himself accused as a plotter and Jesuit in disguise. It was owing to them that, in 1678, when the winter had set in, all the Roman Catholics in London, without regard to age, sex, occupation, or condition, were compelled to withdraw ten miles from the cities of Westminster and London; that the House of Commons was induced to stultify itself and the nation by resolving that there was 'a hellish plot of the Papists to assassinate the King, and subvert the established religion and government;' that a public fast was ordered for our happy deliverance—that even the Church was constrained to put up its prayers to Almighty God for preserving the King and the nation from imaginary dangers.

'This,' says Ralph, whom no one will suspect of leaning too much to Toryism, 'was arming persecution with authority, and destroying the peace of the nation under the notion of preserving it. And yet so hardened or so infatuated were the times, that almost all but the sufferers thought these savage proceedings just. Early in the session, at the instance of the Commons, informers of all kinds had been invited by proclamation to come in and make their discoveries; in consideration of which they were promised not only indemnity, if accomplices in the plot, but a reward for their good service. This had such an effect that scarce a day passed but some strange story was told of armed men marching by night, arms concealed, treasonable letters found, and consultations held, which were not only patiently heard, but actually entered into the Journals of the Lords [before whom the trials took place], as if worthy of the knowledge and attention of posterity.'[3]

The hierophants who presided at this immolation of the national honour, candour, and good sense, were Lord Shaftesbury and his Whig associates.

It was in vain that the King offered to submit to any conditions for securing the Protestant religion they might think fit to propose—'to pare the nails,' as it was expressed, 'of a Popish successor '—provided that the line of succession was left unbroken. He told van Leeuwen, the Dutch ambassador, who was sent by William to protest against his parting with any of his royal prerogatives—for William dexterously availed himself of every opportunity to make capital out of Charles's embarrassments—' Your master is mistaken; he is misled by persons who have views of their own, and who would gladly compel me to pass through the gate I am resolved never to pass. The right of succession is a very essential and important prerogative of the Crown, which my opponents would be glad to induce me to destroy.' ' If,' he added, 'he could have disposed of the Crown, he would have given it to one of his children; but he knew

[3] *Ralph's Hist.*, i. 407.

well it was not at his disposal, and that he must leave it to those to whom it belonged.'[4] He went so far in his distress as to offer to the two Houses to circumscribe the power of his successor, in the event of his being a Roman Catholic; to leave him no control over any ecclesiastical preferments; to guarantee that, in the event of his own death, Parliament should remain sitting for a competent time; and, if there were no Parliament sitting, then the last which was in being should be enabled to reassemble without any new summons; that as no Papist could, by law, hold any place of trust, so, if the King were a Papist, he should have no power to appoint or displace any Privy Councillor, Judge in Common Law or Chancery, Lord-Lieutenants, Deputy-Lieutenants, officers of the Army and Navy, except by the authority of Parliament. It is hard to conceive what stronger safeguards than these could have been devised, or what more the most zealous Protestant could have required, for the security of religion. But, though popery might be the pretext, it was not security against popery, or arbitrary power, which Shaftesbury aimed at. He was far too keen-sighted to share in the vulgar delusion; too indifferent to all religions to care for any; too well aware of the miserable numbers and miserable condition of the Roman Catholics, to imagine that the kingdom would suffer any danger from their encroachments. In England they numbered only one man in two hundred and thirty; in all the three kingdoms, including the Roman Catholic population of Ireland, not more than one in two hundred and five. He did not participate in the panic he had done so much to raise and foment. He had other objects in view. To have admitted any limitation in the succession, to have accepted even the proposal of ministers that the Prince and

---

[4] See *Archives de la Maison d'Orange-Nassau*, by Groen van Prinsterer, vol. v. p. 452, ed. 1861—a book not so well known in England as it deserves to be.

Princess of Orange should be declared Regents, with royal authority, the name and title only remaining in the Duke, would have been an admission of the Duke's right.[5] Nothing short of interrupting the succession, of making the monarchy elective, would satisfy his demands. Whether, if he had gained his ends, he would have set up Monmouth, as Monmouth foolishly hoped and expected; whether he aimed at being the all-powerful minister of an enfeebled king; whether he would have put down monarchy and set up republicanism, no one knows; and he was far too cautious to avow. It suited his purpose with the rabble to cry up, 'A Monmouth, a Monmouth!' but he could talk philosophical treason in his retirement with stiff-backed republicans like Waller, like Algernon Sidney, and the anti-monarchist relics of the old Commonwealth.

Parliament met at Oxford, March 21st, 1681. That ancient and loyal city, it was thought, might be more favourable for calm discussion than the heated, noisy, and factious

[5] 'One of the first things they did' (says Sir L. Jenkins, writing to the Prince of Orange, March 29, 1681), 'was to bring in the old Bill of Exclusion against the Duke. The opposers of that bill offered to their considerations several expedients, or rather one expedient, consisting of several parts; as that the Princess of Orange should have the whole administration and execution of the regal power, under the name of a regent during the Duke's life. They would not so far hearken to it as to turn the House into a committee of the whole House, which was necessary in order to a free debate. The regent was to take a present oath out of hand, and so were all persons in places of trust, to observe and execute the Act for a regency. The Duke was not to be in England, and the Parliament that last sat was to meet again, as soon as was possible, after the King's decease. But nothing of this would be hearkened to. The Exclusion must be had or nothing; and not only that, but, as one of the cabal said openly in the House, they must have the militia, the fleet, the strong places, &c., at their command, and an association to boot.' (Van Prinsterer, p. 488.) See also Lord Conway's Letter to the same personage on the same day (*ibid.* p. 491); only Conway adds that if Monmouth had been proposed for Regent there were probable grounds for believing that the project would have been accepted. It appears from Sidney's Letters (ii. 177) that this device, probably concocted by Halifax, was already known and talked of a month before.

purlieus of Westminster. All the vagabondism of the kingdom had scented the fray, and had been drawn to the metropolis in the hopes of profiting by it. The old disaffected party who had spent scambling lives in shifting from London to Amsterdam, Covenanters, Canon-Hill men preaching treason against the Government under pretence of conscience, framers and vendors of libels, inventors and retailers of scandal, false witnesses ready to swear anything, here picked up noblemen's guineas, and had the chance of being entertained in great houses. The example of Titus Oates, the idol of the Parliament, with his lodgings at Whitehall, and his pension of 10*l*. a week, was not lost upon hundreds of rogues as infamous, if not as successful, as himself. Coffee-houses and taverns offered a safe harbour, where hissing factionists might spit out their venom against the King and the Duke without fear of detection. Here it was that foolish and gaping listeners were assured, ' how the Queen and two of her women had walked three times round the corpse of Sir Edmondsbury Godfrey;' how an invasion was intended by the French and the Spaniards, led by the Papists; how the Government was turning the Tower guns upon the City; how innocent men and women were murdered in their beds by Jesuits and Irishmen: whilst noblemen, like Shaftesbury, dexterously turned these panics to account, and found in them the means for annoying and hampering the Court and its supporters.

The King expected to have found in Oxford an atmosphere less loaded with sedition; materials less likely to kindle the flames of a civil war, to which the nation was now rapidly approaching. He found himself mistaken. The members of the House who supported Shaftesbury and his party advised their various constituencies to send their representatives to Oxford defended by a dozen or ten men well armed with carbines and pistols.[6] The borough of South-

⁶ See the *State Papers* for March, 1680–81.

wark proposed to accompany its member out of London with a cavalcade of two or three hundred burgesses. Monmouth was attended with a hundred horse, Shaftesbury and Salisbury with a numerous retinue. They had agreed to wear purple ribbons on their swords as a party badge, and had provided for themselves, and all who were willing to espouse their principles, hatbands of the same colour, with lackered tin plates, and the words 'No Popery, no Slavery.' Nor were the usual elements of disorder absent. Oxford was astonished to find its quiet cloisters and quadrangles invaded by the refuse of the Westminster coffee-houses; to see libels and caricatures vended about its streets; whilst ribald songs and ballads were thrust into the hands of the passengers. Every device was employed by the popular party to infuriate the passions of the mob, and prejudice their minds against the King and his brother. In one of the caricatures of the times, Charles was represented as a showman, with his box of Parliament puppets at his back, and the Saints pushing him into a ditch, with the motto—

'Help Cooper, Hughes, and Snow,'
To pull down the Raree Show!'

In another the Duke was represented as half Jesuit and half Devil. In one hand, as a Jesuit, he held a firebrand, with which he set fire to London; whilst half a dozen jockeys, booted and spurred, mounted on the back of the Church of England, were riding it as an old hack to Rome.

The King was in a great strait. With the exception of Halifax he had no minister of any ability in his council with whom he could advise; and though Halifax had spoken with great energy against the Exclusion Bill, and personally hated Shaftesbury, he was secretly in the interest of William of Orange. The desire of Charles to find some accommodation, the sacrifices he had professed his willingness to make pro-

⁷ Door-Keepers in the House of Lords.

vided the succession remained undisturbed, had failed to
satisfy his enemies, and filled his friends with dismay. No
one could anticipate when the King would make a stand, or
what concession he would refuse. His apparent vacillation,
added to the notion, deeply rooted in the minds of men, that,
if pressed hard enough, he would eventually yield, and, preferring pleasure to business, throw the reins of government
into the hands of the Exclusionists, promised an easy victory
to his opponents. At last the King was brought to bay, the
prey was in their hands; one more effort, and the day was
their own.

On Saturday, the 26th of March, Charles took his seat in
the House of Lords. Shaftesbury approached him with a
sinister and supercilious smile, the habitual expression of his
pale and haggard countenance. He was a little man, with
ill-shaped legs, and suffered from an infirmity which made
his person far from agreeable. His long and bitter opposition to the Court, now on the eve of its reward, had not contributed to render him more gracious. The curiosity of the
Lords was excited, and the eyes of all were fixed upon him
as, disengaging himself from a crowd of his admirers, he
handed in an anonymous letter to the King. The King read
it with ill-suppressed emotion. It demanded that due
securities should be taken for the Protestant religion, and
that Monmouth should be declared his successor without
delay. The demand was as insolent as it was unusual. It
was calculated to provoke the King's resentment and throw
him off his guard, and that was evidently the expectation of
its framers. Addressing himself to the Earl, Charles said,
with great dignity and moderation, 'I should be very glad
to have a legitimate son, and be able in honour and conscience to see a child of my own capable of succeeding me,
rather than my brother and my brother's children. But no
considerations shall induce me to take resolutions contrary

to law and justice, and other means must be sought for satisfying my people than measures so unjust and odious.' 'Rely upon us,' said the Earl, 'and we will make laws to justify the act.' 'My lord,' replied the King, 'let there be no self-delusion. I will never yield, nor suffer myself to be intimidated. Men become ordinarily more timid as they grow old; as for me, I shall be, on the contrary, more bold and firm, and I will not stain my life and reputation in the little time perhaps that remains for me to live.'[8] From that moment the power of the Earl was extinguished—the tide rapidly turned. The King's party everywhere found their confidence reassured by this one instance of firmness, and monarchy from that day was stronger than ever.

Historians, with Burnet at their head, see nothing worthy of remark or praise in this long and continuous effort of Charles to preserve the succession unbroken. They see nothing in this struggle for law and justice, however mixed up with much confusion in the mind of the King, worthy the attention of the moralist or divine. Of ease, of popularity, of natural inclinations, it does not appear to them that the sacrifice made by Charles for the rights of a brother whom he could not much love or esteem, and who had been the chief cause of all his troubles, ought to form the least item in our estimate of his character. We profess to think otherwise. It seems to us that this is the one great redeeming trait in the conduct of a monarch whose life, even when it was not devoted to pleasure and licentiousness, was apparently so aimless and unsteady, so devoid of all noble purpose. That Charles should have struggled so long and so firmly in behalf of what he felt was right, in spite of all the opposition he encountered, in spite of his love of ease, his own sense of

[8] See *North's Examen,* p. 123, whose accuracy in this matter has been strikingly confirmed by an original letter of Barillon, prin ed by Mr. Christie in the Appendix to his *Life of Lord Shaftesbury.*

the abuse of his functions as a king, and his convictions of unworthiness as a man, was an indication of a better and nobler nature, still existing and still uncorrupted among many debasing vices—a nature which occasionally burst through the clouds that obscured it, and might have been fostered and developed under more favourable circumstances. We see in Charles the example of a man who, in the total wreck of all religious faith, and disregard of the ordinary rules of life, has yet retained some sense of rectitude, to which he clings, all the more firmly and earnestly, because of the confusion of his moral instincts. Such men, though rare, are not wholly imaginary, especially among ourselves. That one intense regard for law and justice we have had to notice in the defence of his brother's rights was to Charles like the Roman soldier's oath to his emperor; it was the last plank the Englishman abandons—the last step between him and irredeemable corruption. That it was not lost upon the nation is clear from the result. If James mounted the throne, without opposition and without a murmur—if his subjects, notwithstanding all their previous disquietude and excitements, peaceably acquiesced in his succession—if they felt that it was right and lawful—they had been brought to those sentiments by the efforts of Charles II.

James was not young when he ascended the throne, as other monarchs had been before him—not young like Edward II., Richard II., or Henry VI.—and he had never had the reputation of being a rash man. He was now in his fifty-second year; had been long trained in the school of adversity; had had many more years' experience at home and abroad than any king that ever ruled in England. When he was only nine years old he was sent by his father to demand the surrender of Hull from Sir John Hotham; the same year he served under his father at the celebrated battle of Edgehill; four years after he fell into the hands of the Parliament, was carried to London, and after various attempts at escape, showing even then great presence of mind, he contrived to regain his liberty and landed in Holland in 1648. In 1652 he entered the French army, and served under Marshal Turenne with great gallantry. In 1660 he returned to England with his brother, a zealous Protestant. In his office as Lord High Admiral he distinguished himself by his close application to business. He reformed the navy, he studied trade, he gave encouragement to the East India and African Companies. In the wars that followed with the Dutch he displayed the utmost coolness, presence of mind, and rare qualities of seamanship. Whatever might be his excesses in earlier years, he had of late, at all events, assumed a more grave and steady demeanour. His industry, his frugality, and the austereness of his manners, formed a striking contrast to that ease, indolence, and love of pleasure which in Charles seemed rather to increase than diminish with his age, and pointed out James to the eyes of the nation as a much fitter ruler of a great people. Comparisons were drawn in his favour to the disadvantage of his brother. He was not only thought to be more grave, steady, and temperate than Charles, which was undoubtedly true, but to possess genius superior to his brother. 'He was,' says Burnet, '*naturally* candid and sincere, and a firm friend!' He had a great desire to understand affairs, and spared no pains, no labour, to become thoroughly acquainted with them. All these good qualities he was thought to have lost by his conversion to the Roman Catholic religion, or, to speak more correctly, by his open profession of it in 1672. His own account of this matter is so important and so curious that we give it here from his own narrative :—' It was about this time, in the beginning of the year 1669, that his Royal Highness, who had it long in his thoughts that the Church of England was the only true Church, was more sensibly touched in conscience, and began to think seriously of his salvation. Accordingly he sent for one Father Simons, a Jesuit, who had the reputation of a very learned man, to discourse with him on that subject; and when he came he told him the good intentions he had of being a Catholick, and treated with him about his being reconciled to the Church. After much discourse about the matter, the Father very sincerely told him that, unless he would quit the Communion of the Church of England, he could not be received into the Catholick Church. The Duke then said he thought it might be done by a dispensation from the Pope, alleging to him the singularity of his case, and the advantage it might bring to the Catholick religion in general, and in particular to those of it in England, if he might have such dispensation for outwardly appearing a Protestant, at least till he could own himself publicly to be a Catholick, with more security to his own person and advantage to them. But the good Father insisted, that even the Pope himself had not the power to grant it, for it was an unalterable doctrine of the Catholick Church *not to do ill that good might follow.*'[9] Finding evasion impossible, he resolved openly to embrace the Roman Catholic faith, not, however, without consoling himself with the thought that the step was, after all, not so perilous as he had imagined; that 'the Church of England men' were not 'very averse to the Catholick religion;' that 'many that went under that name had their religion to choose, and went to church for company's sake;' that the troops and officers then on foot would serve the crown and ask no questions; and that the prosecution of the Nonconformists by the rigorous members of the Church of England would encourage the former to demand toleration.

This is no uncommon delusion among converts of King James's stamp; but they are not in general so rapidly or

* *Life of James II.* vol. i. p. 440.

cruelly undeceived as was James. He honestly refused to
conceal his religion ; he resolutely withstood the repeated
exhortations of Charles to moderate his zeal and make concessions to popular prejudices. Had he only been willing
to attend his brother occasionally to the Chapel at Whitehall ; to have offered the shadow of a concession ; to have
enabled the courtiers to hold out hopes of his re-conversion,
or to have made it appear that he was not so much of a
Roman Catholic as people apprehended, he would have saved
himself, his brother, and his friends a world of trouble and
annoyance. No Popish plots, no Exclusion Bill, no enterprise
of the Prince of Orange, had it been devised, would then
have had the least chance of success. But James, in matters
of religion, was as firm and unbending as Charles was the
opposite. In the days of his youth he had been a sincere
Protestant ; he had resisted the efforts of his mother to bring
over the Duke of Gloucester to that faith which in his later
years he considered himself bound in conscience to avow and
protect, and, as some think, to promote at all hazards. *Qui
nescit dissimulare nescit regnare* was never more applicable
to any prince than to James. It was the only quality he
wanted to have ensured him success. He was the only
prince of his age who had not the least skill in dissembling
his feelings, his thoughts, or his intentions, and he was
surrounded by the profoundest adepts in that art ; he was a
naked and open prey to all around him—to Louis, to Barillon,
to William of Orange, to Sunderland, to Halifax ; even to
bunglers in hypocrisy, such as Churchill, Prince George of
Denmark, and Princess Anne. There might be something of
pride in this ; it is not impossible that he despised the power
of his opponents, and was apt to underrate danger, partly
from his undoubted natural courage, partly from his utter
inexperience of human nature, and his inability to penetrate
the characters of men. If there was the smallest crevice in

other men, Charles managed to peer through it; if they had been as transparent as glass, James would never have discovered them. Rochester said of the two royal brothers, and his saying is repeated with commendation by Burnet, that Charles 'could see things if he would, and the duke would see things if he could.' The fact was just the reverse— Charles would see things if he could; was always on the alert and watchful, when he appeared utterly careless and indifferent; but James never would see things, even when he could; and that paved the way to his ruin. So far from wishing to see things, he had the habit of resolutely shutting his eyes against them. He would never believe that Protestantism had any strong hold upon Englishmen; he would never believe that his son-in-law, the Prince of Orange, would attempt to dethrone him, or his daughters forsake him; he would never believe that the nobility of England would enter into treasonable correspondence with an usurper; he would never believe that the Church of England could be otherwise than submissive to the Crown; or that the army and the officers of both services would go over to his enemy for a point of religion. He would never believe that Churchill, whom he had loaded with favours and trusted implicitly, could desert him for William, and, therefore, he refused to seize his person. He would never believe that Sunderland, who most grossly betrayed and abused his confidence, was any other than a sincere and honest adviser. But worst of all for himself and his own happiness, he would never believe, when the selfish and dishonest had betrayed him, but that all his subjects were equally bent upon his destruction. No king ever came to the throne of riper age than James; with more warning, more experience, had he been willing to turn it to account, of the temper and disposition of the people he was called to govern. But experience, though purchased at the cost of much suffering, was lost upon him. He thought himself a much greater adept in government than his brother was; he thought the concessions made by Charles to popular wishes were a sign of weakness, and a desire to avoid collision with Parliament was a diminution of the royal authority. He thought the easy, undignified manners of his brother impaired the majesty of the Crown; therefore he pursued an opposite course. He was stiff, formal, and ceremonious; he gave audience with his hat on, and only in the presence chamber; he kept his nobles at a distance; he treated his parliaments with rigour, and received the applauses of his people without courtesy or condescension. And whilst his natural manners were ungracious, his rigid adherence to his new faith, and the dislike he could not help exhibiting to those who opposed it, shut him out from the confidence and sympathy of all, except the narrow circle of his queen and his father confessor, and the small knot of flatterers who were interested in keeping from him all information, except such as was agreeable to him. Kings at the best find great difficulty in coming to a right understanding of their subjects' wishes and dispositions, but James took every precaution to increase those difficulties. When the blow fell, he was utterly unprepared for it. He had listened to no advice, and he now found himself without advisers. He had given his confidence to none but those who had abused it.

The last scene of his reign was an exhibition of the most pitiable vacillation and imbecility. He did not want for resolution. It was one of his maxims that 'a king should never recede;' yet he took no step before his fall that he did not retrace, nor resolve on any measure he did not almost immediately retract. He was not deficient in courage. Had he attacked William on his first landing, he could have compelled him to re-embark, or at least have prevented many of the disaffected from joining him. Under Turenne and Condé he had displayed skill and presence of mind; in his engagements with the Dutch he had fought successfully against great odds. Now he forsook his kingdom, without striking a blow; or, rather, he was driven out of it like a dog by fictitious reports. He was pitied for his hardships, his misfortune, the treason of his ministers, the undutifulness of his daughters, the duplicity of his son-in-law, but he contrived to stifle that pity by a flight of which it is not easy to affirm whether it was more ignominious or more impolitic. Even at the last it was said of him by a shrewd observer, 'that he might have kept the crown upon his head as easily as his hat in a high wind. That wind indeed would have borne hard upon it, but would only have carried off those superfluous ornaments which were too weakly riveted, and too little united to bear a storm.' But James could never understand the salutary truth, that he was really most powerful when abandoned by his friends and advisers, and most strong when he was most defenceless. It may be said in his excuse that, like his brother Charles, he was undoubtedly haunted by his father's fate, though the effect of it on the conduct of the two brothers was totally different.

One remark in conclusion. Unlike as the two brothers were in almost all respects, grave and numerous as were their vices and their failings, they had this one virtue in common—they were both prepared to suffer for what they thought a righteous cause, and they gave most unmistakable proofs of their willingness to suffer. No threats, no intimidations, no discomfort, could have induced Charles to abandon or betray his brother's rights. It is clear to us that, as he sacrificed his ease and pleasure, he would have sacrificed his crown and, if need had been, his life in their defence. And the same may be said of James. He may have been weak, he may have been bigoted, he may have pursued his purposes with an arbitrary disregard to the rights and opinions of others. He may have thought that in securing tolerance for those of his own faith, 'he was,' as he said, 'growing old and must take *large steps*, else if he should happen to die, he might leave them in a worse condition than he found them.' But that he was honest and sincere in his religious convictions; that no dangers, no temptations, no political necessity or interest could induce him to abandon or conceal or modify them, is beyond contradiction. Such a man cannot have been the grim, melodramatic tyrant that Macaulay has painted him. He was punished bitterly enough for his wrong deeds; but, so far as this nation is concerned, the greatest wrong that he did was that he found the monarchy hereditary, and left it at the mercy of a faction.

Charles I., by his death, sanctified the cause he had mismanaged in his life, and contrived to associate with the monarchy a sense of personal and romantic attachment which nothing could obliterate. In Cromwell, the man triumphed, but his cause was lost; the inevitable fate of all rebellions attempted 'with a reasonable prospect of success.' Without a soldier at his back, or a guinea in his pocket—without one single commanding excellence, moral or material—Charles II. raised the monarchy from its ruins, and transmitted it to his brother with its hereditary laurel untarnished and undiminished. But James II., through his imbecility and folly, lost all the advantages thus bequeathed to him. Worst of all, he enabled his Whig and republican opponents— *O facinus indignum!*—to lay the crown and liberties of this great nation at the feet of a stranger, to take them or reject them on his own conditions! Who then can wonder that, whilst William's Dutch guards dined at his table, Marlborough and the Whig leaders crouched behind his chair?

But we must here leave our authoress for a while, until her subsequent volumes enable us to pursue the fortunes of the Stuarts in their exile.

SHAKSPEARE.[1]

THE two works at the head of this article are samples of what has been done for Shakspearian literature within the last few years. It is a matter of congratulation to all students of the great dramatist that the appliances of modern science should have given us an exact facsimile of the first collected edition of the poet's works, and thus have enabled all readers to judge for themselves of the state and arrangement of the text as it first left the hands of the poet's literary executors. Mr. Neil's little book has done good service in presenting the facts of the poet's biography, and the most material documents relating to it, in their strict chronological order. The value of the slenderest notices derived from original papers in illustrating not only the life of the poet, of his family, and his neighbours in Warwickshire, but the spirit and manners of the period, can never be fully appreciated until the whole mass of evidence has been thoroughly sifted. Availing ourselves therefore of what has been brought to light by the indefatigable diligence of the poet's admirers within the last few years, and of such papers as still remain unpublished in the Record Office, we propose to lay before our readers a sketch of Shakspeare's life and times, carefully eliminating from the former those supposed facts and theories which

[1] From the *Quarterly Review* for July, 1871, under the following heading :—*Shakespeare : The first Folio Edition of* 1623. Reproduced under the immediate supervision of Howard Staunton, by Photo-lithography. Folio. *Shakespere : a Critical Biography*. By Samuel Neil. 12mo. London, 1861.

have gathered round it on the faith of documents now generally regarded with discredit.

Of Shakspeare's great contemporaries, by descent as well as by feeling, Spenser was intimately connected with the aristocracy of England. His life was spent at a distance from the metropolis. During his long residence in Ireland he treasured up the impressions he had received in his youth of the glories of Elizabeth, and the grandeur of Protestantism,—its heroic sufferings, its eventual triumph over all forms of falsehood and deceit, moral, religious, social, scientific, and political. These impressions were never disturbed by too close an approximation to realities. Happily, it was never the poet's lot to witness the party and personal squabbles in which his knights indulged too freely in the court of his Gloriana, or to see prelates and Puritans divided, and both equally forgetful of mutual charity, in bitter controversies about square caps and white surplices. Hooker, on the other hand, owed his descent to the burgher class. The chief part of his life was spent in the quiet seclusion of the university. If Spenser was mainly indebted to his imagination for his knowledge of the external world, Hooker judged it by his books. His mind was as deeply tinctured with fathers and schoolmen—with an ideal Christianity enshrined in the past—as Spenser's imagination lingered over mediæval romances and Arthurian legends. Over both the past had a stronger hold than the present; the τὸ καλὸν of the one and the τὸ δίκαιον of the other are equally heroical—both equally transcend the capabilities and the limits of poor, failing, common-place humanity.

It was otherwise with Shakspeare. Like Spenser, he was allied by his mother's side to gentle blood;[2] like Hooker, he was linked to the burgher classes by the stronger parent.

[2] 'She was one of the heirs of Robert Arden of Wellingcote.'—*Grant of Arms*

Brought up in the country till the age of manhood, thrown early upon his own resources, obliged to no college-fellowship like Hooker, to no diplomatic appointment like Spenser, he was tossed on the seething waves of the metropolis, or rather cast himself upon them, with the same boldness, perhaps the same apparent recklessness, as he had entered on a marriage at eighteen, when he was no better than a poor apprentice or foreman to a failing glover in a poor country town. Of his life-struggles—and they must have been many—he has left no sign. Of his patience, his endurance, his solitary determination, whilst unassisted and unadvised he carved out his way from the safe obscurity of Stratford to the highest pinnacle of fame, he has told us nothing. This early familiarity with the hard realities of life left no trace on his mind, as these things leave scars and traces on inferior intellects, beyond perhaps that sympathy with humanity, that profound appreciation of it in all its forms, which is one of his greatest characteristics as a poet.

How far the circumstances of his life and times may have determined or assisted the development of his genius, it is not easy to ascertain. Of no other English poet can it be said with greater justice: 'Poeta nascitur non fit.' Many indeed, of Shakspeare's enthusiastic admirers will not allow that he owed anything to art or to learning. They claim for Nature and for natural inspiration alone those great masterpieces of invention in which others have professed to find traces of the most profound philosophy, the most acute physiological knowledge, the clearest distinctions of races, the fullest appreciation of all forms of poetry, the exactest study of man and of nature.

That Shakspeare owed most to nature, that his obligations to learning or accidental circumstances were but slight, we may fully concede, without at the same time entirely over-

looking the obvious advantages afforded by the times for
dramatic composition, and the traces of classical education
to be found throughout the poet's works. The same keen
and unerring instinct which from a single glance could body
forth and project in a visible form the whole life and character of a man, however remote from ordinary observation,
would by a similar power extract from books—poor and
meagre in themselves—the quintessence of a life rich and
varied, instinct with thoughts and feelings, such as inferior
intelligences would fail to gather from the most perfect
productions of the greatest genius. The dreary chronicle,
the blundering biography, the vapidest translations of Cæsar
or of Sallust, were instruments sufficient to set at work that
innate power of the poet which, like Nature itself, develops
the most perfect and glorious results from the most contemptible and unworthy materials. That is what we mean
by genius. With ordinary men the instruments by which
they work must bear some proportion in dignity and value
to the end to be produced; but genius is divine and mira-
culous in this, that it is not tied to the order, methods, and
instruments by which common men are bound. Admitting,
then, that no amount of training or study can account for
Shakspeare's plays, admitting also that the poet was little
indebted to school learning for his wonderful productions,
that would not necessarily invalidate the importance of his
education, or the beneficial influences of his peculiar times.
Brought up at the grammar-school of Stratford, he would
acquire as much knowledge of Latin and French as fell to the
lot of most of his contemporaries. Before the great public
schools had attracted much attention—before, indeed, they
were accessible to the large majority of the English country
gentlemen, owing to bad roads and inefficient means of
travelling—the grammar-schools of our country towns furnished the only means for the training and education of the

gentry and richer citizens throughout the largest extent of England. Were the results poor and unsatisfactory? Can any period be pointed out in our history which provided on the whole abler schoolmasters or scholars more deeply interested in learning? It is impossible to open any popular book of those times without being struck with its rich abundance of classical allusion. If this be attributed to pedantry, that pedantry was universal. But we have a more unsuspicious testimony. Not only did the dramatists of the age freely borrow from classical antiquity their plots, their quotations, their witticisms—and that for dramas intended for a popular audience—without scruple, without dread of being misunderstood—but in the humours of Eastcheap, in the busiest haunts of life, 'the honey of Hybla,' 'pitiful Titan,' 'Phœbus the wandering knight,' 'Diana's foresters,' 'homo is a *common* name for all men,' are freely bandied from mouth to mouth, with not so much as a thought on the part of the author that his allusions will not be fully understood by his audience.

If Shakspeare, then, had, as Johnson observes, 'little Latin and less Greek,' the admission at least implies that he had some knowledge of both—enough of Latin to read ordinary Latin books and translations, and more than enough of genius to extract from what he did read the pith and substance. It was an age throughout of Latin cultivation. Greek, with few exceptions, was unattainable, except to men of fortune, or rare scholars at the universities. In fact, Shakspeare was the poet of an age that loved learning for its own sake—an age that had come into a new inheritance of breathless wonder and interest—

> 'Like some watcher of the skies,
> When a new planet swims into his ken,

and he would not have been the man of his time, nor the poet that he was, had he been wholly indifferent to learning or wholly unacquainted with it.

Nor were the times less favourable to him as a dramatic poet. The Reformation had done much to develop individual character. The feeling of a common Christendom, the sense of submission to the Church as a great society, the duty of not diverging widely from the authorized limits of religious opinion and belief, had all passed away. Each man felt bound to carve out a faith for himself, and to discard as worthless—at least, as suspicious—whatever was recommended or received on authority or tradition. Bacon has said that time, like a river, brings down on its surface the straw and the stubble, but the solid and the gold have long since sunk to the bottom. What seems like a paradox to the philosopher, was accepted by the reformers as an undoubted and undeniable truth. Authority was the test of falsehood, not of truth. Uniformity of belief was not to be found in nations or in single men. No two agreed. Diversity of faith led to diversity of character; and if there be one phenomenon more striking than another in the reign of Elizabeth, it is the strange humours, the extravagances, the conceits, the motley exhibition of dress, manners, sentiments and opinions, admitting no central authority, bound by no restraint beyond the caprice of the individual. There was, besides, no standard of taste, no school of criticism, no public opinion, literary or otherwise, to which men could defer, or, probably, if there had been, would have cared to defer. There were no settled forms of English—no deference to classical models, which all consented to accept. No long-established rules imposed a wholesome restraint on the teeming invention and luxuriant wit of the Elizabethan writers.

But while the Reformation had been thus powerful in developing individual character in its widest extent; whilst men revelled in their new-found liberty, and cared not to determine when it degenerated into licentiousness; whilst nature avenged herself on the dry, logical studies of a preceding age by a reaction which sometimes trespassed into animalism, the material forms of the old world and the old religion still held their ground. In the parish church the service was in English, not in Latin; but the ceremonies, the dresses, the fasts, and the festivals, though curtailed, remained essentially the same. Sermons were scarcely more frequent than they had been in Popish times; men and women went to confession—paid their Easter offerings—looked up to the parish priest as their spiritual guide. Most of these priests had been in their livings when Edward VI. was crowned— had complied with Queen Mary—had re-complied with Elizabeth—accommodated their new to their ancient faith— doubtless retained many of their old Romish practices and predilections—and were winked at by their bishops, especially in distant provinces. How could it be otherwise, unless the rulers of the Church were prepared to see nine-tenths of the parishes of England deprived of all spiritual instructors, and churches and congregations falling into irremediable decay? Though Puritanism was creeping on with rapid and stealthy pace towards the close of the century, it numbered as yet a contemptible and unnational minority. It had not yet contrived to inspire men with one intense and narrow sentimentalism; to force upon their unwilling acceptance its straitened notions of a straitened creed. It had not yet taught them to look with sour suspicion on all forms of amusement as ungodly, or to suspect Popery in mince-pies and cheerful village festivals. So ancient customs remained as they had remained ages before. Christmas, with its pageants and processions, its mummers and its good fare; Twelfth-night, Midsummer's Eve, St. Mark's, St. Valentine's, and All Saints' days, were duly observed. No inductive philosophy had yet appeared to disturb the popular belief in fairies or in witchcraft, in ghosts or in spectres; no ruthless geographer had stripped 'the still-vexed Bermoothes' of its Ariel and its Caliban, or buried the wand which raised such potent marvels.

By the ingle-nook, especially in country towns like Stratford—half a century behind the metropolis, and exempt from those changes to which a great metropolis is subject—men still talked of elves and goblins, and still devoutly believed in them. They repeated from father to son the local traditions of their own and the neighbouring counties. They knew the battle-fields of Tewkesbury; they had heard tell of the encounter when the Severn hid its head in fear of the blood-stained combatants. Kenilworth and Coventry, Gloucester and Northampton, were studded with historical associations. And many an anecdote, many a feat, a trait of manner, of person, and character, of English worthies would thus be handed down which would be sought in vain in the chronicles of Hall or of Hollinshed. For, unlike the wars of modern times, the civil wars of England were fought by the tenants and labourers of the lord, who returned at the close of the struggle to the plough and the spade, to live and die, in most instances, at no great distance from the scene of their military exploits. So sons and grandsons learned to repeat the stories of meek Henry VI., of the fierce and forbidding Richard III., of the hateful De la Pole and the gracious Edward.

The exact year in which Shakspeare abandoned Stratford for the metropolis cannot now be ascertained, nor yet the motive or the manner of his departure. It has been assumed that he quitted his native town shortly after his marriage with Ann Hathaway. The birth of a daughter, Susannah, in May, 1583, followed by twins, Hamnet and Judith, in 1585, has been adopted as a sufficient reason why he should leave a place and occupation in which his father had not apparently prospered, and enter upon a profession more congenial to the bent of his genius. A story, handed down by the parish clerk of Stratford in 1693, who was then upwards of eighty years old, contains the only trustworthy record of this period of the poet's life. According to this statement, Shakspeare was apprenticed to a butcher, left his master, went to London, 'and there was received into the playhouse as a servitor, and by this means had an opportunity to be what he afterwards proved.' That the substance of the story is correct, though it may have suffered from the manner of the telling, can hardly be doubted, considering the authority from which it emanates. A parish clerk in a country town, generally the depositary of the local traditions of the place, and living so near the poet's own times, was hardly likely to have invented such a tale, though he may have disfigured it. That Shakspeare's father, combining a variety of kindred occupations—no very unusual practice in a country town—at once glover, maltster, farmer, appraiser, frequently engaged in litigation, and therefore not unfrequently in debt, should not have considered the occupation of a butcher in a country town as a derogatory employment for one of a family of ten children, may be naturally assumed. Nor by the word 'butcher' is it necessary to understand exactly what that word implies now. Popular tradition associated the poet with his father's occupation; and if Shakspeare had never left Stratford he would, like others of his contemporaries, have grown old in his native town no more than glover, butcher, or maltster, as his father had been.

As for his running away to London and leaving his wife and family dependent on the casual charity of others, that story can only be accepted with many modifications. The distance of Stratford from the metropolis, the difficulties of travelling in those days, the improbability that his father would or could have advanced him the necessary means for so doing, and burthened himself with his son's family, must be taken into account. It is much more probable that if Shakspeare did not join one of the many companies of actors who periodically appeared in Stratford or its vicinity he was brought to London by the Catesbys or the Cloptons, or some one of the powerful families in the county, who had as sufficient reasons for hating the Lucys as Shakspeare himself.

And here, before we pass on to trace the future career of the poet, it will be as well to allude to the anecdote first published by Rowe and repeated by most of the poet's biographers. 'He had, by a misfortune' (says Rowe) 'common enough to young fellows, fallen into ill company; and amongst them some that made a frequent practice of deer-stealing, engaged him more than once in robbing a park that belonged to Sir Thomas Lucy, of Charlecote, near Stratford. For this he was prosecuted by that gentleman, as he thought, somewhat too severely, and in order to revenge that ill-usage he made a ballad upon him.'[3] And though this, probably the first essay of his poetry, be lost, yet it is said to have been so very bitter that it redoubled the prosecution against him to that degree that he was obliged to leave his business and family in Warwickshire for some time and shelter himself in London. Omitting the modern decorations of the story, we may admit the facts of the deer-stealing in the poet's case, as in that of many others of his contemporaries. It may be hard to point to any direct evidence in the poet's works in confirmation of this act of youthful delinquency; but we think that the impression left on the minds of most of his readers will warrant the belief that the poet had been a lad of spirit, of no 'vinegar aspect;' popular—boy, youth, and man—among his contemporaries, and taking life easy

[3] Compare the expression: 'An I have not ballads made on you all, and sung to filthy tunes.'

in all its stages, laughing heartily at a jest, and perfectly willing to bear his part in one. So complete and perfect are the harmony and unity of his dramatic characters that we cannot safely derive from them any hypothesis as to the poet's dislikes and predilections; yet the humours of Eastcheap, the mad pranks of Prince Hal and his associates, the reckless adventures of hair-brained, hot-blooded youth, are painted by the poet with such a zest as can scarcely be held otherwise than an indication of his own temperament. But deer-stealing, though a perilous offence, was too popular and too common in all ranks to entail disgrace or compel an offender to flee from his native town. That Shakspeare entertained a personal dislike for the Lucys, we can well believe; and the more so, as of all his signal and numerous opportunities to take poetical vengeance on his unfriends, that of the Lucys is the only prominent instance.[4] But the feud between the Lucys and the natives of Stratford was of earlier date than this affair of the deer-stealing, and crops out on various occasions. The Lucys were arrogant and imperious Puritans; the good town of Stratford, with the Cloptons and the Catesbys, were zealous adherents of the ancient faith. In the reign of Henry VIII., William Lucy, the father of Shakspeare's Sir Thomas, the friend of Bishop Latimer, had more than once endeavoured to bring down the king's displeasure on the citizens of Stratford for religious differences; and more than once a riot had ensued, in which the Grevilles and the Combes, in conjunction with the Lucys,

[4] That the Lucys were fond of litigation is implied by the opening lines of *The Merry Wives of Windsor*, and justified by history. In the conversation between Shallow, Slender, and Evans, Slender says, 'They may give the dozen white luces in their coat.' To which Shallow replies, 'It is an *old* coat,' evidently referring to the family pride of the Lucys, as well as their antiquity. Evans: 'The dozen white louses do become an *old* coat well; it agrees well, passant.' (That being their heraldic characteristic; 12 luces, passant.) 'It is a familiar beast to man, and signifies—*love*.' Excessively comical in the mouth of a Welshman!

would have ridden roughshod over the burgesses, of whom
Shakspeare's father was afterwards high bailiff, if they had
not been supported by the Cloptons and the Catesbys.⁵ The
Lucys were powerful at the Court of the Tudors, for they
had blood-royal in their veins; and as many of their opponents were Roman Catholics, or had relapsed from
Protestantism to the old faith, one of their most effective
instruments for satisfying personal pique, under the garb of
patriotism, was to put in force the penal laws and the power
of the Crown against their rivals. In a commission issued
in 1592 for persecuting and presenting recusants, directed
to the Lucys and the Grevilles, and obtained apparently by
their means, it is curious to observe that they presented
as a recusant Mrs. Clopton, 'widow of Wm. Clopton, Esq.;⁵
but in their second return they proceed to rectify their con
venient mistake by the naïve admission: Mrs. Clopton,
presented as a recusant, was 'mistaken, and goeth now to
church!' In the same presentment, next to Henley-in-
Arden, occurs the parish of Sombourne, with this notice:
'Mrs. Mary Arden, widow, presented for a wilful recusant
before our last certificate, continues still obstinate in her
recusancy,' and is accordingly indicted. By the same commissioners, John Shakspeare, the poet's father, is returned
as a recusant; but this note is subjoined in his case and
in that of eight others: 'It is said that the last nine come
not to church for fear of process for debt.'⁶

Now, though it is true that already, some six years before the date of this commission, Shakspeare's father had
fallen into difficulties and was deprived of his alderman's
gown, it is hardly probable, had he been notoriously affected
towards the Protestant religion, that his name would have
been inserted in the return of the commissioners; for the

¹ Unpublished papers in the Record Office.
² MSS. in the Record Office.

object of the commission was not so much to learn who absented themselves from the parish church, as to discover Jesuits, seminary priests, and papal emissaries, now, more than ever, busily engaged in sowing disaffection among the people of Warwickshire, and those who harboured them. The government of the day—as is clear from the cases cited by the commissioners—required attendance at church once a month; that done, it did not trouble itself with inflicting further penalties, or requiring more distinct proofs of the recusant's loyalty. John Shakspeare was a recusant in this sense, and the note was appended to explain the reason why he had not complied with the requirements of the government. If then he were a recusant in the ordinary use of the term, this might account for the pecuniary difficulties into which he fell some years before, when the government of Elizabeth exacted the fines for recusancy with unsparing severity.

That the townspeople of Stratford cordially hated the Lucys, and were particularly anxious to avoid incurring their displeasure, is apparent from the records of the town, printed by Mr. Halliwell. He selects numerous items of sack and sugar for the lips of Sir Thomas and his chief friends, Sir Fulke and Sir Edward Greville. In one entry, dated 1598, the chamberlain very bluntly records: 'Paid to Sir Fowle (*sic*) Greville, for nothing, 40s. !' And again in 1601, in an action for trespass brought by Sir Edward Greville against the burgesses of Stratford, the name of John Shakspeare appears as a witness on behalf of the defendants.

We are, therefore, inclined to believe that Shakspeare's departure from his native town was a more deliberate act than Rowe's anecdote of the deer-stealing and the vengeance of the Lucys would lead us to expect. It is impossible that the poet, living so near to Coventry, should not often have witnessed the crude dramatic representations of the times, and equally impossible that the dramatic genius within him, that was never crude, never less than powerful, should not have been mightily stirred by what he saw. 'Mute, inglorious Miltons' may have died unseen; but that was because their Miltonic genius was neither all-powerful nor lasting. It was the slave, not the master, of circumstances. But overpowering genius, like mastering passion, admits of no repulse, and suffers no cold obstruction. Besides it must be remembered that in Shakspeare's time—before Puritanism had done its work—the profession of an actor as well as of a dramatist led to fame and opulence. The stage had not yet been regarded as the illusion of antichrist. It still shared with the pulpit the task of instructing the people. It still bore upon its features the marks of its ecclesiastical origin. It still reckoned among its authors and patrons bishops like Bale and Still.

On Shakspeare's arrival in London all accounts concur in asserting that the poet embraced the profession of an actor; and the old clerk's account—that 'he was received into the playhouse as a servitor'—is not without probability. Such a practice was not unusual. Mr. Halliwell has referred to an instance in Henslow's diary in which it is stated that 'he hired a covenant servant, William Kendall, for two years, after the statute of Winchester, with two single pence, and to give him for his said service every week of his playing in London 10s. and in the country 5s.'

Of the theatres then in vogue the most eminent was the Globe, on the Bankside; and with this or the Black Friars, belonging to the same company, Shakspeare was connected, and in one or other of these all his plays were subsequently performed. In 1603 the company consisted of Laurence Fletcher, William Shakspeare, Richard Burbage, Augustine Phillipes, John Heminge, and Henry Condell,

Shakspeare's literary executors, and several others; the most eminent performers of their age. The theatre, an hexagonal wooden building, was partly thatched and partly exposed to the weather, and the performances generally, if not always, took place in the afternoon, then the idlest time of the day. Rooms or boxes were provided for the wealthier classes, the admission to which varied from a shilling to half a crown, whilst the frequenters of the pit either stood or sate on the ground. The wits and critics of the times were admitted on the stage; and so far was this practice from detracting, as might be imagined, from the interest and illusion of the play, this identification of the audience with the actors, at a time when the scenery was of the simplest kind, and the costume of the actors differed not from that of ordinary life, must on most occasions have given to the scene a lifelike reality to which we are strangers. Such briefly were the theatres in which Shakspeare—

'Made those flights upon the banks of Thames
That so did take Eliza and our James.'

Such, also, in the dearth of clubs and coffee-houses, of novels, newspapers, and other means of information, were the studies as well as the entertainment of the age, where men picked up, in the main, whatever they knew of foreign countries and distant times, of classical lore and English history. And here, by the great good fortune of that age, were brought together the court and its statesmen, from Nonsuch House or Westminster—the Sidneys, the Raleighs, the Essexes, the Cecils, and the Bacons; the soldier of fortune, like Falstaff, the grave citizen, the humourist and man of pleasure, the weather-beaten adventurer of the water-side just landed from Guinea or Bermuda;—all to see set before them every shade of human character—their own among the number—every exhibition of human passion, affection, and caprice; from the most daring and subtle intellect to the poorest driveller; genius at one time taking mystic flights, at another flickering on the verge of imbecility and madness.

At the time when Shakspeare set foot in the metropolis the stage was passing through a new epoch. The Moralities which might in his childhood have satisfied a less critical audience at Coventry or Stratford, and the dumb shows and pageants provided for the Virgin Queen at Kenilworth or Windsor, had lost their attractions.[7] The diffusion of classical learning, numerous translations of the dramatic poets of Greece and Rome, intellects sharpened by the great theological controversies in which they had been lately engaged, the stronger sense of national and individual freedom, had prepared men for a keener relish of the higher productions of art in all its branches. The result is seen in every direction. It would have violated all experience had it not been seen in that form of literature which represented more fully than any other the condition of the national mind, and more than any other appealed to the sympathies and experience of all classes in the nation. A people brave, resolute, and energetic, who had passed, by extraordinary exertion, through so fearful an ordeal, scarcely of less duration than 150 years, and then emerged safely on the firm ground, as they looked back on the stormy ocean from which they had so recently escaped, would expect in their poets and teachers an earnest-

[7] Thus in Greene's *Never too Late*, the strolling actor says to Roberto: 'Why, I am as famous for *Delphrygus* and *The King of the Fairies* as ever was any of my time. *The Twelve Labours of Hercules* have I terribly thundered on the stage, and played three scenes of the Devil in *The High Way to Heaven*.' 'Have ye so?' said Roberto; 'then I pray you pardon me.' 'Nay, more,' quoth the player, 'I can serve to make a pretty speech, for I was a country author passing (good) at a Moral; for it was I that penned the Moral of *Man's Wit*, *The Dialogue of Dives*, and for seven years' space was absolute interpreter of the puppets. But now my almanack is out of date.
    The people make no estimation
    Of Morals teaching education.'

ness and reality of treatment, a vividness of perception, a power of reproduction, wholly different from the mere didactic attitude and philosophic musing into which poets are permitted to fall in more tranquil times. They would forgive any errors rather than those of tameness and insensibility. Regularity of form and harmony of design would be less attractive to them than freedom of movement. Liberty they demanded, even if, as in our early dramatists, it degenerated at times into extravagance and licentiousness. Thus, within a very brief space, English literature as represented by the drama experienced a sudden and entire transformation, such as no other period affords the like. Nor are the dramas of Shakspeare further removed from those of his immediate predecessors than theirs are from the Moralities and Mysteries which they had superseded in their turn.

Of the competitors for public favour when Shakspeare appeared at the Black Friars, in his new capacity as servitor, the most eminent were Lilly, Peele, Greene, and Marlowe. All of these men had been educated at one or other of the two universities, and all took to writing for the stage, with no higher object than that of relieving that poverty into which they continually relapsed from their folly and intemperance, or perhaps, as in Lilly's case, to obtain court-favour. They must be entirely acquitted of any purpose to grasp those deeper questions which confused and perplexed the age; still less of endeavouring to discover the true solution of them. To attempt to enter upon that vast theatre of human experience now displayed before them, to comprehend the various purposes and phases of human life, and its relations, in its novel position, to the past, the present, or the future—this was a task for which they had neither the requisite faculties nor the necessary sympathy. If they could represent the passing and grotesque humours of their age, if they could point some moral lesson against its more obvious transgressions, they aimed no higher. And often, like men of meagre genius and less subtle perception, they mistook the mere transitory phenomena for the cause; their feebler imaginations were taken captive by the disastrous effects of vice and passion, whilst the subtler and more spiritual incentives they never fathomed. So, living in times which were favourable to poetry—and to dramatic poetry especially—when men were still inspired by the excitement of past and of passing events—when individual characterism had not yet crystallized into one dull uniformity by fixed systems of education or engrossing commercial monopoly—when the old had not so far been parted from the new as to lose its vitality and fade into the unrealism of archæology—these dramatists, with all their ability and advantages, produced nothing which could serve beyond the amusement of the hour: not a passage, not a line, not a single happy expression, could take root in the memory of their contemporaries, and secure eternity for itself among the unwritten traditions of the people. Whilst unnumbered hosts of Shakspeare's phrases, often the most plain and artless, the least obviously remarkable for any peculiarity of sound or antithesis, or for those factitious qualities which catch the undisciplined fancy, have grown into household words, only less numerous than those of the Bible, it is impossible to trace any similar fortune in Shakspeare's contemporaries, or his immediate predecessors. And as it is inconceivable that any possible revolution of public taste should ever give life or animation to their writings, it is equally impossible to conceive that any revelations of science, before which the proudest of our present achievements must fade like the baseless fabric of a vision, should consign Shakspeare to oblivion, or render him less worthy of the profoundest study, less fresh, less striking, less instructive, less philosophical, in the truest of all senses, than he is now, than he was before gravitation or the laws of Kepler were discovered, when Copernicus was esteemed no better than a dreamer—a new but ignoble Phäethon driving the earth about the sun.[8]

Yet these men's labours were not without their use. Steeped in classical literature, deriving their rules from classical models, guiding their judgment exclusively, though with small discrimination, by classical authority, they inexorably determined the form and style of dramatic art. They developed the poetical capabilities of the English language. They refined it to those higher purposes of poetical literature for which, even at their time, and still more emphatically before their time, it was considered wholly unsuitable. The world was still divided between the learned and the laymen. Latin associated with the religious sympathies and scholastic supremacy of the middle ages had not yet resigned its special dignity as the only organ of inspiration. It had entered on a new and more splendid career by the revival of letters and the labours of the revivalists. The English tongue, rough, confused, unmetrical—the tongue of business and of the vulgar—was, in the lips of the educated, a condescension to vulgar ignorance and infirmity;—a pharisaic uncleanness, which the scholar and the gentleman must contract in his associations with the unlearned, in his pity for their blindness, but of which he washed himself up to the very elbows in his communion with his fellows.[9] It may be easy to smile at these things now; but, to those who think deeply on the subject, it

---

[8] 'Those new carmen which drive the earth about.'—*Bacon.*

[9] Mr. Collier has printed a letter in which the authorities of the University of Cambridge request they may be excused from complying with the royal request to act a play in English. They are contented to represent a Latin play, but an English one they consider derogatory, and the students are highly offended at the notion.

must seem wonderful how a language constantly associated with ignoble uses, intensely businesslike and prosaic, despised by men of taste and learning, could pass, and that so rapidly, into the radiant sphere of poetry. What is the task of a great artist, embodying his conceptions with a piece of black charcoal and a stick, compared with that of the poet who has to clothe his most subtle thoughts, his nicest, his most incisive and accurate perceptions, in words never trained by usage to such purposes, never adequate to his needs, falsified in their true significance by carelessness and stupidity, always spilling over or falling short in the due adjustment of their popular acceptation to their etymological exactness?

These men, then, did that for Shakspeare which it is very possible the poet, great as he was, could not have done so well for himself. They had familiarised men's minds with the laws of the drama, in the concrete; they had accustomed the ears of men to a stately blank verse, essentially and exclusively English in its character—indelibly associated with all our noblest poetry—and yet evidently suggested by an intense study of its classical forerunner.[1] Language, in their hands, was intensified and elevated, however deficient it might be in suppleness and versatility—qualities at that time less required. For stateliness and dignity, combined with strength and fervour, passages may be extracted

---

[1] This is evidently on what poor Greene prided himself—and justly so—in his dying hours. Thus in the well-known passage referring to Shakspeare: 'There is an upstart crow beautified with our feathers, that with his tiger's heart wrapt in a player's hide, supposes he is as well able *to bombast out a blank verse as the best of you.*' Beautified with our feathers means, as he expresses it, to write blank verse, and imitate the rules of dramatic composition, to which Greene and his friends had contributed so much popularity. That a country lad like Shakspeare, not of the craft, without fame, friends, or a University education, 'should bombast out a blank verse' as well as the most experienced writers of the age, was a fact sufficient to alarm the jealousy of Greene and of his contemporaries.

from our elder dramatists which are not surpassed by any of their successors, Shakspeare and Milton excepted;—and how much the latter was indebted for many of his excellences to a careful study of these early writers, no one can doubt who has taken the trouble to study the subject. If these excellences are marred by startling incongruities; if in their best passages they run into extravagance, or,

'all unawares,
Fluttering their pennons vain, plumb down they drop
Ten thousand fathoms deep,'—

that was incidental to their task. It was no more than, in their case, might have been anticipated. As they could not all at once pull up their audience to their own altitude, they descended to their audience. The mere Latinists, as they were called, proud of their scholarship and defiant of all departure from classical types, died in their theory, and left no mark behind them;—but these men, mixing with the world, too often steeped in its excesses, and sounding the lowest depths of its misery, had more sympathy with their fellow-men and their ways. Their own experience, as they found, was of more worth to them as dramatists than their learning, if they wished for popularity. So with their classical tastes and predilections they mixed up, often incongruously enough, the homely and coarse scenes of their own daily experience, in the homeliest and least idealised forms.

From 1585, when Shakspeare is supposed to have taken up his residence in London, to 1598, we have very few data to determine the poet's circumstances, conduct, or specific employments. That he was assiduous as an actor and a successful dramatist from the very first is clear from the concurrent testimony of the times, scanty as it is. Already in 1598, a writer named Francis Meres, 'Master of Arts of both Universities,' in a 'Discourse of English Poets,'[2] mentions Shakspeare in the following terms: 'Shakspeare, among the English, is *the most excellent* in both kinds (tragedy and comedy) for the stage. For comedy, witness his " Gentlemen of Verona," his " Errors," his " Love's Labour's Lost," his " Love's Labour's Won," his " Midsummer-Night's Dream," and his " Merchant of Venice." For tragedy, his " Richard II.," " Richard III.," " Henry IV.," " King John," " Titus Andronicus," and his " Romeo and Juliet."'

From the language of Meres it would be naturally inferred that he did not propose to give a complete list of Shakspeare's writings in 1598, but of those only which bore out his assertion that he was 'the most excellent' in tragedy as well as in comedy. Thus, within twelve or thirteen years after Shakspeare's arrival in London, Meres could point to twelve plays of Shakspeare so generally well known and universally applauded that, in spite of the popularity of Greene, Peele, and Marlowe, or even Ben Jonson,[3] Meres made no scruple to claim for Shakspeare the palm as a dramatist above all his contemporaries. Even admitting that Meres's list is complete, this would give a year for a play; and for such plays as 'Richard II.,' 'King John,' 'Henry IV.,' the 'Midsummer-Night's Dream,' and 'Romeo and Juliet.'

But this is not all; for, in 1593, Shakspeare had given to the world his two poems of 'Venus and Adonis' and 'Lucrece.' To the same period must be ascribed the three

---

[2] *Palladis Tamia*, printed at London in 1598. The testimony of Meres is the more valuable because from his reference to Shakspeare's 'Sugred Sonnets among his private friends,' which were not printed until long after, Meres must have been either one of those 'private friends' or well acquainted with them.

[3] Johnson's best comedy, *Every Man in his Humour*, appeared two years before Meres's book, in 1596, the year in which Shakspeare lost his only son.

parts of 'Henry VI.,'[4] and at least so many of the Sonnets—if they were written, as some critics imagine, at different intervals—as to justify Meres's encomium of them, which we make no scruple of repeating here, were it only to disabuse some of our readers of the notion that Shakspeare's contemporaries were insensible to his greatness. 'As the soul of Euphorbus' (says Meres) 'was thought to live in Pythagoras, so the sweet, witty soul of Ovid lives in mellifluous and honey-tongued Shakspeare. Witness his "Venus and Adonis," his "Lucrece," his Sugred Sonnets among his private friends.'

The rapidity with which Shakspeare poured forth his wonderful conceptions, the meteor-like flight with which he emerged from the throng of his contemporaries, the endless profusion of his genius, the most consummate judgment and knowledge of his art and its requirements, combined with a luxuriant energy and a teeming imagination that seemed utterly inexhaustible, might well have provoked the wonder and envy of his less favoured rivals. Their most careless and irregular productions, thrown off under the pressure of necessity or on the impulse of passion, could not keep pace with the creations of Shakspeare, in whom the deliberate energy, the studiousness, the conscious reticence of the artist are as conspicuous as the fertility of his imagination and the impetuosity of his genius. 'In beauty,' says Lord Bacon, 'that of favour is more than that of colour: and that of decent (becoming) and gracious motion, more than that of favour.' In the plays of the poet's contemporaries, it is the beauty of colour, of graceful and harmo-

---

[4] On the authority of Greene, in his 'Groatsworth of Wit,' published in 1592, in which the line—
  'O tiger's heart wrapped in a woman's hide!' (3 *Hen. VI.* i. 4)
is travestied into—'tiger's heart wrapped in a player's hide.' It is also supposed that the first part of *Henry VI.* is alluded to by Nash in his *Piers Penniless*, written the same year.

nious language; their stateliness never moves; the action never advances, or by fits and by intervals, like human mechanism. In Shakspeare, on the other hand, the action, like nature, is ever advancing, never still; rapid, but imperceptible; 'like the summer grass—unseen, but crescent in its faculty.' Even in the feeblest of his plays—if such a term can be applied to them—this quality is remarkable. He gets over the ground with astonishing rapidity—an excellence lost to us, who read Shakspeare in the closet and never see him on the stage. He never loiters or lingers in some cool nook, or wastes his time over subordinate details, or turns out of the current to strand in muddy or shallow water, enamoured of his own wit or his own sublimity. But as he rushes straight on in a fuller, more rapid, and ever-increasing volume, sparkling and dashing like a river, all sorts of colours, of sights and sounds, grave and gay, pathetic and joyous, glittering and transparent, dance along the surface; now gleaming fathoms deep to the bottom, now startling and now amusing, now freezing us with emotions of uncontrollable delight, now calling up tears from some sealed and unbroken deep within us.

That the judgment of his contemporaries, though often faulty, was not always at fault, is clear from the notices illustrative of Shakspeare in the scattered literature of his times. It is certain that the greatness of his genius as a dramatist was recognised from the first. Greene would scarcely have warned his associates of their approaching eclipse by this 'new Johannes Factotum,' alluding to the universality of the poet's genius, had Shakspeare's audience shown themselves indifferent to these his earliest productions, or slow in recognising their sterling merits. Nor would Meres have ventured to speak of Shakspeare in such high terms of admiration had not popular estimation guided and sanctioned his judgment. We have, besides, the admission of Chettle, a contemporary playwright, the friend of Greene, and editor of his 'Groatsworth of Wit.' In defending himself from his supposed share in Greene's malevolent insinuations, which had given just offence to Shakspeare, Marlowe, and others, Chettle says: [5] 'With neither of them that take offence was I acquainted; and with one of them (Marlowe) I care not if I never be. The other (Shakspeare) whom at that time I did not so much spare as since I wish I had;—that I did not I am as sorry as if the original fault had been my fault, because myself have seen his demeanour no less civil, than he *excellent* in the quality he professes. Besides, divers of worship have reported his uprightness of dealing, which argues his honesty, and his facetious grace in writing that approves his art.'[6]

These testimonies alike to his genius and the spotless integrity of the poet's conduct, so different from that of most contemporary dramatists, are unimpeachable. The poet's worldly prosperity kept pace with his reputation. The occupation of an actor alone was a profitable one in those days, and with ordinary prudence was sure to lead, not only to competence, but to wealth.[7] But with his occupation as

[5] 'Kind Hearts' Dream,' published in 1592.
[6] Euphuism all over.
[7] Thus, in Greene's *Never Too Late*, in the interview between the player and Roberto (*i.e.* Greene), on the latter asking how the player proposed to mend Roberto's fortune—' Why, easily,' quoth he, ' and greatly to your benefit ; for men of my profession get by scholars their whole living.' ' What is your profession ? ' said Roberto. ' Truly, sir,' said he, ' I am a player.' ' A player ! ' quoth Roberto. ' I took you rather for a gentleman of great living ; for if by outward habit men should be answered (judged), I tell you, you would be taken for a *substantial man*.' ' So am I, where I dwell,' quoth the player, 'reported; able at my proper cost to build a windmill.' He then proceeds to say that at his outset in life he was fain to carry his ' playing fardel,' that is, his bundle of stage properties, ' a foot back ; ' but now his show of 'playing apparel ' would sell for more than 200*l*. In the end he offers to engage Greene to write plays for him, ' for which you shall be well paid, if you will take the pains.' We know from the sequel that though Greene was extravagant, and never to be

an actor Shakspeare combined that of a successful and prolific dramatist; and the two together soon raised him from the condition of a needy adventurer in 1585 to that of a well-to-do possessor of lands and houses.[8] In 1597 he purchased *The Great House* at Stratford-upon-Avon, described as 'one messuage, *two* barns, *two* gardens, and *two* orchards, with appurtenances.' The same year his father, formerly in declining circumstances, applied for a grant of arms, and passed from the condition of a yeoman to that of a gentleman; and the same year he filed a bill in Chancery against the son of the mortgagee who unjustly detained Ashbies, the hereditary property of the poet's mother.[9] Next year the poet is assessed for a tenement in the parish of St. Helen's Bishopsgate, valued at 5*l.*, and is asked by his friend Richard Quiney for the loan of 30*l.*

From this year until 1602, when the fertility of his invention poured forth some of the grandest of his productions, and popular judgment placed him far above all his contemporaries, his progress to wealth and fame was equally rapid. In 1602 he purchased 107 acres of arable land in Stratford for the sum of 320*l.*, somewhat more than 1,000*l.*

trusted if paid beforehand, ' seldom he wanted, his labours were so well esteemed.' See the quotation in Dyce's preface to *Works of Greene*, p. 20, ed. 1861.

[8] No account is to be made of the document which professes to describe Shakspeare as holding a share in the theatre as early as 1596. With that falls to the ground the whole modern hypothesis that as sharer or manager his time was employed in patching up the productions of other dramatists, older or contemporary, and fitting them for the stage. What with sonnets, poems, plays of his own once a year, and acting in his own plays and those of his contemporaries, what room, occasion, need, or opportunity could Shakspeare have had for such an employment?

[9] In the grant he is called 'John Shakspeare, now of Stratford-upon-Avon, in the co. of Warwick, gent., whose parent, great grandfather and late antecessor, for his faithful and approved service to the late most prudent prince Henry VII., of famous memory, was advanced and rewarded with lands and tenements given to him in those parts of Warwickshire, where they have continued by some descents in good reputation.'

in modern computation; five months after, in the same year, one Walter Getley surrendered a house to the poet in Dead Lane, Stratford; at Michaelmas term, William Shakspeare, gentleman, as he is now generally styled, bought from Hercules Underhill, for 60*l*., a property consisting of a messuage with two orchards, two gardens, two barns, and their appurtenances. In May 1603, when James I. came to the crown, a privy seal was granted by the king to his servants 'Laurence Fletcher, William Shakspeare, Richard Burbage, Augustine Philippes, John Hemmings, Henry Condell,' and the rest of their associates, 'to use and exercise the art and faculty of playing comedies, tragedies, histories, interludes, morals, pastorals, stage plays, and such other, like as they have already studied, or hereafter shall use or study,' in their usual house, the Globe, or elsewhere within the king's dominions. And James, who was by no means the fool that posterity represents him to have been, showed his discrimination by frequently commanding Shakspeare's plays to be acted at court.[10] In 1605 the poet added to his property at Stratford by purchasing the unexpired lease of the tithes of Stratford and the adjoining hamlets for the sum of 400*l*. sterling; in modern computation, 1,400*l*.

It is not known at what period he retired from the stage and settled finally in Stratford. By the spring of 1613 he had lost his father, his mother, and his only son. Two daughters remained: Susanna, married, in 1607, to Dr. Hall,

---

[10] In the account of the Revels at Court, notices are found of the following: *Othello, Merry Wives of Windsor, Measure for Measure, Comedy of Errors*, in 1604; *Love's Labour Lost, Henry V., Merchant of Venice*, twice in 1605; at Whitehall, *King Lear*, which had already in 1608 passed through three editions; in 1611, *The Tempest* and *The Winter's Night's Tale*. In 1613, on the marriage of James's daughter Elizabeth with the prince-palatine, the representation of Shakspeare's plays furnished a great part of the entertainment. Among them are *The Tempest, The Twins' Tragedy* (supposed to be the *Comedy of Errors*), *Much Ado about Nothing, The Winter's Tale, Sir John Falstaff, Othello*, and *Julius Cæsar*.

a physician at Stratford; and Judith, married to a vintner named Quiney, of the same place, in 1616. During the last three years of his life notices of his purchases and employments become more rare. In 1613 the Globe Theatre was burnt, and it is gratuitously assumed that many of the poet's manuscripts perished in the flames. Had it been so, we should hardly have failed of finding some notice of such a disastrous loss in the preface and dedication to the first collected edition of his works. Nor, considering the poet's immature death, his various employments, and the number of his plays which have come down to us, is it probable that any considerable portion of his writings has perished.

The manner of his death is uncertain. His will, still preserved in the Prerogative Office, is dated March 25, 1616. The poet's handwriting, never very good, if we may judge from the few signatures that have been preserved, and fifty years more antiquated than that of Sir Thomas Lucy, is feeble, shaky, and imperfect; very little like what might have been expected from one whose practice in writing must have been considerable, and who had in his time filled many reams of manuscript. His death did not occur until the 23rd of April following. It would seem, therefore, that his death was far from sudden; and this alone would suffice to invalidate the tradition, circulated forty-five years after, that the poet died of a fever contracted at a merry meeting with Drayton and Ben Jonson. His bust in Stratford Church, his portrait by Droeshout prefixed to the first folio edition of his works, and the whole tenour of his life, contradict altogether the supposition that the poet was intemperate. If the opinion of competent judges may be taken, the bust was executed from a cast taken after death. It was certainly coloured after life, and until it was painted over by Malone—a greater crime to Shakspeare's memory than Mr. Gaskill's destruction of the famous mulberry tree

—it represented the poet exactly as he appeared to his contemporaries. The eyes were a bright hazel, the hair and beard auburn; the doublet was scarlet, covered with a loose black sleeveless gown. As in Droeshout's portrait, the forehead is remarkably high and broad; in fact, the immense volume of the forehead is its most striking feature. The predominant characteristic of the whole is that of a composed, self-possessed, resolute, and vigorous Englishman, of a higher intellectual stamp than usual, but not so far removed from the general national type as we should have been inclined to expect from his writings.

'Of the several works of Shakspeare—plays and poems—there were prior to 1616 in circulation, in all, no fewer than between sixty and sixty-five editions. Some of these reached as many as six editions within a period of not more than twenty-one years. This argues of itself an extensive popularity, especially when we reflect on the small number of the reading public of his day. If we take the lowest estimate of the editions (sixty), and suppose each issue to have consisted of the lowest possible paying number (300 say), we should have in circulation no fewer than 18,000 copies of the productions of the great dramatist in print during his lifetime.'[1] This ingenious computation applies only to the plays and poems printed before the *first* collected edition of Shakspeare's works in 1623. That folio contains thirty-six plays; one half of these, so far as is known, never got beyond the footlights; and, therefore, we may presume were printed by the editors of that volume from the author's manuscript. Among that number are to be found 'Macbeth,' 'Timon of Athens,' 'Cymbeline,' 'The Tempest,' all the Roman plays, 'Twelfth Night,' and 'The Winter's Tale.'[2]

[1] 'Shakespere, a Critical Biography,' by Samuel Neil, p. 59.
[2] The following is a list of the 4tos and their various editions, before

No collected edition of Shakspeare's dramatic works appeared until 1623, seven years after the poet's death. The volume was ushered into the world by two of his former dramatic associates, John Heminge and Henrie Condell, to whom in conjunction with Burbage, the famous actor, Shakspeare had left in his will '26s. and 8d. a piece to buy them ringes.'[3] But Burbage died on March 16, 1619;[4]

the folio of 1623. The letter *M* is prefixed to those mentioned by Meres.
M 1594. *Titus Andronicus*, entered at Stationers' Hall Feb. 6, 159$\frac{3}{4}$; first edition not known to exist; 2nd ed. 1600; 3rd ed. 1611.
    1595. *Henry VI.*, Part III., 1595.
M 1597. *Romeo and Juliet*, 1597, 1599, 1609 *bis*?
M „ *Richard II.*, 1597, 1598, 1608 *bis*, 1615.
M „ *Richard III.*, 1597, 1598, 1602, 1605, 1612, 1621? 1622.
M 1598. *Love's Labor's Lost*, 1598.
M „ *Henry IV.*, Part I., 1598, 1599, 1604, 1608, 1613, 1622.
    Henry IV., Part II., 1600.
    1600, *Henry V.*, 1600, 1602, 1608.
M „ *Merchant of Venice*, 1600 *bis*.
M „ *Midsummer Night's Dream*, 1600 *bis*.
M? „ *Much Ado about Nothing*, 1600.
    1602. *Merry Wives of Windsor*, 1602, 1619.
    1603. *Hamlet*, 1603, 1604, 1605, 1611.
    1605. *Lear*, 1608 *bis*.
    1609. *Pericles*, 1609, 1611, 1619.
    „   *Troilus and Cressida*, 1609 *bis*.
    1622. *Othello*, 1622.
            Contention of York and Lancaster.
  Old plays; *Richard III.*, 1594; *Taming of a Shrew*, 1594, 1607.

[3] 'And to my fellows, John Hemynges, Richard Burbage, and Henry Cundell, xxvjs. viijd. a piece, to buy them rings.'

[4] Burbage, or Burbadge, according to Malone, was one of the principal sharers of the Globe and Blackfriars theatres. In a letter written in 1613 (Harl. MSS. 7002), the actors at the Globe are called *Burbadge's Company*. In Jonson's *Masque of Christmas*, 1616, the year that is of Shakspeare's death, Venus, in the character of a deaf tire-woman, is made to say of Cupid: 'I could have had money enough for him, an I would have been tempted and have let him out by the week to the king's players. Master Burbage has been about and about with me, and so has old Master Hemings too; they have need of him.'—*Shaksp.* iii. 230, ed. 1803.

Heminge and Condell are said to have been printers as well as actors, but Malone thinks that there is no authority for this statement. Probably it arose from their connection with Shakspeare's printed works. At all events, had they been printers by occupation, it is reasonable to surmise and if, as is not improbable, he had been originally associated with Heminge and Condell in preparing Shakspeare's dramatic works for the press, his death before the appearance of the volume prevented his name from being joined with theirs in their glorious task. Not one word appears in Shakspeare's will as to the disposal of his papers and manuscripts, or of his shares in the theatres, if at the time of his death he possessed any. If Ward's statement be true that Shakspeare during the closing years of his life furnished annually two plays for the stage,[5] if it be true that the poet's income was considerable, that he made no purchases of any moment after 1605, that he was besides in the very zenith of his fame and the most popular author of his times, it will be difficult to account for two things: how was it, if he sold the copyright of his plays to his fellows of the Globe and

---

that their names would have been found on the title-pages of some of the earlier copies of Shakspeare's plays. All the payments made by the Treasurer of the Chamber in 1613, and subsequently, for plays performed at Court, are 'to John Heminge and the rest of his fellows' (Malone, *ib.* 234). In his will Heminge directs that if a sufficient sum cannot be raised from his ordinary chattels towards the payment of his debts, a moiety of the profits which he has 'by lease in the several playhouses of the Globe and Blackfriars' shall be set aside for that purpose. In another legacy he says: 'I give and bequeath unto every my fellows and sharers, his Majesty's servants, which shall be living at the time of my decease, the sum of 10s. a piece, to make them rings for remembrance of me.' Heminge died in 1630.

Henry Condell, whose name appears in the privy seal of James I., 1603, in conjunction with those of Shakspeare, Burbage, and Heminge, died in 1627. Malone thinks that both Burbage and Heminge were natives of Shottery, near Stratford (*ib.* 233).

[5] That Ward's statement was not very far wrong will appear from the following considerations:—Shakspeare wrote in all 37 plays, including *Pericles*. Meres mentions 12 plays as existing in 1598. If to these be added *Pericles* and the three parts of *Henry VI.*, that would give 16 ; or 19 to be written in the seventeen years and few months following. From 1597 to 1605, or 1606, seven plays only, including the first sketch of *Hamlet*, appear to have been published, five in 1600, one in 1602, and *Hamlet* in 1603. Between *Hamlet* and *Lear* five years elapsed (1602-1607) without any entry of Shakspeare's writings at Stationers' Hall. Had he ceased writing all that time, or ceased to attract publishers?

Blackfriars, that he was no richer in 1616 than in 1605? Or if he was richer, how did he dispose of his wealth? From the tithes which he had purchased at Stratford he derived an income of 120*l.* a year, not less than 400*l.* a year, according to our present computation. He was not careless or extravagant in his habits, had one daughter only, after 1607, and his wife dependent on his exertions. Did he then retain the copyright of his plays, in his own hands, during this later period of his life, intending to publish them himself, like his contemporary Ben Jonson? Or was he as indifferent to money as he is said to have been to literary fame? The former of these hypotheses is set at rest by the various documents produced by Mr. Halliwell and others, all of which go to show that the possession of the most transcendent genius is not incompatible with the virtues of economy, regularity, and despatch. His supposed indifference to literary fame finds no countenance in his writings, still less in the evidence of his contemporaries.[6] Thus we find Chettle apologizing to Shakspeare as one of those who had taken offence at the disparaging remarks of Greene in his 'Groatsworth of Wit,' to the publication of which Chettle had been instrumental. Again, Heywood in his 'Apology for Actors,' published in 1612, alluding to the trick of a publisher named Jaggard, who had brought out a copy of 'Venus and Adonis,' with two love epistles between Paris and Helen, under the general title, 'by Wm. Shakespere,' says, in reclaiming his property: 'I must necessarily resent a manifest injury done me in that work by [its] taking the two epistles of Paris to Helen and of Helen to Paris, and printing them in the name of another

[6] That Shakspeare permitted inaccurate copies of his plays to be circulated in print is one thing, to assume that he must have done so from indifference to literary distinction, is another. Moreover in this case, as in that of many others, literary fame was money, to which he was certainly not indifferent.

(Shakspeare); which may put the world in opinion I might steal them from him; and he to do himself right hath since published them in his own name. But as I must acknowledge my lines not. worthy his patronage under whom he hath published them, *so the author I know [was] much offended with Mr. Jaggard, that altogether unknown to him presumed to make so bold with his name.*' Such words are not compatible with Shakspeare's presumed indifference to the fate of his writings.

With these remarks we return to the consideration of the first folio and Shakspeare's connection with it.

It is a very handsome volume, on which no expense has been spared in respect either of paper or type. It consists of 962 pages in double columns, not including the dedication, preface, or introductory verses. Taking 60 as the average number of lines in a column, the lines in all would amount to 116,402. All circumstances considered, it was one of the most sumptuous and expensive works which up to that time had appeared from the English press in the English language. For size, costliness, and beauty, there had been few works like it; certainly no works of fiction. So far therefore as concerned expenses of this kind, Heminge and Condell had not shown themselves unmindful of what was due to Shakspeare's memory.[7]

Nor in other respects had they shown themselves careless or inconsiderate in the execution of their task. It is not pretended even by those who have been most severe in condemning their labours that they omitted from their collection any genuine drama of Shakspeare, with the exception of 'Pericles.' Modern research from that time to this, shar-

---

[7] The sale of Foxe's *Martyrs* was secured by government. Hollinshed's *Chronicles* and the works of Sir Thomas More occupy the next place in size. Then came the bulky translations and histories of Grimstone, North, and others, generally published by Islip or Bill, the royal printers.

pened with all the anxiety of achieving distinction which could not fail the man that discovered a single new play or even a few lines from the poet's pen, has added nothing to the list of the dramas as they have come down to us since the first edition by Heminge and Condell. Very few dramatic authors have been so fortunate in this respect; very few writings have been so much indebted to posthumous care. Supposing it were true that these editors admitted into their collection plays of doubtful authenticity, does any one imagine they would have done better if, like some of Shakspeare's more recent critics, they had rejected ' Titus Andronicus,' the three parts of 'Henry VI.,' or 'Henry VIII.'?[8] Or if, laying down a theory of their own as to what was or was not worthy of their great contemporary, they had exercised a principle of selection according to their own principles of criticism, would they have deserved so well of posterity as they have done? We are under infinite obligations to them for what they did; that obligation being no less than this— that whatever emanated from the poet's hand ' they would not willingly let die.' The work was a large one, and unusually costly. The poet's family could not undertake the task, and it is probable never would have done.[9]

The editors' labours could scarcely have been other than disinterested. ' We have but collected them [the plays],'

[8] *Pericles* does not appear in the first folio.
[9] The only person competent to the task was Dr. Hall the physician, married to the poet's eldest and favourite child, Susannah. But he seems to have been wholly indifferent to the fame of his great father-in-law. Yet Dr. Hall was not an unlettered man.
 Shakspeare's widow died in 1623, the year when the first folio appeared; Dr. Hall in 1635; his wife, Susannah, in 1649; their daughter Elizabeth, remembered with a legacy of 100*l*. in her grandfather's will, and afterwards Lady Barnard, in 1670. Judith, his other daughter (who signs but does not write her name), died in 1662; her husband some time later. Yet not one of them thought of recording a single fact or anecdote of their relative's life, or of preserving a scrap of his writing. Was it indifference or ingratitude? Or had Puritanism taught them to be ashamed of the name of Shakspeare?

they say in their dedication of the work to the Earls of Pembroke and Montgomery, 'and done an office to the dead to procure his orphans guardians; *without ambition either of self-profit or fame:* only to keep the memory of so worthy a friend and fellow alive, as was our Shakspeare.' Nor is there any reason for suspecting the sincerity of their statement. What pecuniary advantage was to be expected from so costly an enterprise? The impression of the book could not have been large, and when the expenses of publishers and printers had been paid, very little profit would remain for the editors; if, indeed, editors in those cases received any remuneration.

What motives then could they have for undertaking so responsible a task beyond that of friendship for the dead? As we have said, Shakspeare left no directions in his will touching the disposal of his writings. Were they then acting in their corporate capacity as managers of the Globe Theatre, or merely as personal friends of the deceased, guided solely by the dictates of personal affection? Why publish in their corporate capacity that which could bring them little or no corporate profit? Why divulge to rival theatres dramas of which the exclusive copyright and privilege of acting were so valuable? Their language is scarcely susceptible of any other than one plain and obvious interpretation. They say in their Dedication: 'Since your Lordships have been pleased to think these trifles something heretofore, and have prosecuted both *them* and *their author*, living with so much favour; we hope that they, outliving him, and he not having the fate, *common with some,* to be *executor to his own writings,* you will use the like indulgence toward them, you have done unto their parent.' And in their notice to the reader:—

'It had been a thing, we confess, worthy to have been wished, that the author himself had lived *to have set forth and overseen his own writings.* But since it hath been ordained otherwise, and he *by death* departed from that right, we pray you do not envy his friends the office of their care and pain to have collected and published them: and so to have published them, as where before you were abused with divers stolen and surreptitious copies, maimed and deformed by the frauds and stealths of injurious impostors that exposed (sold) them; even those are now offered to your view cured, and perfect of their limbs, and all the rest,[1] absolute in their numbers,[2] as he conceived them: who, as he was a happy imitator of nature, was a most gentle expresser of it. His mind and hand went together; and what he thought he uttered with that easiness, *that we have scarce received from him a blot in his papers.*'[3]

Now these expressions certainly imply that Shakspeare had the right, common with others, of being the 'executor to his own writings.' They imply also that he had not parted with that right until he was surprised by an untimely death. Ben Jonson, like Shakspeare, wrote for the stage; like Shakspeare, he received money from the theatre for his dramatic writings; but this did not deprive Jonson of the copyright of his works, or prevent him from publishing his plays with dedications to various friends. It is then equally consonant with analogy, as with the expressions of Heminge and Condell, to infer that Shakspeare possessed the same right, and was as much at liberty to use it as Jonson; and careful consideration of the extracts already quoted will lead us to conclude that Shakspeare did intend

[1] That is, those which had never appeared in print before.

[2] *I.e.* complete and perfect. We might have suspected this Latinism had they not been actors accustomed to such phraseology.

[3] It is to this expression that Ben Jonson refers: 'I remember the players have often mentioned it as an honour to Shakspeare, that in his writing, whatsoever he penned, he never blotted out a line. My answer hath been,' &c. From the censure conveyed in Jonson's remark, it is obvious that he was not the author of this address, as some have surmised.

not only to claim but to exercise that right. It were 'to have been wished that the author himself *had lived* to have set forth and overseen his own writings.' Would this expression have been employed had Shakspeare been so wholly indifferent to the fate of his works as is sometimes assumed? Would his friends have merely expressed a wish that he should have *lived* to superintend the publication of his own works, when upon the ordinary hypothesis such a wish would have been equally fruitless had his life been longer or shorter? Then again their expression, 'we *have* scarce received from him a blot in his papers,' seems to be incompatible with the notion that Heminge and Condell were speaking in the names of the Company, or were referring to their engagement with Shakspeare many years since when he commenced dramatist, and not to more recent and personal events.

This plain and obvious interpretation of their words is the most probable and the most consistent. Their meaning surely is, that Shakspeare had intended to collect and publish his own works, and to rescue them not only from oblivion but from the inaccuracies and deformities of careless and surreptitious copyists; that he had by him at the time of his death manuscripts of those plays which had never been printed, and some of the printed quartos; that he was employed in altering and enlarging or re-casting the latter when death surprised him at his unfinished task; and on his death-bed, by his own directions, his papers were transferred to Heminge and Condell, to prepare for the press. That their statement is true in the main is undeniable; for from nobody, except from Shakspeare, could these editors have obtained the manuscripts of twenty original plays, of which no other copies are supposed to exist except in their edition, and those augmentations of the quarto copies which are found for the first time in their folio. Their credibility has

been disputed, because whilst they inveigh against spurious
copies of Shakspeare's plays, it has been asserted that their
text is in many instances derived from the quartos. The
statement incautiously made by Malone has been repeated
from critic to critic. But all they really say is, that whereas
people had been 'abused with *divers* stolen and surreptitious
copies'—an assertion for which there was abundant evidence,
without supposing that they intended to condemn *all* the
printed copies. Considering the total wreck and devastation
of many early dramatic works, their statement might be
literally true, and yet not be aimed at *any* one of the quartos
which have come down to us.[4]

If the explanation of Heminge and Condell's words, as
here suggested, be the true one, sufficient reason will appear
why the text of the quartos should sometimes be reproduced exactly in the folio and sometimes be widely departed
from. That great inaccuracies should be found in the type
—that words and lines should have been transposed and
make nonsense of that which was sense before—will not show
that the editors' account of their labours is untrue or fraudu-
lent, but that either they did not superintend the press or
were unskilful in the mysteries of typal corrections. Probably
both: they were plain men who had their own occupations
to attend to, and when they had consigned their precious
deposit to the printer's hands, they might naturally think
that their task was ended, and they had fulfilled their debt
of 'gratitude both to the living and the dead.'[5] Such, we

[4] Thus, of the *Hamlet* of 1603, only two incomplete copies are supposed to
exist; of the edition of 1604, only three; of the *Lear* of 1605, one only; of
The Taming of the Shrew, one only.

[5] If Shakspeare's handwriting was at all like his signature, it was by
no means easy to decipher. If we may speak dogmatically upon such
slender proofs as we now possess, he learnt to write after the old German
text-hand then in use at the grammar school of Stratford. It was in this
respect fifty years behindhand, as any one may see by comparing Shakspeare's signature with that of Sir Thomas Lucy, Lord Bacon, or John

fear not, will be the verdict of those who judge their labours impartially.

This folio was ushered into the world, according to the prevailing fashion, by commendatory verses from the pens of Ben Jonson [6] and others. It is divided into three parts, with distinct pagination. The first contains the twelve Comedies, beginning with 'The Tempest' and ending with 'The Winter's Tale;' the second the *Histories* (as they are here called), commencing with 'King John' and ending with 'Henry VIII.;' the third the twelve Tragedies, beginning with 'Troilus and Cressida,' which is not paged, as if its insertion were an afterthought, and ending with 'Cymbeline.' What authority the editors had for this arrangement, or by what principles they were guided in their selection, it is not now possible to discover. It is clear that the order of the

Lilly. The wonder is how with such a hand he could have written so much.

[6] The fact is important; for it at once disposes of an hypothesis started of late, that Jonson, and not Shakspeare, was the author of *Henry VIII.* Is it at all likely that Jonson would have allowed one of his own plays to be inserted in this volume as Shakspeare's without any remonstrance? Or supposing that it was composed in a sort of literary partnership by the two dramatists, would Jonson have failed to notice a fact so agreeable to his vanity? Leonard Digges, a poet who composed two copies of verses, one prefixed to the first folio of the *Plays* and the other to the *Poems* published in 1640, explicitly refutes the notion that Shakspeare either joined in such strange partnerships, or borrowed scenes from his predecessors or contemporaries:—

                      'look thorough
This whole book, thou shalt find he doth not borrow
One phrase from Greeks, nor Latins imitate,
Nor once from vulgar languages translate:
Nor plagiary—like from others glean;
*Nor begs he from each witty friend a scene
To piece his acts with.*'

The same writer insists on the great superiority of Shakspeare in popular attraction to Jonson:

                      'Let but Falstaff come,
Hal, Poins, the rest, you scarce shall have a room
All is so pestered (crowded). Let but Beatrice
And Benedick be seen;—lo, in a trice
The cockpit galleries, boxes, all are full.'

plays was not determined by the dates of publication. Had Messrs. Heminge and Condell thought of ascertaining the strict, chronological order of the plays, they would have furnished us with a clue to the solution of many difficulties, and contributed a most important chapter to the literary history of the poet. For this we have unhappily no sufficient evidence. No two critics can agree precisely on this perplexing question. The arrangement which commends itself to the historical research or critical taste of one inquirer is unceremoniously set aside by his successors as preposterous or untenable. It might have been supposed that as Shakspeare wrote for a livelihood, as soon as one drama was composed he would dispose of the copyright to some theatrical company, and the publication of the play or its entry at Stationers' Hall would have assisted the inquirer in determining the date of its composition, especially as the poet's productions were eagerly sought after. But even this evidence is not wholly reliable. Meres mentions the Sonnets in 1598, though they did not appear in print until 1609. Of 'The Two Gentlemen of Verona,' also alluded to by Meres, no copy is known to exist prior to that of the folio in 1623. The earliest editions of 'The Midsummer-Night's Dream' and 'The Merchant of Venice' are of 1600.[7] But although the editors of the folio did not trouble themselves with adopting any strict chronological arrangement, it may be asserted as a *general* truth that the Comedies belong to the earlier period of Shakspeare's life, the Histories to his maturer years, and the Tragedies, especially the Roman plays, to the succeeding epoch. In other words, whilst 'Hamlet' (as we now have it), 'Lear,' 'Macbeth,' 'Othello,' 'Timon of Athens,' and the Roman plays, belong to the reign of James I., the Histories and most of the Comedies, with the excep-

[7] As they are entered the same year at Stationers' Hall it is unlikely that they should have been printed before.

tion of 'The Tempest,' were composed in the reign of Elizabeth.[8] Born and disciplined in the vigorous, passionate, but practical age of the Tudors, the genius of the poet took a wider range and sublimer flight when the accession of the Stuarts brought the nation into more familiar contact with the great problems of nature and the inscrutable destiny of man. Until the close of the sixteenth century he had failed to put forth all his strength; it was perhaps scarcely known to himself. Flashing with wit and liveliness, inventive, prolific, and versatile, the quaint, the dry, the humorous, the exceptional, were irresistibly attractive to a temperament as yet unsteeped in affliction, that 'doffed the world aside and let it pass.' For the world had upon the whole used the poet kindly—laughed at the sallies of his wit, lent itself with childlike docility to the practical jokes and endless humour of Falstaff, or shed happy and complacent tears over the sorrows of Romeo and his Juliet. Rarely, with the exception of 'Richard II.,' had the genius of Shakspeare travelled into the regions of the sublime and mysterious. In no instance, until the appearance of 'Hamlet' in 1603, had he attempted to show how closely this world of sight merges on the confines of the spiritual, or how there is more than the measured philosophy of mere motives to determine the fate and actions of mankind. Gradually the veil was uplifted; the narrow sphere of the visible—sufficing at one time for all the poet's sympathies, at one time an inexhaustible fund for his keen perception of human passions and eccentricities—was gradually enlarged; and nature presented itself to his eyes in the fulness of its strength and the extremity of its weakness. Sadder and more solemn grows the poet's vision; the humorous and the comical seldom find a place in his maturer productions; but instead of them the

[8] *Titus Andronicus* is Roman only in name, the treatment and colouring are Italian.

omnipresence, the omnipotence (as it were) of evil. Latent infirmity within, dogged, encouraged, and lured to its destruction by invisible wickedness without; momentary weakness trammelling up in its never-ending train gigantic consequences; Heaven holding out no relief, no sign to oppressed innocence; virtue dragged from its height; valour in Macbeth stooping to crime; honour and fidelity in Othello ignoble victims to bat-like suspicion; generosity betrayed in Timon to selfishness; grand resolutions the fool of accident in Hamlet:—these are the themes of his maturer powers. If the poet still deals with the exceptional and uncommon— and that in the mind of Shakspeare is of the essence of tragedy—it is no longer the exceptional or eccentric in humours, manners, diction, taste, but of intellect, imagination, and passion. The subtlest forms of insanity striking its thin and poisonous fibres into the strongest reason, sapping by unseen and unconscious degrees the noblest intellectual faculties, warping the purest affections to its own masterless bias; the broad clear daylight of the mind, now overcast, now yielding to darkness, until it succumbs to total eclipse; the light alternating with the shade; the thin edge separating sanity from insanity; the various shapes and tricks of moodiness, from the dreaminess of unnatural calm, to the frantic rage of Lear and his heart-broken sorrow: these are the scenes on which Shakspeare dwells in the latter epoch of his life, and has described with inimitable power, insight, and fidelity.

Morning and night meet, as in Nature, in the poet's writings—the comic and the tragic. In the full flush and luxuriance of his powers he rises upon us bright, lively, and jocund as the dawn; we know not where he will lead us in the abundance of his poetical caprice, what stores of mirth and wanton wiles, what brilliant and ever-changing hues will sparkle, dazzle, and allure us in his ambrosial course.

But that bright morning—unlike the morning of many of the poet's contemporaries—goes down in a solemn and glorious sunset, canopied with clouds of gold and purple.

For the plots of his comedies Shakspeare was chiefly indebted to French and Italian novelists; for his histories to Hall and Hollinshed; and for his classical plays to the 'Lives of Plutarch,' translated by North, and to such versions of the classical authors as had appeared in the earlier part of the sixteenth century. Old English authors, plays, chronicles, and ballads furnished him with the groundwork of his tragedies; and this readiness of the poet to lean on the inventions of others, however feeble and meagre, rather than rely on his own superior resources for the framework of his plays, has often been quoted as an instance of his carelessness, or at best of his unwillingness to venture upon untrodden ground. He preferred to base the wonderful superstructure of his genius on incidents already familiar to his audience, trusting to his power of investing them with a new character, a more profound or more lively significance, than, like many of his contemporaries, owe his popularity to the horror, the extravagance, the involution, or the novelty of his story. But may not the true solution of this hankering after old and established facts and traditions be found in Shakspeare's intense realism? He had a profound reverence—not Aristotle more so—for everything that carried with it the stamp of popular recognition. His strongest convictions, the highest dictates of his taste and feelings, are not always proof against this 'settled purpose of his soul.' He clung to it with an intense earnestness, as if to abandon it was to commit himself to a sea of doubt and perplexity— a wandering maze without a footing. To Bacon it was enough that any theory, any opinion, any fact should be generally accepted to be unceremoniously rejected. 'A mixture of a lie doth ever add pleasure'; and if truth itself were to become popular, it must be plentifully alloyed with falsehood.[9] The perfect self-confidence of Bacon, who at sixteen passed judgment on Aristotle, as barren and unfruitful, might set him above the necessity of any such fixed points. But then Bacon's vision was limited; his mind and attention, earth-fixed and bound up in the investigation of material laws, were in no danger of wandering and being lost in the regions of infinite space, as the eye glanced 'from Heaven to earth, from earth to Heaven.' His ethical creed might have been comprised in the words, 'Man delights not me, nor woman either.' But Shakspeare, with stronger, wider, kindlier sympathies, as untrammelled by systems as Bacon, working out for himself, in solitude and unassisted, as true a method of inquiry, as profound an observer as Bacon, as convinced as he of a divine order underlying and overlapping the seeming confusions of this world, dreaded quite as much as Bacon could do the danger of mistaking for realities the dreams of his own phantasy. So, wiser than Lord Bacon, and more truly philosophical, instead of despising popular belief, instead of ignoring it, as if it had no foundation except in falsehood, Shakspeare accepted it, probed the foundation on which it rested, brought into clearer light the half or whole truths enveloped in it, and gave form and coherent meaning to the confused and incoherent creeds of mankind.

Perhaps also to one who carved out for himself a wholly untrodden path like Shakspeare, who had little of the countenance of the learned or the confidence of rules and systems to support him, a fixed faith somewhere was the more indispensable. He was living in a sceptical age, when the freshness of faith and that confidence in the rising glories of Protestantism, which had inspired the poetry of

[9] Or, as Bacon pithily expresses it: 'Auctoritas pro veritate, non veritas pro auctoritate sit' (p. 105).

Spenser, were fast dying out. Many had relapsed into Romanism, many had fallen into atheism; the narrow creed of Puritanism could not accommodate itself to the larger sympathies and growing intelligence of the age. It viewed with the utmost consternation and alarm divines like Hooker securely trespassing beyond the pale of its doctrinal conventionalism, and philosophers like Bacon poring over 'the book of God's works,' as a derogation to the 'book of God's word.' Sympathizing with Romanism and Protestantism so far as they were human, Shakspeare could not be wholly satisfied with either. There was something deeper than either, perhaps common to both. And whilst the creeds of neither are distinctly enunciated in his writings, whilst neither can claim him as an especial advocate, both recognize in him a sincere and profound religious element, distinct, positive, permeant through his writings; not thrust forward to catch applause or gild a popular sentiment, but a pure, dry, vestal light, equally free from fanaticism on one side and from infidelity on the other.

Unfixed, unsettled in their faith, the men of the poet's days looked uneasily at the progress of inductive philosophy; at its bold innovations, its new tests, its contempt for antiquity, its hatred of Aristotle. How could the faith hold its ground against the invasion of science? How could men immersed in the contemplation of second causes recognize their sole dependence upon Him who is the first cause? Philosophy might assure them that the province of revelation and the province of science were distinct—that philosophy was as remote from divinity as the terrestrial is from the celestial globe. But the divine felt, and felt truly, that it was not a question of distinct and incommensurate jurisdiction; not whether the field of science might be occupied with earnest and hardy inquirers, and the field of divinity be cultivated in the authorized mode; but how far was it likely or possible, that men who had been rigidly trained to one method of investigation, who deferred to one tribunal, from which they admitted no appeal in matters of science and material utility, could or would divest themselves of these ingrained habits, when not science but faith was concerned.[1] So then, as now, the question was, How shall religion stand before the new philosophy? How shall reason be reconciled with revelation? For this neither divine nor philosopher could discover the true solution. What help may be found for it in Shakspeare we will not undertake to say. But if the clearest and the largest transcript of human experience can contribute to that solution, that help is to be found in the dramatist. The data with which he has supplied us are as sound, as certain, as unerring a basis for axioms and deductions, as those of the inductive philosophy; like them, are founded not on notions, but observation, and have been gathered from as wide a circle of experience. We argue, and we justly argue, upon the characters in a play of Shakspeare, or any sentiment propounded by them, or their exhibition of passions and feelings, not as the poet's creations, but as historic realities. In reading or studying his dramas, we feel that we are surrounded not by phantoms, but by flesh and blood closely akin to ourselves; and no hard deduction of logic, no persuasion of any kind, can make us feel or think otherwise. They may be Romans, or Celts, or Italians, or Jews, living in the dark backward and abyss of time which we cannot realize, compacted of influences long since extinguished; yet whatever they are they are men, to us more real than those who pass before our eyes, or even tell us their own histories. For if our most intimate friends, throwing away all self-restraint and self-respect, were willing to turn themselves inside out for our inspection, neither

---

[1] Bacon anticipated the evil; see pref. to '*Organon*,' p. xcvi.; anticipated, but not otherwise provided against it, except by pointing out the danger.

would they be able to do it nor we to read or understand the confused characters we should find there without some interpreter. We should be just as much unable to distinguish the writing, as the inartistic mind does a natural landscape, or an unscientific one a complex piece of machinery. Shakspeare supplies the scene, supplies the machinery, and gives with them the interpretation; not from his own conceit or any preconceived theory, not because he has any certain scientific bias or philosophic views of art, which he is desirous to work out and set before us in their concrete forms, but because he 'held the mirror up to nature.' That '*nuditas animi*' which Bacon considered indispensable for the acquisition of truth, with which the severest study must begin and end, Shakspeare possessed more than most men. Unlike the dramatists from the University, who came to their task with imperfect notions of the rules of classical antiquity; unlike Ben Jonson, who thought that a dramatist must be dieted by system, and feed and fast by regimen, to attain perfection, it was the reproach of Shakspeare that he owed nothing to art and all to nature. The reproach was unfounded; but if it be meant that he brought to his task no dry theories, no poetical dogmas, no personal prejudices to interfere with his strict and rigid observance of nature, the remark is just. No poet is more impersonal; no poet mixes up with his most admired and successful creations less of his personal predilections. It is impossible to select any one character from the whole range of his *dramatis personæ* of which it can be said, this was a favourite with the poet. In the full torrent of his wit or the excitement of his eloquence, in the successful exhibition of retributive villainy or the defence of injured innocence, he stops at the due moment, never overstepping the modesty of nature. The scene closes, the character is dropped, the moment the action requires it; and however just or true or exquisite the conception, it falls back into the void of the past from which it had been summoned, often to the greatest regret of the reader and spectator, but with no apparent regret on the part of the poet. Artists and painters in general have their likes and their dislikes, as strong but not always the same as the admirers of their works; they can rarely work successfully without such prejudices. It is natural for the artist to fall in love with his own creations, and natural that what he loves and all admire, he should repeat in various shapes again and again. But in Shakspeare this never happens. His is the truthfulness and dispassionateness of a mirror. And if the unfeeling, the erring, and the vicious are not unmitigated monsters in his pages, it is because they are human; not because his sympathies would have concealed their deformities. It is because even the toad, ugly and venomous, wears yet a precious jewel in its head. The utmost vice in this life is not beyond redemption; the utmost virtue not without its flaws.

But it may be thought that these remarks are inapplicable to those creations of the poet which lie beyond the pale of human experience; such as the witches, fairies, and ghosts introduced into some of his plays. Yet it is worth observing how scrupulous even in these cases the poet is of adhering to popular tradition. Only, as popular credulity is always falling before that *idolon* (against which Bacon protests), of determining the unseen by the seen, the spiritual by the material, Shakspeare is on his guard against this error. He raises the vulgar witches, with their popular familiars, the cat, the toad, the storm, and the sieve, into spirits of evil, surrounded with spiritual terrors and endowed with spiritual agencies. The fairies have persons, occupations, passions that are not human, nor are they susceptible of human attachments. The same may be said of Ariel and Caliban; the one above, as the other is below humanity. The habits of each are solitary, not social, and both are alike unsusceptible of friendship or gratitude. The ghost of Hamlet's father is another instance of the poet's wonderful mastery in uniting the vulgar and sublime. How was the poet to combine in the same personality the earthly father calling for revenge with the disembodied spirit—the substantial with the unsubstantial—the 'sans eyes, sans teeth, sans everything,' with voice, motion, armour? But the popular notion of purgatorial fire, and the half earthly, half unearthly creed of the Middle Ages, on which he readily laid hold, were a great assistance. Here too the genius of Shakspeare delights in triumphing over the union of impossibilities. The ubiquity of the ghost is so harmonised with his local personality, that the reader detects no incongruity in the composition. Besides, when he is first discovered, as the sentinels tramp up and down the parapet of the castle, with the sea roaring fathoms down at the foot, who can tell whether the Ghost comes striding along close by in the impalpable air, or on the firm ground? That Shakspeare should have acted this part we can well believe, for none but he could have conceived how a spirit would or should talk. The characters least within the bounds of human probability are Falstaff and Richard III.: the former as the ideal humorist, the type and catholic original of those eccentricities, which Shakspeare's contemporaries tried to draw, but could not; the other as the type of what sixty years of intestine fever and bloodshed must produce—the poisonous fungus generated out of political, social, moral anarchy, all combined. Both are what Bacon would have called the *monads* of nature.

Shakspeare, then, had no idealisms which he wished to present in visible forms beyond those which would be found in the exact representation of nature. If critics have since professed to discover in his works the profoundest revelations

of art and science, that is because those arts and sciences are
found in the facts presented us by the poet, and not because
they were consciously present to his mind.

It is this continued freshness and nudity of mind, ever
open to the impressions of experience, that prevents him
from falling into that mannerism or unity of style and treatment, into which, with his single exception, all other poets
and artists have fallen. His mind is never stationary; he
never contemplates his subject from one point of view exclusively; he is not a narrator, a spectator *ab extra*, or an
epic poet, but he is intensely dramatic; that is, his own personality is sunk entirely in that of his creations. In this
respect he is superior to any poet that ever lived, not merely
in the complete embodiment of the characters he introduces,
but in their number and variety. Every known region of
the globe is laid under contribution; Greeks, Romans,
Italians, French, Englishmen, Asiatics, Egyptians; ancient,
modern, mediæval times. Every rank, every profession,
every age and condition of life passed before his eyes;—once
seen never to be forgotten; once stored up in his memory,
as in a treasure-house, to be summoned forth, not as pale
colourless spectres—

> 'What story coldly tells, what poets feign,
> At second hand and picture without brain,
> Senseless and soulless shows '—

but with their full complement of humanity, action, thought,
feelings, words, infinite shades of expressions and emotions.
More true also to nature than other dramatists, Shakspeare's
characters are never the mouthpiece of uniform sentiments,
passions, or temptations; they are not the living embodi-
ments of abstract qualities which never vary and never grow.
The masterless passion is shadowed off by endless varieties
and transitional modes of feeling. It is deposed from its
seat by inferior motives, and restored when the due time

comes. The brave are not always brave; the cruel not always unmerciful. Though the unity of the character is never lost sight of, it is not a stagnant uniformity, but grows and develops with the action, and is acted on by the circumstances of the play or the influences of others. As in the infinite variety of nature, form, colour, smell, contour, grow harmoniously and simultaneously, and all from the original organism of the plant—are not, as in human mechanism, the result of successive efforts—so it is in Shakspeare. The unity of the character is never lost in its diversity; the widest apparent divergence from its primitive conception and outset may be traced back, step by step, with the accuracy of a natural and necessary law. Action, speech, expression, the colour and metre of the diction, grow out of the original unity of the character, and yet mould themselves with plastic ease to every diversity of its sentiments and feelings.

It is this ever-varying posture of mind, this flexibility in the style, structure, and colour of his language, adapting itself to every movement of the thought, that makes it so difficult to determine on any common measure of the poet's mind, or, beyond the general power they exhibit, to determine what is genuine in his plays and what is not so. Conclusions derived from some supposed type of style and metre must not be trusted. How can they be, unless we shall have ascertained beforehand in any given case that they are incompatible with the poet's purpose or conception? Homer felt no difficulty in putting heroic words and heroic hexameters in the mouth of Thersites; a catalogue of the ships falls into the same rhythm with the anger of Achilles. The common soldier, or the barbarous Thracian, utters his thoughts in as choice Greek, as musical and as sonorous as Œdipus or Agamemnon. But with Shakspeare the style and metre are moulded by the thought, and not the thought by the metre. Common every-day thoughts fall into prose; Dogberry and Sir Toby Belch rise not into the solemnity of verse. Falstaff and the humours of Eastcheap are the prose and the comedy of Henry IV. and the palace.

That such a writer as this could not fail of being popular with his countrymen we may well believe, and the evidence that he was so is full and unquestionable. It is clear from the repeated references made to him in the writings of contemporary poets. It is clear from the influence he exercised upon the stage; for however inferior subsequent dramatists might be to the great original, it requires very little reading to discover how much in style, composition, regularity of structure, delineation of character, they were indebted to his example. It is clear from the number of his dramas, from the repeated editions of them during his lifetime, from the competition of the booksellers to secure the right of publishing them, from the admiration, not to say the envy, of those to whom theatrical audiences were far less indulgent. Nor was this popularity purchased by vicious condescension to the popular tastes :—

'With such a show
As fool and fight is.'

The occasional coarseness of Shakspeare is the coarseness of strong Englishmen, who 'laughed and grew fat' over jokes which might shock the delicacy and moral digestion of more refined ages, or more sensitive and sentimental races, but did them no more harm mentally than their tough beef dressed with saffron and ambergris, or their hundred-herring pies, or tainted red-deer pasties, interfered with their bodily health. Think of an age that mixed sugar with its wines, and frothed its sack with lime; Homeric in its achievements and in its appetites, in its tastes and its enterprises! But Shakspeare is refinement itself as compared with some of his contemporaries and with most succeeding dramatists. He

does not rely for interesting his hearers on the display of
moral or mental horrors, or questionable *liaisons*, in which
so much of the ancient Italian fiction abounded. If we
except ' Pericles ' and ' Titus Andronicus,' there is throughout his plays an absence of the monstrous and the horrible;
and the poems of the poet are wholly employed in delinea-
ting action and character, either within the ordinary reach
of probability, or sanctioned by historical evidence.

But his popularity is also evidenced by his extraordinary
profusion. For six-and-thirty years successively he kept
possession of the stage, and riveted his claims to popularity
by producing seven-and-thirty dramas within that period:
not of mere farce or incident—not hasty, incorrect, and
tumultuous—but as much superior to the dramas of others
in their ease and elaboration as for still higher qualities of
genius. Not one of these plays was reproduced in another
form: scarcely a word or sentence in any of the thirty-seven
can be traced to other sources. This is as wonderful as anything else in Shakspeare. Other poets 'toil after him in
vain.' Tears and laughter, the inseparable attendants of
surpassing genius, are equally and at all times, and in all
degrees, at Shakspeare's command. The wit of Dogberry
and the sailors in 'The Tempest,' the wit of kings in ' Henry
IV.' and 'Love's Labour's Lost,' the wit of Falstaff and of
Hamlet; native wit, philosophic wit, the wit of the fat and
of the lean man; wit in the half-glimmerings of dawning
reason trenching upon madness; the wit of temperaments
like Mercutio's, of topers like Sir Toby Belch, of mischief
as in Maria and Cleopatra, of confident villainy as in Richard
III.—all these, and many more, flow from him with inexhaustible fertility. Nor is the pathetic and the tragic
exhibited under less multiplicity of forms. Nor is it less
sudden and meteoric than the wit. The reader is taken by
surprise. It flashes on him with the suddenness and vivid-

ness of an electric flash. He is prostrated and melted by it, before he is aware. Whether the reader be prepared for what is coming, whether the poet in the consciousness of his might forewarns him that he may be forearmed, or whether he darts on him by surprise, the result is the same, it is inevitable. In Falstaff's ridiculous exploits, though the whole scene is inexpressibly comic, the burst, 'By the Lord, I knew ye, as well as he that made ye,' &c., is as sudden and surprising as if it had flashed upon us out of the darkness—out of the most serious scene; as in 'Lear,' whilst every fibre of the heart is quivering with irrepressible emotion, one expression in his dying speech, 'Pray you, undo this button,' standing conspicuous in its commonplaceness against the rest, sweeps away the little self-restraint that .remains to us with the suddenness and overwhelming force of a torrent.

Yet as if the ordinary construction of the drama did not furnish employment sufficient for his unbounded energies;— as if he could not crowd his conception and his characters within the allotted range, Shakspeare is fond at times of multiplying difficulties. For it is to this tendency that must be attributed the double action in some of his plays. The principal action has its shadow in some contemporaneous and subordinate one. In 'Hamlet,' avenging his father, is another Hamlet; in 'Lear,' exposed to filial ingratitude, is a Glo'ster equally ill-treated and betrayed by his bastard son —the moral and the natural bastardy. Lesser examples may be seen in 'Taming the Shrew,' and in Falstaff personating Henry IV., a comic presentment of the serious interview between that king and his son;—as if the poet mocked his own tragedy by comedy, or lowered it by an obtrusive parallelism of inferior scale and interest. What writer besides Shakspeare would have ventured on so hazardous an experiment? Yet always certain of his victory, always sure of producing whatever effect he desires to produce, he is indifferent to any waste or profusion of his powers. How, indeed, could there be waste where the wealth was inexhaustible?

And as the theme of the poet extends to the furthest verge of human experience, and sounds all the surging depths of human consciousness, Shakspeare is equally master of the many moods and voices in which that consciousness expresses itself. He is dramatic as in 'Henry IV.,' or epic as in 'Richard II.,' or lyric as in 'Romeo and Juliet,' melodramatic in 'Titus Andronicus,' farcical in the 'Comedy of Errors,' subjective and philosophic in 'Hamlet,' a master of scholastic logic in Pandulph, of rhetoric in Mark Antony, pastoral in Perdita, elegiac in 'Cymbeline.' His songs are unapproachable; there is nothing like them, or near them in the whole range of English literature, abundant as that literature is in this species of composition. And the beauty of these songs consists not merely in the sentiment or the exquisite adaptation of the expression, or their display of broad and obvious feelings, as opposed to those subtleties and metaphysical conceits of a later age, or in their musical structure —all of which they have in perfection—but also in their appropriateness to place and occasion. As contrasted also with later lyrics, the impersonality of Shakspeare is as strictly preserved in his songs as in other parts of his dramatic writings.

It seems then absurd to suppose that such a poet wrote in vain for the nation— that he was not appreciated in his own day. Such insensibility would have been a national disgrace and misfortune—a proof that Shakspeare was not an Englishman, or had materially failed in understanding his countrymen; the only race he did not understand. But, putting aside the praises of Ben Jonson and others, how stand the facts? The folio of 1623 was followed by the folio of 1632, and with it the sonnet in Shakspeare's praise by Milton. The poem entitled 'L'Allegro' represents Shakspeare as the favourite, not merely of the Puritan Poet, but as the general favourite of the stage. It is Milton that accuses Charles I. of making Shakspeare the companion of his solitary hours. One hears, again, of the memorable Hales of Eton, of the accomplished Lord Falkland, of the favourite Cavalier poet Sir John Suckling, discussing at their social meetings the merits of Shakspeare as compared with the Greek dramatists. Of Selden, Chief Justice Vaughan, and Lord Falkland, this anecdote is preserved, 'that Shakspeare had not only found out a new character in his Caliban, but had also devised and adapted a new manner of language for that character.'[2]

For though Shakspeare is familiar with all forms of human experience—ranges at will through all the provinces of history—re-invests with life the most confused, apathetic, shrivelled traditions, and compels Time 'to disgorge his ravine;' be it Lear or Macbeth, Cæsar or Cymbeline, he is never antiquarian. The presentment of his characters is essentially English; their stage is the 16th century. This is the meaning of his anachronisms, the puzzle and the triumph of small critics. The whole range of past experience had been gathered up, not as broken remnants, to be pieced together by the laborious ingenuity of a learned mechanism —not to be flaunted in the eyes of readers and spectators as

[2] As Shakspeare was mentioned and studied by almost every poet and man of genius in succession from his own days until the Puritans for a time put a stop to dramatic representations, and refused to license dramatic writings, it is hard to say upon what grounds the supposed neglect of Shakspeare is founded. Jonson, Drayton, Suckling, Herrick, Milton, Dryden, Fuller, the wittiest of historians, and a host of others, are unimpeachable evidence of the uninterrupted popularity of Shakspeare : of no other poet can as much be said. Even Bacon, though he hated poets, and thought poetry was no better than *vinum dæmonum*, without mentioning Shakspeare seems to allude to him in his *Adv. of Learning*, p. 83; whilst his essay on *Deformity* is little else than an analysis of Shakspeare's *Richard III*.

an ornament to be proud of—but fused and melted by the intense imaginations and lofty aspirations of the poet's times into the reach and limits of the present. The past reappeared to the apprehension of that age as much related to itself, as much a part of the common humanity of Englishmen in the reign of Elizabeth, as the Armada itself, and the perilous rivalry of the two female Sovereigns. To Ascham, Cicero and Demosthenes were not merely statesmen of all times, but of his own times especially—as much as Burghley and Walsingham, or even more so. The whole age was dramatic to the core. In set speeches, in conversation, in grave State papers, the mythical and the legendary were mixed up with the historical and the present, as if all were alike real, and all ultimately blended with one another. The vivid imaginations of men supplied the connecting links and brought the picture home to the mind, instead of setting it off at greater distance, as is the tendency of modern criticism to do. The common ground of all was the supposed humanity of all; varying, indeed, according to time, climate, circumstances, but in all essentials one and the same with themselves and those around them. And this habit of self-identification with past events and principles, with ancient races and parties, with the same zeal and vehemence as they infuse into current politics, has ever been, as it was then, characteristic of Englishmen. If Shakspeare availed himself of this feeling, he did much to foster it. He is comparatively careless of the tiring-room of antiquity,—indifferent, like his age, to the niceties of archæological costume. Humanity is to him, wherever found, of all time, and equally at home to him in all its fashions; and though he never deals with abstractions, like Spenser, seldom idealizes like him; his realism rests on a broader basis than local manners, personal eccentricities, or historical minuteness. Whilst his Greeks, his Romans, his Italians, his ancient Britons, are true to their race, their country, and their times, and could never be transposed, as in other dramatists, without utter confusion to the whole meaning and conception of the poet; they are intelligible to us, because the poet makes us feel that, however remote they may be, they are of our own flesh and blood of like passions, temptations, strength, and weakness. It may be said of his genius what Hamlet says of the ubiquity of his father's ghost, *hic et ubique*; the *ubique* is never disjoined from the *hic*; however wide the rays of his poetical fiction travel, they all converge in one point. Shakspeare is above all other men the Englishman of the 16th century.

Moreover, dramatic poetry, especially dramatic poetry of the Shakspearian drama, is the poetry of Englishmen: first, because it is the poetry of action and passion, woven out of the wear and tear of this busy world, rather than the poetry of reflection; and, secondly, because it is peculiar to Englishmen not merely to tolerate all sides and all parties, but to let all sides and parties speak for themselves; and to like to hear them. It is part of the national love for fair play, part of its intense curiosity and thirst for seeing things and men from all points of view and in all aspects, of preferring to look at things as they are, even in their nakedness and weakness, to any theories, or notions, or systems about them. Not only is the drama most pregnant with this variety, but no drama is ever successful that neglects it. The fair play in Shakspeare is scarcely less remarkable than the infinite range of his characters. There is no absolute villainy—no absolute heroism. He takes no sides; he never raises up successful evil merely for the pleasure of knocking it down, and gaining cheap applause by commonplace declamations against it. He pronounces no judgment; in most instances he commits his characters wholly to the judgment of the spectator. This judicial impartiality is another characteristic of the nation, that hates dogmatism in all shapes, in juries or in judges, in the pulpit or the senate.

In this respect Shakspeare, like Bacon, was guiding the topmost bent of the nation, and in one other especially :—

'There is no art,' says Sir Philip Sidney,[3] 'delivered unto mankind, that hath not the works of nature for his (its) principal object, without which they could not consist, and on which they so depend, as they become actors and players, as it were, of what nature will have set forth. . . . . *Only* the poet disdaining to be tied to any subjection, lifted up with the vigour of his own invention, doth grow in effect into *another nature;* in making things either better than nature bringeth forth or quite anew; forms such as never were in nature, as the Heroes, Demigods, Cyclops, Chimæras, Furies, and such like; so as he goeth *hand in hand with nature,* not inclosed within the narrow warrant of her gifts, but freely ranging within the zodiac of his own wit. Nature never set forth the work in so rich tapestry as divers poets have done; neither with so pleasant rivers, fruitful trees, sweet smelling flowers, and whatsoever else may make the too much loved earth more lovely. Her world is brazen, the poet's only silver and golden.'

Then he proceeds to say, in language no less solemn, true, and beautiful, that, as the skill of every artificer is manifested in his *idea,*[4] 'or præconceit of the work and not in the work itself, so the greatest of all idealists is the poet— and the poet only. Now, as this grand claim, by no mean poet, for the heroical and transcendental in poetry, con-

[3] *Defence of Poesy.* Sidney died in 1586.
[4] So that charming pastoral—

'Come, live with me and be my love,'

with its transcendental images of 'coral clasp and amber studs,' describes what no one has ever realised in nature, but it has its existence as certain in the amorous imagination of the poet as the object to which it was addressed.

stitutes the ablest defence of such writers as Spenser, and the best apology for the popular approbation of the stilted drama of Marlowe and Kyd, it is also the best exponent of the feelings of men like Sidney; men of all others who loved and fought, and died for Gloriana, and carried the nobility, generosity, chivalry of the old Romance into the commonest events of hodiernal life. But when Sidney fell at Zutphen, the last if not the brightest star in this galaxy of men fell with him—the old age of Elizabeth was pestered with the intrigues and selfish plots of noblemen and gentlemen; the round table of Arthur was no more; 'the goodliest fellowship of famous knights' was all unsoldered. There was no one to exhibit in his own person the examples of that type so dear to Sidney and his contemporaries. Besides, the nation was settling down to the 17th century, and to those sterner questions which nothing but the grimmest realism could hope to understand and determine. The high but artificial standing of the earlier age could not hold out against the shock: would not, even if it had not degenerated with the Stuarts. Thus Shakspeare in his unheroism and in his realism was exhibiting to his contemporaries the growing tendency of his own age. The inflexible, almost cruel, impartiality with which he holds out to them the good and the evil, the weakness and the strength, of all men and all classes alike, the sure vengeance which overtakes misdirected but good intentions, equally as it overtakes crime, the Nemesis of extravagant affections, emotions, actions, passions, thoughts, expressions;—the assertion of a law and order in all things, as inexorable as the Fate of the Greek dramatist, which none can break and escape punishment—the world as God made it and not men's passions, partiality, righteousness or unrighteousness would have it—the sun and the rain for the unjust as well as the just—innocence foiled as well as guilt at the moment of its triumph—mirth turned into sorrow—laughter in the midst of tears—light chequered with darkness everywhere—wisdom defeated by folly—manhood corrupted by youthful dissipation—the comic hand in hand with the tragic;—the drunken porter and the murdered king—the convulsive fool and the heart-broken father—earth gibbering whilst heaven is rent with 'sulphurous and thought-executing fires'—fools and wits, innocent and guilty, high and low, kings and pickpockets, the proud and the mean, the noble and ignoble—this is the warp and woof—the tangled web of good and evil composing what men call the world, and set forth by Shakspeare to his contemporaries. With so broad and varied a theme as this —so terrible, pathetic, ridiculous, vulgar, and sublime, the heroic of Sidney is incompatible. Rather it shrinks into nothing on the comparison ; and the life of the imaginary is less full of wonders than of the ordinary hero of every day.

One more characteristic has to be noticed which stamps Shakspeare especially as an Englishman, and an Englishman of the reign of Elizabeth : and this is the prominence given by him to his female characters, their variety, and the important part assigned to them in his dramas. It has been said that, if Shakspeare paints no heroes, the women are heroines. If in Spenser the knights fail to accomplish those enterprises which are accomplished for them by the other sex ; if Una and Britomart and Belphœbe are the guides and the advisers of their different champions; if male courage is unsexed, except it be regulated by purest devotion to women ; in Shakspeare, Imogen, Hermione, and Desdemona stand forth in shining contrast to their faithless, wavering, and suspicious consorts. But in Spenser woman is little else than ideal ; she is too good for human nature's daily food and daily infirmities. Shakspeare's women are strictly real; their very infirmities, like the tears of Achilles, are not a foil, but an ornament to their perfections; their failings spring from the root of their virtues. The criticism which condemns Desdemona and Juliet is as monstrous as it is mistaken. The women in Shakspeare suffer as they suffer in the world and in real life, because, in following the true instincts of true nature, they fall sacrifices to the experience, the selfishness, the caprices of the stronger sex. If parents are careless and imperious like Brabantio, or impure and worldly like old Capulet and Polonius, Shakspeare saw too well that such muddy cisterns, hide their corruptions as they will, cannot prevent the subtle contagion of their own ill-doings from staining the pure fountains of their household. Youth pierces through their flimsy disguisings with a sharp and divine instinct wholly hidden from their purblind vision. With the exception of Lady Macbeth, there is no female character in Shakspeare which comes near the atrocities of Iago or Richard III. The fierce natural affection of the injured Constance excuses her occasional excesses; the weakness of Ann, like the palpitating bird, is not proof against the basilisk-like power and fascination of Richard III.; Miranda falls in love at first sight with a being she has dressed up in her own perfections; even Lady Macbeth has steeled her nature above that of her sex in admiration and devotion to her husband. Look out upon the world, and the same is going on every day: woman complying with the law of her creation, and man transgressing his.

And as Shakspeare differs from previous dramatists in his conception and representation of the real, not the colourless ideal, of woman, he equally differs from Ben Jonson, from Beaumont and Fletcher, with their mere animal instincts and their coarser delineation of the purpose and destiny of woman. Nor is it merely in the purity, refinement, and feminine grace of his female characters that the great dramatist so far surpasses his contemporaries; for 'The Virgin Martyr' of Massinger, and 'The Faithful Shepherdess' of

Fletcher, though rare and unusual, have something of the same excellence; but the woman's nature and instincts are never lost sight of by the poet. If faith, love, constancy, purity, are beautiful even in the abstract, they are more beautiful still in the concrete; and the hardness of the abstract is rounded off when they are presented to us not as fixed and isolated qualities or all-absorbing influences, but'in the tenderness, weakness, and alternations of flesh and blood. The heroism of strength may delight the hero-worshipper; but the heroism of weakness is far more human and attractive. The faint resolve, springing forth as a tiny blade from unpromising ground—now seemingly contending unequally against the blast—now gaining unseen strength and vigour from the contest;—the moral purpose exposed to the storm of passion and the inveiglement of temptation; like a frail craft at sea—now hidden by the waves—now apparently foundering hopelessly—then rising to the storm—creating in the spectator the contending tumults of pity, hope, and fear—appealing to the strongest and most inexhaustible sympathies in the hearts of men—these are the triumphs of the dramatic poet. And it is in this exhibition of moral strength and weakness, whether in man or woman, that Shakspeare excels, even in his less complex characters; whilst in the impersonation of a character of more complex elements, such as Cleopatra, any comparison of the great master with any writer of fiction, in ancient or in modern times, would be altogether absurd. What must that imagination have been that could conceive, or that power which could so perfectly delineate, three such types of womankind as Juliet, Desdemona, and Cleopatra? Whose but his, who, without losing his own personality, seeing with other men's eyes, and feeling with other men's feelings, understood the universal heart of man, and has become the tongue and voice of universal humanity?

But we must forbear. If there be one omission in the great dramatist, if we have one cause of complaint against him, it is his almost rigid, his Baconian, resolution not to look beyond the region of human experience : for to this remark we cannot consider his fairies, witches, and ghosts, his Ariel or his Caliban, as forming any exception. In his days, at all events, popular faith in these ultra-human creations accepted them as beings of this world. But, when we compare Shakspeare with Spenser; when we consider how brief is the interval separating him from Luther; how deeply and how recently the religious heart of England had been stirred ; how all her noblest sons had associated trust in God with loyalty to their nation and their sovereign ; we wonder why the poet should never have exhibited the influences of religious faith and resignation, or so cursorily or so coldly as scarcely to deserve the name. Men and women are made to drain the cup of misery to the dregs; but as from the depths into which they have fallen by their own weakness or the wickedness of others, the poet never raises them, in violation of the inexorable laws of nature, so neither does he 'put a new song' in their mouths, or any expression of confidence in God's righteous dealing. With as precise and hard a hand as Lord Bacon did he sunder the celestial from the terrestrial globe, the things of earth from those of heaven ; resolutely and sternly refusing to look beyond the limits of this world, to borrow comfort in suffering and injustice from the life to come. Such expressions of faith might be out of place in ' Macbeth,' or ' Cordelia,' or ' Lear ; ' but we should have expected them in Richard II. and his queen, in Desdemona, and still more in Hamlet, who had been a student at Wittenberg. Yet Hamlet, who had pondered more than most men on the great questions of life and the destiny of man, when unexpectedly overtaken by death, has nothing more to say than those ominous words: 'The rest is silence!'

Even the vindication of God's order and judgment, of which he is made the instrument, leaves him as darkling as it finds him. Must we then think that the godly spirit and faith of Luther had departed? that Protestantism had failed as well as Romanism? or that Shakspeare, in thus ignoring the great central truth, like Bacon, was, like Bacon, unconsciously exhibiting the Calvinistic tendency, the downward and disorganising progress of his age, by substituting man for God as the great centre of this universe, as the sole and engrossing subject of human interest?

THE STUDY OF SHAKSPEARE.

AN INAUGURAL LECTURE DELIVERED BEFORE THE SHAKSPEARIAN SOCIETY OF KING'S COLLEGE, LONDON.[1]

GENTLEMEN,—I must first congratulate you on your success in forming this Society; and, secondly, on the purposes for which it has been established. You propose to read carefully and aloud among yourselves some great English author; and you have chosen for this purpose the greatest of all English authors—Shakspeare. It is the first time, I believe, that any such resolution has been taken in this College—certainly it is the first since I have been connected with it; and I expect from this Society many useful results. The value and the merits of this new mode of study would appear at once, if for the name of Shakspeare I were to substitute that of Sophocles or of Homer. You and everyone else would see directly how much might be gained for a thorough appreciation of either of these authors, if they were to be studied in the way in which you propose to study an English poet. If a number of you were to unite, and dividing the poems of either of these great writers among

[1] Neither the subject nor the publication of this Lecture is of my own choosing. The Students of King's College requested me to deliver an Inaugural Address on a subject in which they were deeply interested; and as I thought that they had a just claim on any reasonable services I could render them, I would not oppose their desire, notwithstanding my numerous engagements and the little time I had for preparation. The same motive which induced me to comply with their first request, has induced me to consent to their second request, and suffer the Lecture to be published.—J.B.

yourselves, were diligently to examine and master them, each one of you bringing his quota of observation into a general fund, nothing would more conduce to the understanding of your author than such a living conference. It s only because we undervalue classical authors and philology in general,—because we do not see the deep truths which underlie their words,—because we are not moved by the calm, the simple, the manly, the majestic beauty of the thoughts they are endeavouring to reveal unto us,—that we have not yet approached the task of mastering the classical authors with due reverence, hardly even with the sense that they were living men like ourselves. It is only for these reasons that we have never yet felt but that we were all-sufficient to interpret whatever they might have to say to us; and that a grammar and a lexicon, and a few German notes, were competent ministers, and priests enough, for these great apostles of Humanity.

Gentlemen, how august that Humanity is, you, I think, can have no doubt. Your ordinary studies in this place, and the careful study of that poet whom you now propose to examine and sift more deeply for yourselves, have not been without their use in helping you to the knowledge of this truth. You have, I think, been led to feel in the study of one play of Shakspeare, that we are not to call that common or unclean which God has cleansed; that in the highest, and the weakest, and the most unintelligible aspirations of the poorest as well as of the noblest humanity, there is some thing much too deep and sacred to be trifled with; that that Humanity has been taken into God, and that if the firstfruit be holy, the lump is also holy; and second only in importance to the actual indwelling was the expectation of God's incoming to His temple. If then, as I believe, the whole ancient world was lying in sorrow, groaning and travailing for that great deliverance; if that deliverance is, as

I believe, the centre, the gravitating point of all history and all literature, old or new; if it be the insensible law which, in spite of themselves, was shaping men's acts, and thoughts, and words, towards one end; and if the clearest exponents of those thoughts—if the truths underlying all that confusion are to be found in those great writers whom you mainly study within these walls—you will confess at once how solemn a task that study is. You will feel that much is needful for the due fulfilment of it, beyond the mere mastery of the formal grammar or vocabulary of a language—that if it were possible for you to institute a sort of division of labour for the reading of a great Greek or Latin author, as you now propose to do for Shakspeare, appoint a chairman, confer with one another, and invest the whole subject with a truly practical interest, much more would be gained for the understanding of your author than any grammar or lexicon, more than any private study in your own chamber, could accomplish.

Now, I hope it will not be imagined from these remarks that I think you might have chosen some author of the ancient world, instead of your own great countryman. I do not; I think you could not have made a better choice than you have done. I recognise the claim most heartily which your own language and literature have upon your attention. You must think it strange indeed if I did not, considering the position which I hold. And in all the literature of this country, there is no author more deserving of the preference you have given him than Shakspeare. But I have made these remarks in order to set forth more distinctly what appear to me to be the general objects of your Society; why they have decided upon this course, and in what spirit they propose to carry out their plan; not as a mere amusement, as it might be thought—not to read Shakspeare as he is too often read—not to realise imperfectly the dramatic effect of his plays; but to study him thoughtfully, examining him with the same minute care and attention as you would have done had you selected a classical author.

First, then, permit me to make some remarks upon the advantages you will derive by reading Shakspeare aloud; and next, upon the author you have chosen, in reference to your immediate object and your general studies. Many of those advantages have, I doubt not, presented themselves to your minds already, and many more will occur to you in the course of your practice: first, in the mere exercise of the voice, one of the most neglected and yet most divine of human faculties. Go where you will, the singular indifference with which the human voice has been treated is most striking. In the senate, in the pulpit, in the lecture-room, and even on the stage, this neglect is most apparent. The capabilities of the voice are never cultivated, its functions never developed, its treasures of music and eloquence never mastered. As the Romans, when they first fell in with our forefathers, were offended, somewhat needlessly, at their hoarse, thick, and undisciplined tones, so I doubt whether they would be better pleased now. I am afraid that if Cicero, or Virgil, or Horace, could hear our orators and actors declaim, they would scarcely believe that we were nineteen centuries older in arts and civilisation. We have abandoned the rude adornments in which our fierce Teutonic fathers delighted; we have parted with the undressed skins in which the stout limbs of the stalwart Germans displayed themselves to the gaze of shrinking and sentimental Italy; but the hoarse and undisciplined voice remains still, and time has made but little difference. The husky orator, with his unmastered organ, hovering through all incredible notes of the gamut, within these very walls and other walls not far distant, insensibly reminds one of the rudeness, without the freshness, of the primæval forest.

Now much of this is to be traced, I believe, to the extinction of an excellent custom which once prevailed universally in educated households in England, and remained till a very late period; I mean, the custom of reading aloud in families. No long time has elapsed since the evenings, in this country at least, were devoted to this occupation. The book circled from hand to hand, the voice of the readers was heard in succession, the rest sate by, and worked or listened. The scarcity and dearness of books might have done something to foster this practice, but it did not do all; for the custom had grown up from earliest times; it was linked with homely associations; and it lingered in this country longer than elsewhere, because of its connexion with those feelings. Like many other economic and domestic habits, it passed over from the monastic institutions to our English households. In all monasteries, which had been framed originally, as near as the founders of them could conceive, on the model of a holy household, this practice of reading aloud in the dormitory or refectory prevailed universally. At their meals the fathers and mothers of England generally appointed one or other of their children to read aloud to them. King James had all the controversies of Bellarmine read aloud to him at his dinner time. In the poems of Cowper, we have references to the same pleasant habit, not as peculiar to himself and the fireside of Mrs. Unwin, as indeed it was not, but as a common characteristic of a winter's evening throughout the country.

Now this habit alone, without any pretensions to what may be termed fine reading, was of no little service in training the voice, and giving it an air of cultivation and refinement; that inexpressible charm, which in well-bred men and women engages us in spite of ourselves, and is often far more prevailing than the most forcible rhetoric. It was almost impossible for the men of that generation, when they came to speak in public, to express themselves awkwardly, or mar the excellence of their matter by the vulgarity and barbarism of their delivery. Accustomed to read aloud the best writers of their country, habituated to the sound of their own voice, insensibly trained by the surest of all methods to use it in a simple and unaffected manner, they were never apt to lose, as many speakers now do, the grace and the mastery of it in the most disturbed and impassioned moments. A very little acquaintance with the lives of Lord Chatham and other great statesmen of that generation will bear out the truth of this statement; if, indeed, it needed such a confirmation; and there is no reason to suppose that he or his contemporaries had any other training than that to which I am alluding.

Something has indeed been done of late to meet this deficiency in our modern schemes of education; reciting and learning to read now make a part of college and school instruction—with what degree of success I cannot say. But, not to insist at present on the difference in intellectual training of the present system, as compared with the old habit of reading a book or poem through with those who love and understand us—not to insist on the elocutionary scraps and extracts, often indifferently chosen, often more rhetorical than poetic, often dull, and not less often vulgar,— permit me to say that the two methods are widely and essentially distinct in other respects. They do not proceed at all from the same principle. The main and almost the only principle of modern elocutionists is emphasis. The first thing which they teach is, to lay the right emphasis on the right word. Examine their books, attend to any of their exercises, and emphasis is the main gist of their teaching, modulation of the voice the second, and that at a great interval, and, moreover, inefficiently mastered and applied. Now, the first impression upon hearing what is called an emphatic reader is a disagreeable surprise, a sense of unreality, an obtrusive artificialness. Nothing is more tantalizing to a man of sensibility, than to have his understanding continually pulled up, checked, and thwarted, by a reader whose emphasis forms a constant running commentary on the text which he is reading, and a very objectionable distortion of the sense which he requires you to put upon his author. I have been infinitely more offended by the emphatic reading of St. Paul's Epistles or of the unfathomable words of the Gospel, than by the most monotonous sing-song.

But the truth is, that the whole principle of emphatic reading is a false one. Reading ought to be like style, a colourless medium, beautiful only because it is clear and transparent. A reader, like a writer, should remember that he is only an interpreter, no more. This emphasis can never be; for it isolates certain words, dislocates them from their connexion, and crystallises round them not the feelings of the poet, but the sense and understanding of the reader. Besides, in many frames of mind the lips are not emphatic; the deepest passions are often the dreariest and most monotonous in their outward expression; it is only in the cells of the voice that they seem to lurk, eddying round them with a tremulous but scarcely perceptible reverberation. Ordinary readers will be surprised to be told, though you will not, that a people of so delicate an organisation as the Greeks, and so susceptible to the charm of oratory, never permitted the most impassioned dialogues or soliloquies in their tragedies to be otherwise than modulated. The madness of Hercules, the griefs of Antigone, the despair of Œdipus, were regulated by the flute; and it was mainly if not exclusively by the modulation of the voice that the actor expressed the various passions of the soul. If emphasis were used at all, it must have been very subordinate.

The mechanism of the Greek language would lead us to infer that it was utterly superfluous, and therefore was never thought of.

Modern reading, on the other hand, proceeds on an opposite principle; and it is not unusual to hear an emphatic reader keeping his voice in the same note or key, whilst by his emphasis he would have us infer that he is animated by a succession of different emotions. Thus, whilst his emphasis is varying with the varying emotions expressed by him, his modulation remains unchanged. This is both false and contradictory; and this, as it seems to me, is the reason why emphatic reading soon grows heavy and monotonous; why, for any lengthened reading, the natural modulations of a home-taught and sensible reader infallibly charm us much more than the most artistic reading framed upon modern principles.

Hitherto, Gentlemen, I have spoken exclusively of your proposed readings so far as they will assist you in cultivating a faculty very much overlooked at the present day. I have told you in what way I think this exercise may prove of more service to you, in this neglected branch of education, than the most approved modern training; but valuable as I believe that result to be, it is by no means the sole, it is not the highest advantage you will gain. To the full understanding of all great authors, prose writers or poets, but of poets especially, reading aloud is indispensable. I doubt much whether *any* author ever composes a sentence without having some conception in his own mind of its rhythm, and of the effect which he thinks that rhythm is likely to have on the minds of his readers. Certainly this is so much the case with some writers, that we plainly see that the meaning of their sentences is modified by the sound, and they are enslaved by the modulation of their own oratory. But this law, which mischievously enslaves the prose writer, becomes in the hands of a great poet subservient to higher purposes. With him the sound is not merely, as Pope has expressed it, 'an echo to the sense,' but a vehicle of the sense; and you can no more separate from a poem the spirit of music which runs along the verse without detriment to the sense, than you can change the imagery of a poem into dull and decent prose.

We have the confession of a great poet of modern times (Wordsworth), that his lyrics required the natural recitative of the voice. We have plenty of instances of poets showing a feeling of that necessity by reading aloud their poems to others, and of the pleasure they take in so doing; and this is not to be attributed to vanity or love of display. We know to our cost that the loss of the musical accompaniment to the Greek choral odes has wonderfully obscured to us their beauty and their meaning. Nay, I doubt if some poems of a very high order could ever be thoroughly understood unless they are read aloud. I doubt if Tennyson's 'Maud' could; at all events, if I may judge from my own experience. Parts of that poem were unintelligible to me, until I happened to read them aloud to others. Besides, I may appeal to your own experience, whether it is not a fact, however much you may have read and studied a poem by yourselves, that you have gained a deeper insight into its meaning by hearing it read aloud, or by reading it aloud to others.

This is a deep and mysterious subject, as indeed all music is, and all that is connected with music, and with that which is the most spiritual and divine of all music—the human voice. It is that voice, more even than its words, which sounds the depths of the heart, and penetrates the recesses of the brain. Why is it that in the solitudes of nature a man can listen to all sounds, however unearthly, however unaccountable, with comparative calm, but a disembodied human voice would be full of mysterious awe?

Why is it that 'the *voice* of one crying in the wilderness' is so impressive an image? Certainly there is a mysterious power in the human voice over the souls of men, which would be almost intolerable were not its effects impaired by being so common. Now, whether it is that in certain emotions the intellect of man is more clear and penetrating, and approaches at such times almost to the power of divination, as we often see that it does; or whether it is that the music springing from the poem when read aloud forms a subtle commentary on the poem itself, supplying a sense and meaning which words cannot; or whether it is that sounds, by associating to themselves certain ideas, serve as silent guides to the fuller understanding of the poem, I cannot determine. Perhaps all combine; but the fact is certain; and you, Gentlemen, who have had the opportunity of hearing this subject touched upon in an excellent essay, read to you by one of your own body, will be least inclined to doubt it. You have been shown how much the rhythm of Tennyson's 'Maud' serves to connect the different stages of the poem; how by the music of the verse we are at once brought back, from every variety of emotion through which we have passed, into whatever state of feeling the poet considers requisite for the better understanding of the parts of the poem. You have seen how, by the modulation of his lines, even more than by the meaning conveyed in them, Tennyson has connected those various states of feeling, which otherwise would have appeared incongruous or disjointed; just as a great musician winds out from a simple air, or a few solemn bars of music, all sorts of melodies, wild or plaintive, grave or gay, sublime or complex—

'in many a bout
Of linkéd sweetness long drawn out;'—

then brings us back again at pleasure to the frame of mind in which he started with us, developing a most wonderful and mysterious law, which he enables us to follow, but not to comprehend. And, certainly, I must say that in this respect Tennyson's 'Maud' is a marvellous poem; as a lyric, it is the most perfect in the language. No other poem generates its own proper musical accompaniment as this does. The music that rings through it, as you read it aloud, comes back to you audibly on the ear, as you may have sometimes experienced in the notes of a choice singer; beautiful because it is so aerial, like the invisible music of the Tempest.

But I must pass to the other division of my subject. I have spoken of the value of the exercise which you propose for yourselves in reference to the training of the voice; I have spoken of it next as an excellent and almost indispensable help for the perfect appreciation of poetry. Now, I must say something of the writer whom you have selected for this purpose; not indeed in the way of praise, for that would be quite impertinent, but in reference to yourselves and your studies. Shakspeare is the priceless inheritance of Englishmen of all ages and of all times, in his own days and now, when we are young and when we are old, when we need relaxation, or when we are craving for more earnest study. Nay, I do not fear to say that I believe him to be the most religious poet in the language, as much or more than Milton himself, except in one particular. I do not hesitate to say that since we have been reading him together more carefully in lecture, this impression has forced itself more strongly than ever upon my mind, as I believe it has done upon yours. I must also say that when I compare him with Hooker, Spenser, and Lord Bacon, his great contemporaries, the more has this feeling increased upon me. I thought that I ought to read lectures upon him as the great English poet; as one who deserved to be studied as such; as one of whom English men and boys had reason to be proud;

as a great classic, without some knowledge of whom no English education could be complete. I am not ashamed to say that I have learned more from my lectures than I fear you have learned from them. I have learned to feel, though yet far from fully, the inexpressible value of Shakspeare as an interpreter and a guide, not for his own time only, but for the present; not only as the great seer of those sons of Anak in the sixteenth and seventeenth centuries, but for the men of this nineteenth century. And now, at the hazard of appearing somewhat tedious, I will strive to tell you why.

Queen Elizabeth came to the crown of this country at a period of great depression. The reign of her predecessor had unnerved the spirits of the people; without were fightings, within were fears. The graver qualities of the English mind had degenerated into a sort of grim despondency, shared alike by the two parties who then divided the State. In the religious persecutions which disgraced that reign, the dominant party went about their task of vengeance not like men exulting in the triumph of the truth, not moved by religious enthusiasm, but like men enforced by others to deeds of butchery, as they really were, and urged not by their own spontaneous suggestions, but by the bidding of a stern and despotic master. There is evidence enough to show that even the English Roman Catholic prelates who took part in these scenes were reluctant agents; they felt the falsehood of their position, the denationalising and demoralising struggle in which they were engaged. It was a sad sight to behold a queen of this country losing all sense of her position and of her responsibilities, forgetting even her individuality, and transformed into the dark shadow of Philip II.

Not less sad was it to see the nobles and the bishops of this land not the mere agents of a spiritual power, but the trembling vassals of a temporal monarch, who felt that the spiritual power had no existence but for the temporal. A terrible cowardice reigned everywhere; the false Duessa had done her work; valour was separated from truth, and truth had parted company with valour. It is, perhaps, the only occasion when a craven spirit ever came over the heart of so brave a nation. Men looked on at the executions at Smithfield, not as they might have done had some notorious criminal or some terrible emissary from the Inquisition been the victim. They saw nothing but old men, feeble women and children, heart-sick, loathing the light, muttering curses of despair. Deliverance dawned suddenly.

It is impossible to conceive the instantaneous change which followed on the accession of Elizabeth. It was like that of men who felt that a horrible incubus had been taken off them. Nor is that change to be attributed solely or primarily to the different faiths of the two sisters, for the new queen was welcomed by both parties. True, Elizabeth was a Protestant, and Mary a bigoted Romanist; but then Elizabeth was by no means forward in expressing her Protestantism; some of her subjects even questioned her sincerity. There were symptoms enough to induce those who were distant from the court to believe that in her religion she more resembled her father Henry VIII. than her half brother Edward VI. One great difference consisted in this, that Elizabeth was a brave woman and Mary a timid one. The moment Elizabeth ascended the throne, she asserted her rightful authority as the free queen over a free people; she would suffer no dictation; she rejected all the offers of Philip; the people were all to her, and she was all to her people. In Mary, the cold suspicious qualities of Henry VII. had degenerated into jealousy and timidity, though she was not without a spice of the Tudor bearing. In Elizabeth, all the Tudor courage shone out without any of those reserves or those uncontrollable fits of rage and jealousy which transported Henry VIII. The result was extraordinary, not merely as regarded the temper of the nation, but still more as it regarded a class of men who seemed at once to spring out of it as if by magic. The men of this reign were the growth of this reign; we catch not a glimpse of them before, and they disappear when this reign comes to an end. I mean not merely the Burleighs, the Walsinghams, the Leicesters, and the Howards, but that class of worthies who even more than these are characteristic of the reign of Elizabeth: the Sydneys, the Essexes, the Raleighs, the Carews, the Grenvilles, and the like. One is inclined to ask, 'Whence did these men come, and how did they grow? How did they manage to stamp their own image so strongly on this reign? What was the secret of that influence?' Look at them, Gentlemen, as they appear in the pictures of that century, with their high oval-piled foreheads, their delicate lips, their clear olive complexions, their lofty and somewhat Spanish bearing. Look at their exquisite hands and long tapering fingers, neither too white as indicative of effeminacy, nor coarse as indicative of low breeding. Look too, as a type of their minds, at their lace ruffs and gold-studded corselets; strength, beauty, and grace united, not without a spice of foppery. What is it that these men cannot do? For what of valour, of strength, of agility, of grace, of wit, of wisdom, of poetry, of policy are they not sufficient? At their ease in Queen Elizabeth's presence-chamber, dancing a corranto in pearls and murrey-coloured velvet, exquisite in the falls of a ruff and the adornments of the last new sword-belt, more than a match for the bench of bishops in scholastic theology and abstruse divinity, competing with Spenser in all the varieties of English metre and rhythm, slicing up wild Irishmen under Sir Arthur Gray, and seeking the bubble reputation across the Spanish Main; wits, warriors, and gentlemen, dutiful sons, passionate lovers, firm friends, and ready—aye ready, Gentlemen, if Queen Elizabeth only looks upon them, to carry her name and her colours on their sleeve to the utmost corners of the earth.

Can you wonder that men like these, strung up for some great enterprise, both by the peculiar position of their nation and their own hopes, the subjects of a virgin queen, the sworn enemies of all that was mean, underhand, grovelling, or vulgar, should think that they were born to signalise themselves? They are to be knights and paladins, and keep an ideal world before them; not indeed to spurn—no, not that —but to look upon the humbler tasks of life, and even their humbler fellow-men, as objects more of their courtesy than their sympathy. Could they ponder over the favourite authors of the day—Tasso, Ariosto, and Spenser—and not think that the road to glory lay far beyond the ordinary paths of life, that the ideal beauty which they worshipped made its abode in some distant region?[2] Could the wondrous discoveries, far more beautiful than the imagination of decrepit Europe and its dark ages could comprehend, fail of fostering these visions? And, finally, could the mere external differences of forms, manners, education, tastes, hopes, studies, fail of forcing the conviction on their minds that they were not as other men, that they were bound to act not like vulgar men, to think or talk like them? For—

> 'By solemn vision and bright silver dream
> Their infancy was nurtured. Every sight,
> And sound from the vast earth and ambient air
> Sent to their heart its choicest impulses.
> The fountains of divine philosophy
> Fled not their thirsting lips; and all of great,
> Or good, or lovely, which the sacred poet
> In truth or fable consecrates, they felt
> And knew.'

And now, Gentlemen, I beg you to notice the dangers of this state of mind. One sees how soon this aspiration for an

[2] See Arthur's dream in Spenser, F. Q. i. 9.

ideal excellence may degenerate into the ridiculous—how
slight may be the chasm between Platonic love and sen-
suality—how Don Quixote is the conclusion of Spenser's
" Faërie Queen." In these men the danger was greater than
in any others; for they were not men of the sword only—
Christian men, but no scholars—like the knights of an
earlier age ; they were not like the carpet cavaliers of Louis
the Fourteenth's time—courtiers and scholars, but no
Christians. They united in themselves all that can go to
the composition of a true gentleman—knights, scholars, and
Christians, with all the genuine refinement and grace which
the union of these three can produce in their perfection.

Shall they then fall back again into the invisible world
of the middle ages, and contemn the visible? Is it desirable for themselves or their nation ? Is it desirable that
they should inadvertently even, from the very loftiness of
their thoughts, separate themselves from the common
sympathies of humanity? Could this ideal world of theirs,
and this sense that they were to be heroes in it, remain pure
or lasting? Could they do this sort of violence to those
laws and those relationships which bind us together, without
suffering from the process? It does not require much fore-
sight to answer these questions. Theirs was a natural error,
one that is common to ardent minds, though not so common,
nor so bewitching, now as it was then. But who has not
experienced in his life somewhat of the same feeling ? Who
has not felt that he could be a hero if he could have an ideal
world of his own to figure in ; and that it was better, and
easier, and a more glorious thing to seek for honour, and
beauty, and immortality, as poor Shelley did, in some imaginary island, some interlunar cave, some outlying region of
the fancy, than in the ordinary duties and lowliest relations
of life ? After all that has been said about them, there is
something to me of a melancholy in the lives of those great

Elizabethan worthies of whom I have spoken—a melancholy surely not exceptional, but running through the whole tissue of that reign, becoming more sad and sombre at its close. I cannot see how possibly it could be otherwise, or how men with one great mistake underlying the whole fabric of society and the sacred relations of life, could be otherwise than melancholy. The most cursory examination of the portraits of that age will put this statement beyond contradiction.

And now, Gentlemen, this brings me to speak, in conclusion, of Shakspeare's relation to this age and this state of feeling.

It is customary to hear men talk of Shakspeare's heroes, and of his fondness for heroic characters. If they mean by this, heroic characters in the sense in which the Elizabethan worthies would have understood those words, nothing can be more erroneous. Shakspeare's characters in that respect are sedulously unheroic; they have nothing extravagant or imaginary, nothing of King Arthur's or Ariosto's knights, about them. Quite the reverse. The singular thing in Shakspeare is, that his heroes are intensely human—that they are continually treated by him as men of like passions with ourselves, tempted as we are, naturally no stronger than we are, and falling as we do. And what is more, their whole lives and fortunes turn upon the ordinary events and the passions incidental to us all. In that respect Shakspeare stands forth a most remarkable contrast to his contemporary dramatists. He never deals with the exceptional—he never delights in the tragical for its own sake—he does not fill the stage with unnatural crimes, or with amazing wickedness —he does not delight in tracing their progress or their punishment. And it needs not. He has infinitely higher aims in view; he is in reality dealing with those things that 'come home to every man's business and bosom.' If to do that be commonplace—if it be commonplace to show how the minutest transgressions of God's laws—how disobedience to parents, in cases where the world would be indulgent—how ill-assorted matches—how fatherly affection urged too far—how idleness in the streets—how misplaced indulgence —how the main of our happiness and our misery depends on the most ordinary duties and the most familiar and common events of our life,—if this be commonplace, then is Shakspeare the most commonplace author that ever existed, in this or in any other nation. But if, Gentlemen, in these common duties and relations of life—resting as they do on a divine foundation, and imaging the most divine and awful of all mysteries—if, I repeat, in these relations there is more strength and beauty, more loveliness, more true heroism, more real and genuine exaltation of feeble human nature, than in the most sublime of all human inventions, or in the purest ideal that ever entered the heart of man, then is Shakspeare also the most divine, the most deeply religious and the truest, of all poets that ever existed. And all true poets, and all true moralists and philosophers, if they would enter on the same inheritance, must take Shakspeare for their guide and their interpreter. In proportion as they have felt with him the value of the common facts and duties of life—in proportion as they have been able to see and assert a divine law running through all those facts and duties, vindicating itself, it may be, often at the cost of blood and suffering, but always in the correction of wrong, always in that correction approving itself divine, and bringing humanity nearer to divinity, and making it instinctive of divine and mysterious truths—as they have felt this, in that proportion have they been and will be great poets.

And now then, Gentlemen, can you fail to see what was the relation of Shakspeare to the men of his age? or what he was doing to dispossess their minds of what was distorted or baseless? or what he was doing to guide them and interpret to them the meaning of those facts and difficulties which lay around them? Surely, in thus enabling them and all men to see that there was a divine foundation in the common laws and relations of life—that they rested on a divine sanction and appointment—that through them God was making manifest His divine order—that these are the ways, and the ways only, in which we can catch a glimpse into a diviner order than any we have yet seen—that our instinctive love of the strong, the beautiful, and the harmonious, can be gratified only in this appointed way, and not in ways we would carve out for ourselves—in this, I say, are to be found the most magnificent functions of a poet, far more than to suppose that Shakspeare's main concern was to show his own cleverness, or even, in the language of Coleridge, to create a character, or skilfully anatomise the mutilations and diseases of our moral and intellectual being. I cannot but think that he was performing a more noble task in enabling us to perceive, as he does perceive for himself, an order in the disorder around us; and what is more, in showing us the cause of that disorder; and what is higher still, in giving us a clue to escape from it. I cannot help thinking, that in proportion as he realised this calling of his, he was doing God's work; for His work is certainly to bring man to the knowledge of Himself and His works—to enable us to see His works as He sees them—to rejoice in them as He rejoices, in their order, harmony, and beauty. Not in this way or in that—not in the visible world without the invisible—not in the moral world without the material—not in the soul without the body—not in the new merely but in the old; for He sees them all at once, those mighty works which He worketh from the beginning, and 'behold they are very good.'

And now one word in conclusion. The worthies of Shakspeare's times saw as well as we can see, and admired as much, perhaps more than we do, the grand and the heroic; they, more than we, worshipped greatness—great acts of sacrifice, great acts of munificence, great acts of valour. They needed not to be twice asked to lay down their lives for a great principle—to leave homes and wives and children when their country bade them, or her glory or even her gains were at stake. We are all of us, even the least romantic and heroical, ready enough to see the divine and the admirable in these great actions. But it is not in these grander matters, which can happen but seldom, and comparatively to few, and form the exceptional cases, and not the staple of life—it is not, I say, in these that we need encouragement, that we require a higher light than they afford, but it is in the small things and the ordinary duties, in those which belong to every man, and are common to our common humanity. It was the ambitious father who required to be told that his authority over his daughter was to him the representative of God's authority over himself—that it was only this divine authority which gave strength and sanction to the natural obligation. It was the worldly suitor who required to be told, that however respectable his motives, marriage was a sacrament of love as well as faith. It was the brilliant and witty Mercutio of the day who needed to be told that life was too precious a talent to be employed in nothing better than flashes of wit and harmless frivolity. Lastly, all men needed to be told that they were linked together in a mysterious way, and that no actions of their life were indifferent. All men needed to be told that out of their commonest obligations, out of their least noticeable deeds, one touch of sorrow or of suffering could bring forth all that was tenderest, noblest, or most beautiful —that the heroic as well as the true lies at our feet, and not in the extremities of earth or heaven.[1]

[1] See Note on *Romeo and Juliet* at the end of this Essay.

There is one other relation in which Shakspeare stands to the men of his times not less necessary to us now, which I forbear to insist on, as it will properly occupy us in the lecture-room. If these remarks shall in any way assist your object, their purpose will have been answered; if they enable you to study Shakspeare in a way more satisfactory to yourselves, because bearing more immediately on the deeper questions of your lives, I shall not regret my labour; though, I confess, that with the multitude of my avocations I could have wished that your choice had fallen on some other Professor. I have now only to wish you success, and to express my hopes that you may reap from this exercise the advantages which it offers. Of this I am certain, that no careful reading of Shakspeare or any other great poet can ever be wholly in vain.

SHAKSPEARE'S 'Romeo and Juliet' gives us the deepest insight into the strength and weakness of Elizabeth's reign, as 'Hamlet' does into that of her successor. Compare the first act of that drama with the last; consider the difference and the cause of it. With consummate skill the poet brings before his hearers the hollowness and confusion prevailing at the outset of the poem. How idle are those retainers loitering about the streets! how devoid of all serious employment! By their half-jesting, half-earnest biting of their thumbs, the whole city is set on fire; and their idleness and disorder are reflected through the whole town. Nobler characters appear upon the stage, but with the same radical defect. Escalus is a prince with no high sense of his authority; it is not connected in his mind with any nobler principle than the enforcement of peace — nay, scarcely that. Then we have Romeo, whose love is the creature of his fancy, which he must keep alive by flying from his family to a grove of sycamores; he shuts up his windows in the daytime, and makes for himself an artificial light. Then we have the two Capulets, mother and father, devoid of all real love or respect for their child; evidently the mother does not know how old her daughter is. She has been left to the care of the nurse, and the wonder is that Juliet does not show the result in her conduct and conversation, as we have so clear an insight into her most secret thoughts. Even Juliet herself reflects in one way the hollowness of her parents. She is asked about her marriage, and makes an answer with a mock simplicity, which is not of the heart, and is far from her character, but such as any well-bred young lady might have made, who had known all the world and its ways, which Juliet did not: and this, be it observed, to her mother, not to her lover. Then we have Mercutio, the man whose wit is the result of animal spirits, and therefore is a true exponent of his mind, such as it is; he has no seriousness in him, and no deep interest in anything earnest or serious. Singularly enough, he is always in a mistake; he does not and he cannot understand the true character of anyone with whom he is brought into collision. The whole world is manifestly a puzzle to him with all its contradictions; his own life is a puzzle; but he can find amusement in all, and that without being ill-natured. It is only when he comes to die that the reality breaks in upon him in those most bitter words, which all his spirits and his native politeness cannot keep down—'A plague of both your houses!' I need not pursue these remarks any further—my readers can do that for themselves. But what strange materials are these, and how unpromising, from which the poet intends to work out the deepest truths, and build up the most serious realities of this life! How very differently would they have been treated by an inferior dramatist!—by Ben Jonson or Massinger, for instance.

Now, compare this act with the last act of the play, and observe how all this confusion has disappeared. A solemn feeling and sense of order impresses itself upon us, notwithstanding the sorrow and suffering which all the actors in it have been working out for themselves. Observe, too, that that order is not of human creation; on the contrary, every one has been adding his quota of confusion to obscure and retard it. The friar - the religious element—has been doing a little harm to secure what he considers a great good; he has been augmenting the evil which he wished to cure. He has been trying by evil to do good—to justify bad means by the benevolence of his intentions. The two lovers feel that love has changed their being; it has commended itself to their true and natural sympathies; they feel its necessity; and they, too, add to the confusion by a clandestine marriage. The parents, who have been negligent before, now add to their fault by forcing their daughter's consent to a marriage hateful to her, and unholy in itself. The respectable morality of Paris tends to the same end.

Yet this order has established itself—it has manifested itself—and that, too, out of strange elements, and in a way inscrutable to us! The disorder and hollowness in the outset of the play have given place to order and reality at the close; the city is at peace, the families are reconciled, the lovers are united, and in the same grave lie Romeo, Juliet, Paris, and Tybalt.

What has brought out this result? The wedded love of the man and the woman. Bitter it is undoubtedly, in some aspects, to human feelings and ordinary reasonings; but I think Shakspeare makes us feel that, even with all its bitterness, it harmonizes with a truth within us—it is a better and a happier state than the first. As the Mercutio of the first act might pass easily into the fanciful Romeo, and from Romeo, had he lived long enough, into Tybalt, so one feels in the last act that one touch of reality and true suffering has exalted even the most commonplace characters of the play into beings above themselves. There is no comparison between the interest felt for Mercutio and Paris; and yet the most simple words of the latter, as he falls by the hand of Romeo, have more true feeling, and interest us more deeply, than all the wit and bickering of the former :—

> 'Oh! I am slain. If thou be merciful,
> Open the tomb, lay me with Juliet.'

Then observe that in proportion as this reality comes out in men, in proportion as the light and the fanciful are superseded by that which is true and earnest, in the same proportion are they brought into conformity with an order external to themselves. In that proportion the confusion disappears which had seemed to prevail around them. It is an abiding sense of the realities of this life which enables men to recognise more truly the realities of the next. Mere declaiming on the hollowness and vanity of things around us ends in total infidelity; if the present is a dream, the future is no better. Whilst the love of Romeo is merely fanciful, he is no true man; he is not true to himself, to his family, or to his friends. When the rest of the city is raging with party strife and bloodshed, he, a young man, the chief of his family, an Italian with hot blood in his veins, observing the blood on the ground, passes it over with the remark,—

> 'Where shall we dine? O me! what fray was here?
> Yet tell me not, for I have heard it all.
> *Here's much to do with hate—but more with love.*'

Words wonderfully prophetic, though not at that time to the mind that uttered them! But the moment he sees Juliet, his whole nature is changed—he has lost to find himself in her. His true passion makes him true to himself and to all around him. His love is no starveling, to need the artifices of the fancy. His eyes and his sympathies are open to all that is around him, to nature, and to his fellow-men—courteous to the nurse, witty with Mercutio, a true friend, a loyal gentleman. Intense as his love is, it has not overlaid but developed his better qualities. Even the love of Juliet cannot induce him to be untrue to his friendship, though there is a sore temptation to be so. He feels that even that love is lost if it makes him unmanly.

With what truth and skill has Shakspeare worked all this out! How has he again shown us what a poor shrunken thing this world is—what a mere 'beggarly account of empty boxes,' where love is not! How deep a truth, and how much needed it to be insisted on in the age of Elizabeth! This wedded love was not what Bacon said of it,—' Nuptial love maketh mankind, friendly love perfecteth it;' not as Rome had taught, a concession to man's weakness; not as the Elizabethan heroes would have persuaded themselves, a commonplace substitute for a mere ideal friendship, but the perfection of the sexes, the type of the deepest Christian verities, the foundation of whatever is sound, healthy, and lasting in the social and political relations of man.

Looking then at that time, and at other times in history, I cannot help feeling that this is a truth ever needful to be prominently stated; that whenever it is neglected, or disfigured, or placed upon an unnatural or erroneous basis, all sorts of error and confusion follow; it becomes the root of every kind of derangement and bewilderment. This Milton felt, and this he taught when he wrote his 'Paradise Lost' as a commentary on his own age, and showed that the disobedience of Eve to the law of her husband was the prelude of Adam's disobedience, and the rupture of the marriage tie between God and man. This is obvious also from the fact, that marriage was eclipsed of its glory and highest sanctions in the old world, and does not reappear in them until Christ's incarnation. Of this remark the struggles of the old world furnish a wonderful illustration.

To conclude this overgrown note. Mr. Maurice has stated that by a careful consideration of this relation between the sexes, and from having the truth of it brought home to their minds by peculiar visitations, some men have been enabled to see in that great eternal verity of the Holy Trinity, not a mere doctrine to be believed, but a substantive reality, lying at the foundation of all the relations of life, and of this of marriage primarily. For as all things outward are of God, and in His Unity all things subsist, so on the relations of the Three Persons in One God all other relations depend. The old jurists and the schoolmen exemplify this remark. With a statement of the relations of the Three Persons in One God every one of them commences his work; on the truths contained in that profession every one raises the superstructure of all laws and all knowledge, divine as well as human. But there is, I think, another important conclusion to be drawn from the remark of Mr. Maurice, and it is this. The discredit thrown upon marriage by the Roman Church was one main reason why not only the schoolmen in their speculations, or rather in the treatment of them, are so far removed from our ordinary sympathies —(a strange thing if you consider the men themselves, their unwearied patience, their strong labour, their gigantic self-denial, their superhuman strength of intellect)—but this discredit was the reason why the outward realities of life and the world of nature were to them a sealed book and a dead letter. They were unable to realise the visible. It was not until the Reformation restored marriage that it restored the intercourse between man and nature, thus giving the first impulse to that truth .to which the great reformer Bacon dedicated all the powers of his mind, *commercium mentis et rerum.* From that time the book of nature has been to man the word of God; or, in the words of Hooker, 'an authenticall or an originall draught of the law written in the bosome of God Himselfe.'

THE ROYAL SUPREMACY, AND THE HISTORY OF ITS INTRODUCTION.[1]

THE anxiety of the Episcopal Bench to get rid of Bishop Colenso by some legitimate means brings us once more face to face with the Act of Supremacy and its authors. Hitherto, Churchmen have upheld that Statute with as much vehemence and tenacity as if the existence of the Church itself depended upon it. The greatest of English theologians, from the days of Hooker, have flourished it in the face of their enemies as a weapon of proof not less effective against Romanism than Dissent. To the old thick-and-thin supporter of Church and State the royal supremacy seemed a tower of strength. He was not ashamed to be told that he belonged to a Church which owed its superiority solely to its political advantages. He would not have flinched from the assertion that the Reformation was a political movement; that the State Church was under greater obligations to the King than the Bishops. He rather gloried in the fact. He saw in this alliance a pledge that the powers of the State should be employed in securing for the Church a supremacy above all other religious societies. However they might fluctuate and decay he was perfectly secure. It was the business of the State, not his, to see that the Church sustained no damage, to prevent any attacks upon its outworks, and put down the promulgators of schism from within. It was a comfortable doctrine; it saved a world of thought, of labour, and of

[1] From the *National Review* for October 1863, under the title: 'State Papers of Henry VIII. published by Royal Commission. Correspondence of Cromwell in the State Paper Office.'

reading; better than all, it saved him from the necessity of forming a judgment on the difficult problems sometimes thrown in his way. It is pleasant to have others to think and provide for you; it is especially pleasant when thought and labour bring with them no other reward than 'laborious days,' and the imputation of singularity.

There did, indeed, happen times when the Church ran off the accustomed rails, and this State-support became oppressive. The yoke, which bore equally on the necks of both animals in the straight furrow, fell in rougher ground with disproportioned weight on the shoulders of the smaller beast. It was hard for the non-juring clergy in the reign of William III. to stand up and hold their own against the whole bench of bishops; still more hard when the whole weight and influence of the Crown were thrown into the scale of the stronger. Then the clergy began, if not to disavow the royal supremacy, at least to question its true and legitimate limits. The same authority which seemed unfavourable to Dissent when it pleaded for liberty of conscience was equally unfavourable to the exercise of the same liberty on the part of the clergy. Their strength was to sit still. The moment they attempted to stir a hand's breadth beyond the established formularies of the Church, the moment they attempted to walk alone, without recognising the support of the State—that moment they received unmistakable warnings of their helplessness. The Church of England claims in its Articles the right of every individual Church 'to decree rites or ceremonies' as it shall think needful; and the State endorses that claim. It claims authority to determine what is right or wrong in 'controversies of faith;' and the State, with equal complaisance, sanctions that authority. It denounces the man who is cut off from the unity of the Church as 'a heathen and a publican:' and the State has not a word to say against so wholesome and so charitable a doctrine. But the moment the Church attempts to put these abstractions into practice, the State steps in with its Act of Supremacy; and woe to the unhappy Churchmen, singly or collectively, who, deluded by these fair promises, should venture to act upon them. With authority to decree rites and ceremonies, rites and ceremonies have remained precisely as they were more than three centuries ago. The whole nation has been torn with controversies of faith, almost without intermission, from the Reformation to the present hour; but the Church has never ventured to interpose an authoritative voice in these matters. And as for denouncing a Dissenter as 'a heathen and a publican,' we take it that a jury of twelve enlightened citizens would very soon show the denouncers how far such advice was allowable. In fact, the state-support is very much like Sancho Panza's state-physician in his island of Barataria. 'He had hardly put one bit into his mouth, before the physician touched the dish with his wand, and then it was taken away by a page in an instant. Immediately another with meat was clapped in the place; but Sancho no sooner offered to taste it, than the doctor with the wand conjured it away as fast as the first.' Any actual exercise of authority on the part of the Church is neutralised by the State, whether it relates to doctrine or to ceremonies; and therefore, like Sancho Panza, compelled to solace his hunger, in the absence of more savoury and substantial dishes, ' with a hunch of bread and some four pounds of raisins,' the action of the Church rises no higher than to a crusade against pew-rents or the recommendation of thanksgiving for a plentiful harvest.

Sooner or later the whole subject will provoke, as it has long since demanded, grave consideration. Not that, in the present distracted state of religious parties, we are anxious to see those restrictions removed from the independent action of the Church, for such a relaxation would be inevitably turned to mischief and end in its total ruin. But, as we have stated, we are brought face to face with the practical difficulties of the question by the case of Bishop Colenso. As the law now stands, the Church can pronounce no judgment on the Bishop of Natal. It has no jurisdiction over him or any other bishop, heretical or orthodox. He may write and preach as much Hoadleyism or neologianism, or any other *ism*, as he pleases. The Church is absolutely powerless. Long before the Reformation the right of punishing a bishop had been vested solely in the Pope. The Act of Supremacy transferred this, with other ecclesiastical privileges, to the Crown; and we might live to witness the anomaly of a bishop, ordained to drive away false doctrine, maintaining it in his own person, without any power in the Church to restrain or to punish it. In fact, the time cannot be long distant when a much greater amount of freedom of opinion will be claimed both by bishops and clergy. In the rapid advance of art and science, it is impossible that theology alone can remain stagnant. It is equally impossible for the clergy of the Church of England, brought up at the Universities, accustomed to the broader and profounder views which a philology unknown to the sixteenth century has opened to mankind, to remain satisfied with the theological axioms of the Reformers, often based on a total misapprehension of the original language of the New Testament, and always more or less crippled by those narrow habits of thought in which they had been trained. Of the Fathers of the Reformation, as they are called, to whom we are indebted for the Articles and Homilies of the Church of England, who is there that would now be quoted as an authority in any great question of ecclesiastical history, of philology, of philosophy, or even of theology? It is impossible to turn over a single page of their writings and not be struck with the total absence of power and originality. Even in the most learned, such as Cranmer, the learning consists mainly in scraps and commonplaces from the Latin fathers, or miserable translations of the Greek, valued solely for their apparent efficacy in the pending controversy against Catholic opponents, but indicating the smallest possible familiarity with the true spirit of antiquity. It is impossible that the clergy can be long content to walk in the theological gyves of the sixteenth century. And unwilling as the Church of England may be, and, in its present relations with the State, unable to grapple satisfactorily with the question, the time is not far distant when it must be prepared to reconsider its past decisions on many theological difficulties, and claim for itself and its adherents a greater liberty of expression and of action.

Of the history of that Act, which has produced such important consequences and modified the whole existence of the Church of England, we should have been glad had Mr. Froude furnished us with a little more explicit information in his history of Henry VIII. To us it is far more interesting, and in itself infinitely more important, than Anne Boleyn's robes or the feuds of the Geraldines. Whose genius was it that upset the traditions of fifteen centuries, and devised an organisation without parallel in ancient or in modern times? Who first conceived the bold idea—not of a parity of power between the spiritual and temporal jurisdictions, not Warburton's figment of an *imperium in imperio*, not modern Anglicanism, watching to steal a feather out of the tail of the imperial eagle—but a transfer of the whole authority of the Church from a spiritual to a temporal ruler? Who was it that, with one stroke of the pen, to use the phrase of Bishop Andrews, 'transubstantiated Henry VIII. into the Pope' and converted the Church from an independent rival to a ready and submissive dependent on the State? With all the papers and documents before him needful for the satisfaction of such an inquiry, we should have been glad if Mr. Froude had availed himself of his precious opportunities; if he had told us by what steps the authors of such a policy arrived at this result—how they emancipated themselves from the long prejudices of ages—how they ventured, not only in the teeth of Roman Catholic tradition, but of that new ecclesiastical liberty then awakening in the breasts of Continental reformers, to set up an ecclesiastical headship which was neither old nor new, foreign nor Anglican, Catholic nor Puritan. Whose ingenious brain conceived, who shaped into practical form, this alliance between Church and State, wherein both should seem to be equal, but one in reality was extinguished? Was it the natural consequence of English constitutional tendencies? Was it the inevitable result of English Protestantism? Did it find acceptance with the mass of the people from its own intrinsic excellence, or was it forced upon them as a State necessity by the subtle ingenuity of Cromwell, or the iron resolution of Henry VIII.? Every man who cares to read the history of those times feels at once that this is *the* question, this is the keystone of the Reformation; all other topics dwindle into insignificance beside it. This is the real point at issue between the advocates of the old and the new system; this, and not purgatory, not pilgrimages, not transubstantiation; not what Mr. Froude seems ever and anon to suppose, the different degrees of loyalty and morality in Romanist and Protestant. There were men as loyal and pure-hearted as More whose consciences would not suffer them to acknowledge that Henry VIII. was 'Head of the Church;' there were men as vulgar and worldly as Bonner, leaders of rebellion, like the Bigots, the Husseys, and the Constables, who were ready to die themselves, or at least put others to death, in defence of the King's supremacy. The coronations of kings and queens, the pomp of Cardinal Pole's ceremonials, even the death of the unhappy monks of the Charterhouse, sink into nothing in comparison with this. They were but temporary ; they scarcely stirred the heart of men familiarised with such spectacles, and too much occupied with their own griefs and perplexities to spare much sympathy for others. This, on the other hand, has spread its broad shadow across the range of centuries. It has fallen like a thing of evil on Romanists and Puritans alike. If it brought More and Fisher to the scaffold in the reign of Henry, it wrung the hearts and wasted the life-blood of Cartwright and the Puritans in the reign of Elizabeth. If it hung like a sword over the heads of the Tudor bishops, and prevented all relapse to Rome, it equally drove out from the pale of the national Church every conscientious Nonconformist, who was a zealous Protestant in everything with the exception of this one Article. It kept the Church obedient to the Sovereign and to the first principles of the Reformation, but it effectually prevented all organic expansion, whatever the circumstances of the times.

We do not hope to throw much light upon these topics ; a full elucidation of them must be left to the historian of the Reformation. The Acts which transferred to the King the supreme headship of the Church made it treason in anyone to dispute or to doubt it in writing or conversation. Further than this, and with a stretch of arbitrary power unknown even in the darkest times, it was not necessary to prove any overt offence against the Statute ; it was enough to involve a man in the penalties of high treason if, when examined by oath *ex officio*, his answers were not deemed satisfactory by his judges. Such powers concentrated in the hands of one man, or one set of men, could hardly escape abuse even in the most peaceful and regular times. But the great minister of Henry VIII., whose genius conceived these measures, and whose ability directed them, was, Mr. Froude tells us, beyond the passions and temptations of ordinary statesmen. The severities occasioned by them might be bitter, but they were in his estimation necessary and salutary. He entertains a charitable hope that these powers were not abused, and that those who passed these measures were not 'betraying English liberties in a spirit of careless complacency.' He finds a necessity for these proceedings, and excuse in the insecurity of the times; and as Romanists had been persecutors in the days of their ignorance, he reconciles himself with a sigh to the righteousness of this retaliation: 'the even hand of justice was but commending the chalice to the lips of those who had made others drink it to the dregs. They only were like to fall under the Treason Act who for centuries had fed the rack and the stake with sufferers for opinion.'[1] In the present condition of historical literature we are not so unreasonable as to expect that no materials should escape the notice of the historian which can throw light on his inquiries. A few years only have elapsed since the judicious liberality of the Master of the Rolls has thrown open to the student the true sources of English history, and many years must still elapse before those sources can be fully explored. But when Mr. Froude wrote his history there were materials within his reach which we think he ought to have consulted; materials of which ample use had been made by Sir Henry Ellis—we mean Cromwell's own correspondence, formerly in the State Paper Office, now at the Record Office. The authenticity of these letters cannot be disputed. They furnish the most complete insight into the life and history of this wonderful man.

'Cromwell,' says Mr. Froude,[2] 'the *malleusmonachorum*, was of good English family, belonging to the Cromwells of Lincolnshire. One of these, probably a younger brother, moved up to London, and conducted an iron-foundry, or

[1] *History of England*, ii. 330. [2] *Ibid.* ii. 108.

other business of that description, at Putney. He married a lady of respectable connexions, of whom we know only that she was sister of the wife of a gentleman in Derbyshire, but whose name does not appear. The old Cromwell dying early, the widow was re-married to a cloth merchant named Williams; and the child of the first husband, who made himself so great a name in English story, met with the reputed fortune of a stepson, and became a vagabond in the wide world. The chart of his course wholly fails us. One day in later life he shook by the hand an old bellringer at Sion House, before a crowd of courtiers, and told them that "this man's father had given him many a dinner in his necessities." And a strange random account is given by Foxe of his having joined a party in an expedition to Rome, to obtain a renewal from the Pope of certain immunities and indulgences for the town of Boston; a story which derives some kind of credibility from its connexion with Lincolnshire, but is full of incoherence and unlikelihood. At length we catch for a moment an accurate sight of him. In the autumn of 1515 a ragged stripling appeared at the door of Frescobaldi's banking-house in Florence, begging for help. Frescobaldi had an establishment in London, with a large connexion there; and seeing an English face, and seemingly an honest one, he asked the boy who and what he was. "I am, sir," quoth he, "of England, and my name is Thomas Cromwell; my father is a poor man, and by occupation a cloth-shearer; I am strayed from my country, and am now come into Italy with the camp of Frenchmen that were overthrown at Garigliano, where I was page to a footman, carrying after him his pike and burganet." Something in the boy's manner attracted the banker's interest; he took him into his house; and after keeping him there as long as he desired to stay, he gave him a horse and sixteen ducats to help him home to England. If this story is true, the future

x

minister must have had a rough training; and in the midst of it this noticeable fact further shows itself, that he knew by heart Erasmus's translation of the New Testament. After his return from Florence, he found employment in the household of the Marchioness of Dorset in some uncongenial capacity; and at length found his way into the general asylum of ability in want of employment, the service of Wolsey. Here he made rapid progress. Wolsey soon discovered the nature of the man with whom he was dealing, and in 1525 employed him in the most important work of visiting and breaking up the small monasteries.'

Circumstantial as this narrative seems to be, there is hardly a statement in it correct, with the exception of the last. We cannot disprove every assertion made by Mr. Froude, because we cannot always discover when he speaks from authority. Having assumed that the minister of Henry VIII. belonged to the Cromwells of Lincolnshire, Mr. Froude assumes the probability of Foxe's story, borrowed from Bandello. And though he doubts in his notes, as reasonably he might, how Cromwell could, according to Foxe, be at the storming of Rome with the Duke of Bourbon in May 1527, when he was employed in Wolsey's household in England, Mr. Froude is inclined to prefer the more dramatic but unsubstantial narrative of the martyrologist to the drier but indisputable testimony furnished by official documents. We are sorry to dissipate such a pleasant illusion. But the whole account is little else than a mistake. If the story told by Camden and Broke, and repeated by Fuller, be true, it is certain that Cromwell did not belong to the Cromwells of Lincolnshire. 'Formerly there flourished,' says Fuller, 'a notable family of the Cromwells at Tattershall in Lincolnshire, especially since Sir Ralph Cromwell married the youngest sister and co-heir of William the last Lord Deincourt. Now there wanted not some flattering heralds (excellent chemists in pedigrees, to extract anything from anything) who would have entitled this Lord Cromwell (minister of Henry VIII.) to the arms of that ancient family. His answer unto them was, " that he would not wear another man's coat for fear the right owner thereof should pluck it off over his ears," and preferred rather to take a new coat.' Mr. Froude describes his widowed mother as marrying again to a cloth merchant named Williams, ' and the child of the first husband, who made himself so great a name in English story, met with the reputed fortune of a stepson, and became a vagabond in the wide world.' But this part of the story he fails to authenticate. Cromwell had a sister married to a man of obscure parentage, named Williams or Williamson, who died about 1533, leaving a daughter, whom the minister was anxious to place under the care of some noble lady, and induct her into the manners of fashionable society. It is possible that the mother may have been a widow and married a man of the same name as her daughter's husband, but not very probable. At all events, until better authority be forthcoming, the statement must stand for what it is worth.

The facts known of Cromwell's life, so far as they can be drawn from the indisputable data furnished by his own correspondence, are briefly these. The first notice that occurs of him is that of a merchant, trading, in 1512, at the mart of Middleburgh, to all appearance a member, even at this early period, of the Society of Adventurers who had dealings with the Low Countries. Sir Henry Ellis has published a letter addressed to him, at a later date, from Antwerp, in which the writer wishes to engage Cromwell in a speculation for buying cheese; and the whole style of the letter shows that the future minister was perfectly well versed in such operations. In 1520 and the following years he was practising in London as a scrivener and attorney, combining with his other occupations that of a cloth-dyer. He was then living in Fenchurch Street. On wandering scraps of dirty papers, and dry-as-dust heaps in the Record Office, quite beneath the notice of the hero-worship of history, we stumble upon queer bits of information relating to his early career. Here is the back of a bill for cloth dressing and facings mixed up with items paid in the course of his business at the law courts; here the draft of a petition in Chancery, or a list of creditors, hopeful and desperate. As early as the year 1521 he was flourishing in business and lending money. In 1525 Lord George Grey is his debtor for 30*l*., and Lord Harry Percy, Anne Boleyn's unfortunate suitor, for 40*l*. in 1527. Here, again, is a letter sent to him by one T. Tressell, dated from Worcester, 20th October, 1522: 'Mr. Cromwell: I commend me unto you, and I trust that ye have dressed my cloth long ere this time. I pray you to send me word what ye paid for dyeing of my cloth. But, sir, I do suppose unkindness in you that you do not send unto me my pouch of velvet, &c. Commend me unto Mr. Wodall and Anthony Bonvyxy.' This reference to Antonio Bonvyx, a wealthy Italian merchant, to whom Sir Thomas More addressed his last letter from the Tower, is worth observation. He continued a constant correspondence with Cromwell long after his greatness. And possibly it was this connexion with Bonvyx which gave occasion to the rumour that Cromwell had been an agent to the Italian merchants in Lombard Street.[1] Mr. Froude refers with scorn to the conversation narrated by Cardinal Pole between himself and Cromwell in the house of Cardinal Wolsey. Pole states that in the excitement caused by the divorce, and the differences of opinion existing among the King's councillors, Cromwell

---

[1] 'He was a merchant's clerk,' says Pole, 'and kept his accounts, and I know the merchant well, a Venetian, in whose employment he was.' This merchant was undoubtedly Bonvyx.

took occasion to sift Pole's sentiments, then just returned from Italy. At that time it must be remembered that Wolsey was moving heaven and earth to accomplish the divorce, nervously conscious that all chance of retaining Henry's favour depended on his success. It is piteous to read his earnest appeals to the Pope, and witness the excitement which dragged the omnipotent minister out of his bed before daybreak. All other business was forgotten in the one absorbing topic. If successful, he might still hope to retire and spend his declining years in the service of God, and in watching over the welfare of his growing colleges; if unsuccessful, no past services could protect him from the resentment of an implacable master. In this state of things Cromwell and Pole met. 'I told him,' says Pole, evidently alluding to the Cardinal and those who shared his sentiments, 'that it was the duty of a councillor to consider above all things the honour and interests of his sovereign; I enlarged on these subjects as they are enforced by the law of nature and the writings of pious and learned men.' Cromwell replied, that he did not deny that what I had urged were popular topics in the schools, and were received with great applause when uttered from the pulpit; but, he said, in the secret councils of princes such arguments were insipid; whoever attempted to urge them at the council table must change his tone, or bring his counsels and himself into discredit; and he added, that such principles rarely agreed with the tempers of sovereigns, and were entirely out of fashion at Court. It was a wisdom, he said, not to be gained from the schools; and they who come fresh from college to the councils of princes often make shipwreck against these rocks from want of this experience.' In the end he advised Pole to give up his studies and read Machiavelli.[1]

[1] After giving in his text the story of Cromwell's appearing, in 1515, at

If this story be a mere invention of Pole's, it displays an insight into character and a power of imagination not usually found in his writings. The sentiments expressed in it are too much in accordance with the times, and the great change then rapidly approaching, to be altogether imaginary. Nothing could mark off in stronger relief the statesmen of the old and the new era. It is precisely the feeling which would reign in the heart of the new man, who owed his advancement solely to his knowledge of the world, and despised the less practical wisdom of the schools. Nor does it need much insight into Cromwell's character to perceive that there worked in his mind this sort of contempt for learning; as a factor to Antonio Bonvyx, he had made himself master of Italian, probably the only language with which he was familiarly acquainted besides his own. We find him recommending the study of it to Bonner, and lending him 'The Triumphes of Petrarche in the Italian Tongue.'[1] But it was to his knowledge of men and his experience of the world that he owed his advancement. These were the qualifications which placed him at once above all his clerical rivals in the court of the Cardinal. Though his person was

the door of Frescobaldi's banking-house in Florence, Mr. Froude adds, 'this noticeable fact further shows itself, that he (Cromwell) knew by heart Erasmus's translation of the New Testament.' The fact is more noticeable than Mr. Froude seems to be aware of, and adds one more marvel to Cromwell's marvellous career; for by Mr. Froude's account he must have learned Erasmus's translation of the New Testament by heart a year before it was published. But, unconscious of his blunder, Mr. Froude continues: 'A fact (this reading the translation of Erasmus) which qualifies Reginald Pole's accusation of Machiavellism against Cromwell. He says Cromwell told him to read Machiavelli. If he did, there is no occasion to be surprised. Men may read and learn from books which they do not wholly admire.' A platitude no one would dispute.

[1] We doubt if he understood Latin beyond what was necessary for his legal business. The letters addressed by him in that language to persons in official employment might be written by the regular clerks. But if he did, this would be an additional presumption against his shoeless and neglected condition. Very few boys in his rank of life would be taught Latin at that time.

plain and ungainly, even to ugliness, the flexibility and fascination of his manners were universally admitted. His contemporaries could attribute it to nothing less than magic. And there is still preserved at the Record Office the confession of a simpleton charged with resorting to necromancy for the purpose of obtaining a magical ring such as that by which Cromwell had risen so rapidly in favour. Traces of these qualities are to be found in the following letter, which we insert entire, not only as disproving the absurd stories of Foxe, which Mr. Froude is too fond of reproducing with little embellishments of his own, but also because we believe it is the earliest letter now preserved in Cromwell's handwriting. It has other claims to attention. It gives an account of the Parliament held in 1523, where Cromwell sat as a burgess. That Parliament was remarkable as the scene in which Sir Thomas More, then for the first time chosen Speaker, is said to have hit upon this singular device of outwitting the Cardinal and preserving the privileges of the Commons: 'It fortuned at that Parliament,' says Roper, 'a very great subsidy to be demanded, which the Cardinal fearing would not pass the Commons House, determined for the futherance thereof to be there present himself. Before whose coming, after long debating there, whether it were better with a few of his lords, as the most opinion of the House was, or with his whole train royally, to receive him there amongst them—"Masters," quoth Sir Thomas More, "forasmuch as my Lord Cardinal lately, ye wot well, laid to our charge the lightness of our tongues for things uttered out of this House, it shall not in my mind be amiss to receive him with all his pomp; with his maces, his pillars, his pole-axes, his crosses, his hat, and the Great Seal too; to the intent that if he find the like fault with us hereafter, we may be the bolder from ourselves to lay the blame on those that his Grace bringeth hither with him."'

But here is Cromwell's own account of the matter, addressed to 'his especial and entirely beloved friend, John Creke,' then residing at Bylbowe in Biscaye:

'Maister Creke, as herteleye as I can I commende me, and in the same wise thanke yow [for your] gentill and lovyng lettres to me at sundrye tymys sent; and wher as I accordinglye have not in lyke wise remembrid, and rescribid, it hath been for that I have not hade anything to wryt of to your advancement; whom I assure yow yf it were in my lytyll power I coulde be well contentyd to preferre as ferre as any one mann lyvyng; but at this present I being at sum layser, entendjng to remembre and also remunerate the olde acquaintaunces and to renew our not forgoten sundrye communycacions, supposing ye desyre to know the news curraunt in thes partyes, for it is said that news refresshith the spy[rit] of lyffe; wherfor ye shall understonde that by long tyme I amongist other have indured a parlyament, which contenewid by the space of 17 hole wekes, wher we communyd of warre, pease, stryffe, contencyon, debatte, murmure, grudge, riches, poverte, penwrye, trowth, falshode, justyce, equyte, discayte, opprescyon, magnanymyte, actyvyte, force, attempraunce, treason, murder, felonye, consyli[s], and also how a commune welth myght be edeffyed and a[lso] contenewid within our realme. Howbeyt, in conclusyon, we have done as our predecessors have been wont to doo, that ys to say, as well as we myght, and lefte wher we begann. Ye shall also understond the Duke of Suthffolke, furnysshyd with a gret armye, goyth over in all goodlye hast; [whit]her I know not: when I know I shall advertyse yow. Whe have in our parlyament graunytd unto the Kinges highnes a right large subsydye, the lyke wherof was never grauntyd in this realme. All your frends to my knowlage be in good helth, and specially thay that ye wott of; ye know what I meane: I thinke it best to wryt in parables be caus[e]

I am in dowt. Maister Vawhan fareth well, and so doth Maister Munkcaste[r]. Maister Woodall is merye withowt a wyffe and commendyth hym to yow ; and so ys also Nycholas Longmede which hath payd William Wilfforde. And thus as well f[are] ye as I woolde do my self.

'At London, the 17th daye of August, by your frende to all his possible power,

'THOMAS CRUMWELL.'

Of his other belongings at this period it is not easy to speak with precision. But there is not a tittle of evidence to justify belief that he was an erratic and shoeless adventurer. In fact, all evidence points to an opposite conclusion. He was a steady thriving merchant, married and settled in life, at the very time when he is supposed to be wandering in Italy, dependent on the charity of the Frescobaldi. So fall Mr. Froude's anecdotes of the bellringer at Sion whom he shook by the hand, and told the crowd of courtiers that 'this man's father had given him many a dinner in his necessities;' of the manner, still more romantic, in which he repaid Frescobaldi, who afterwards came to poverty—a story dressed up with great dramatic effect by Foxe.

To speak of his family. Of his wife frequent notice occurs in his correspondence ; and the 'tattered stripling' must have been married at the time he is described as appearing before Frescobaldi. He had a son named Gregory, a dull boy,[1] not very well educated, who had already been under several masters, while he was placed at Cambridge, under a tutor named Chekyngs. This could not have been later than 1528 or 1529, when Cromwell was in Wolsey's service. Supposing Gregory was the eldest child, and was between thirteen and fourteen at the time he was sent to the University, we must

[1] He was 'almost a fool,' says Hills, a stern Puritan, writing to Bullinger.

assign his birth to the year 1515, or at the latest 1516—a date much too early for Foxe's story. We find Mr. Chekyng dunning the future great man, then a wealthy merchant, for the shabby sum of 6l. and the repayment of 30 shillings, which he had been out of pocket for Gregory's commons ; and to add to the shabbiness of the whole affair, Cromwell, who had innumerable bags of ducats to relieve the imaginary poverty of Frescobaldi, pays the poor schoolmaster only a part of his bill, under the plea that Gregory had not 'got on well with his learning.'

How Cromwell was taken into Wolsey's service we have only conjecture to help us. But we cannot be far wrong in supposing that he owed this advancement to his knowledge of business, and his skill as a lawyer. From early times he had been employed in this capacity. The numerous drafts of leases and agreements in his handwriting, now at the Record Office, add probability to this conjecture. He was not admitted to any part in Wolsey's political negotiations. The Cardinal was at this time busy in suppressing the smaller monasteries, and conferring their houses and estates upon the two colleges he was then erecting at Ipswich and Oxford. The transfer of the property, the settlements with the tenants, the adjustment of different claims fenced in by canon and by common law, was a work of great intricacy— far more than the Cardinal had anticipated. The suppression of the smaller religious houses roused up a host of powerful enemies, not only among the abbots and bishops, but among the most influential nobility, whose progenitors had been the founders of these houses, and who still claimed a sort of right over them by virtue of these foundations. It wanted but this one act of aggression—for aggression it was then considered—to fill up the measure of Wolsey's unpopularity, and provoke the vengeance of those who were already bent upon his destruction. Stories were industriously circulated of unhappy monks who had been turned out of their ancient homes and sent adrift upon the world to starve. The nobility and the bishops regarded the act as an unjustifiable aggression on their property, to be followed by others not less alarming. Had he succeeded in effecting the divorce, it is possible that Wolsey might have outlived this storm; defeat boded irretrievable ruin. Still this mighty man kept on his way, and concentrated all his energies for this last effort. Shorn of his strength, hated by Charles, deceived by Rome, betrayed by Suffolk (of all betrayals the most ignominious and disgraceful), detested by Anne Boleyn, and coldly supported by the King, he was not to fall an inglorious victim. His despatches, always bold, vigorous, and comprehensive, are at this time infused with the energy and rhetoric of despair. It was his last appeal; the die was cast; the world was against him. Men looked tamely on his dying struggle with a sort of curiosity, not unmixed with awe and even satisfaction. No wonder the effort was too great; and the overstrained nerves of the expiring minister gave in their reaction no other proof of what he had been except tears and imbecility. But under these overwhelming cares he had little thought or time to spare for the adjustment of leases and the settlement of rents. It was a relief to find an able man, not unambitious to please, to whom he could delegate the business. His concern for his colleges survived all other considerations. They were the last thought of his dying moments; and if any of his old affections still survived from the wear and pressure of political life, they survived to fix themselves with exclusive energy on that one object which, to Wolsey's apprehension, seemed the sole relic of his herculean labours and better aspirations. His greatness had passed away never to return; the purpose to which he had devoted his life had been shipwrecked; his colleges still survived to embalm his memory and pray for their founder. With this anxiety strong upon him, even in the heaviest moments of his life, it is not surprising that Cromwell should have attained a high place in his favour; still less that he, then a burgess in Parliament and accustomed to parliamentary business, should have been selected by the Cardinal to watch the bill of attainder preferred against his master, which Mr. Froude rightly characterises as 'violent, vindictive, and malevolent.' It was much too violent and vindictive to have any chance of passing the House. In fact, his enemies— even the Duke of Norfolk, the most formidable—had already begun to relent. Satisfied with humbling the Cardinal and removing him from the Court, they had no wish to proceed to extremities. Mr. Froude is rapt in admiration at Cromwell's chivalrous and disinterested conduct on this occasion, and speaks of the gallant service rendered by him in serving Wolsey. We have no wish to detract from the merits of that service; but what other line of conduct could he have pursued with decency, and what disgrace or peril did he incur by its espousal? It might have been inferred from Mr. Froude's language that Cromwell stood alone in this respect, but others were equally forward, and certainly quite as disinterested in their intercessions: 'Master Russell told me,' says Chapuys, an authority to whom Mr. Froude will readily defer, 'that, on account of a few words in favour of the Cardinal which he had reported (*porté*) to the King, the *Lady* (Anne Boleyn) had held him in great displeasure, and refused to speak to him for a whole month; and that a week ago the Duke of Norfolk told Russell how much the *said Lady*, his niece, was irritated with him, and also against the Duke, because he had not done his worst against the Cardinal.' We have the same authority for the assurance that, the irritation of the moment once over, the King's favour was rapidly returning. 'A gentleman told me,' says Chapuys, writing on the 27th of November, 'that a short time ago, the

King was complaining to his council of something that had not been done according to his wish, and exclaimed, in great wrath, that the Cardinal was a very superior man in managing business to any of them. And he repeated this twice. Since then the Duke, the *Lady*, and her father have not ceased from their machinations against the Cardinal, the *Lady* especially, who does not cease to bewail her lost time and her blemished reputation, threatening the King that she will leave him. They say that the King has had trouble enough to quiet her; and that he prayed her most earnestly, *with tears in his eyes*, not to talk of leaving him; but nothing would satisfy her without a promise that the Cardinal should be arrested.' That the King therefore should not be sorry to see that justice done to the Cardinal he had not the firmness to do himself, was natural enough. Mr. Froude says, with an air of solemnity, commenting on this part of Cromwell's history, 'I cannot call him ambitious; an ambitious man would scarcely have pursued so refined a policy, or have calculated on the admiration which he gained by adhering to a fallen minister.' Mr. Froude seems to us simply to misapprehend the real position of parties. Such magnanimity has been as frequently exhibited in the nineteenth as it was by Cromwell in the sixteenth century. It was a struggle for pre-eminence between two factions: that of the nobles headed by Norfolk, backed up by Charles, and supported by Anne Boleyn; and that of the Cardinal—a head without followers. Till the day of Wolsey's death, it was almost universally expected that he would be restored to favour; and the paroxysm of fright into which his enemies were thrown the moment the King exhibited any signs of relenting only show how well these apprehensions were founded.[1] What

[1] James Clyffe, a priest, writes to Bonner, Wolsey's chaplain: 'My Lord of Wiltshire is in the French King's Court. Mr. Leye is come home; it is thought he hath not brought such news as have been longed (longyt) for. In divers pleas, wherein my Lord Card. grace is communed of, and among

could Cromwell expect by throwing himself into the arms of
Wolsey's opponents ? He had no favour to anticipate from
that quarter. He would have been looked upon as a deserter ;
and he had other inducements of a personal nature we
cannot now stop to insist upon. He chose the more graceful
and the more generous path—that of supporting the cause
of his old master ; but in serving him he served himself.

From Wolsey's, Cromwell passed into the King's service,
but how soon and by what steps we have no evidence to tell.
We find him, in the Michaelmas term of 1531, addressed as
the King's trusty Councillor, if the date be correct, and
appointed to confer with the King's learned 'Counsaell'
much on the same business as he had been employed in by
Wolsey. The candidates at this time for royal favour were
the Duke of Norfolk, who had been mainly instrumental in
Wolsey's downfall, and Stephen Gardiner, Secretary of State
and Bishop of Winchester. Probably both looked upon the
new pretender with infinite disdain ; one as a mere upstart,
the other as his former inferior in Wolsey's household.
Norfolk had the reputation of being hard and imperious ; his
treatment of Wolsey had not heightened his popularity; to
Henry he was never acceptable, though he did everything in
his power to secure the King's good graces. But besides the
influence of his rank, his services, and his riches, he had the
support of Anne Boleyn, of her father and brother, and, such
as it was, of the Duke of Suffolk. Gardiner, wily, ingenious,
and supple, had recommended himself to the King by his zeal
and ability in conducting the negotiations for the divorce.
The confidence reposed in him by the King was unbounded,
and his great experience as a diplomatist, picked up under
Wolsey, gave him signal advantages. Had he combined his

Lords of the Council specially, they fear that they shall of necessity be
compelled to ask for my Lord Card. grace again. God continue their
minds in that behalf. The King's grace and the Queen as this day lie at
Hampton Court, and my Lady Anne. 29 May (1530).'

forces with Norfolk, the two together might have succeeded in excluding Cromwell from power. But why should they? Who would ever have dreamed of such an advancement? Had it not been the boast of the King to surround himself with scholars, to have about his Court the best educated ambassadors and ministers in Europe? No one up to this time had ever been preferred to any post of importance who did not seem to possess some claim to it from the eminence of his attainments, or who did not command it by the eminence of his birth. The whole administration of the reign had been managed by scholars and nobility. Here was a new man who could lay claim to neither distinction. He had been unknown when he made his appearance at Court, except for his damaged reputation and his faithful adherence to a disgraced minister. He had no friends, and apparently he looked to none. He does not seem to have paid extraordinary court to Anne Boleyn, or any of her numerous relatives and hangers-on, who now monopolised the King. Perhaps he did not expect favour from one whose resentment was sharp, if not lasting, and who would not forget that he had been the confidant of the man she hated above all others. Possibly Mr. Froude may set down this indifference to the sense of virtue, and to a conviction in Cromwell's mind of the Queen's immorality. We attribute it to lower motives; for we cannot, after due examination, accept his estimate of the character of this minister. To Mr. Froude we must apply the language he has used in examining and condemning the conduct of Queen Anne:[1] 'If Protestant legends are admitted as of authority, the Catholic legends must enter with them, and we shall only deepen the confusion. The subject is one on which rhetoric and rumour are alike unprofitable. We must confine ourselves to accounts written at the time by persons to whom not the outline of the facts only was known,

[1] ii. 462.

but the circumstances which surrounded them.' We accept these conditions with pleasure, and only regret that Mr. Froude himself should so often have departed from them.

Certain it is, then, that the new candidate for power regarded Anne Boleyn with indifference, if not with positive dislike. He is even accused by Alexander Ales, the Scotch reformer, then resident in London, with having poisoned the King's ear against her.[1] But whatever may be thought of this charge, this very isolation of Cromwell turned to his advantage. He had but one anxiety—to please the King; and in this he was eminently successful. Whilst his two grand and learned rivals were despatched on foreign missions, he, much too humble and obscure for such splendid employments, remained at home in close attendance on the King. He might have found a dangerous rival in Sir Thomas More; and a few years before no one bid so fair as More to engross the favour of Henry. The smiles for which other men grovelled in the dust, and bartered their faith and their principles, fell unsolicited on More. On no man's neck did the King hang with greater familiarity; in no man's conversation and society did he take so much delight. If he attempted to be familiar with Wolsey, there was something in the very character and surroundings of the Cardinal, something perhaps in the supremacy of his intellect, which forbade ease and raised up a shadow between them. If the King was willing for a time to forget his crown and his dignity, Wolsey never forgot, in the proudest achievements of diplomacy, that he was the King's 'most humble chaplain and bedesman.' But More, witty, charming, easy, and refined, would not bate an iota of his principles; he had turned a deaf ear to the blandishments of Courts, to employ himself in writing against heretics. His opinions on the divorce were too well known;

[1] In a letter addressed by him to Queen Elizabeth, September 1, 1559.

and he hastened to get away from the uncongenial atmosphere of a palace. So the whole field was left to Cromwell; and he was not a man to let his opportunities lie idle. In the autumn of 1532 he attended the King to the interview with Francis at Calais; in 1533 he was Chancellor of the Exchequer, master of the jewel-house, and recorder of Bristol; in 1534 he was Secretary of State, and Master of the Rolls; in 1535 and the next year Visitor of all Monasteries, Vicar-General, or King's Vicegerent in all ecclesiastical matters, and Lord Privy-Seal. Within these few years he had engrossed in his own hands powers such as no subject and no sovereign in this country had ever possessed before or will ever possess again. As Secretary of State he had the ear of the King exclusively; he opened the despatches of ambassadors and dictated their instructions; he issued commissions, filled up appointments; disciplined and dictated to the House of Commons. As Visitor of Monasteries he appointed abbots and priors, disposed of monastic pensions, corrodies, and leases; interfered with discipline, punished offenders. As Vicegerent in ecclesiastical matters he presided in person or by deputy over Convocation, taking precedence of the Archbishop of Canterbury; he summoned, dissolved, managed it at his sole will and fiat. To him archbishops and bishops rose up and bowed down as to the great golden image which Nebuchadnezzar the king had set up. He disposed of livings, he granted church leases, he regulated the punishments and promotions of ecclesiastics from the highest to the lowest. Great and unconstitutional as were these powers, wielded at the will of one individual, without the check of public opinion or the control of an independent House of Commons, they were infinitely increased by the Acts of Supremacy and High Treason. By these Acts, any man's house could be ransacked without notice at any moment, his papers and books seized and sent to London and himself committed to prison and the rack,[1] on the most frivolous accusation. If at any time, in the carelessness of conversation or the heat of discussion, he had dropped an incautious or angry word which could be construed as expressing a doubt of the King's marriage, or the spiritual nature of the King's supremacy; if he possessed a book or paper, however secret, in which these topics were discussed; if he had by carelessness failed to obliterate the name of the Pope or Thomas à Becket from every MS. which he possessed; if he expressed commiseration for Queen Katherine, or questioned the virtues or good qualities of Queen Anne, he fell under the penalties of high treason; and if he did not forfeit his life, he was committed to prison, there to remain for an indefinite period, until Cromwell sent down an order for his release or execution. Nor was it necessary that the unhappy culprit should know the offence precisely with which he was charged, or be confronted with his accuser. Malice, ignorance, even a blunder, were active causes in bringing many to gaol.

But Mr. Froude will tell us these powers were seldom abused; at least he has so much confidence in the goodness of Cromwell as to assure us, if any mistakes were made or any undue severity shown, they fell only on those who had monopolised for centuries religious persecution. We cannot accept such an assurance. We do not see how it would excuse the arbitrary proceedings of the times if we did. We do not believe that the punishment fell only on men who, themselves or their forefathers, had been actively engaged in persecution, or that these considerations weighed with those who administered the laws. Far from it. Men like Bonner and Gardiner escaped, not because they abhorred persecution,

---

[1] Notice of the use of the rack is found more than once in this minister's papers and correspondence. Few were able to resist such an argument in support of the King's supremacy.

but because if they had scruples of conscience they swallowed them, and took the oath. More and Fisher, and men of tender and scrupulous consciences—and there were thousands such —whose objections to the King's supremacy did not, as Mr. Froude terms it, consist merely in sarcasm, but in a real difficulty—these men, we say, were executed, not because they or their fathers had been persecutors for centuries, but simply because they refused to forswear themselves. A very superficial acquaintance with the correspondence of the times will show how bitterly these laws were carried into execution; how every parish bailiff, headborough, justice of the peace, and knight of the shire, was forward to recommend himself to the great man and his favour, and his multitudinous means of preferment, by hunting down unhappy subjects. The more numerous the victims, the more unquestionable the loyalty of the persecutor, the better his chances of promotion. Even the officious zeal of modern policemen has to be kept in check by magisterial caution and restraint; what was it, then, when the whole kingdom was converted into spies, informers, and sharp executors of the law, stimulated to their task by the hopes of gain or distinction at Court. The correspondence of Cromwell is filled with cases of this kind. Here is one instance of administering justice for which Sir Roger Townshend doubtless expected the thanks of the minister:

'Please it your good Lordship to be advertized that there was a poor woman of Wellys beside Walsyngham that imagined a false tale of a miracle to be done by the image of our Lady that was at Walsyngham, sith the same was brought from thence to London; and upon the trial thereof by my examination from one person to another, to the number of six persons, and at last came to her that she was the reporter thereof and to be the very author of the same, *as far forth as my conscience and perceiving could lead me.* I committed her therefore to the ward of the constables of Walsyngham. The next day after, being market day there, I caused her to be set in stocks in the morning; and about nine of the clock, when the said market was fullest of people, with a paper set about her head written with these words upon the same, *A reporter of false tales,* [she] was set in a cart and so carried about the market stede and other streets in the town, staying in divers places where most people assembled, young people and boys of the town casting snowballs at her; this done and executed, [she] was brought to the stocks again and there set till the market was ended. This was her penance, for I knew no law otherwise to punish her but by discretion; trusting it shall be a warning to other light persons in such wise to order themself. Howbeit, I cannot perceive but the said image is not yet out of some of their heads. I thought it convenient to advertise your Lordship of the truth of this matter, lest the report thereof coming into many men's mouths might be made otherwise than the truth was: therefore I have sent to your Lordship by Robert Touneshend the said examination. Thus I beseech Almighty Jesu evermore to have your good Lordship in his best preservation. Written the 20th of January.'

In another letter, written about the same time, from Sir Thomas Blount, we find eight poor men and two women hanged for offences against the Act of Supremacy, and a poor tailor, Miles Denison of Kidderminster, for expressing his indignation at the proceedings, was committed to prison. 'Your Lordship shall be advertised that Dr. Taylor, chaplain unto my Lord Bishop of Worcester (Latymer), was one which preached on Saturday 27th July last past, at the place of execution, where eight men and two women suffered death. And his sermon did set forth the King's authority of supremacy, and persuaded the prisoners to take their death charitably and to take the same death for the satisfaction to the world only, and Christ for the satisfaction of their sins, by reason of which sermon the prisoners so did, and gave thanks to the King and his officers for their just execution and death.' The offence of the tailor consisted merely in passing a very unceremonious remark on the preacher: 'This is a foolish knave priest, come to preach of the new learning, the which I set not by.' A pewterer of Hereford was committed to gaol by the mayor for saying, 'I trust to see Queen Katherine's banner spread again, and she shall be Queen of England in her old place, by the grace of God.' These are but a few of the numerous instances of the way in which the statutes were enforced against the laity. Those against the clergy are more numerous, but equally disproportioned to the offence. One priest is committed to prison for saying that he thought the King could not be supreme head of the Church, 'for he could not give a man that thing that he should have when he came into the world, nor when he went out of it'—*i.e.* the sacraments; a remark which at least indicates, what no careful student of these times will deny, a persuasion in the minds, even of the educated, that the King did claim by his supremacy precisely the same spiritual powers which had been exercised by the Pope. On another occasion, a schoolmaster was sent to gaol for having a Bible in his possession of which three or four lines in the preface relating to the supremacy were cancelled and blotted out, though he denied it was his doing. Two friars are subjected to the same penalty for saying that they would not for a year or two buy new habits, for 'by that time perchance there will be another change.' A Cambridge undergraduate is imprisoned for saying, what nowadays few would deny: 'If the Pope would have consented that the King might have married Anne Boleyn, he would have been Pope still, and been called Holy Father.' Two active magistrates write to Cromwell to inform him, that they had committed to ward a curate who had confessed his 'conscience would not serve him to speak against the papal supremacy, " because he heard that the Bishop of Rochester and the fathers of Sion had suffered death for it." But he confessed to us that he prayed every Sunday in the pulpit, where he was curate, for our Sovereign Lord King Henry VIII., supreme head of the Church of England, and for Queen Anne his wife, and the Lady Elizabeth princess, their daughter.' He professed his sorrow for his omission, and offered to comply ; but notwithstanding he was sent to prison. Richard Thompson, a clerk, is committed to the King's Bench, for praying for the Bishop of Rome ' at the compulsion of his parishioners, whom he durst not contrary at that time.' In some cases the Statute assumes a more aggravated form. Clerk, the Bishop of Bath and Wells, whose sympathies leaned to the old religion, informs Cromwell that he had imprisoned a priest for not having preached to his parish 'against the Bishop of Rome's usurped authority.' Another had been committed to gaol, there to continue until Cromwell's pleasure be known, for omitting to erase the Pope's name from his own private books. One minister, apparently a Puritan, is brought up before the justices for exclaiming in his pulpit, ' the King is naught, the bishops and abbots are naught, and himself was naught too.' Another for tripping on a similar occasion— ' that the holy Bishop Urban, sometime *Pope* of Rome,' and then he advised himself and said, 'holy Urban, *Bishop* of Rome, had granted pardon,' &c. Sir Anthony Brown is examined by the Council solely for expressing a wish ' that God would give the Lady Mary grace to submit herself to the King;' and this was interpreted 'as bold talking of the King's succession.' In fact, the whole land swarmed with informations. Malice or ignorance might convert into high treason the most innocent or the most careless expressions, and men found themselves hopelessly immured in the walls of a prison, and their goods confiscated, for crimes they had never committed, solely because they had no friend at Court to recommend their case to the consideration of the minister.

It is difficult to see in any of these instances, and they might be easily increased, on what fair principles of construction such offences could be legitimately interpreted as offences against the Statute; and it may be urged that Cromwell must not be made accountable for the blunders and misapplied zeal of country justices and incompetent magistrates. But no one who has studied the phraseology of the Act can doubt that it was thus loosely worded in order to allow of its widest possible application. It was a net intended to catch the weak equally with the subtle; an instrument which threw into the hands of an arbitrary minister indefinable powers of oppressing his enemies. This is a harsh judgment we admit. But even those who take a more favourable view must acknowledge that, though these instances of the perversion of the law were brought immediately to the notice of Cromwell, and are found in his correspondence, no attempt was ever made by him to correct the evil or moderate the intemperate zeal of his informers. In fact, the reverse is true. He grew more arbitrary; he endeavoured to surround himself and his exorbitant authority with a sanction that should make it high treason to dispute his acts, or breathe a censure on his character. Far as the crime of treason had been extended by his legislation, he sought to extend it yet farther. There is a draft of an Act among his papers, in his own hand, in which, among other offences to be punished as high treason, we find that of leaving the realm without a licence; living in the dominions of a foreign prince; annoying the King, his ambassadors or servants; causing them to disclose the King's secrets—offences even more vague than those included in the Act of Supremacy. And therefore these arbitrary extensions of the Act, already too vague and comprehensive in its penalties, are not to be attributed to the subtle interpretation of the Crown lawyers, as Mr. Froude would have his readers believe,[1] but were part of the original intention of its framer; and Cromwell is the first and, we believe, the only minister, who placed himself on a level with the Sovereign, by bringing offences and words against himself under the Statute of High Treason. Magistrates were taught to make no distinction. Was it likely they would? Expressions against Cromwell were visited with the same penalties as words against the King, his crown, his marriage, his supremacy. We find the justices of Ludlow acting upon this understanding. They write to Cromwell to say that they have apprehended a priest for speaking words against him, sealed his house and taken an inventory of his goods, and delivered his plate and property to certain persons for the use of the King. They had searched his house and examined his papers, to find if there was 'any untruth' to our Lord the King, but had found nothing. From a bag belonging to the priest, containing 76*l*. 16*s*., they had taken 20*l*. to pay their own expenses, 10*l*. for engrossing the inventory, and 10*l*. for the messenger appointed to carry this information to Cromwell!

We could easily fill the whole of our space with instances of such arbitrary proceedings, but we must press on. They show a systematic attempt to force the consciences of men, to punish them for their religious convictions, and strain the law to its utmost for this purpose. Mr. Froude will excuse it as a State necessity; he will draw a subtle distinction between punishments inflicted for offences against the State and punishments merely for religion; he will contend that these were civil, not religious crimes, and were only punished as dangerous to the safety of the State. We, on the other hand,

[1] ii 329.

contend that no such distinction existed at the time in the mind either of Sovereign or of people; that the King, as spiritual head of the Church, assumed to himself the right of punishing such offences, not as contrary to the laws of the State, but as contrary to what he was pleased to determine was the law of God—offences as much against his spiritual as against his temporal power. He never stopped to consider how far this or that creed might be excused or condemned, and its assertors brought to the scaffold as rebels or as heretics. That was a distinction first set up by the subtle statesmen of the reign of Elizabeth, when persecution for religion was growing unpopular. It had no place in the mind of Henry. The passing of the Six Articles, and the punishment of those who transgressed them, the persecution of Tyndal, and the death of Frith and Barnes, all show this. When he transferred to himself the supremacy of the Church, he transferred with it all those powers which the Church had ever exercised for the punishment of heresy or disobedience to its authority. If the Pope was the Bishop of bishops, so was he; if the Pope could of himself determine controversies of faith, so did he. Whether the doctrine of purgatory, or the sacrament of penance, or the worship of saints were or were not to constitute part of the creed and of the teachings of the Church of England, depended upon the King alone. It is true that he did not administer the sacraments and ordain priests and bishops, but if any man had questioned his power to do so, he would have incurred the penalty of high treason. 'A bishop,' says Cranmer, 'may make a priest by the Scripture, and so may princes and governors also, and that by the authority of God committed to them.' In common with other reformers, Cranmer looked to all spiritual functions as absolutely dependent on the will of the King, as temporal commissions, like those of any other magistrate; and consequently, when Edward VI. came to the Crown, he made an offer of resigning his bishopric as if it had been extinguished by the death of the Sovereign. And precisely as the power of the Pope was supposed to over-ride that of the ordinary, so were the clergy taught to believe that obedience to their diocesans was superseded by the Act of Supremacy. Thus Adam Becansaw, one of Cromwell's visitors, writes to him that it was considered that 'no man is obedient to any ordinary immediately, but only unto the King's highness, as unto the supreme head, *which is one of our chief articles of visitation.*' If these facts indicate the utmost confusion in the minds of men of real religious convictions like Cranmer, to what dangerous purposes might they be applied by a minister like Cromwell, who, as Mr. Froude seems to admit,[1]

[1] Mr. Froude says of Cromwell: 'His Protestant tendencies were unknown as yet (1530) perhaps even to his own conscience; nor to the last could he arrive at any certain speculative convictions. He was drawn towards the Protestants as he rose into power by the integrity of his nature, which compelled him to trust only those who were honest like himself.' What Mr. Froude means by 'speculative convictions' must be left to others to explain. Does he mean to say that while Cromwell passed for a Protestant, and allowed his partisans to believe that he was the great champion of the reformed doctrines, he was in fact opposed to them? Are we to assume that though Cromwell was a Catholic, yet, on finding that all Protestants were honest men and all Catholics dishonest, he was drawn to the former by the integrity of his nature and persecuted the latter in spite of his religious convictions? That is precisely what Foxe might have said in his honest, blunt, and immovable bigotry. Meanwhile, there is this difficulty. Supposing that so shrewd an observer as Cromwell could have passed his life among the merchants and aldermen of London without paying any attention to the great controversy of the times, it is certain he had been in correspondence with the favourers of the new doctrines (among others, with Miles Coverdale) some years before 1530. In the first draft of his will, dated June 1529, he leaves 20s. to every one of the five orders of friars within the city of London, to pray for his soul; and he enjoins his executors to engage a priest 'to sing for my soul three years next after my death, and to give him for the same 20l.' The will was corrected by himself throughout some years after, to make the alteration required by the death of his two daughters and by other circumstances. The bequests are in general increased one-third throughout, and in some instances doubled. Added to the fact of these alterations having been made in a later hand, we must infer that they were inserted some years after the original draft, unless this augmentation of his wealth was gained by indirect means. Suppose the period to be five or six years, this would bring the

had no clear religious principles! They were used by him as political engines; they were employed to damage and crush his political rivals; they were made the instruments of his hate, the furtherance of his worldly interests—not exclusively, we allow, but still they were misused to these purposes. And just as he never scrupled at the means he employed, however unconstitutional, to carry his measures in the House of Commons, so he never scrupled to make use of the spiritual power, when by so doing he could obtain his purposes more speedily and more securely. If he packed the House of Commons with his own creatures, would he be more scrupulous in packing a jury? If he interfered with the functions of the bishops, was he likely to be more reserved in interfering with the freedom of elections? These are not hypothetical cases. We find him writing to the King in 1539:[1] 'For your grace's parliament I have appointed your majesty's servant Mr. Morisson to be one of them; no doubt he shall be ready to answer and take up such as would crack (boast) or face with literature of learning, or by indirected ways, if any such shall be, as I think there shall be few or none; forasmuch as I and other your dedicate councillors, be about to bring all things so to pass that your majesty had never more tractable parliament.' What those means were of making parliaments 'tractable' we need be at no loss to divine, but they were such as had never before entered the head of the most arbitrary sovereign. It was not merely undue influence at elections, it was not bribery, it was not intimidation; it was even more. On the 20th

date of them to 1534-5—after the passing of the Act of Supremacy and the death of More and Fisher. Yet, in its amended form, not only are these two bequests for his soul retained, but in the latter the term is enlarged from three years to seven, and the money from 20*l.* to 46*l.* 13*s.* 4*d.* To us the inference seems to be incontrovertible—viz. that while Cromwell, like his master, was a political Protestant, he adhered in his religious belief to the ancient faith. If there was one tenet to which the Protestants of that period were most opposed, it was that of prayers for the dead.

[1] State Papers, i. 603.

May the corporation of Canterbury write to Cromwell, then Chief Secretary, to say that they have complied with the King's command certified to them in Cromwell's letter, and according to the King's pleasure have chosen as their burgesses in Parliament Robert Darknall and John Bryges, notwithstanding that on the 12th of May the sheriff had returned two other burgesses as already duly elected—John Starky and Christopher Levyns—whose election was thus disregarded and set aside by this unconstitutional interference. We could produce instances scarcely less flagrant of his tampering with juries and escheators in relation to Crown property, but we must forbear. We have already put the patience of our readers to a severe test, and are therefore almost ashamed to beg their attention to the following paper addressed by Cromwell to Cranmer. It shall stand in its colours of good and evil without any comment, for we know of no document which sets forth in so true a light the real feelings of the nation at the time on the principles by which its rulers, civil and ecclesiastical, were actuated. We will only premise that it was written just after the marriage of Henry VIII. and Anne Boleyn—that marriage which Mr. Froude insists was earnestly demanded by the people, out of deference to whose wishes the King was driven into measures often otherwise inexcusable. It is endorsed—but the endorsement is not contemporary—

'*Reasons to clear the Clergy for condescending to the King's second Marriage, and for abolishing the Pope's Supremacy.*

'There be (I think) in this realm that be not in their minds full pleased and contented that our Sovereign hath married as he hath done, some bearing their favour to the Lady Katharine, Princess Dowager, some to the Lady Mary, some because the Pope's authority was not therein; and for this they lay the blame alonelie in some of the prelates. And albeit that the prelates have none otherwise done in this matter but as it became them, and according to the very law of God, yet many of the inconstant commons be not therewith satisfied. And though they forbear to speak at large for fear of punishment, yet they mutter together secretly, which muttering and secret grudge within this realm, I think, doth not a little embolde the King's adversaries without the realm. And forsomuch as this muttering and grudge is not against our most gracious Sovereign Lord the King, for every man seeth that he is the most gentillest prince, and of the most gentillest nature, and the most upright that ever reigned among men, but only against some of the prelates, and specially against the Archbishop of Canterbury; therefore I would deem it right expedient, that he should show himself to have done nothing (as he hath not in very deed) but according to the very law of God. And although the suspicion and muttering be both false and untrue, and of the people unreasonably conceived against him, yet must he endeavour himself to pluck it out of their heads, and that by loving manner. And also if the Pope be excluded out of this realm, the Archbishop must be chief of all the clergy here, the which will not lightly be accepted in the people's hearts, because it hath of so long time continued otherwise, except that the people perceive themself (by reason of the said alteration) to be in better case than they were before. Wherefore I think it were very necessary for those considerations that the said Archbishop should make out a book, not over long, to declare that it that he hath done is not only according to the law of God, but also for the great wealth and quietness of all this realm; and this book would be from him written to all the clergy of this realm. And in the said book let him exhort in charitable wise all the said clergy, and specially such as be in great authority and advanced to dignity in the Church, as Bishops, Abbots, Priors, Deans, Provosts and such other, that they at length now call to

their remembrance that they be not called unto those rooms
and dignities for their own sakes, but for the people—not
for their own ease, rest, and quiet, but for the quiet, rest, and
ease of the people—not for their own winning and lucre, but
to make the people rich and plentiful—not to the intent to
eschew labour and travail, but by their labour and travail to
ease the people of their burthens—not to reign in abundance
of all delights and pleasures and the people in misery, but
by their temperance and sober living to help the people at
the least to plenty of suffisaunce—and finally, not to be
served worshipfully, but for Christ's sake (like as He did) to
serve other; for woe to us (let him say) if we do not thus!
and let him thunder out here and there the vehement excla-
mations of the prophets, and specially of Jeremie, against
spiritual pastors; and let him persuade the said clergy to
avoid clean all pomp, all pride, all vain glory, and specially
all manner of covetousness that hath been occasion of so
many evils in the Church of Christ. Let them avoid all
ambition, all delicate fare, and to be ready with heart and
mind to depart and dispose among the people of this realm
lands, goods, money, and whatsoever other thing they now
possess superfluously; and that they never hereafter seek for
the riches or lordship of this world, nor show themselves
desirous of any honour in this world, but diligently to seek
for the kingdom of heaven, and there to make their treasury,
and clene cast away all care of this world. And let him say:—
"Most dear brethren in Christ, let it never be seen in us that
we seek for any ease or for any pleasure in this world, but
only to joy in the cross of Christ and in the health and
salvation of the people both in body and soul; for this is our
charge, and for this we shall give a straight accompt. If you,
most dear brethren, will gladly go with me this way at my
loving exhortation, ye shall greatly merit for your obedience,
but in case ye will not I will compel you by the law of God

thus to do, and then ye shall lose your merit of obedience. Thus our Lord Jesus Christ send us grace, both you and I, to accomplish this mine intent to the wealth of all the people both in body and soul. Amen."

'I am very sure if he would set out a little book after this tenour, though he could never bring his purpose about, yet should he by this mean greatly content the people's minds, and make them think that they be happy thus to be rid of the Pope's oppression, and that the Archbishop is a perfect and a good Bishop, and that he intendeth truly according to the Word of God, and that he never did anything for his prince's pleasure so much to win him promotion as he did for the truth's sake, seeing he pretendeth to stamp under foot all pleasure, all ease, all delight of this world, and utterly give himself to travail and pain in this world: for my mind is and ever hath been that the King's highness should not be seen to be most busy to defend his most righteous cause himself, but let the Clergy specially do it, and namely, the Archbishops. But if there be any so stubborn that he will not believe the truth, then the King's highness to punish him according to the laws in that case provided. For I wote well if it come to the hearing of the Pope and the Emperor that the whole clergy of England is fully bent to defend our Sovereign Lord the King's cause to the very death, they will not meddle much further.'[1]

There are other points in the inquiry on which we should gladly have entered had our space permitted us; inquiries for a satisfactory solution of which we have searched Mr. Froude's pages in vain. The hero of his story is Henry VIII., and yet he seems to attribute the conception and execution of the

[1] With a view of making the clergy more dependent on the Crown he proposed to confiscate the episcopal revenues, and make the bishops pensioners on the State. Each one of them, with the exception of the Archbishop, was to receive 1000 marks a year. Had he lived longer, the bishops would have followed the abbots and priors.

most eventful and characteristic measures of the reign to the genius of Cromwell. We are told by Mr. Froude 'that Cromwell struck the line on which the forces of nature were truly moving—the resultant, not of the victory of either of the extreme parties, but of the joint action of their opposing forces. To him belonged the rare privilege of genius, to see what other men could not see.' And yet in a page or two after it is the Tudor spirit that wakes, it is the King that speaks. We should be glad to know which was the wheel, and which the index; which the substance, and which the reflection. Did Henry set his seal to measures suggested to him by his minister, or did his minister merely carry out the ideas of his master? Mr. Froude will point out to us letters and sign-manuals; he will call our attention to passages in which he feels 'the noble spirit' of the monarch breathing in every line. We confess we cannot be satisfied with these evidences; and we fancy—though it may only be fancy—that we trace in the laboriously corrected drafts of the Secretary indications of those qualities which Mr. Froude regards as the exclusive attributes of the Sovereign. It may be that the Secretary was writing to dictation; it may be that he was no more than the hand upon the dial-plate. But this is the point we desire to see cleared up. If Henry was indolent and disinclined to business; if he was engrossed in his amorous passion for Anne Boleyn; if Mr. Froude's favourite metaphor of his 'waking up' is to be construed literally—then it might happen that his able and obsequious servant would not willingly obtrude on his master's slumbers. He might be satisfied with a general conception of his master's wishes; he might shape out his policy after his own fashion, satisfied that the King should affix his signature, or that he himself should apply the signet to Acts bearing the King's authority, and running in the royal name, but of which the King himself had very little cognisance. If this seems a hazardous supposition, it must be remembered that it was his theory that the King should not be seen too much in his own causes. And even if it were not so in all measures, it is probable that the King would confine himself mainly to questions of foreign politics and leave domestic reforms to his Vicar-general and Vicegerent. To Henry it was of much greater moment what the Emperor thought of his doings, or how he should draw Francis I. into following his own example of renouncing the Pope, than to punish discontented subjects for calling Queen Anne 'a churl's daughter,' or setting curates in the pillory for haggling over his title of supremacy. At all events, the doubt is as old as the days of Cromwell. 'They that rule about the King,' said people, 'make him great banquets, and give him sweet wines, and make him drunk; and then they bring him bills and he putteth his sign to them, whereby they do what they wish, and no man may correct them.' 'That Cromwell,' exclaimed one John Hampson, in a street-brawl at Oxford—'that traitor hath destroyed many a man ; an I were as nigh him as I am to you, I would thrust my dagger into the heart of him.' Whether these prejudices were well founded or not, there can be no doubt that they existed ; and, in fact, Mr. Froude admits that Cromwell was the most unpopular man of his time, without a friend in either party; but then he falls back on the poetical commonplace that he was friendless from the excess of his integrity.

On that point we must conclude, and then leave our readers to judge for themselves. We have shown before with what unexampled rapidity this minister rose from the utmost obscurity within six years to the highest honours of the State, how in less than three years he saw all his rivals at his feet, whatever their rank, their abilities, or their advantages—he, a man in trade, not distinguished by learning, not trained to politics, a subordinate in Wolsey's household. If he owed this rapid promotion solely to his virtue, then should Mr. Froude comfort himself that virtue is sometimes highly rewarded. But these are questions which will immediately occur to men of ordinary sense, and to which they will demand a satisfactory answer before they consent to surrender their convictions to the most bland and graceful of historians. When Cromwell entered Wolsey's service he was a thriving merchant, but no more; when he entered the King's service, on the death of the Cardinal, he had given up business. To live at Court, and that so splendid and extravagant as the Court of Henry VIII., required a fortune; the mere presents that every minister must distribute—the New Year's gift alone—would have swallowed up a moderate income. His official emoluments as Secretary of State were of the scantiest kind; yet we find him early launching out into great expenses. Within a few years he has five establishments—one at Austin Friars, another at Hackney, another at Stepney, another at Mortlake, another at Canonbury, besides his official residence at the Rolls. At Austin Friars, Hackney, and Stepney he was carrying on extensive repairs and buildings all at the same time, and employing upon each of them from fifty to seventy workmen at 6*d.* a day. Not long after, he was erecting a mansion at Ewhurst, of which his steward reports that it was 'the goodliest and the mightiest he had ever seen.' He kept from three to four stewards, he had a staff of clerks, servants, hunters, hawks, and all the expensive *impedimenta* of a noble establishment. In July 1537 the expense of his household, not to mention wages, was 101*l.* 13*s.*; in August 98*l.* 9*s.* 6½*d.*; in September 240*l.*[1] Next year, in the same month, it had increased to 300*l.*, not including 133*l.* 6*s.* 8*d.* for provisioning Lewes Priory, which had then come into his hands. On November the 19th, 1537, he paid 2,000*l.* for a diamond and a

---

[1] These sums must be multiplied by ten to bring them near to modern computation.

ruby. In June 1538 he purchased Sir George Somerset's house at Kew; in November following the manor of Brampton for 1000*l.* In January the next year he bought the demesnes of the priory of Folkestone; next month the manor of Holden for 3450*l.* The same year he lent Gostwick 2000*l.*, the year before 2253*l.* for the King's use. Besides these outlays, he lost money at dice and cards, in sums varying from 20*s.* to 20*l.* Nor were his outgoings as a courtier inconsiderable. On the birth of Prince Edward he gave the messenger 6*l.* 13*s.* 4*d.*; to the ladies attending on the Prince 20*l.*; and 3*l.* 10*s.* to the poor of St. James's. To the King he presented a gold cup and an ' outlandish beast,' with a velvet collar; to the poor Queen herself his New Year's gift in 1537 was a cup of gold and 22*l.* 10*s.* With these exceptions, his liberality was most conspicuous to the Princess Mary. In 1537 he sent her 24*l.* as a New Year's gift; then 11*l.* 5*s.*; and immediately after 6*l.*; and next month, as her ' fallantyne ' (valentine), 15*l.* In November of the same year he paid Wriothesley 38*l.* 6*s.* 8*d.* ' to make my Lady Mary a New Year's gift,' and in December a 'salt of gold and 10 sovereigns.' Her only acknowledgment of this bounty was 'a dish of quinces,' for which the minister rewarded the bearer with 5*s.* Whether she remained inexorable, or money grew scarce, her next New Year's gifts were only 11*l.* 5*s.* Besides these he was fond of masques. In the January of 1539 he exhibited a masque before the Court which cost him 30*l.* 7*s.* 6*d.*—the stuff 13*l.* 7*s.* 11*d.*, the copper-plates and disguises 9*l.* 2*s.* 1*d.*; and among the curious items is one of 21*s.* 2*d.* 'paid for the trimming of Divine Providence when she played before the King.' To Woodhall, the schoolmaster at Eton, he gave 5*l.* for playing before him at Christmas; and to Bale, afterwards Bishop of Ossory, and his fellows, on a similar occasion, 30*s.*; to Grafton, the furnisher, 10*l.* for masks. His installation as

Knight of the Garter in 1537 cost 25*l*., his gown 6*l*. 13*s*. 4*d* . his collar and George, 7*l*. 6*s*.¹

When Churchmen were ministers, the scanty emoluments of office were supplemented by bishoprics, but Cromwell could enjoy no such advantages. Henry was not unkind to his virtues, and he had numerous grants from the Crown ; but such grants brought in little ready money, certainly none adequate for such heavy expenses. Then how were these expenses defrayed ? A glance at his correspondence explains. In Wolsey's service he had learned to take *douceurs*—we should call them bribes—to obtain the Cardinal's favour for suitors. When he became chief minister to Henry VIII., he continued the practice ; and his letters furnish ample evidence of the extent to which this practice was carried. His appointment as Visitor and as Vicar-general gave him ample opportunities of enriching himself by indirect means ; and the numerous applications made to him afford ample indications—even if we had not his private accounts to produce— that his virtue was not impregnable. Sir Ant. Cope writes to him to say that seven convicts had escaped from the Bishop of Lincoln's prison in Banbury, and this will be a good opportunity to extort from the Bishop the fee-farm of the hundred of Banbury, which he holds of the King, and bestow it on one of Cromwell's friends ; and he ends by offering Cromwell 200*l*. to obtain it for him. Sir Simon Harcourt writes to him to procure him from the King a little house of Canons in Staffordshire : ' His Grace shall have 100*l*., and your mastership, if it be brought to pass, 100*l*. for your pain,

---

¹ There are curious items, for which we cannot afford space ; *e.g.* such as ' ribbands for his George, 8*d*., and a lace for his spectacles, 4*d*.; two stools to set his legs on, 1*s*., and 20*d*. for a pewter pot to wash a running sore with which he was troubled,' like his master. He was by no means conspicuous for charity. His alms in 1537 were 8*d*. to a poor woman in March, 8*d*. to two poor men in July, 1*s*. to three poor women and 2*d*. at Christmas. Next year he was more liberal, but chiefly to the poor of Putney.

and 20*l.* fee as long as you live.' But if it be dissolved, and Cromwell can obtain the grant of its farm for the petitioner, he will give him 100 marks. Thos. Candell offers him when Privy Seal 10*l.* to obtain the King's patent and seal for a friar's house and lands. Lady Mary Capell offers him 20*l.* to buy a hobby, if he will get the arrears of her annuity paid up. Sir Piers Eggecombe desires the grant of the suppressed priory of Totness. He offers the King 800 marks for it and Cromwell a present of 100*l.* to procure the King's favour. He obtains his request, and then asks for two manors in Devonshire. A wretched constable, employed by him as a visitor of the religious houses, begs him to stay the conclusion of a bargain between one Broke and the Abbot of Bardsley: 'Hear me speak or you conclude with him: it shall be in the way of 200 marks.' Archbishops and bishops, noblemen and widows, purchased his smiles with eager hands. The blackmail which he levied under the name of New Year's gifts, fees, and annuities was enormous: 40*l.* a year from Cranmer, 20*l.* a year from the other bishops, and 10*l.* a year besides in the shape of a New Year's gift; sums of 2*l.*, 5*l.*, 10*l.*, and 20*l.* from most of the priories and abbeys in England; 40*l.* from the Earl of Wiltshire, 20*l.* from Queen Jane Seymour, the same from the unhappy Countess of Salisbury, 20*l.* from Dr. Lee, the same from Dr. Leighton, and 10*l.* from Dr. London, his visitors of the monasteries. The entries in his steward's book reveal the same tale: 6*l.* 13*s.* 4*d.* in a little white purse; 'in a pair of gloves' 13*l.* 6*s.* 8*d.*; 'in a handkercher' 66*l.* 13*s.* 4*d.*; in a black velvet purse 20*l.*; and 10*l.* 'with a purse of silver and gilt.' 'A purse of crimson satin' containing 66*l.* 13*s.* 4*d.*; in 'another crimson satin purse' 20*l.*; 20*l.* 'in a white paper'; 20*l.* 'in a glove under the cushion in the gallery window'; 'under a cushion in the middle window in the gallery' 10*l.*; 'under the cushion in the gallery window, in a purse of white leather,' 100*l.*; 'the same day 50*l.* in a purse of red leather';

'in a purse of white leather' 10*l*.;—all lying close together in those eventful months when nobles and peasants were dissipating and plundering the abbey lands.

We might enlarge these instances almost to any amount. The poor monks at Canterbury who paid him an annuity for his protection had a summer residence at Bekesborne, the envy of the neighbourhood. The King was desirous to have it and offered the prior any lands of equivalent value in exchange. In great trepidation he laid his griefs before the minister: the monks could not consent to part with it on any terms; it was their only place of recreation; nothing could be an equivalent for its loss. The powerful intercession of the minister saved it from the clutches of the Crown, and the monks were profuse in their gratitude; but in his very next letter he demanded and obtained a lease of it for himself. Pensions and annuities from abbots and priors trembling for existence; presents of money from grasping squires and nobles eager to clutch at the prey and forestall each other; hampers of game, fish, and poultry; eggs, cheeses, and venison pasties from less wealthy visitors, all anxious to bespeak the favour of this man more powerful than the King himself, poured in at his gates. The venison sent him fed his servants and saved his butchers' bills, as his thrifty steward informs him: if it got a little damaged by the journey it was baked in a pie, and that was food for the man which was no food for his master. For though he rose to the highest offices in the State, and his income was enormous, the business-like habits and frugality of the merchant still reigned in his heart and his household. No wonder whilst the minister grew wealthy the Crown grew poor. It was thought a great thing that Cardinal Wolsey once in his magnificent administration, with foreign wars and continual loans to Maximilian, to Charles, and, after his captivity, to Francis I., should have demanded a subsidy from the House of Commons; now, in a period of profound peace, with parliamentary subsidies, the enormous fines paid by the clergy to escape the premunire, with annates and firstfruits, which had hitherto rolled a stream of gold to Rome, all turned into the exchequer, the King 'woke up,' after six years, to find himself on the eve of a rebellion, with no funds to meet it, unless he melted his plate and sold his jewels.

These details are not taken from Protestant or from Popish legends, so much deprecated by Mr. Froude; they are not the blind suggestions of malice or envy; they are derived from an authority which Mr. Froude himself will not dispute—Cromwell's own correspondence. We do not contend that they present the whole account of the matter, and that Cromwell's character is to be judged by these facts alone, to the exclusion of others: that would be to fall into the fault we condemn. But whether they bear out Mr. Froude's views, and whether an impartial historian ought to have ignored them, our readers can decide for themselves.

PASSAGES FROM THE LIFE OF ERASMUS.[1]

April, 1863.

THE Dean of St. Paul's (Dr. Milman) has familiarised his readers with the expression, 'Latin Christianity.' The phrase is new, and is apt to suggest a distinction that never existed. Had the patriarch of Constantinople succeeded in his opposition to the rival patriarch of the West, had an imperial court overawed by its splendour and authority the humble palace of the Vatican, Greek Christianity (if that be meant as a correlative to Latin) might have found a centre, in which the thousand varying lights of Greek intellect might have converged. But in fact Greek Christianity, as represented by the later Greek fathers, is little more than a feeble reflexion of the Latin. Christianity, strange to say, awakened no responsive chord of the old Greek mind; the poetical and philosophical elements of earlier days sprang up to no second life. Even that logical subtlety which struck such vigorous root in the Latin Church found no place in the Greek. The intellect, language, and leisure of the Greeks would have seemed to point them out as the most suitable guardians and interpreters of the New Testament. And yet, as if to falsify all human anticipations in these matters, the Greek Church produced no expositors comparable to the Latin, Athanasius excepted. The social forms and economy of Christian life are of Latin growth. Our ecclesiastical ceremonies and dresses are

[1] From the *National Review* for April 1863, under the heading : 1. Unpublished Papers in the Public Record Office. 2. *Erasmi Epistolae*.

Latin; our prayers and liturgies are Latin; our translations of the Scripture are from the Latin; our disputes upon cardinal points of doctrine are founded upon Latin words, and guided entirely by our conceptions of their Latin meaning.

Placed in the van of that battle which Christianity had to wage with the new barbarian nationalities of the North, the Latin mind gained new life and vigour from the struggle. If it be true that there are men whose genius, like aromatic herbs, never gives out its fullest sweetness until they are bruised and trampled on, it is equally true that but for these collisions we might have known the old Latin literature in its strength and majesty, but never in ' its hearselike strains;' never in its more spiritual forms, and that ascetic beauty which haunts and lingers round the memory like a spell. If not the product of the same necessity, at least the most potent aid to that same need, the Latin Church found in the Vulgate an instrument for reaching all hearts and guiding all tongues. For those new races, the founders of the nations of Western Christendom, all their earliest religious impressions were connected with the Vulgate. From the Vulgate all forms of thought took their first direction. What popes and schoolmen never could have done—for securing uniformity of belief and worship; for rooting in the hearts of men the grand idea of one church, one head, one language, binding the old to the new races in unbroken succession, and to him above all who had the keys of death and hell—was done by the silent and irresistible influence of the Vulgate. No wonder, then, that any attack on its authority should have been resisted as a deadly thrust against the very foundation of that system which had grown up with the growth of centuries and entwined itself with every fibre of the heart and imagination of mankind.

It is, then, as the opponent of that authority which till

his time had been held infallible, and for this alone, that Erasmus can be regarded as the precursor of the Reformation. In his jests against the clergy, or rather against the religious orders, the clergy laughed as heartily as himself, secure and heart-sound. It was only when he proceeded to examine the evidence on which the Vulgate rested that they looked grave; when he claimed to apply to the authorised translation of the Scriptures the same rules of criticism as the scholars of his days were applying to Cicero or to Virgil. In this respect his influence on the Reformation was greater than Luther's; as the application of the principles of interpretation introduced by Erasmus must, under more favourable circumstances and in more vigorous hands, lead to consequences more important. At this time, when so much excitement has sprung up on the subject of biblical interpretation, we have thought that an account of this first effort at theological criticism might not be without interest to our readers.

In the year 1509 Erasmus was in Italy, when he received a letter from William Lord Mountjoy, urging his instant return. With more than a significant hint at the parsimony of Henry VII., Mountjoy informed him that the reign of avarice was at an end. 'Our new king,' he added, 'scatters his treasures with a liberal hand; he is more ambitious of virtue and renown than of gold or precious stones.' Considering the numerous attractions which Italy had for Erasmus, it might have been thought that such an invitation, though backed by a present of 5l. from Archbishop Warham, and as much more from Mountjoy himself, would not have proved very seductive. The climate of Italy, its brilliant skies, its books and antiquities, its libraries and learned societies, were exactly suited to a scholar and valetudinarian. Erasmus was fastidious in his diet. He could not endure the sour wines or sourer beer of our northern latitudes. The stoves of Germany and the winters of England filled him with dismay. But though Erasmus might care for Italy, Italy probably did not care much for Erasmus. Italian scholars, the arbiters of literary distinction, were not prepared to admit him into their exclusive circle. They were not satisfied that his Latin style smacked of the true Ciceronian flavour. Nor was Erasmus backward in expressing his contempt for their fastidiousness. He ridiculed their slavish imitation of Cicero, their utter ignorance of all authors beyond their one acknowledged idol, their tumid eloquence and shallow conceits. From the warlike Julius, whom he hated for his roughness, he received no notice; Leo X., whom he had known as a student, was condescending, but offered no substantial favour. From chagrin or other causes his health had suffered in Italy; he hastened to accept the invitation of Mountjoy.

The tediousness of the journey was relieved by casting into form the scenes he had just abandoned; the impressions made on his mind by Roman society may be seen in his 'Praise of Folly.' Arriving in London he took up his abode with Sir Thomas More. Courted and caressed by all who had attained, or were ambitious of attaining distinction, there was no post in the State to which he might not have aspired; no position in the Church which was not open to him. 'There is no country,' he boasts in one of his letters, 'which would not gladly entertain me—Spain, Italy, England, or Scotland. When I was at Rome, there was no cardinal that would not have received me with open arms as a brother. In England,' he continues, 'there is not a bishop who does not think it an honour to be noticed by me, who is not anxious to secure me at his table; who would not gladly retain me in his household. The king himself (Henry VIII.), a little before his father's death, sent me, when I was in Italy, most loving letters, written with his own hand. He addresses me with more respect and affection than anyone else. Whenever I salute him, he embraces me most kindly and looks at me affectionately. You may be sure he thinks of me not less kindly than he speaks. The queen (Katharine) has endeavoured to secure me as her preceptor. Every one is aware that if I would but condescend to live a few months at court, I might accumulate as many benefices as I pleased.'

But Erasmus has devoted himself to letters, and resolutely turned his back on those paths which led others to chancellorships, baronies, and bishoprics. The liberality and undeviating kindness of Warham and Mountjoy placed him above immediate want; and his friend Fisher, chancellor of the University of Cambridge, at that time employed in founding St. John's and settling Lady Margaret's will, induced Erasmus to take up his residence at Cambridge, and give lectures in Greek to the students of that University. The precise period at which he entered on his professorship is uncertain; his correspondence from Cambridge commences with the summer of 1511. At first the novelty of his position, and the hopes of improving it, sufficed to atone for the smallness of his audience and the scantiness of his remuneration. The account he gives of his lectures do not impress us with a very exalted idea of the state of Greek literature in England. 'Hitherto,' he says in a letter written from Cambridge in October 1511, 'I have lectured on the grammar of Chrysoloras to a small class; perhaps next term I shall begin the grammar of Theodorus (a Greek of the Lower Empire) to a larger one.' In other words, he was teaching the elements of Greek grammar.

His expectations were not destined to be realised. The University found it difficult to pay his salary of fifty nobles, and applied for assistance to Lord Mountjoy. His audience did not increase; neither the ambition of the University nor

the influence of his friend the chancellor could secure for
him pupils or a decent remuneration. The great obstacle to
his success with younger students was his total ignorance of
English; with the more advanced, his novel notions of the
duties of a theologian added to his hatred and contempt of
the schoolmen. The grammar of Theodorus had no greater
attractions for Cambridge undergraduates than the grammar
of Chrysoloras; 1512 passed without any visible improvement; 1513 was not more promising. 'As for profit,' he
says in a letter to Colet, 'I see no chance of it. What can
I take from those who have nothing to give?' 'I have not
been here five months,' he says in another letter to
Ammonius, 'and have spent sixty nobles, without receiving
more than one. The expense is intolerable, and the remuneration nothing.' College beer did not agree with his
stomach. College gyps stole his wine, or mixed it with
water. College porters mislaid his letters. Masters of Arts,
divided into rival sections of Thomists and Scotists, scouted
lectures on theology which denuded Scripture of all mystery
and aimed at nothing higher than a literal and grammatical
interpretation. The Scriptures, said they, are levelled to
the capacity of children and laymen. St. Jerome was a
mere grammarian; St. Augustine was a dunce. What could
they or any other fathers know of entity, relation, ampliation,
restriction, formality, hæcceity, quiddity, or the like?
What help can the Scriptures afford for the refutation of
heresy? How is the Church to stand, or the dignity of
theology to be maintained, by the laws of syntax or the aids
of lexicography? To increase his vexation, the war with
France carried away, in 1513, his most intimate friends,
Ammonius and Mountjoy. Engrossed with the bustle of a
great campaign, bishops and noblemen, who in times of
peace might have repaid a translation from Lucian or a copy
of complimentary verses in angels, were either occupied in

mustering their retainers, or in discussing the merits of Almain rivets, apostles, and falconets. Erasmus groaned with disgust. He hated war for its own sake; he regarded it exclusively from its noisy and horrible side. He could see nothing in it, except a disorderly mob of vagabonds and scoundrels bent upon pulling down what the wisdom, patience, and experience of former ages had built up. But he hated it still more because it was incompatible with the cultivation of letters. Unfortunately, also, during the autumn of this year, the sweating sickness made its appearance. Cambridge was deserted, his hearers dispersed. In a pardonable but by no means pleasant mood, he writes to Ammonius (Nov. 28), that he had been shut up in Cambridge for some months, confined to his books, like a snail in its shell. 'Here,' he adds, 'is one unbroken solitude. Many have left for fear of the plague; and yet, when they are all here, the solitude is much worse. This winter I am resolved to turn every stone, and throw out my sheet-anchor. If I succeed, I shall make a nest for myself. If I fail, I shall flit elsewhere. Had I no other reasons, I am resolved not to die in England.'

But although Cambridge had disappointed his expectations, and was not yet sufficiently prepared to do justice to his Greek or his theological lectures, his residence in that University had not been thrown away. The more scanty his audience, the more time was left to his own disposal; and he was not of a temper to let it remain idle. As early as the year 1505, in a preface to Valla's notes on the New Testament, he had ventured to express his approbation of the new rules of criticism applied by Valla to the revision of the Vulgate. 'Where is the harm,' he remarks, 'if Valla, upon the authority of the ancient Greek copies, wrote notes on such passages of the New Testament as he found to be at variance with the original, or had been less correctly rendered by dozing interpreters?' He avowed his belief that the translation of Scripture belonged exclusively to the philologist, and that Jethro in some things was wiser than Moses. 'Grammar, I admit, is employed upon minutiæ; but these minutiæ are small things without which no one can become great. It is busied with trifles, *sed hæ nugæ seria ducunt.* If it be said that theology is too dignified to be restrained by the laws of syntax, and that the interpretation of Scripture rests upon inspiration—I reply, that this is claiming a new dignity for theologians, if they are to have the exclusive privilege of writing nonsense. But I hear it said that the old translators were skilled in the languages of the original, and are sufficiently intelligible for all practical purposes. I reply, that I prefer to see that with my own eyes, rather than with the eyes of others; and, secondly, allowing they have done much, they have certainly left much to be done by those who come after them.'

With views so liberal as these, so far in advance of his age, it is not surprising that he should have entertained the idea of following the steps of Valla, and devoting his time and abilities to a critical revision of the New Testament. In common with others, he may have been influenced in this determination by his classical distaste for the old unclassical version. Yet it must be admitted that he was influenced by a nobler feeling; more than once in his serious moods he has avowed his belief that the only remedy for the vices and disorders of the time was to be found in the careful study of the holy Scriptures. More than once he expressed a wish that the pure oracles of divine truth were made accessible to all. He hoped to turn men from the unprofitable dialectics and noisy discussions of the schools to the more quiet and thoughtful study of philology. He evidently anticipated such a result from the appearance of the New Testament and the aids it would afford to a more certain and speedy study of the original. With these motives, others less pure may have been combined. There was the refinement of the scholar, in common with other classical revivalists, unduly offended with a Latin version which could be referred to no era of established Latinity. Less fastidious than his Italian contemporaries, he yet saw no reason why theology, and still more that work on which all true theology was based, should adhere to the exclusive and unenviable distinction of speaking a more barbarous language than any other science. From the two bodies into which the theological world was divided, he had little reason to anticipate opposition. The revivalists could not be offended if the New Testament appeared in a style of eloquence more conformable with their notions, at least so free from gross violations of classical Latinity that they might read it without fear of vitiating their taste; whilst by Scotist and Thomist, exclusively occupied with their favourite masters, this or any other attempt to promote the study of the Gospels would be regarded with indifference amounting to contempt.

With these views he set to work whilst at Cambridge to collate such MSS. of the New Testament, whether Greek or Latin, as were within his reach. In this task he had the assistance of Lupset, one of his Greek pupils, a *protégé* of More and Colet. He tells the latter, in a letter dated May 1512, that he had already collated the New Testament with the ancient Greek copies, and annotated it in more than a thousand places. His collations were completed and his work ready for the press in the summer of 1513. Concurrently with these labours, either of which alone might have been deemed sufficient for the ambition of the most enterprising and indefatigable student, he was employed in preparing a new edition of St. Jerome. But though his health was suffering from excessive exertion, and the plague was then raging at Cambridge, he tells Ammonius, in September, that his labours were drawing to a close; and so earnestly was he bent upon the task that he felt as if he was inspired.

Suddenly he disappeared from England in the spring of 1514. In a letter from Hammes Castle, dated July 8, of which his friend Lord Mountjoy, afterwards lieutenant of Tournay, was the governor, he informed Ammonius of his prosperous voyage. The Dover boatmen, whose extortions may boast the prescription of three centuries, carried off his portmanteau with all his papers. 'It is the way of these fellows,' he adds, ' to steal where they can conveniently; and when they cannot steal, they extort money and sell you your own property. When I fancied the labour of so many years had perished, I felt as much grief as a mother might feel at the loss of her children.' 'I know not,' he continues, ' whether I told you that I went to take leave of his Majesty (Henry VIII.). He received me with a very friendly countenance. The Bishop of Lincoln (Wolsey) bade me be of good cheer, but uttered no hint of a present; and I did not dare to allude to it, for fear of appearing importunate. Durham (Ruthal) gave me six angels; the archbishop (Warham) took the opportunity of pressing on my acceptance as many more; Rochester (Fisher), a royal. I am now staying a few days with my friend Mountjoy at Hammes Castle, and intend to go to Germany.' He visited Basle in the autumn, and arranged with Frobenius, then rising into celebrity, for the printing of the New Testament. In the winter of 1514 or the spring of 1515, he returned to England; was in London in March, with a view of securing the good offices of Henry VIII. with Leo X. At this time the influence of Henry with the pontiff was supreme. Louis XII. was dead; Charles, not yet emperor, was a young man without influence; Ferdinand of Arragon and Maximilian were in close amity with England; and Wolsey was exerting all his skill to imitate the policy of the League of Cambray, and, by a close union of the chief European powers, attempting to shut out France from all political influence. Of these movements Erasmus was kept well informed by Ammonius, the Latin secretary to Henry VIII. Accordingly, from London he addressed a highly complimentary letter to Leo X.;[1] applauding his political sagacity, his wise efforts for peace, and dexterously contrasting the mildness and wisdom of his rule with the turbulence of his predecessor Julius, he applied to Leo those words in the Apocalypse, ' Vicit *Leo* de tribu Juda.' Then glancing at his labours upon St. Jerome, ' the prince of Latin theologians,' he told the Pope that the fatigues he had endured in editing the works of that father were little less than St. Jerome had experienced in writing them. He expected no remuneration, and only begged his holiness's approbation. The Pope returned a complimentary answer on July 10, but neither invited him to Rome, nor held out hopes of preferment. He accompanied his letter with a recommendation of Erasmus to Henry VIII. ' These scholars,' he said, ' who devote themselves to literature and the arts are not a bad sort of people.[2] I have on more than one occasion found them very honest and trustworthy. I was acquainted with Erasmus, who is one of the best of them, before I was raised to the papal chair; and I beg to recommend him to you. I do not ask any favour for him; but, if it should fall in your way to oblige him, I shall be glad if you will let him know that my recommendation has had its due weight.'

At the end of the summer of 1515 Erasmus hurried off to Basle, dropping an occasional letter to Ammonius full of high spirits. In one, dated October 2, shortly after the battle of Marignano, he writes to say that the printers had

[1] April 29.   [2] ' Minime malos esse.'

commenced the New Testament. 'My health,' he continues, 'has been very good until they began their stoves.' The German stoves were as hateful to Erasmus as afterwards to Wordsworth, and he was obliged to have an English fireplace in his chamber. 'I can neither stay, from the intolerable smell of the stoves, nor leave my work, which cannot get on without me. Our friends the Swiss are in high dudgeon because the French would not civilly allow themselves to be beaten (at Marignano), as they were beaten by the English at Tournay, but dispersed the Swiss with their artillery. They have returned home with tattered ensigns, somewhat fewer in number, torn, mutilated, and wounded. So, instead of a victory, they are holding a funeral. If my health allows me, I intend staying here until Christmas. If not, I shall go to Flanders or Rome. York (Wolsey, then bishop of Tournay) has given me a prebend at Tournay; mere moonshine. His commissary (Dr. Sampson) has been publicly excommunicated in Flanders. Such is the reverence they show York in that part of the world. However, I have accepted it, for nothing is easier than to lose.' In December he was still at Basle, and told Ammonius he intended to stay till March; the printing of the New Testament was nearly completed, and he reckoned it would extend to eighty sheets. The labour was enormous: his health and strength feeble. 'I am overwhelmed,' he tells one of his correspondents in a letter, still dated from Basle, late at night, 'with a double burden, either of which would require rather a Hercules than an Erasmus. To say nothing of other labours of less consequence, I have the weight of St. Jerome and the New Testament upon my shoulders.' On March 7, 1516, he writes to say that the New Testament is out, and the last colophon was then being added to St. Jerome. But all who have had any expérience of the press know too well that the last colophon is seldom the last. Month after month slipped away, and it was not until Whitsunday in 1516 that he was able to write to his friend, the burgomaster of Nuremberg, that the Testament was completed.

He took leave of Basle in a sort of triumph, rejoiced to escape from his prison-house.[1] If he had been delighted above measure with his reception, he could scarcely be less delighted with the respect paid him at his departure. A cavalcade attended him out of the city, and took their leave of him with moistened eyes and heavy hearts. At Antwerp he fell in with his old friends Tunstal and Peter Caraffa, afterwards Paul IV. From Antwerp he proceeded to visit Mountjoy; thence to St. Omer, where he arrived on June 5, intending to cross to England. A slight attack of fever delayed his passage. He had, however, taken the precaution to forward copies of the New Testament to the archbishop and other friends in England. From St. Omer he wrote, in his usual lively strain, to Christopher Urswick, a name familiar to readers of English history: 'Your horse is a genius, and has been very lucky to me. He has twice carried me safely backwards and forwards to Basle, not only a tedious but a dangerous journey. He has visited so many universities that he is grown as wise as Homer's Ulysses:

'Mores hominum multorum vidit et urbes.'

Whilst I have been killing myself the last ten months with excessive fatigue, he has grown so fat and so idle he could scarcely get in at the city gates. I cannot tell you how much I am pleased with Upper Germany and the kindness shown me on all sides. I doubt not you have seen the New Testament. St. Jerome will speedily appear. I have sent four volumes already to the archbishop by your alumnus, Peter, the one-eyed man.'

The day of his arrival in England is uncertain. On

[1] *Ergastulo*, vii. 10.

June 22, Warham wrote to him from Oxford, acknowledging the receipt of the New Testament and the earlier volumes of St. Jerome; and on August 9 we find him in London, writing to Leo X. On the 17th of the same month he was staying at Rochester with Fisher. He tells Ammonius he had been over-persuaded by the bishop to spend ten days with him, and more than ten times had repented his promise. 'I had angled for a horse from Urswick by presenting him with a New Testament; the last horse he gave me died from drink in Flanders—a common complaint in that country. But whilst he is away hunting, my hunting has come to nothing.' The New Testament was warmly applauded by his friends in England. Warham, archbishop of Canterbury, too magnanimous to take offence at the transfer of the dedication from himself to the Pope, wrote to Erasmus to express his great gratification at the immortality he had conferred upon him, and sent him sixty nobles. He was profuse in his commendations of the work; was sedulous in showing it to his brethren the bishops, and to the most eminent theologians of the day, 'all of whom,' he said, 'had concurred in praising it.' Colet, dean of St. Paul's, writes: 'Your New Testament is bought with avidity, and read everywhere. You have many approvers and admirers. Some, however, carp and disapprove, and urge the same objections as Dorp did;[1] but these are only such theologians

[1] Dorp had written to Erasmus some time before, to dissuade him from his design of editing the New Testament. The arguments he employed are curious as showing how old are the prejudices, and how little Protestant the objections, repeated at this day against biblical criticism.

'If I prove to you that there is no error or falsity in the Latin translation, will you not admit that their labour is superfluous who try to mend it? I insist, then, on the correctness and integrity of the Vulgate. For is it likely that the whole Catholic Church would have erred so many centuries, seeing it has always used and sanctioned this translation? Is it probable that so many holy fathers, so many consummate scholars, would have been mistaken; who have relied on the authority of the Vulgate for their decisions in councils, their defence and explanation of the faith, and the

as you describe in your " Moria " no less truly than wittily. Their censure is praise, their praise censure. For myself, I am variously affected by it. At one time I lament that I have never learned Greek, without which *nihil sumus;* at another I rejoice that I have lived in the light of your genius.' In Germany the excitement was equally intense. 'The abbess of St. Clare and her sister,' says Pirkheimer, ' are assiduous students of your writings. They are greatly delighted with your New Testament, and are wonderfully affected by it. They would write you a Latin letter, did they not think that such letters as theirs would be unworthy of your perusal.'[1]

One college at Cambridge refused to join in the general commendation. It signalised itself in the cause of bigotry and bad sense by passing a decree that the New Testament of Erasmus should not be brought within the college precincts on shipboard or horseback, by waggons or porters !

---

framing of those canons, to which all rulers have submitted ? You know it is an established axiom that General Councils cannot err. Do you suppose that the Greek copies are more correct than the Latin ? Have the Greeks, who have often fallen into heresy, taken more pains for the preservation of the sacred oracles than the Latins—the Greeks, who affirm that there are errors in all the Gospels except the Gospel of St. John ?' After further arguments in this strain, he adds: 'But you will say, "I do not intend to introduce any changes; I do not assert the Vulgate is incorrect; I only show what I find in the Greek copies, and where they differ from the Latin; and where is the harm in this ? " Great harm, my dear Erasmus ; for if people once begin to learn from your work, or hear you only assert in conversation, that there is ever so small an error in the authorised version, they will begin to discuss and to doubt, and the whole authority of the Scriptures will be lost.' Who could have anticipated that the learning of this day would have borrowed its lessons from such quarters ?

[1] A copy of this first edition is preserved in the British Museum. It may be distinguished from all others by its fantastic title of *Novum Instrumentum,* which Erasmus afterwards dropped. Nothing, we think, can give a better idea of the popularity of the book than the fact that this copy, as appears by a contemporaneous inscription, was the property of Robert Elyston, a monk of St. Mary's Fountains, and was given by him to a relative named Christ. Tatum.

With this exception, the objectors were either few or undecided. In the paucity of Greek scholars it was not easy to find men able or even willing to enter upon the task of examining the critical merits or defects of the new edition. The two centres of orthodoxy abroad were Louvain and Cologne. But the latter had already been handled severely for its persecution of Reuchlin, and was not inclined to engage in a fresh controversy. Erasmus tells Ammonius in a letter from Brussels, where he had resolved to spend the winter of 1516, that his enemies were anxious to have an examination of his book delegated by royal commission to the schools of Louvain and Cologne. 'They will have enough to employ them for two years if they do,' he adds. He wisely anticipated the danger by taking up his abode at Louvain in the April of 1517. 'You can scarcely imagine, my dear Ammonius, the danger I was in from the malice of the theologians in this place. In their quarrelsome humour they had prepared their approaches, and, under the leadership of the vice-chancellor of the University, who is the more mischievous because he is an enemy in disguise of a friend, they had formed a conspiracy against me. I have, however, taken up my abode here, and dissipated all this smoke; and am now on the best terms with them all, from the highest to the lowest.' By degrees, however, ugly rumours gained ground. As early as October 31, 1516, one month only after he had left England, More wrote to tell him that Latimer[1] was highly pleased with his New Testament; 'in which, however, you have been too scrupulous for his approval. He is not pleased with your retaining the word *Sabbatum*, and the like. He would not admit a single word that has not the sanction of classical authority. I agreed with him, so far as Hebrew idiom and usage would allow, and begged him to send you a list of such words as

[1] Professor of Greek at Oxford.

he would have translated otherwise. But, my dear Erasmus, there are others here who have conspired to read your work with very different intentions; whose design, I confess, fills me with alarm. Don't, therefore, be in a hurry to bring out a new edition. Very sharp critics here have determined to sift your book to the uttermost, and lay hold of all occasions for condemning it. Who are they? you will say. I am afraid to name them; it will strike you with despair. I must tell you, however, that that consummate theologian the Franciscan friar,[1] of whom you have made such honourable mention in your preface to St. Jerome, has entered into a conspiracy with others of his order to note down your blunders. For the more speedy execution of their task, they divided the work between them, and decided after reading it through with the greatest attention not to comprehend a word of it. You see your danger. They came to this resolution over their cups in the evening; but in the morning, as I hear, forgetting what had passed, rescinded their determination and betook themselves to mendicancy,—a trade they understand much better than criticism.'

But notwithstanding this banter, it was necessary for Erasmus to hasten forward a new edition. The first had been produced under very unfavourable circumstances; and when the excitement occasioned by its appearance was over, no one was more ready to acknowledge its imperfections than Erasmus himself. The work had grown upon him, and assumed a dignity and proportion he had never originally intended. At first he had designed to restrict himself to very brief notes, not exceeding two or three words, on such passages of the New Testament as seemed most imperatively to need explanation. When the work was ready for the press, he was persuaded by his friends to correct the

[1] Dr. Standish.

grosser errors of the Vulgate, and occasionally change the style into a purer Latinity. 'This little additional trouble, as I then thought it,' he writes to Budæus, 'proved most oppressive. I was next persuaded to increase the length of the notes. The work had to be recast entirely. Another labour succeeded. I had imagined that I should have found more correct copies at Basle. I was disappointed, and compelled to revise the sheets beforehand for the use of the printers. Two persons, one a lawyer, the other a theologian, acquainted with Hebrew, had been engaged to correct the press. But as they had never been used to this employment, they could not fulfil what they had undertaken, and I had to read the proofs. The work of the editor and that of the printer proceeded simultaneously, and a sheet was finished daily. I could not give my undivided attention to the New Testament, as I was at the same time engaged on St. Jerome. I had resolved to bring out the work before Easter, or die at my post. Again, I was deceived in the size of the volume. The printer assured me it would amount to thirty sheets only; it exceeded eighty-three. Worn out with these labours and occupied with things which properly did not belong to me, I had to proceed to the notes. I did the best I could, considering the time and the state of my health. Some errors I passed over intentionally; some I connived at, in the publication of which I dissented from my own opinions. I am now preparing a second edition, and shall be glad of your assistance.'

In the first edition he had admitted corrections with a sparing hand. In his versions of the Gospels he had closely adhered to the Vulgate. The evangelical narratives were so clear and so simple, written in such a plain and unaffected style, that he thought there was no room for error. Translator and copyist could scarcely go astray. It was otherwise with the Epistles. The difficulties and obscurities of St. Paul demanded a greater mastery over the Greek than could be expected from those under whose hands the Vulgate had assumed its present shape. Here there was greater need of revision and explanation. He was urged by his friends, especially in England, to give freer scope to his criticisms; to express his judgment more fully, where before he had been brief and obscure. The success of his paraphrase of St. Paul's Epistles, published about this time, and universally applauded, gave him confidence to make his revision of the Gospels correspond with his previous version of the Epistles. Greater facilities were at hand, especially the appearance of a new Greek lexicon, for the more successful prosecution of his task. But he entered upon it with manifest reluctance. He dreaded a return to Basle; and his weak health made him naturally reluctant to expose himself to a repetition of those fatigues and privations from which he had so recently escaped. 'There are three things in Germany I detest,' he says in one of his letters: 'the stoves, the thieves, and the plague,' which was then raging. He could not make up his mind, notwithstanding the high opinion he had of Frobenius, whether to go to Basle or to Venice. He would much rather have gone to neither. Had Greek types been accessible in Louvain or Brussels, he would have consulted his own ease and inclination by remaining in his lodgings. He would rather have forfeited three hundred golden crowns than undertake the journey. 'Oh, how I wish you had a fount of Greek types!' he writes to Badius Ascensius,[1] a printer near Brussels. 'Now, at the hazard of my life, must I go to Basle, to superintend in person the printing of the New Testament.' But Badius had no types, and there was no alternative.

Before his departure, he sent word to the two best Greek

[1] April 17, 1518.

scholars of the day, Latimer in Oxford, and Budæus in
Paris, requesting their advice and assistance. But Latimer
was formal and pedantic, Budæus envious and conceited.
'You know,' says More, 'how stiff and obstinate are these
philosophers. I suppose it is because they take so much
pride in their consistency.' Whether More was right or
wrong in his conjecture, their consistency would not thaw,
or not in time to be useful. Once more, then, single-
handed, Erasmus wended on his road to Basle, reluctant
above all things to stoop his neck to the collar. 'Once
more here I am in this odious mill,' he tells his correspondent De Berghes. By the latter end of 1517 he was hard
at work. Next year, on April 25, he writes to Henry VIII.,
who had sent him sixty angels and a pressing invitation
to return to England, that he must devote four months to
the second edition of his New Testament, but he would
leave Basle in the autumn. Before, however, he committed
his labours irrecoverably to the press, he had taken the
precaution of fixing his wavering friends at Louvain. If
he could not prevent, he might anticipate opposition by
securing their approbation to his proposed revision. The
two whom he had most cause to fear were Dorp and the
vice-chancellor; the latter for his insincerity, the former
for the flexibility of his temper. Dorp had once attacked
him and repented. The vice-chancellor he held 'like a
wolf by the ears,' to use his own illustration. Ostensibly
civil whilst Erasmus was at Louvain, he would join any
conspiracy against him when his back was turned. 'The
time was drawing near,' he says in one of his most remarkable letters to Barbiri, 'when I had to start for Basle with
the second edition of my New Testament. On the eve of
my journey, the vice-chancellor invited me to supper. Eg-
mont was there and Vives. I informed the vice-chancellor
after supper that I must leave for Basle in a few days. I

begged, protested, besought him to do me the favour to tell me if there was any change he would like to see made in the work, or anything in it prejudicial to good manners or the Catholic faith.' He replied he had read over the whole, and it seemed to him pious and learned. 'I would rather be admonished than praised,' replied Erasmus; 'admonition will profit me, praise will not. Now I have opportunity for altering: hereafter it will be too late.' He reiterated his applauses. 'If you are sincere, said I, why did you join in the outcry against the first edition?' 'Before I had read it,' he answered, 'many unfavourable criticisms were reported to me; but on reading it I found reasons for changing my sentiments. I approve hugely of what you have done; I cannot say what you may do.' 'Then,' said Erasmus, 'if you like the first edition, I will lay my life you will approve of this. He then bade me God speed on my pious labours and my efforts for the advancement of the Christian religion.'

He started for Basle about May; how far satisfied with having muzzled the wolf we cannot undertake to say. He is not the only scholar who has tasted such experience. He is not the only divine who has shown notes and prefaces to Christian friends, and found that his unguarded confidences were afterwards so many counts in the charge against him. Vice-chancellors, divinity professors, principals of colleges, the whole battle-array of orthodoxy, with its guns charged and its spears in rest, were for the next four months consigned to oblivion. Even the pleasant summer months were shut out, as he stood in the grim printing-house of Frobenius, buried up to the ears in copies of the fathers, damp sheets, and groaning forms. But the wit, the good humour, the lively sallies, the sparkling repartee, which played and flickered about his lips, no labour could shut out. 'Gracious Heavens!' says Frobenius, in a letter prefixed to his epigrams; 'have we not seen Erasmus, when he was with us a year and a half ago, partly employed in turning Greek into Latin, partly in correcting the Epistles and Gospels; now compiling his notes to the "Novum Instrumentum," anon penning scholia upon St. Jerome? What laborious, what incessant study! What fatigues were his daily portion! In the midst of all, visitors of rank would make no scruple of calling on him and interrupting him about some trifle or another; one would try to wheedle him out of an epigram, another to gain immortality by a letter. And how did he, the most easy, good-natured man in the world, act on these occasions? Did he refuse? did he manifest impatience? He was fully occupied in writing— break off his employments he could not. Yet write he did, at odd moments, as he went backwards and forwards to mass —anything to oblige.'

Erasmus returned to Louvain in September, with the first instalment of his work wet from the press. He had left Basle in languid health, occasioned by long confinement. It was a pleasant sail down the Rhine, but the autumn was hot, and at noon the sun was oppressive. At Brisach he was annoyed by the stoves and the abundance of flies—two plagues he detested. His appetite failed, and his somewhat fastidious taste recoiled from the coarse fare of an inferior German hotel; 'nasty plates, nasty pies, nasty salt meats, which had already been served to previous customers,— *meræ nauseæ.*' At the next stage he sat down to supper with more than sixty travellers in a small heated kitchen. 'If there be any God,' said Luther,[1] 'for whom the Germans of my days entertain a profound veneration, that is the god *Qwaffe.*' His orgies were celebrated with an inflexible constancy, known only to Teutonic appetites. No guest was allowed to rise from the table before the clock struck

[1] *Table-Talk*, p. 527.

ten; and as the devotees grew hot and noisy over their orgies, the ears and nose of Erasmus, the most sensitive of mortals, were not agreeably entertained. At Spires his English horse [1] knocked up from bad treatment. At Mayence he embarked on the Rhine; took an open carriage at Cologne, in a terrible storm, succeeded by a rainy night, and reached Aix completely knocked up. Here he was compelled, by the officious courtesy of his friends, to dine off fish—a diet he could never endure.[2] In great pain he reached Louvain, where a stupid physician pronounced that he was suffering from the plague—a signal for all to abandon him. Happily he was compelled to take his case into his own hands. A cup of chicken-broth, rest, and quiet effected his cure. 'Who could suppose,' he exclaims, 'that this frail body of mine, for I am now turned fifty, so slim and so delicate, after such laborious journeys and so much hard study, could have borne up against so many afflictions?'

Just then the dispute between Luther and the Dominicans on the subject of indulgences was deafening the world by its noise and its acrimony. Suspicion was aroused. It was impossible to anticipate how far the mischief might spread, or to what perils this permission of the laity to interfere in theology and pass their judgment on the Scriptures might lead. His enemies in England had not been idle, and his new edition gave them an advantage of which they were not slow to avail themselves. So long as Erasmus had been contented to confine his notes and revision to the text of St. Paul's Epistles, there was no great danger of the dispute extending beyond the ranks of the learned. People at large understood little and cared less

[1] Urswick's present.
[2] He used to say of himself, that though his soul was a good Catholic, his stomach was a Lutheran.

for nice points of scholarship. The most potent of orthodox champions would have failed to blow up the excitement beyond blood-heat. Greek particles, minute distinctions between Greek verbs and their tenses, are but poor faggots to kindle a fire with. What cared the uninitiated whether Œcolampadius, who superintended the sheets and lent his Hebrew acquirements to the undertaking, had made a blunder in some point or not? What did they know whether ὡς Θεός was more fitly rendered by *tanquam* or *quasi Deus*? Erasmus might have gone on to the end of his days with his learned affectation of ' Novum Instrumentum,' free at least from popular clamour and danger. Lord mayors and aldermen, the corporation of London, the Court of Arches itself, would have slept on, and turned a dull ear to the rhetoric of Standish and the vitriolic orthodoxy of Lee. In an evil hour Erasmus had descended to popular ground. He not only enlarged the scope of his notes, and trenched on many delicate topics of doctrine and manners, but he had modernised the Latin version of the Gospels. First and foremost he had changed the expression in St. John's Gospel, already sanctified by long usage, and the acknowledged antidote of Arianism, from ' *In principio erat* Verbum,' into ' *In principio erat* Sermo.' He had spoken of the histories of the Old Testament (that of Samson, for instance) under the questionable expression of *fabulæ*. He had accused St. Paul of having recourse to Hebraisms from inability to express himself in correct Greek.[1] Christ's equality with the Father he had referred to his human and not his divine nature (Philipp. ii. 6). In his notes to St. Matthew (ch. ii.) he had insinuated that the writers of the Gospels might have erred from not examining books, but

[1] 'The Greek of the Apostles,' he says, ' is tinged with the peculiar idioms of their native tongue.' Elsewhere: ' Their Greek is not that of Demosthenes, but *e vulgi colloquio*.'

trusting too much to their memories. As the climax to all
these offences, he had struck out from the Epistle of St.
John the celebrated verse of the Three Witnesses. Women
and children, the most ignorant, the most indifferent, could
understand and shudder at the danger when Erasmus was
charged with reforming the *Magnificat* and the *Pater
Noster*. When Carmelites and professors of theology, in
their violet-coloured hoods, thundered out anathemas from
the pulpits against that profane learning which, discontented
with the simplicity of the divine oracles, sought to remodel
them to the caprices of itching ears, who could remain unmoved? The days of Antichrist were at hand, and these
were the signs of his coming.

Foremost among his opponents were two Englishmen,
Dr. Standish, provincial of the Franciscans, about this time
appointed bishop of St. Asaph, and Dr. Edward Lee, afterwards archbishop of York, the patron of Roger Ascham.
Both these prelates played important parts in the reign of
Henry VIII. Standish was descended from an ancient
family of that name long settled in Lancashire. He had
studied at both universities; had entered the order of Gray
Friars, and became warden of their convent in London, now
converted into the Blue-coat School. The readers of Burnet
will remember that this Standish was the chief actor in that
notable dispute at the outset of Henry's reign between the
king and the Convocation. Standish is represented on that
occasion as standing up against the bishops and clergy in
behalf of the king's supremacy. And if that account is to be
trusted, he was more than a match for Warham, Fox, or
Wolsey. The story has its difficulties, like many others in
this reign. To find the friars the uncompromising advocates
of the king's supremacy, and exalting the temporal over the
spiritual power, is a fact not easy to be reconciled with our
modern notions of these orders. This is clear, however, that

the old animosity between the bishops and the religious remained unabated.

We regret we have not room for a graphic account given by Erasmus of the feuds and squabbles which prevailed at this time between the Franciscans and their rivals, but the limits of our space admonish us to be brief. Supreme over all the mendicant friars in England, Standish was a formidable opponent; if not for his talents, for the means he thus possessed of rousing the passions of the people. The exclusive privilege of the mendicant friars to hear confession gave them a hold over every household in England. They were accused of ruling the husband by the knowledge thus obtained from the wife. The female sex, more devout than the male, listened readily to their suggestions. They were the popular preachers; had great social powers; combined in their own persons the qualifications of the home and foreign missionary. In Chaucer's sketch of them, which remained unaltered till they were swept away by the Reformation, they are described as skilful in playing the fiddle and telling good stories; and no one who has looked into their sermons will doubt the correctness of the poet's description. Whilst the Dominicans kept possession of the schools and the monk was confined to his cloister, the friar wandered at large in the towns, and made himself agreeable in the pulpit and out of it. As his reputation with his own order depended on the amount of alms he collected from day to day, all his arts of wheedling and intimidation were thus brought into play. Bare heads and naked feet, tattered russet coats girt with a knotted rope, appealed irresistibly to the charitable feelings of all classes, especially the lower. The poor Carthusian monk of Sterne was in fact a begging friar of the better sort; and they who escaped the cajolery of the importunate, or defied the unscrupulous, could scarcely stand unmoved before the eloquence of silent poverty, which proffered its claims in the meek accents of pallid faces, uncomplaining grief, and pious resignation. There might be pretenders to sanctity among them, but we have the most undeniable evidence that they preached and prayed where no others of the clergy ventured.

In a most remarkable state paper, written at the commencement of this reign, giving an account of the wretchedness, confusion, and misgovernment of Ireland, the writer says:[1] 'What common folk in all this world is so poor, so feeble, so ill beseen in town and field, so bestial, so greatly oppressed and trod under foot, as the common folk of Ireland?' And this among other reasons is assigned:—'Some say that the prelates of the church and clergy is much cause of all the misorder of the land; for there is no archbishop ne bishop, abbot ne prior, parson ne vicar, ne any other person of the church, high or low, great or small, English or Irish, that useth to preach the word of God, *saving the poor friars beggars.*' Even Henry himself, though fond of learning, keenly sensible of the ridiculous, and possessed with more than a Tudor's dislike of popular commotion and disaffection, would not allow the friars to be crushed by the superior clergy. This very Dr. Standish was upheld by him against the whole influence of Convocation; against all hostile influence afterwards (and that was not slight), he was advanced by the king to the bishopric of St. Asaph. Nor was it otherwise with Katharine. All her devotional predilections ran in favour of the friars. When she expected a prince, she had recourse to their prayers and their intercessions. The friars of Greenwich, Oxford, and Cambridge received, from her pious hopes and fears, many a charitable dole and many a pound of wax. At all events, like most of her sex, we may be quite certain that she sympathised more with Standish than with Erasmus, and believed, like half the good women

[1] *State-Papers of Henry VIII.* ii. 10.

in England, that this new method of interpreting Scripture was little better than covert infidelity.

These were the men who were now to signalise their opposition against Erasmus. Shortly after the appearance of the second edition of the New Testament, Standish was appointed to preach at Paul's Cross before the lord mayor and corporation of London. After prefacing his sermon with some general observations on charity, he suddenly broke away from the main topic, and launched forth, to the astonishment of his audience, in bitter denunciations against Erasmus. He declared that the total extinction of Christianity was at hand, unless these new-fangled versions of the Scriptures were suppressed. It was intolerable that Erasmus should venture to corrupt the Gospel of St. John, and transform the old reading, '*In principio erat* Verbum,' to which the Church had adhered for so many centuries, into the new style of, '*In principio erat* Sermo.' Then turning to the lord mayor and corporation, he told them that St. Augustine had given very good reasons for the use of the old word *Verbum*. ' But,' added he, ' that pretentious and shallow Grecian could not comprehend the arguments of the holy father. And, oh ! ' he exclaimed, ' that I should have lived to witness these times—I, a doctor of so many years' standing; I, who have all my life read "*In principio erat* Verbum," to be sent to school and compelled to read "*In principio erat* Sermo."' With that he wept, to the astonishment of the men and the edification of the women.

It was his fortune that day to dine at the palace; and after the meal was over, Standish was introduced to the royal circle. A large assembly of bishops, nobles, and scholars surrounded Henry and Katharine. Bustling through the crowd, Standish fell on his knees, and, raising his hands to heaven, broke forth into loud praises of the king's royal progenitors, who had always religiously defended the Catholic church against heresy and schism. Most perilous times, he exclaimed, were at hand; Erasmus was daily publishing some new book; and unless a firm resistance were made to such innovations, Christianity was at an end. Then, turning up his eyes to heaven, he begged Christ to assist His forlorn spouse, though all else forsook her. One of the circle, probably More or Mountjoy, watching his opportunity, slipped down on his knee before the king, and, mimicking the theatrical tones and attitudes of Standish, besought him, as he had inspired their majesties with so much fear and anxiety for the safeguard of Christendom, to be good enough to tell them what were the perilous heresies and schisms to which he alluded in the writings of Erasmus. Then, stretching out his hand, Standish began to reckon them on the tips of his fingers. 'First,' says he, 'Erasmus denies the resurrection; next, he annihilates the sacrament of marriage; thirdly, he derogates from the eucharist.' These assertions occasioned great sensation. His opponent requested him to produce the passages on which these accusations rested. Standish began with his thumb. 'First,' said he, 'that Erasmus denies the resurrection I prove thus: Paul, in his epistle to the Colossians' (he mistook Colossians for Corinthians) 'says: *Omnes quidem resurgemus, sed non omnes immutabimur*; but Erasmus, out of his Greek, reads it thus: *Omnes quidem non dormiemus, sed omnes immutabimur*. It is clear, therefore, that he denies the resurrection.' The other explained that Erasmus had professed to adhere strictly to the Greek text; and as the word 'resurrection' should have been retained by him in so many other places, it was absurd to say that in this change, which he had adopted on good authority, he had denied the resurrection. 'Ah, yes,' said Standish, 'you mean the authority of St. Jerome; but Jerome took this from the

Hebrew.' Hereupon another friend of Erasmus, advancing through the circle, dropped on his knee before the king, and, after reverence done, addressed himself to Standish: 'I cry your mercy, reverend father: will you repeat what you said just now, as I was not paying much attention.' Standish repeated his remark. Then his opponent, to draw attention to its absurdity, rejoined: 'That is no trivial argument which his reverence has advanced; but I should like to reply to it, if his majesty will permit me.' Queen Katharine, twitching the king, called his attention to the speaker. 'I don't see,' says the objector, with assumed gravity, 'what answer can be made to his reverence's argument. I don't suppose he imagines that the epistles of St. Paul were written in Hebrew, when every schoolboy knows they were written in Greek. What purpose could St. Jerome possibly have in correcting them from the Hebrew, when no Hebrew copies of them ever existed?' Henry saw the bishop's discomfiture, and, with kingly grace, changed the conversation.

But the opposition of Standish, though vexatious enough, was confined to England. A more bitter and formidable enemy sprung up in Edward Lee, chaplain and almoner to Henry VIII. He had written, or more probably had put together, the floating objections of the times against the first edition of the New Testament, and circulated the book in manuscript, among his own friends and those of Erasmus. On the return of the latter from Basle, before the notes to the second edition had appeared, he had requested Lee to allow him the sight of his criticisms: if not, he begged Lee to publish them at once, that he might make the necessary corrections in his forthcoming edition. Lee resolutely refused. He was bent on securing a reputation by an attack on the most remarkable author of the age; and his book would have been worthless had Erasmus anticipated his objections. The matter might have ended there, with little credit to Lee's generosity. But Erasmus could not forbear expressing his irritation. He spoke of Lee in terms of great contempt, to more than one of his numerous correspondents. 'The earth had never produced anything more arrogant, venomous, or foolish.' He stigmatised him as a conceited young man and a sciolist. With still greater indiscretion, finding all other means ineffectual, he wrote a letter to Lee, in which he had the bad taste to threaten him with the vengeance of his friends in Germany, 'who had not yet,' as he added, 'dropped all their native ferocity.' Lee waited for no further provocation. He immediately brought out his book, and prefaced it with the following calm and sarcastic letter. 'Edovardus Leeus Desiderio Erasmo salutem. En! nunc demum habes, Desideri Erasme, nostrarum annotationum librum, quem tantopere efflagitasti—opus, spero, cum primis tibi gratum et jucundum, si non quod nostrum sit, tamen quod tuo nomini nuncupatum, et te annum jam totum hortante emissum: vel forte, eo potius nomine, quod inde orbi nostra prodetur ignorantia, quam tu nullis non modis studes propagari; ut omnes cognoscant me talem esse, qualem tu fingis.'

It was evident that the author of such a letter could not be the puny and contemptible adversary Erasmus had represented. Nor was he. Roger Ascham has done justice to the learning of Lee. More and Fisher were inclined to think he had been unfairly treated, and, after the provocation he had received, he could hardly be expected to remain silent.

Lee took exception to the hasty and perfunctory manner in which Erasmus had introduced emendations into the New Testament. He accused Erasmus of rejecting readings, confirmed by long patristic usage, on the slender authority of a Greek manuscript, as to the age of which and its general accuracy grave doubts existed. He taxed him with citing passages from the Greek copies which were not to be found in them, and omitting such as were. In some instances his Latin version did not correspond with the Greek; in others the true meaning had been misquoted or misrepresented. The rest of Lee's objections related rather to matters of doctrine and opinion. Erasmus had spoken contemptuously of previous commentators; he had condemned the Church for admitting the Epistle to the Hebrews into the canon; he had asserted that the Gospel of St. Mark was nothing more than a compendium of St. Matthew's. But it was his gravest and most substantial charge that, in the Apocalypse, Erasmus, to supply the defects of his Greek MSS., had ventured on the extraordinary license of turning certain verses into Greek which he had found only in the Latin copies. Objectionable as such an act undoubtedly was, and subversive of all sound criticism and literary honesty, Erasmus had not intended to impose upon his readers. He had acknowledged the fact in his notes. It was indeed much to be wished that Erasmus had candidly admitted these accusations, instead of attempting to recriminate. They were true in the main; they could not be denied. Had he fallen back upon that line of defence which he had taken up at first; had he admitted that in so laborious a work, too rapidly completed and surrounded by numerous obstacles, it was scarcely possible to avoid omissions and errors, he would have diminished nothing of his fair fame. He chose to stand upon the defensive—to hurl back invectives at the head of Lee; and thus he gave an importance to these charges they did not intrinsically deserve. His best friends looked sad; to his enemies he had exposed an advantage of which they were not slow to avail themselves; whilst to the Gallios of this world, who regarded with supreme indifference the real question at issue, it afforded a fund of delight to see the great biblical scholar tormented by petty and malicious assailants. Stunica and Caranza, the successors to Lee and Standish in this inglorious warfare, were as amusing as Pasquin to infidel bishops and classic cardinals at Rome, if not for their wit, yet for their unceasing virulence.

But we must draw these observations to a close. Of the editions of the New Testament which appeared in the lifetime of Erasmus, the fourth, published in 1527, is the most complete, as he had the advantage of the critical aids afforded by the Complutensian. In the third edition, which appeared in 1522, he reinserted, from an English MS., the verse of the Three Witnesses. But, except for the interest which must always attach to first experiments, the Greek Testament of Erasmus has little value for the biblical scholar of the present day. Much beyond his contemporaries in his conception of the duties of an editor, and of the philological requirements for establishing and explaining the text of an ancient author, he fell far below the modern standard. He understood quite as well as later scholars do, that the text of the New Testament must be determined by the ancient Greek copies, supported by the earliest Latin versions and the Greek fathers. He was in some respects even less fettered than modern critics are by prejudices in favour of an authorised text or established translation. He had no leaning to the Vulgate. He was not inclined to attribute to it the praise it unquestionably deserves. The necessity of a careful description of the age and condition of the MSS. and authorities employed by him in forming his text—an indispensable part of an editor's duty—he almost entirely overlooked. Consequently, beyond his own critical judgment and sagacity, his text rests on no satisfactory or determinable authority. He would have done more had he done less,—had he been content with a careful edition, resting on one or two good MSS. Therefore, unlike the early editions of the Greek classics, the New Testament of Erasmus is absolutely worthless for all critical purposes. Yet, strange to say, until within a very late period, it remained substantially the only form in which the original was known to the world. It was not in the execution, but in the conception of his work that he deserves our praise. He had not health, patience, or inclination for the tedious and laborious process of collating MSS. He was much more at his ease in compiling notes and bringing his vast and multifarious reading to bear on the elucidation of the history and antiquities of the New Testament. So far as vast learning can be of service, in this respect no commentator can be compared to Erasmus. With the whole region of Latin literature he was familiar, and scarcely less at home with the most eminent of the Greek and Latin fathers. At a time when the Greek scholars in England might be counted on the fingers, his notes to the Greek Testament abound in quotations from Homer, the Greek tragedians, Herodotus, Aristophanes, Aristotle, Athenæus, Lucian, and others.

Whatever judgment we may now be inclined to pass on his work, it must be allowed the praise of being the first attempt to introduce a more diligent study of the New Testament. Luther used his labours, and proclaimed his contempt for them, in his noble commentary on the Galatians. Erasmus, he complained, stuck too much to the letter: 'humana prævalent in eo plus quam divina.'[1] Yet, in spite of this dictum, are we not entitled to say, after three centuries' experience, that the surest sign of a barren and unreal theology is not over-attention to the critical meaning of the original, but carelessness of the life that is in words? The slow induction, the careful sifting comparison, the spiritual sympathy, so to speak, which alone enable a scholar

[1] *Luth. Epist.* 29.

to understand Plato, or a philosopher to read the material world, must surely be applied to the Greek of the New Testament if we would know its true compass and significance by a profounder insight than we have. The severe beauty of the Vulgate and our own homely and noble English versions have partially set aside and obscured their original by the chain of words that come native to our thought and the long link of household associations. Such work as Erasmus's was is dreaded by many as a wanton iconoclasm, a defacing, if not a destruction, of the holiest forms of faith. Perhaps the very fear is the best argument that the task needs to be done again. Of all phases of bibliolatry, that which prefers the copy to the original is surely the strangest. For ourselves, we can only express our firm confidence that the Gospels will never lose by being studied in the very words of the Evangelists.

THE STUDY OF HISTORY.[1]

WHAT is History? What does it profess to teach us? How is it to be studied? These are questions which will spontaneously occur to my hearers who are interested in the subject of this lecture. The word History is ancient enough. It belongs to that people who first understood the value of History, and who were the first to set the example of this kind of writing—the Greeks. History, then, in the words of the first Greek historian, Herodotus, means *Inquiry*—an inquiry into facts. 'These are the inquiries (he says), that is, the history of Herodotus of Halicarnassus;' —and he tells us, furthermore, what he considered was the purpose of history;—'that the deeds done by the Greeks in their wars against the barbarians should not go out of memory, and be forgotten.' He felt a truth which thousands of men before him had not felt—or had not attempted to realise—that all men owe a debt of remembrance to those who have gone before them, especially when those predecessors of theirs have been their benefactors, especially when the blessings of moral, intellectual, social, and political freedom have been worked out by *their* blood and *their* endeavours. And the same feelings which prompt a true-hearted man to preserve the memorials of his father and mother, would prompt him as a citizen to preserve and remember the memorials of his fellow-men, who stand to him in the next relation to that of parents, as teachers, rulers,

[1] A Lecture delivered at the Working Men's College.

liberators, preservers of his and their common country. And there is more in it than mere thankfulness:—for there is not a man that hears me this day, and there will not be for all future time, who has not been benefited by this book of Herodotus. This simple act of love and duty— the endeavour that so far as he was concerned the deeds of his countrymen should not be forgotten—has issued in the most wonderful consequences to all generations.

But his own example furnishes the best comment on what he meant by History, and in what spirit he thought that such inquiries should be conducted. We should expect that in proportion to the love and faith in which he undertook this task, he would prosecute it with earnestness. And so he did. He was unwearied in his researches after the truth; he spared no pains. To get at the facts, to disentangle them from the misrepresentations in which his own prejudices, or the passions or the ignorance of others, might have obscured or entangled them—this was his great object.

We have then in him an example of the duty of a historian, and of all who, without being historians, are bent upon the study of history. They are to be inquirers, seekers after truth, and, as such, earnest in their pursuit of it— and earnest especially that they do not mistake their own notions or conceptions of it for the truth which it has to reveal.

You see that in thus asking ourselves what 'History' is, we have glided insensibly into the second question—'What does it profess to teach us?' If it be a painful inquiry into facts, that is at once the meaning and the object of History. So far then it is leading us into an acquaintance with the truths and facts which concern our race, which concern our predecessors, which concern ourselves; which are lying about us and around us; in all the questions of the day; in the institutions and governments under which we live; in the words we are now using; in the most familiar habits and usages of our lives. As the science of medicine brings us to the knowledge of the facts and laws which regulate and concern our health; as astronomy to the laws which determine the motions of the heavenly bodies; as other physical sciences introduce us to the consideration of laws which regulate the material universe; history brings us to the knowledge of those facts and those laws which concern us as men and citizens. It tells us how men have grown from barbarism to civilisation, from separate and contending masses to a sense of national life and unity; how that national life has expressed itself—in what forms, actions, languages; what causes have fostered or obstructed that national union; how men have struggled for truth and righteousness; what mistakes they have made in so doing; how they have been punished by them, how they have recovered from them. It brings before us, moreover, the lives of those who were most instrumental in advancing or retarding these events.

If it be important to know these facts, then is it important to know history, from which alone they can be derived. And history is thus a part of that great revelation which all arts, all sciences, and all literature is gradually unfolding before our eyes. It is helping us, like these other branches of philosophy, to see things as they are; it is helping to disencumber us of those images and delusions—that slavery to present sense and present objects—which stand between us and the truth. Nay, more, it is bringing us to the knowledge of what is true, permanent, and substantial, apart from the mere outward forms and phantoms we are so apt to mistake for it; enabling us to disengage the errors, dogmas, and systems of men from the truths which they sought to maintain; to see a light in the thickest darkness, an order not of human but divine appointment vindicating itself among the loudest clamours and deepest confusions of our race.

There is a passage in Lord Bacon so much to this purpose that I cannot forbear quoting it. 'Although' (he says) 'we are deeply indebted to the light, because by means of it we can find our way, ply our tasks, read, distinguish one another; and yet for all that the vision of the light itself is more excellent and more beautiful than all these various uses of it; so the contemplation and sight of things, as they are, without superstition, without imposture, without error, and without confusion, is in itself worth more than all the harvest and profit of inventions put together.' And so may I say of History; that useful as it may be to the statesman, to the lawyer, to the schoolmaster, or the annalist, so far as it enables us to look at facts as they are, and to cultivate that habit within us, the importance of History is far beyond all mere amusement or even information that we may gather from it.

But when I say that History is a revelation of facts as they are, do not suppose that your whole task consists in stringing all the facts of a period together, or that when you have got the facts you have necessarily mastered all the truths involved in them. Remember that when you have possessed yourselves of all the facts—supposing that you have done so—there is yet another process to come, not less laborious; that is, to look at the facts steadily, to make sure that you *do* see them. For you know that many people think that they see things when they do not; that nothing is more common than this self-deception; that the habit of seeing, and seeing accurately and carefully, has to be taught, not to children only, but to grown people, when first introduced to objects which are strange to them or new. You know, too, that a man may look a hundred times at a common object and see nothing in it—and then all at once the truth of it flashes upon him, and he is astonished that he never saw it before. You know, too, that a cold or indifferent, is as bad as a bigoted or prejudiced observer in discovering the fact. For instance, here is before me a son or daughter who has at home a father or mother; or a parent who has a child. Do they not see under the outward decaying form the inward and eternal spirit—that which is beautiful and immutable—which eyes less anxious and affectionate than their own cannot discern? Does not the poet, the man of genius, the true man, be he where he may, see beneath the besmirched and fading forms of humanity around him, the truth and beauty and goodness which others cannot? Not because he has put it there; not because it has no other existence than his own fancy; but because he has the power, partly natural, partly acquired, of seeing more deeply than other men into the inner life of things about him. That is why I say, that when you have the facts which history furnishes, there is yet something more required—a power of insight into these facts and their meanings, which, if not native, is only to be acquired by patient and humble study.

Now I have already pointed out to you the danger in this, as in all other pursuits, of substituting opinions about facts for the facts themselves; of setting up the idols of a man's own mind in the place of those truths and realities which lie around him. You will ask me, then—How are you to set to work? How are you to fix your eyes on these facts and try to interpret them? And how can you be sure that after all you are not falling into this mistake? I answer, that probably you will, and that very often; for no man comes into the clear light of any truth without falling often, and making many mistakes. But as when a man falls into moral untruths and into temptations, he must not lie there in his untruth and his sin, but get upon his legs again and press forward to the truth—be he dirty or clean —so is it here. He must never lose sight of the facts; he must keep up the intercourse between his mind and them; he must keep walking up and down in them, always bearing this truth about in his thoughts—that he has not exhausted and cannot exhaust them; that let him live as long as he will, they will always have something to tell him, if he is humble and thoughtful; and be he the wisest philosopher that ever lived, some one will come after him to whom it will be granted to see in them what he could not, and that too without a tithe of his abilities.

Besides, however, this general caution, there are some few practical rules suggested by it. As the characters and principles of men would give us the closest insight into their actions, so it is with History;—national characteristics are the best interpreters of national history. It is important therefore to remember that English history is one thing and French history is another; and therefore to understand them aright, you must shift your point of view accordingly. Plain as this truth is, it is very often neglected; men are accustomed to carry their own principles and notions with them, and apply them indifferently to all history alike. But this observation is valuable not only as furnishing us with a clue to the interpretation of history, but as enabling us to divide history into portions, to study each of them by themselves, and then in their relations to each other. In modern history it is the only method which can prevent us from falling into confusion. Let me apply this to the subject so far as the limits of a lecture will allow, and you will clearly perceive its value.

History is divided into two great portions, ancient and modern. Ancient history has no other difficulties than those which are presented by its remoteness from present times, and our consequent inability of adequately representing to ourselves the thoughts and feelings of people living in a state so very different from our own. Christianity, new races, a new world, great inventions, have been moulding for many centuries all our notions, pursuits, manners, speculations. It is hard for us to divest ourselves of these influences and to go back to a simpler and less complex period, when one division only of the globe, one race, or one nation only challenges consideration. But Ancient History has this advantage over Modern, that it does not distract us with a multiplicity of details, or bring at the same time a number of different nations and actors on the stage, each of whom is demanding and distracting our attention, each of whom has something to say which must not be disregarded. On the contrary, Ancient History goes on in one simple and uniform tenor; either presenting to our view one country, one people, one literature, exclusively and successively, or if it brings forward other nations at the same time, it is only in reference, and in subordination, to a single people which is predominant at the time. In the History of the Hebrews we hear of Egypt, in the History of Greece of the Persians, but instead of confusing our views, these occasional glimpses assist in bringing out more clearly the condition of the chosen nation with whom they are brought into connection. Thus Ancient History has a unity in it denied apparently to Modern History. It requires no arbitrary divisions of our own invention; we have but to follow the law thus clearly marked out, and consider each epoch successively. So Ancient History falls into a series of easy and natural divisions. First the Hebrew, then the Greek, and then the Roman; and each of these people, though engaged in numerous wars, exposed to various temptations, and exemplifying a vast diversity of actions in their career, have in them a unity of character; are penetrated by one strong and predominant principle of action, which serves as a light—a clear and steady one—to interpret the most obscure passages in their history.

Take the Hebrew, for instance, with which we are all familiar. Here we have one people with whom is connected the earliest records of the world; there is but one book in which their history is contained, and in it we are made to feel how strong is that unity of the Jewish people, and upon what truth that unity is based. Now what is that Book? We call it the Bible—that is the Book of all nations; as it is; but we call it also a Revelation—the Word of God. And so it is. But you will also remember that it is the book which contains the national annals of the Jews—that is, of 'God's people.' But it is not less God's word, not less His revelation of Himself to them, as the Jews, as the nation. Whatever else this Jewish history may contain, it contains these facts—these which lie at the foundation of their national life. First, that God was revealing Himself to them more clearly than he did to any other people; that that revelation brought them nearer to Him than any other people; that it made Him the Ruler of the nation, and them His people, in a sense such as no others enjoyed; and that on the recognition of this truth, that they were His people—nation and rulers, prophets and workmen— their happiness and their welfare as a nation depended. They might forget that truth, and they did over and over again. The people might think that they had a right to take their own way without consulting His will. The prophet might prophesy in his own name, and turn his gifts to his own interest and aggrandisement; the king might rule as of his own authority, forgetting whose minister he was. But they were made to feel the consequences of these transgressions, not only in themselves but in the sufferings and distractions which they entailed upon their nation. This then is the principle of the Jewish life, whatever else may be—individual and national—that the people are in covenant with God. He is their ruler, they are His servants.

I have not time to extend this to all its various ramifications; nor yet to show you how it must never be forgotten in interpreting the history of this people. Let me show you in passing how it throws light on the history of those nations with whom this people are brought into connection, and with whom they have been of late not wisely confounded. Two of these are the Assyrian and the Egyptian, for whom, as you know, modern history has done so much, and of whom such wonderful records are preserved in the British Museum. You have seen these records. What are they? Winged bulls and lions, memorials of conquest, types of the power of the great king. Nebuchadnezzar brings their meaning home to us: the man whose pride was exalted, who set himself up above the stars of heaven. In him are united the temporal and spiritual authority, a danger into which the East is continually falling. The Egyptian, on the other hand, is ruled by his priests; he deals in magic, and uses the mysterious powers of nature to secure his authority over the people. In one the ruler, in the other the priest, are forgetting the Jewish principle that they are God's ministers, and that their gifts are to be exercised for Him. Each found their representative in the Jewish nation; and each, we know too well, led that people into their own peculiar temptation.

We pass to the next people of the old world—these are the Greeks. They are in many respects the very opposites of the Jews; the Jew permitted no representations to be made of the Unseen God—the Greek delighted in them. Everywhere he multiplied these representations, everywhere he tried to reduce to sight spiritual things by shadowing them forth in the likeness of men. Nay, the more Greek he was the more he essayed to do this. If he thought of wisdom it was under the emblem of Minerva; if of strength, Hercules; if of abstract beauty, Venus; if of empire, Jupiter; if of light and inspiration, Apollo. Of the mysteries of nature in which the Egyptian delighted he thought nothing, or only so far as they related to mysteries in himself. Man and the powers of man, man as the master over matter and the ruler of the world, were the objects of the deepest thought and speculation to the Greek. Whatever fell within the limits of this inquiry he pursued with increasing avidity: his government, his institutions, his philosophy, his poetry, had this for their object. Every problem which could concern the soul or the body, or their connection, or their faculties, or their habits, or the exercise of their several powers, never came amiss to him. No wonder that the Greek magnified the courage, the strength, the wisdom of man; that he claimed for him a distinction from brute matter around him—a life of his own and a personality—as the Jew was witnessing to the nations that God was not to be confounded with the invisible powers of Nature. Though different, both were asserting a necessary truth; and the evils and idolatry of both arose not from the truths which they held, but from the falsehoods which they mixed with those truths. To the Greek we still go for instruction in all that belongs to the dignity, the powers, the beauty of man, for examples of brave deeds, for heroical recitals, for noble struggles against tyranny in all forms, whether of brute force, or ignorance, or pain, or as he called it, destiny. The great enemy to the Greek is the Persian, as the Egyptian was to the Jew; and yet as there was a most extraordinary attraction of the Egyptian to the Jew, so was there of the Greek to the Persian. The Greek was naturally tempted to adopt Persian manners and customs, the Persian would offer every kind of temptation to induce the Greek to settle in his country. There were also, opposite as they might appear to each other, points of resemblance between them which render this mutual attraction and repulsion the more remarkable. The Persians were an heroic people like the Greeks. They thought much of their ancient heroes, Cyrus, Darius, Xerxes. Like the Greeks they hated a sacerdotal caste, who used their influence to blind and mislead the people. Like the Greeks also, the sun was the chief object of their national worship. But to the Persian his God, though a power infinitely removed from himself, and the Light of the World, was a light and no more. He had none of the attributes of a God in the sense of the Greeks; he had no personality. He was not, it is true, made with hands, and He dwelt not in temples; but neither did He draw near to His worshipper, nor did His worshipper feel that he could draw near to Him. There was no feeling that He could sympathise with humanity; that He could or would make a covenant with His people. Thus not only the evil powers of the world and the instruments of darkness were to the Persian more definite, comprehensible, and formidable; but his extreme reverence for his king as the sole representative of all authority, as the ruler, the sole dispenser of justice and judgment, converted the Persian into the mere tool of despotism. He is the willing instrument of conquests, the enemy of national independence, the champion of a universal monarchy of which the Great King is the head. To him the Greek, striving for individual independence, never forgetting his native land, never blending with the people among whom he settles, is as much a mystery as his own reverence for kingly authority and his feeling that he has no existence independent of his king is to the Greek. But that the Persian had hold of a truth which the Greek needed, much as it might be perverted, is clear from the fact that Greek history comes to an end with the destruction of Persia. And this truth is verified in more than one instance in the histories of men and nations.

We have reached the history of another people more powerful than any we have yet seen—I refer to the Romans. They too are a religious people, they have their auguries, their priesthood, and, like the Hebrews, a belief in the invisible God, who has been the founder, and is the father of their nation. They too are strongly impressed with a sense of their own power, and of the value which it possesses in bringing the nations of the earth into order and regularity. They too, like the Greek, set a high value on the freedom of man; and, like the Persian, they feel that there is some paramount and paternal authority, superior to all the rest, on the acknowledgment of which the strength and unity of their nation depend. The history of the Roman people tells us of the virtues of fathers and mothers, the obedience of sons, the chastity of daughters. The founder of their nation is the dutiful Æneas who saves his father from the flames of Troy. Is he in doubt what to do, he flies for advice to his father; after death it is his father's spirit that guides, it is his father's household gods who extend their protection and guardianship to the son. It is the parental authority that is shadowed forth in all the forms of the Roman government; it is the sense of reverence and obedience which the son owes to the father, that is at the root of all their discipline, their civil order and subordination. It is this which gives a dignity and intensity to their civil disputes, and to the contentions of senators and plebeians. We feel that they are not mere ordinary broils, like other popular tumults, but that the deepest principles are involved in them; and out of such confusion they are to come forth stronger and more united than before.

Wherever the Roman sets his foot he rouses up his own sense of law and social order among the nations, even though he cannot raise up among them a true feeling for those principles which had led himself to a true appreciation and knowledge of self-government. Whatever the nations, whatever their condition, savage or civilised, no sooner does the Roman appear among them than they too are led to feel a value for right and order, as they had never felt before. Permanent forms of government start up, towns are built, roads are made, people are taught to live together, to co-operate, to depend upon one another. They were a stern and severe people it is true; they were often guilty of great acts of tyranny and oppression in carrying these lessons to the nations round about them; but we must not for that overlook the great good that they did; we must not forget to recognise the fact, that with all his failings, the Roman in his manliness, in his love of right, in his unswerving adherence to justice, in his patriotism, in his regard for the laws of his country, has been an example to all the world. No nation has done more to imprint the names of its great citizens on our memories and to make them familiar in our mouths as household words. We may know little of the personal histories of Decius, of Regulus, of Brutus, or of Cato, but so long as self-devotion, self-denial, patriotism and unconquerable rectitude are admired, so long will these names be remembered as the brightest examples of those virtues.

I have thus endeavoured to mark out for you the great epochs of ancient history. I have endeavoured to show you how, in studying each of these epochs, you will gain much for the better understanding of the history by considering primarily the people who are predominant in each epoch, and studying carefully the great principles which lie at the root of their national character. First we have been brought to the knowledge of a people to whom nature is a mystery, an inexplicable puzzle. With all his civilisation, his wonderful mechanical skill, the Egyptian is a slave to the external world. Then we see the Jew, to whom God is revealed as the Lord and Creator of this external world, with all its beautiful and mysterious objects, and in that truth the Jew feels that though in one sense the subject, he is in another the superior of that external world. Then comes the Greek, fully impressed with the superiority of man, taking his stand on that pre-eminence, looking at all things calmly from it, and referring all things to it. Man, his character and his attributes, engage his exclusive study. Then comes the Roman, caring little for the individual character, but regarding men in relation to an organised whole, to a great and symmetrical system: and desiring most to know by what laws that system can best be held together. Let us now ask, are there any such helps for Modern History; because if there are, they would deserve to be thoroughly considered, and the plan which is pursued in the study of Ancient History points out the course for the study of Modern History. But before we can settle this, we must first of all remember that we have not determined these epochs in Ancient History, nor their main characteristics, nor marked out the people who distinguish for us the point of view from which each epoch is to be studied. That has been done for us; all are agreed upon that head, and no subsequent discoveries can possibly alter this method. But how stands the case in regard to Modern History? Are we all agreed as to its divisions, as to its order, as to the main features of each period? Does not every man look at it from his own point of view, which is determined sometimes by his nationality, sometimes by accidents of birth, religion, and education? The German has one theory, the Frenchman another, the Englishman a third. The Roman Catholic and the Protestant, the Whig and the Tory, have their respective points of view. Which is in the right, and which ought we to follow? Abstractedly, we, as Englishmen and as Protestants, can find no great difficulty in answering the question. But then, we must remember that if we set out upon our task, valuing everything according to these two national principles, we may very possibly miss many truths which history has to tell us, and end, as many others have ended, no better and no wiser after our labours. There is a wise remark of Coleridge, applicable to this mistake:—'He who begins by loving Christianity better than truth, will proceed by loving his own sect or church better than Christianity, and end in loving himself better than all.'

Let us first examine the difficulties, and then consider how they are to be mastered.

In the first place, Modern History is much more complicated than ancient; instead of one nation being supreme and ruling the rest, it presents us with many nations, all standing on their own independence, all having their own languages, their own modes of government, all occupying countries of the utmost diversity, all engaged in different pursuits. New portions of the world have been brought in to add to this diversity—India and the extreme East, America with all the regions of the West. And we cannot shut our eyes to the fact that these have been and are exercising day by day, and hour by hour, permanent and mighty influences, not merely on the commerce of the world, but on its thoughts, its literature. Instead of becoming more like the ancient world, and showing its unity and singleness of character, it would appear as if Modern History were daily becoming more complex; daily its centre of unity becomes more hidden in the multiplicity of competing influences. Above all, as distinct from the nations and the national society, often opposed to it, often allied with it, but never totally merged in it, Modern History shows us the progress of another society—that of the Christian Church—as difficult and as important as any other part of history, as necessary to the clear understanding of the rest. How then shall we find a clue for this labyrinth, how find the law which will bring these multifarious and conflicting details into order? How shall we be saved from putting our own interpretation upon them, and making them deliver up to us, not their own oracles, but ours? You see the difficulty and importance of the subject, you see also the danger into which the most ingenious and the most thoughtful men are apt to fall.

Well, happily, in Modern History, as in ancient, there are some great landmarks and divisions which we have not to determine for ourselves. Of these we must make the most. Some of them will occur to you at once; others will appear to you as you grow more familiar with the subject. The first great division is that of history before and after the Reformation. Now, whatever other effects may have been worked out by this great event, these facts are undeniable: that the papacy has ceased to be the centre of Europe, or European history; there is no longer one Universal Church, under one Visible Head, speaking one language, distinct from the national languages of Christendom; there are no longer two classes, the spiritual and the temporal, separated from each other by an impassable limit, and taught to consider themselves as the denizens of two distinct worlds. With the depression of the Papal Supremacy has ceased not only the exaltation of the foreign over national authority, not only of the spiritual over the temporal, but the antagonism between the two, and all the train of consequences which followed upon that antagonism; not only the exaltation of the religious over the laity, of celibacy over marriage, of the Church over the State; but, what is of more importance, the errors which grew out of this exaltation—the notion that the layman could not be religious, that marriage could not be holy, that the State had no better than worldly sanctions. It dispersed the mischievous error that the kingdom of God is not within us, that the spiritual world is not nigh at hand, that the visible world is not the door to the invisible, nor the relations of this life the training and discipline for the next. And all the pangs, the confusions, the contradictions in men's thoughts, feelings, pursuits, and actions which grew out of this fatal mistake disappeared, with all that formalism which had its roots in this pernicious distinction.

But as these things constitute the difference between the periods before and after the Reformation, they serve also as marks to characterise the two, and are guides to the study of the history. The rise and influence of the papacy, and the relations of other nations to it, will always form an important consideration in the study of mediæval history, as the independence of nations under their national sovereigns will belong to the second period.

But there are still narrower limits. The first period, notwithstanding that unity in its characteristics which I have pointed out, has another natural division. It shows a time when the nations were struggling alone without any sense of co-operation ; it has a period when they were all brought together, all united for one great action ; I mean the Crusades. And this period subdivides itself into others. So, without any arbitrary divisions, we may mark off this period into the following epochs :—First, The Roman period, from the first century to the end of the fourth ; when the East and West were permanently divided, and the West fell a prey to the Barbarians. Secondly, The Barbarian period, when the German tribes came in and occupied the finest provinces of Europe; while the Mahometan occupied those of Asia and Africa. Thirdly, The Union of the German and Roman under Charlemagne. Fourthly, The breaking up of this empire, and the rise of distinct nations from its ruins. Fifthly, The coming together of these at the Crusades, under one common authority, the Church. Sixthly, The new position of the Church in reference to these nations, and her attempt to rule them for her own aggrandisement, binding their consciences to her dictates. Seventhly, Their emancipation by the Reformation. Eighthly, The relation of kings to their people. Ninthly, The era of Louis XIV. Tenthly, The French Revolution.

These—or divisions analogous to these—have this advantage: first, that they are not arbitrary; they do not depend on the cleverness of the reader or student, however clever he may be, but are determined by general consent. That general consent not only decides upon their importance, but it shows that they are in a special measure the movements and turning-points of *general* interest. They occupy then the same position as the several acts of a great drama— as indeed they are; and they are to be studied in the same way. Consider what an act is, as shown to us in one of Shakespeare's plays, and you will understand what I mean. An act is not merely an arbitrary division of the drama invented for the poet's or the spectator's convenience—not so. It is a real action, a real progress; and the poet by means of it brings his characters together; shows how they are affected by it, and how they are affecting one another. He gives us, therefore, different scenes of his action, presents it to us on different sides, and lets us see how his different characters will regard it in a different light, and be variously affected by it. And so it is in this world: each man and each nation have their peculiar tempers, characters, energies of mind and body; and these peculiarities, whether of good or evil, are brought out by the circumstances in which they are placed, by the actions of others and of themselves. Now, what the act is in a drama, a great epoch is in history; it affords the means of testing the nations, of comparing them, of observing their strength and their weakness. And a succession of such epochs, or acts, enables us further to trace their progress. We can not only ascertain their relative condition at different intervals, but see their failures and their successes, and the causes. What is but weak, doubtful, and precarious at one epoch is seen in its full bloom and development at a later one; the temptation which appears so alluring at an earlier stage is seen in its native ugliness and its direful consequences at a subsequent interval; the weakness and the strength, scarcely appreciated in their infancy, show themselves in their true character as men and nations come more and more into contact with one another and the outward world.

Take a common instance, often a mournful one, as an illustration of this remark. Suppose the members of a family were gathered round the family table once a year during all their lives. How would the father of them all, as he looked upon the moral, the physical, and the worldly condition of his sons, be able, not only to compare them with one another, but to trace with unerring precision the causes of their happiness or misfortune! How clearly would he perceive the laws which had determined their respective conditions! How would he see the unerring development of consequences from causes! Would their lives appear to him full of confusion? Would he think that their destiny was in their own hands—that all was the work of chance? Quite the reverse; would he not see that the moral world was as strictly ruled as the physical world, and that men's lives, and men's history, were not a mere chapter of accidents, but the most unmistakeable testimony to a divine order and harmony which is always manifesting itself—to our happiness if we strive to discover and obey it, but still going on and asserting itself in spite of our crimes, our follies, and our disobedience?

Great epochs of history do this: they enable us to gather

the nations together, to consider them in reference to one and the same great action, and in reference to one another; to trace their growth and decline, to see what great truths they have neglected, what laws they have broken, what opportunities they have lost. We may see how their pride, or presumption, or tyranny, have been followed by punishment; how their love of right, of truth, of liberty has been rewarded. Sum it all up, and, though we may be sometimes at a loss to vindicate God's justice in the case of individual men, in the case of nations there is no difficulty. There crimes and sins work out their visible consequences; there honesty and virtue are always in the end rewarded; there the neglected talent is taken away; there, without any exception to the rule, faithfulness in few things is rewarded with the trust of many things. So far then is history from being an obscure, vague, uncertain page in the book of knowledge, it is a most faithful and unerring record; it is a revelation of the laws of the Unseen God, which like Himself are perfect, eternal, and immutable.

I might confirm these observations by a special instance— by an application of this method to any one of those epochs which I have pointed out. But I have already trespassed long upon your patience, and I am anxious to conclude this lecture by one remark. I warned you at the commencement of it against interpreting the history of other nations by your own predilections or principles or faith as Englishmen exclusively. I did not mean that you were to put off your nature, and study history as if you had no such personality. Quite otherwise: men must study themselves first, and all that is English is to an Englishman the greatest aid to help him in the puzzles which he will be sure to meet; and if he neglect to study history as an Englishman—supposing that were possible—he would deprive himself of the greatest light which the history of his own country affords for the understanding of history generally. Consider this island in its position—'a swan's nest in a silver sea'—an island, isolated and yet set near the mainland, jealously watching and working out its own independence, permitting no foreign interference, and yet continually, by God's blessing, not suffered to sink into selfish bigotry or sullen independence, but compelled to take a prominent part in all Continental movements. This is a type of its history; it is this which gives that history so much value. In it you have the history of an individual nation; but you have, besides, a reflex in it of all that greatly interests or changes Europe. You see, too, how those general questions are affecting its character as a nation. In other words, you have a great drama worked out on this favoured soil, of which the chief character is England. For the main events of history in general, but still more for the clearer understanding of those events in their bearings upon nations and upon men, there is no history, no study, which can serve your purpose so well as the careful study of the history of your own country. There are other reasons why English history demands this of you, especially as it is illustrated by an uninterrupted lamp —I mean its literature. But these considerations I have not time to pursue at present. We have already skimmed an immense space. Will you permit me to hope that my task has not been altogether unprofitable?

ON THE STUDY OF ENGLISH HISTORY.[1]

I PROPOSE to address some remarks to you this evening on a very wide and difficult subject, almost too wide and too difficult, I am inclined to think, for us to be talking about on Saturday night, of all nights in the week; for you have been working hard all the week, and so have I; and instead, therefore, of trying to find out a method for working harder, and grappling with so tough a subject as the Study of English History, we might fairly be excused if we had devoted this hour to some lighter and more enlivening pursuit. One hears a great deal of talk just now of the 'Martyrs of Science.' I believe there have been more books than one put out under that head. But the truest Martyrs to Science, I conceive, are working men, who, after labouring hard all day with their hands, come and lay their heads together here of an evening, above all on a Saturday evening; and above that, if it be possible, over English History. Doing this may, I think, be justly called the pursuit of knowledge under difficulties—a sort of Saturday-evening martyrdom.

I have a very conscientious respect for your feelings and my own; and I am quite aware that I ought not by any adventitious dulness and prosiness of mine to add to the gravity of your task, as I feel I inevitably shall do. At the same time the blame is not entirely mine. You will be pleased to lay some portion of it—I don't mean of my prosi-

[1] A lecture delivered at the Working Men's College, Great Ormond Street.

ness, but that I am here in the place of better men—on the broad shoulders of our friend Mr. Shorter. I have the satisfaction to think that if I am here to-night to speak on the Study of English History, a good share of the responsibility rests upon your secretary.

You are aware that a great deal of discussion has of late taken place on this subject, and that gentlemen who have lectured within these walls have borne a distinguished part in the controversy. The question in dispute is whether history is tied down by any such fixed and positive laws as those which regulate the material universe. The discovery of certain great laws (as they are called) in physics has given to natural philosophy a steady progress and development, not so apparent in other branches of knowledge—not for instance, in history. Has history its laws, like astronomy, chemistry, and geology? Can it be reduced to a science as they are? Can we get at these laws, and so attain to some sure and certain method for the study of it, instead of floating about in a maze of facts and vague generalities? It seems, say the advocates of this notion, that human progress follows certain laws. History, therefore, as a record of that progress, must be employed in illustrating those laws, must follow those laws; and all that the enlightened historian has to do is to look out for those laws, and they will determine his method.

Well, no doubt, if there were any such laws for history, it would be very useful if they could be found out and applied. We might then hope to find one universal method for the study of history, just as we find in the physical sciences. I should not be here groping about in the twilight to find a method for studying history and recommending it to you as a great discovery. And you, had you more patience in hearing me than even you now have, would hardly come to listen. We should both have taken for granted that

the laws of history once discovered would have left us
nothing else to do except to accept and apply them. All
honour, say I, to those who have entered this thorny field—
who believe that history has its fixed and unerring laws—
and that these laws are to be discovered and followed. I
have so long felt the difficulty myself—so long have I been
perplexed, and so no doubt have some of you, with the
difficulty and uncertainty attending on all historical studies,
that we should gladly pay all homage to the man who could
find out for us the laws of history and a sure and scientific
method for the study of it. I think you and I would do him
as much honour as Plato proposed to do to the poets in his
model republic. We would reverence him 'as a sacred,
wonderful, and gracious man;' we would pour myrrh upon
his head and place on him a crown. But not, as Plato,
would we beg of him to go out of our city; rather we should
say to him: 'Oh! generous man, you must lecture to us,
not on Saturday evenings only, but on every evening of the
week!' At the same time, when he professed to have discovered the laws of history, he must tell us the laws. We
could not allow him, you and I, to go on speculating on the
laws of history, and giving us his speculations for the laws
themselves. If he had found the laws and was sure about
them, then the laws by all means; if not, we can't take
theories in the place of them—that would only add to our
difficulties and perplexities. With such a man we should
have to do after all what Plato did with his poet; and tell
him our College was too grave and severe a place for him.

Well then, until the divine man comes who shall have
found out the laws of history, as Newton did the laws of
motion, I am afraid we must go by the old beaten road, and
get at the laws of history by studying the facts of history.
There seems no other way. If, when this controversy be
ended, it is decided by competent judges that history has its

laws like other divisions of human knowledge, we shall have to get at these laws by careful observation and collation of facts; if it be decided that though those laws exist they are not unvarying, that men break through them or rise above them, we shall be where we were before. Both alternatives lead to the same result. There is nothing for us to do but patiently to collect and watch the facts.

But here is the difficulty—how to get at the facts; how to be sure, when we have got them, we have not only got the facts, but got them in the order and proportion in which they stand. The order of the facts is as important as the facts themselves; for—understand me—supposing a man who had never seen a watch in his life had got hold of all the several parts of a watch, and in putting it together judged of the relative importance of the parts by their size and apparent complexity, would he not turn the watch inside out? Would he not be liable to neglect the most important mechanism for its apparent insignificance? Would he not mistake the meaning and nature of each subordinate part, as well as of the whole? He could not understand or know the value or the meaning of any one part except he had some notion of the order in which all the parts ought to stand. Some knowledge of the whole is indispensable, and of the relation and arrangement of each part in and to the whole, before the meaning and purpose of any one part can be fairly understood. So it is in man's life; so it is in history. Isolate the facts from the whole, and you falsify their meaning and proportion.

Or, suppose some intelligent inhabitant of the sea—a mackerel or a merman—had found at the bottom of the ocean the legs and arms and various portions of a man, and endeavoured to find out their purposes and put them together according to his fish-theory of man; how would he arrange them, how would he judge of their relative importance?

His theory of equilibrium would be sorely tried. If he put the man's head upon his shoulders, his specimen of humanity would, by the law of gravitation, float with his legs uppermost; it would be worse if he tied it to his feet. He would put it into the man's stomach, as the most convenient place for floating such a senseless lump of ballast. And other members would be arranged, not in their natural order, but according to his hypothesis of their meaning and importance.

You see, then, not only the importance of the facts themselves, but also the importance of understanding the order in which they lie. The one cannot be understood without the other.

Now, in science, the physical philosopher has this advantage over the historian: he has the facts, and he has the order of them. He cannot substitute an order of his own for the natural order; at least, when he experimentalises before you, he submits to your eyes the facts, and the order in which he finds them. You have the facts submitted to your observation; you see the process, step by step, by which he arrives at his conclusions. His deductions may be wrong, or they may be partial; still the data for correcting them are open to all. You have the same facts to work upon as he has, all arranged in an infallible order—the order of Nature itself. The geologist puts before your eyes the specimens of strata; he analyses them before you; he begs you to observe the position in which they lie. There they are—they are his book; he begs you to look at the pages of it, and he tells you how he interprets it. These are the facts; this is the way he reasons upon them. His facts cannot be wrong—you are sure of it—though his reasonings about them may. The writing is the handwriting of Nature; it is sure and unerring. The only question is whether he construes it right. When Professor Huxley lectures to you on the formation of the lobster, he brings the animal before you; he shows you the shell and the claws; he tells you, by reference to the things themselves, of what material they are composed, how they are formed, for what purposes, at what period. The facts are the same to you and to him, and will be to all comers, now and hereafter; only he sees more than you do into their meaning. Another may come with a different interpretation, but his facts will be just the same —neither more nor less—and their order will be the same, No subsequent discovery of lobsters will alter them, though it might possibly assist in the interpretation of the facts already before us.

However, the illustration which I have just used from geology will show that the order of the facts is as important as the facts themselves; to the geologist the order in which the strata lie is as important for understanding the history and purport of the strata of the earth as the strata themselves. Alter the arrangement of the strata to suit your notion of the fitness of things, like the philosophical mackerel of which I spoke, and you falsify the whole interpretation. The strata are the same ; you may have departed very little from the natural order ; you may, like popular historians, have picked out and put together the most striking and brilliant bits; but, for the purposes of truth, you have perverted and confused it all, and the farther you proceed the more hopeless grow your error and confusion.

Here, then, the historian differs widely from the scientific enquirer. For the historian has to take his facts in the main on the testimony of others. It is very difficult for him to be assured that they were exactly such as they are reported. And then he himself exercises a principle of selection and rejection, as the scientific enquirer does; but with this difference, that you do not know what he rejects, and cannot easily get at it. The omissions are not so obvious—

not in the way, like the facts of Natural History. Besides, the historian rarely follows at the rear of his facts. He leads them, not they him, at least in modern histories. He has some notion to. work out beforehand; some hero whose acts are to be put forward with prominence; and he is apt, in consequence, to measure the importance of things and persons accordingly; to form a picture of his own, arranging his personages and grouping his scenes according to his own conception. The artistic feeling, even in writers of a high order, leads them to give a completeness and roundness to their work which is not found in nature. The historian can seldom separate himself from the artist. In science it is otherwise. And, in this difference of the two, one is reminded of the caution of Lord Bacon: 'If the great Work-Master had been of human disposition, He would have cast the stars into some pleasant and beautiful works and orders, like the frets on the roofs of houses, whereas one can scarce find a posture in square or triangle or straight line amongst such an infinite number; so differing an harmony there is between the spirit of man and the spirit of nature.'

I dare say some of you, who have been engaged in studying history, have felt these perplexities. You have found the difficulty, first, of getting at the facts; next, of getting them in their true order and not substituting an order of your own. You have found the difficulty of getting anything like a tolerable sketch or notion of the period, and the relation of its different parts and their proportion. And, unless a man is very much in love indeed with some one line of enquiry or some one-sided view, the more he ponders over it, the more he feels the want of being able to trace any fact in connection with all its bearings and surroundings. He gets a suspicion that he may have exaggerated its proportions, or at least that he cannot completely master its significance by looking at it in its isolation. You'll understand what I mean by an illustration. Suppose a man had a cutting before him from a geographical map of a range of mountains and of them only, and he kept this constantly before his eyes. By watching it narrowly and considering it again and again, he would draw out of it much valuable knowledge—the height, the shape, the formation of the range. He would begin to see how the rivers spring in it that watered the earth; how the clouds collected about it and modified the temperature and the currents of the wind; how the rain and the storms washed down its sides and carried a fertile soil to the valleys below; how people collected about the slopes or the foot of it; how all sorts of animals and vegetation were thus possible, which would not be possible in more level or exposed regions; how, in short, in one way or another, the whole condition of the material world and even of man himself was dependent on these mountains. And he would naturally think that mountains were the most important things to study in geography; and, being thus important, he would be inclined to exaggerate their importance. But he must extend his map. He cannot understand these mountains well without seeing their relations to the surrounding country. He gets a map, and he finds that, important as these mountains are, there is another element, less obvious perhaps to first sight, the most yielding and soft and impassible, which is here more active and energetic, out of which these mountains have been thrown up. And, perhaps going farther, he finds other powers at work, still more subtle and hidden in their influence, and more potent than those which in his less experienced glance seemed to him all-powerful. If this is not like the error into which the skilful historian falls, who devotes himself to illustrating a particular side of English history, it is a common error into which the unskilled enquirer falls. This or that side, this or that portion of the history, seems to him the all-in-all important. And he has not the safeguard which the geographer possesses. The geographer's map saves him from this danger. He cannot isolate for consideration any one physical peculiarity of the earth without his eye having wandered consciously or unconsciously over the whole. He, like the geologist, has the advantage of a fixed natural order to keep him steady; and he feels that that order is as important to the mastering of Nature as the facts themselves. It prevents him from substituting the harmony of his own spirit for hers.

These, then, are the difficulties of the student of history; these are the two things he has to master—the facts and their order; for, as to theory and speculation about them, they will come fast enough without being provided for. And fast enough will come laws and philosophy of history—too fast, even before the facts, if you call for them. You, readers of John Bunyan, remember how Mr. Talkative intrudes himself unbidden and unwelcome on Christian and Faithful, and what smooth and convenient theories he has for the great realities with which the two pilgrims have to grapple—theories, like French kid gloves, made to fit all fingers, large, small, clean or dirty. You will remember how hard they find it to get rid of this respectable but pertinacious elector of the good town 'Destruction.' That's like all theories—theories of history in particular—they come unbidden, and make such a dust and a clatter about a man's ears, the poor miserable little facts have no chance at all, and generally slip away or get strangled in the mêlée; the orators of 'Destruction' have it all their own way. And you, friends, must pardon me for saying that these sturdy and independent electors of the City of Destruction are quite as apt to find favour with you as with us. The world is pretty fairly divided between the men who have brains and no facts, and the men who have facts and no brains.

But suppose that you and I don't want theories about history, but the history itself; suppose that we are willing to bring our brains to the facts, or, if you like, facts to our brains; in Bacon's quaint metaphor, to solemnise a marriage between the mind and external realities; to find the order of nature and not make one. Is it possible? It were worth trying, even if the possibility were a small one. A man who knows only a few facts about a small portion of the earth, is better off in his knowledge than he who has the finest and most magnificent theory with no such basement of fact. If we could do a little only, that little would be worth doing. And it seems to me that something may be done. I have no theory to propound. I can give you nothing more than the result of my own experience and observation. Not worth much, you will say, at the best—worthless if it be taken for a fixed rule or system, and be not modified according to each man's wants and requirements. But what I say is perfectly feasible, not only to the man of much leisure, but for you, who have not much leisure and cannot command many books. I hope the time will come when libraries of good books will be more generally established for working men in various quarters of our large towns. That ought to have been done long since; it used to be done some centuries since, in all parishes in England, though in a more restricted form than is desirable now. But what I say will not be much affected by the absence of such a provision, especially to the members of this College, who have a useful library at their command.

Plutarch has on more than one occasion in his numerous writings compared history to geography, and the comparison has often seemed to me both just and useful. Now supposing you had to teach a child the geography of Europe or any other quarter of the globe, how would you proceed? I suppose somewhat in this way. First, taking a map of the world, you would endeavour to give the child some general idea of it as a whole. You would show the position and size of Europe, or of any other quarter of the globe which you wish to illustrate, and its more striking and obvious characteristics by a comparison with the other portions. Then dropping them, you would draw the child's attention to that quarter of the globe, let us say Europe, which is to be the subject of your instructions. Beginning with a map of Europe, which you would demand of the child to keep steadily in his eye, you would then begin to point out to it the broader features—the general shape, the coast line, the ranges of mountains, the rivers and lakes. You would descend to its subdivisions into kingdoms, then to its great cities, and show where they were placed. You would then take one great city, speak of the number of its inhabitants, their occupation, their government, the great quarters into which it was divided, the more remarkable buildings, the antiquities, the historical associations connected with them, and the like. You would go on again and again, repeating the same process, advancing from larger to smaller divisions; from the whole to the several parts.

Now this analogy appears to me to offer a very valuable hint for the study of English history, whether for yourselves or for the purpose of teaching it to others. First of all, it follows the natural order; secondly, it avoids arbitrary divisions—a great snare in all pursuit of knowledge; and, thirdly, it keeps before the mind the relation of the parts of the subject to the whole and to one another.

Of course we have no map in English history as we have of England or Europe. It cannot be represented before the eye as the map represents it; and any attempt to construct such a map for the purposes of history would be ineffectual. But let us consider the matter in this way. Let us, in the first instance, take the history of England as a whole. Well, then, that is the history of nineteen centuries, of a country standing by itself, yet on the very verge of the Continent, growing with a prosperity that has seldom known any check from century to century—from the first hour when Christ was born to this present hour in which we are met together in this room. That is a wonderful reflection, if we could adequately grasp it. Like the island itself, the history of this country stands on the verge of the Old World; but the vigour of its race, the knitting up of its bones and sinews, the growth of its stature, have been all along in these new centuries of the Christian era. Other countries, like Spain, France, and Italy, started before; their cradle is in old pagan Roman times—when Rome was at the strongest, and stamped its character and its literature and its modes of thought with a heel of iron on its subject provinces. The old national life had died out before the tramp of the conqueror; and when he died too, there was nothing but his feeble and fearful ghost to take his place. Other countries, like Germany, started later; the history of England was never parallel with the rest of Christendom. But not to insist on this, what will a thoughtful man, pondering over this fact—the totality and continuance of English history—gain? You see, I am not asking you to hunt after abstruse facts and theories about English history; I ask you to do, as you would ask another, to whom you might wish to teach geography—to keep your eyes and thoughts steady upon the open and obvious facts, and try to spell out their meaning. A man whose hands are well occupied, and who has little time to turn over books, can do this. He can try to master the great divisions of English history, and its prominent facts, at his work, or walking backwards or forwards to it, or at odd intervals. Now this long history of nineteen centuries, what does it mean? Well, first, that this is an old country, not a new one; that it has the rich experience of past years to fall back upon; that, on the whole, it has no reason to be ashamed or unthankful for its past history. It may stand up among the confederacy of nations and not be abashed. But how will these things affect the general character and the actions of the nation? If, in the hackneyed phrase, 'the child is the father of the man,' the very history of a people who have remained upon the same spot generation after generation must have very potent effect on the succeeding ages. The influences by which the present race of men are surrounded, the treasures of art and polity and literature gathered up for them by the care and forethought of their forefathers, form the most subtle, because the least noticeable impressions. Here is an institution which takes us back to the days of King Alfred; there is a House of Commons which has talked and argued and kept Argus eyes on the public purse since the days of the first Edwards. Here is a bit of a wall contemporary with the times when a Roman garrison was posted on Cornhill, and an altar to Apollo usurped the site of St. Paul's. Here is an abbey where the first missionary preached the news of the Gospel under an oak to our Anglo-Saxon forefathers. Here is a cathedral which grew out of that new-born faith, connecting with the highest development of the spiritual nature of man the most spiritual embodiment of Christian art. Follow a crowd of workmen on a holiday to Westminster, 'and here,' one says to his children, 'is the tomb of Edward the Confessor, the last of the Saxons; and here is Edward the Black Prince, who fought at Cressy and Poictiers; and here is one general or naval worthy who carried England's flag by sea or land over countries never traversed before; and here are worthies not less renowned who built steamers, wrote history, cured the small-pox; or poets, gone to their rest ages ago, as freshly remembered as if they were living among us to-day.' We are not monks, but we do not want to part with our abbeys and cathedrals, nor yet with the good they may have wrought out for us; we are only plain men here—the Harrises, the Joneses, the Tom Browns, working hard, with no visions of garters or coronets; but we do not want to sweep away from their tombs, pedestals, and niches the old worthies of England, whose names run deep down into the peerage. I suspect we are not all Conservatives here, but we are conservative enough to preserve the glories of England intact and entire, and save the memories of those who have been instrumental under God in making her what she is. And more than once have I seen the most uncompromising of radical reformers, with his head and tongue full of the evils of things established, turn a very sincere because a very unconscious Conservative in Westminster Abbey or some old cathedral.

These are some, not the least important, results of a history like ours, which measures its length through so many centuries; has in it the elements of so much stability connected with so much of progress, as a man would see by comparing the things already mentioned with the no less wonderful effects of our vast colonial possessions; so much of the staidness, unity, fixedness of the old, with the rapidity, energy, variableness of the new; so much of the tranquil grandeur, quiet simplicity, calmness and contemplation of the old order, with the vigour and creative energy of the new.

But I must leave this part of my subject, as my object is only to illustrate. I only want to show that a working man by thinking over the great facts of English history may draw out of them, by his own single strength and without the help of books, the very life of the history. I give you these examples of my meaning. But pondering over the facts yourselves, you will bring out of them at every new effort much better results than these.

Now you have got your loaf; and turned it carefully

over, weighed it and measured it as good economists do; looked at the upper crust and the lower, before you begin to break it up; and on looking at it carefully, and turning first one way, then another, you find it separates itself quite naturally into two parts—before and after the Reformation. This is the broadest and simplest division of English history. But before you lay aside either part, or proceed to their separate examination, it will be as well to compare them and see how they differ from each other. For these differences will run throughout them and affect all their other characteristics. They will be great features in your historical map, to apply my old illustration. What are those differences? They are all so important, it is hard to say which is the most so. Well, the most striking are these: In the earlier portion there is a sense of a common Christendom under one spiritual and visible head. Not so in the latter: instead of it we have a national sovereign, acknowledging no superior under heaven—an independent sovereign ruling over an independent people, considering that their spiritual welfare is his concern as much as their temporal, and that for both he is accountable to God alone. It is impossible to overlook the importance of this new theory of kingly government—or rather this new development of it in all the great political, moral, and religious discussions since the Reformation. It is impossible to take up an ordinary newspaper paragraph at this day, to attend any debate about church-rates, or education, or separation of Church and State, or the duties of the Church, or the duties of the State, and not see that all of them are intimately connected with the apprehension or misapprehension of this doctrine of the Royal Supremacy. It marks off sharply the history of England before and after the Reformation.

With this fact of a common Christendom under one spiritual head, there was necessarily connected the persuasion, not only of the superiority of the spiritual to the temporal authority, but of the essential disparity between them, as if the one were of heaven and the other of earth; and of the laws, as if the laws of the Church rested on a divine sanction, not so the laws of man. The spiritual was not the life and soul of the temporal, but separated from it by a broad and impassable line. I cannot stop to point out how deeply this conviction was at the root of all history and all the great disputes in history before the Reformation. For with this spiritual head of a common Christendom there was another great fact connected—the existence of a common language in which its teachings, decisions, and proceedings should be conveyed, which should be associated with it, which should be the special distinction and privilege of its ministers and all who are appointed to carry out its functions;—I mean the Latin language, which thus became the inheritance of the learned, and distinguished the learned man from the lewd man or the layman. And thus learning became the peculiar privilege of a few; was circumscribed to those subjects which are in the main only interesting to the few; and was tied up to those forms which are only used or understood by the learned. And here is a difference incredibly wide between our history before and after the Reformation—not merely that literature is now in the vulgar tongue and then was in Latin, not merely that all its forms and subjects are more popular now, not merely that it deals with subjects which come home 'to all men's business and bosoms,' but that it may and ought to do so; that it is as much the inheritance of the laity and the unlearned as of a special class; that it is a gift for all, and not confined to a favoured few. Conceive what an impregnable buttress it would be to ignorance and bigotry at the present moment if the old pre-Reformation notion could be revived, that there was something unholy and unspiritual in communicating to the unlearned and the vulgar the reasons and mysteries of learning; that books were not intended for them; that this was casting pearls before swine; that if they had any books, they were to be such husks as only swine might eat, and no clerical man ought to peruse. And then consider what effect such notions as these would have upon lewd men's literature—how impossible it would be to persuade the learned that there could be any good in communicating the precious gifts of knowledge to men who delighted in garbage—how sharp the distinction between them!

Well, there are these and other characteristics, or rather broad facts, distinguishing the history of England before and after the Reformation, on which I cannot now stop to insist. I will suppose, however, that you have examined the two halves of your loaf to make yourselves masters of these differences. You see it is not a matter of much book-learning; I have stated only the ordinary facts you knew before, and which any man with a little trouble might pick up for himself. I repeat I only require of you to take the ordinary indisputable facts, which lie on the surface of every child's History of England, and then to compare these facts one with another, not setting up for yourselves any theory or assuming arbitrary arrangements and divisions, but to torture these facts and make them give you an answer—to pin them down, and not let them out of your sight, till you have got their riddle out of them!

Now, then, to proceed to the further examination of these two divisions—the history of England before and after the Reformation. My remarks will apply equally to both divisions; and if any student has the time or the inclination to master both, I would advise him to apply the same method, or nearly the same, to both. But if he has not, and if he desires to study the earlier period no farther than is necessary to master the more recent, he must apply the rule already laid down, contenting himself with an acquaintance with the more prominent details. What I mean will appear more evident in the sequel.

Now, on examining these two divisions, we find them easily and naturally dividing themselves into dynasties and reigns. But the earlier portion divides into epochs, which the latter does not; and for the student who does not interest himself much in this early period, it will be advisable to study these epochs without breaking them up into reigns. As thus; the earliest of these epochs is the Roman, extending to the middle of the fifth century; and to understand this he need do no more than read the life of the Roman governor of Great Britain under the Romans—Julius Agricola; if possible, some English translation of his Life by the historian Tacitus—this by all means, I repeat, if possible. For it will give him the best idea of a cultivated Roman nobleman in the days of the Empire; it will let him into the secret of the influence of the great Republic; it will show him what sort of Romans these were, to whom St. Paul wrote, with their high sense of law, justice, and subordination, and by what arts they conquered and they cultivated. Read, therefore, by all means, this Life of the great Roman by the greatest of Roman historians; it will repay your perusal every way, as the most important historical illustration of the occupation of England by the Romans, as the most masterly biography that ever was, as great in its way as one of Shakspeare's plays; read it in Tacitus, and when you have read it once read it again. You can get a map of Roman Britain for two or three pence, and with this before you, and a workman's eye on the division into provinces, the camps, the roads, the rudimentary towns, and Tacitus in your hands, you will get a clearer insight into this period of history than by any other means. Then comes the Anglo-Saxon epoch, from the middle of the fifth century to the Norman invasion in the middle of the eleventh. Milton called this period of our history a battle of kites and crows. Well, it was not quite that. The order of it, after a little observation, is not so confused as it seems at first sight It will be enough for you to remember that it is eventually a struggle for supremacy between the settlements along the south coast of the island, consisting mainly of pure Saxon blood; along the east coast, where the old Danish paganism was strongly mixed up with the Anglo-Saxon settlers; and the middle counties, where Roman, Celt, and Saxon were welded together. The struggle ended in the supremacy of the South Coast and the establishment of the line of Alfred. The reign of this king stands out with unmistakable prominence: if any man has heard of English history, he has heard of Alfred. This, then, is the life for you to study. You may read it in Knight's Penny Cyclopædia—in fact, in any tolerable cyclopædia or biographical dictionary; and if you add perhaps to this the life of St. Dunstan in Knight, you will understand the prominent features of Anglo-Saxon England. Of course, if you wish to go farther you must read Bede's introduction of Christianity into the island, but that is not to be done yet.

We come to the Norman era, beginning with William I. and ending in Stephen. Now your method expands a little. It is worth while to look at the three kings, William I. and II. and Henry I., as exemplifying different sides of the Norman character. And here, for those who wish to work out the history carefully and are not afraid of a little trouble, my advice is that, putting aside for the present all English histories, long or short, epitomes or not, they should set to work and make out their history for themselves. There are thirteen kings before the Reformation, reckoning that event to begin with the Tudors, and fifteen after, to the close of William IV.—in all twenty-eight. Now if a man would buy twenty-eighth penny memorandum or blank books—not all at once, I don't ask him to expend so much capital on any advice of mine, but eight-and-twenty penny blank books for eight-and-twenty weeks in succession, he might set to work as follows. Let him first make a list of all the names of the Kings of England from William I. with the dates of their accession. With his penny memorandum book before him, let him look out in Knight's Cyclopædia or a good biographical dictionary the life of each king in succession, one life for one book, and, having read the life attentively, let him take down into his memorandum book, and in their order, a note of the principal dates and events of that king's reign, and leave one side of the pages blank. I can't tell you exactly what things you ought to take out, but I suppose they would be something such as these:—Of what race the king was by father and mother, and what sort of father and mother they were; how old he was when he came to the crown, and whether before his accession his youth had been in any way remarkable; what were his acts for the improvement or enlargement of his kingdom; if he fought any battles, where they were and for what ostensible purpose; with what nations he was at war; any great laws passed in his reign—any great institution or remarkable usage. And you are to take down these notes not as a formal history, but merely to help the memory—briefly, as you can best recollect them, as you would do in business or for work. Having made your memoranda, look them carefully over and see you have got them all right. Then put your book in your pocket, and go home and have your supper, if you eat supper, or go to drill with Adjutant Furnivall. Next morning when you get up read over your notes; read them again now and then as you have a minute to spare—before dinner, after dinner—any time; a minute or two now and then, keeping your book in your pocket for convenience.

That's enough for a week's work—for a fortnight if you are not in a hurry. I say again keep the facts—the great facts—steady in your memory, and leave the small ones for the present—and that in their order and relative position. 'Take care of the pence,' says Dr. Franklin, in his advice to thriving young men, 'and the pounds will take care of themselves.' But in the study of history and literature the converse is true; take care of the great facts and they will take care of the little ones; study the great authors and you will easily exhaust the little ones.

It is probable that some time will pass before you see the advantage of this method. These facts won't light up all at once into very brilliant theories, and enable you to fathom and explain all the mysteries and secrets of the British Constitution. It is not improbable they may lie dormant and not choose to speak a long time. They say that facts are stubborn things. So they are, in more ways than one; for they won't speak always when and as men would have them; and sometimes they won't speak at all. How you are to treat them to make them civil and docile I can't advise you, except generally to keep your eyes upon them. And as in the case of which I am now speaking; see at what they point in the feelings, thoughts, and morals of the people or the king in whose reign they happened; see how they hang together—compare and contrast them one with the other. Well, let us suppose that a man has done this for a month, and so he has come to the end of the Norman dynasty. Hitherto he has worked it out reign by reign—a reign a week; giving the leisure of a week to think over his memoranda of each single reign. Now he has got a whole period complete—a great drama in four acts. Now he can compare the end with the beginning; trace what causes established the Norman, what causes led to his fall ; what progress the nation made during the period—what were the main characteristics of that race—what their strength, what their weakness—what they did and what they left undone—what they destroyed, and what permanent traces of themselves they left in English history.

Now this is the way I would have a real man of work go on working out for himself, reign by reign and era by era; first studying attentively and thinking over each several reign in itself, then in its relation to the whole epoch of which it forms an individual portion. And I would advise him to note down on the blank sides of his memorandum-book any thought that struck him, whether it occurred to him of itself or was derived from books or conversation. The process here marked out is to be carried on through all the succeeding epochs of English history—through the Plantagenet, beginning with Henry II. and ending with a subdivision of the York and Lancastrian disputes, from Henry IV. to Henry VII.; through the Tudor, beginning with Henry VII. and ending with Elizabeth; through the Stuart, beginning with James I. and ending with Queen Anne; through the Hanoverian. And as he will find great advantage in comparing one king with his predecessor and successor, he will derive as great advantage in comparing dynasty with dynasty.

In these remarks I have said nothing of those great questions on which many books have been written—questions of the deepest interest to Englishmen; such as the constitutional history, or the social; or the rise and progress of certain classes in the community; or of momentous periods such as those of Magna Charta, the Barons' Wars, the House of Commons, the Reformation, the Puritan or Non-juring controversies, and many others. I have done so intentionally. I would not have the student of English history isolate them from the times or reigns in which they appeared, if he would grasp their true significance, and not substitute his own or nineteenth-century notions about them for their true meaning, or a hard cut-and-dry theory for the real theories and agonies which gave them birth. When the grim skeleton of dry facts which the student has thus brought together, not without pain and toil, begins to live and smile; when he can look upon it as a great organic whole, and not as a clever machinery put together by the vices, wants, caprices, or even the benevolence of mankind; when, as a man, he can sympathise with the struggles, the aspirations, the despair and triumph of humanity, in ages long gone by, and under forms very different from those with which he is familiar, then he may turn to systematic histories of constitutional, ecclesiastical, and social questions and disputes, always remembering that these are no more than the outward expressions of the great soul of humanity, its blood and tears, its throbs and living pulsations written down on the pages of history—its training and discipline, under the guidance of some absolute and unfathomable Will, so dark and so mysterious, yet withal so full of sadness, wisdom, and sober delight.

I have but little more to say. My remarks have been intended chiefly for those who are anxious to pursue the study of English History with somewhat of that order and certainty which they see is, and can be, applied to physical inquiries; and I have endeavoured to point out such a way, and to show how it is practicable to men of little leisure, and few books, like yourselves. It does not preclude the reading of historical works, if you can command them on any periods or questions of interest to English history. I believe it will enable you to read such books with much greater advantage and less fettered judgments; but if any man thinks that the labour I have suggested is too great, and he only cares for history as a rational amusement, my remarks, I admit, can be of no use to him. He has nothing else to do than surrender himself at discretion to whatever author tickles his fancy or his sentiment; only it is better to surrender to a man of some genius and nobleness of mind than to a blockhead or a bigot. And therefore all such a one will have to do, will be to be careful of making choice of the best authors; and, as a general rule to go with an historian when he praises and magnifies the men, actions, principles, and parties he is endeavouring to set forth to the admiration of mankind, and to withhold from him your sympathy and judgment when he falls into a humour of condemnation; for love is more quick-sighted than hate, and for one instance of unmerited praise you may find ten instances of undeserved censure.

ANCIENT LONDON.[1]

'ONE generation passeth away and another cometh'—so comes, so occupies the place of its predecessor, so passes again into oblivion, that neither the memory nor the imagination can bring it back, except in its faintest and feeblest outlines. Carry your thoughts back to the last generation, the last hundred years; what do we know of them? Are they not as far off from us, and far beyond our reach, as much faded into the dim past, as if, instead of being our immediate predecessors, they had drifted away from us, on the stream of time, ages and ages ago? Take this great city, for instance, and strip it of the things which have grown up in and about it during the last hundred years; reinvest it with its old fashions and customs; try by a trick of the imagination to put it back again into what it was in the days of George III.—and that is not very far—and what a strange place it seems! how far removed from our present notions and conceptions! how utterly impossible does it seem to us that it could ever have existed at all in such a shape! A lady, some little time ago, who had carefully preserved her wedding costume, showed me the bonnet in which she was married. She was a lady of some wealth, and her costume was made by the most fashionable milliner. Of the dress she wore, the bonnet was considered as profoundly elegant; it was precisely in the style of a coal-scuttle, and

[1] A lecture delivered at the Working Men's College, Great Ormond Street.

protruded three feet at least from the face. You may have seen such bonnets in old pictures. I have; and have thought they were caricatures. But though the thing was before you, it was impossible to credit one's eyes; you could not believe that such a dress had ever been possible, that it would not have led to a thousand inconveniences, and been immediately abandoned. And so it is with all old fashions and uses. Instead of belonging to the lady I saw before me, instead of having been part of the veritable dress of one not much older than myself, it might have belonged to a female of the Anglo-Saxons, or some British chieftain when Cæsar invaded these shores.

Well; now think of London in its old-fashioned condition sixty years or a hundred years ago, and you experience similar feelings of vagueness and impossibility. Strip it of its gaslights and policemen, and recall the dim oil-lamps and sleepy watchmen, the miry, ill-paved streets; the straggling suburbs, when ladies and gentlemen went backwards and forwards to Hampstead and Shepherd's Bush under protection of an armed escort. Bring back the days of the old stage-coaches, when all the conveyances that existed for transporting the inhabitants of this huge metropolis from town to country consisted of a couple of dozen or so of stage-carriages carrying four inside and ten out. Why, a single Brighton excursion train now conveys more passengers at one journey than all the mails combined did in their four-and-twenty hours of sixty years ago. Cram back into those couple of dozen stage-coaches all the travelling and locomotion of these days. It seems impossible for the world to have got on at all with such a state of things.

Or to take a nearer instance. This house, this room for example, sixty or a hundred years ago. Shut your eyes, and fill it once more with its old inhabitants. Then it was a most fashionable mansion, in the extreme West End, surrounded with notability and nobility; the Belgrave Square of the eighteenth century. Fancy it on some gala or reception day, filled with gentlemen; ay, in this room, sipping their coffee, or engaged in a game of ombre. It may be that some one or more of the party have ridden over that day to Hyde Park Corner, to where the Marble Arch now stands, to see some Jack Sheppard or Jonathan Wild drawn along in semi-triumph through Oxford Street—then a flaunting and irregular suburb—to make his exit at Tyburn; and here they are discussing the events and perils of the day. Was there ever a more useless or ridiculous costume? Powdered wigs, knee-breeches, silk stockings, long ruffles and shoes. Here is a gentleman whose whole ingenuity for a month past has been expended in contriving and adjusting the curls of his wig; here is another in plum-coloured satin coat and peach-coloured small-clothes, talking to his neighbour in colours equally bright and varied. Here a third is grinding the high-backed chair on which he is sitting with the hilt of his diamond-studded sword. One is astonished how the gentlemen of those days could have taken the air at all. Their silk and satin dresses would not keep them warm or fence off the weather; their three-cornered hats, not made for the head but the hand, afforded no protection from the rain, or from the long gutters and water-spouts, which shot their contents from the roofs of the soaking houses into the streets below, on the heads of unwary passengers.

Then those wigs! worn universally by all classes, high or low. No matter how poor the man, or how low his finances, a wig was indispensable. No citizen on a Sunday, no clerk, no skilful mechanic, would think of appearing without this appendage. He would just as soon have thought of walking about in his nightcap, or in no clothes at all, as show himself abroad without his wig. Those were the days when barbers flourished; when the spruce apprentice brought home his master's wig carefully suspended on a species of light block, with its last puff of powder and last turn of the curls, ready for church on the Sunday morning. Ah! those wigs, what consternation did they make among the ladies! How many a rich widow, how many a proud heiress, whom no sighs, no protestations could move, yielded to the charms of a handsome wig! The barbers were the most important men in England. Nay, so universal was the fashion, so indispensable was this ornament, that, as I have heard my father say, it gave rise to a particular occupation; and on the Saturday evenings, when men had left their work, and they were thinking of their Sunday dress, and their wives of their Sunday dinners, Jews used to go about the streets with bags full of wigs, crying out, 'A dip for a penny.' That is, every one who paid a penny dipped his hand in the bag and took his chance of the first wig that came up. It would happen that the man fished up a wig too big or too small, or a black-haired man got a red wig, or the reverse; or a most outrageous fit, in which no decent citizen or artisan could appear. Why, then he gave another penny and dipped again; and no doubt in this as in all other lotteries, he found more blanks than prizes. In those days wigs afforded great temptations to thieves. In the ill-lighted streets the gentleman returning from the theatre, or from a carouse— for men were not very temperate then—was a rich prize; if he had gambled away his money, his wig was more valuable than his watch. A brawny fellow, sometimes with two or three more, is passing by with a basket at his back; he seems a gardener or porter on his way to Covent Garden Market—the great centre of public amusements. In this basket a little boy is concealed, who suddenly clutches at the wig of the unsuspecting passer-by, and wig and boy disappear in a moment. These things look like fables; they are facts of a past age, not far removed. If we cannot realise them, it is because our own times and manners, though so near, have drifted away from them, and seem so much further from them than they are.

And to those ancestors of ours undoubtedly the manners and fashions and usages of *their* immediate predecessors would have appeared equally unreal, ridiculous, and antiquated as those of the last generation appear to us—as strange and as unreasonable, as they in their turn would have considered it, could *they* have been suddenly transplanted to the time when all this street and all its neighbourhood was covered with wood, and the howling of wolves and foxes resounded, as at this hour, and was carried on the winds to the ears of the distant city. Far away stretched the wood sloping down to the banks of the Thames; far away, mingling with clear streams, and skirted by green meadows. And long before the holiday folks came here to enjoy the fresh air, or delight themselves with the landscape, unobstructed by house or building of any sort, miles on miles, possibly as at this season of the year—(I am speaking now of earliest times)—came the Druid to collect from 'the signal oak' the sacred mistletoe. Here, after offering two white bulls with many ceremonies (is this the origin of eating roast beef on Christmas Day?), he ascended the tree in his white garment and cut down the glistening mistletoe with a gold knife. Or here, perhaps, at stated seasons, if Cæsar's account be true, he came to offer human victims on greenest turf; and amidst all things instinct with life and gladness, thought that the God of gods could not be satisfied except the life of man was shed for man.

We have come by a wide leap to the point from which we are to start—these Celtic forefathers of ours, who ranged the woods and wilds more than eighteen hundred years ago, before Cæsar came and dragged this island at the chariot-wheels of Rome, and forced it to enter into the career of

history and civilisation. What was the condition of the
country then, and of London in particular, is hard to say.
Forests and marshes everywhere. Great swamps in and
about London; so much is certain. Look from the rising
ground of Hampstead or Highgate, and see in what a basin
the city stands, surrounded with hills in all directions, and
every hill pouring down its tributary stream into the low
grounds. Then mark the number of freshets and pools of
which the names are still preserved, as Holy*well*, and
Clerken*well*, and Lamb's Conduit, and Holborn (or the Old
Brook), and Twy*burn*. Or ask the excavators of the Metropolitan Railway how many brooks have impeded their progress. If any city in the world, London might well be
called 'The Queen of Many Waters.' Abundance of waters
for fish; abundance of wood for game. Hares, geese, wild-
fowl; wild cattle, and with them wild boars, wolves, and
foxes. The beech, the fir, and the oak; milk, butter, and
cheese in plenty. Here and there a patch cleared at distant
intervals for corn; not much. For the forest served, by its
depth and intricacy, not merely as the best shelter and protection for the cattle in time of danger, but as a natural
fortification for the towns. A wooded enclosure, a deep and
impassable morass, which the nature of the country itself
suggested and supplied, were the main defences of London
and the neighbouring town of St. Albans, which Cæsar found
on his landing here. In fact, the forest itself constituted
the town. A deep ditch drawn across it prevented the
cattle from straying. All the towns in England, but London
especially, long retained this primeval character. Long
straggling streets and disjointed suburbs intersected with
parks and gardens; old trees, the relics and sole survivors of
larger patches of woods; whole trunks of mighty trees, and
horns and bones of wild animals found below the surface of
so many parts of London, seem to recall the description of

Cæsar: 'The Britons call that a town, when they have drawn round a wood a rampire and a foss; and into it it is their custom to retire to await the incursion of an enemy.'

To London, under the name of Trinovant, Cæsar is supposed to allude: 'the strongest city in those parts;' that is, in Middlesex. It was governed by a petty king who had slain his predecessor. The whole island was divided under such kings and chieftains; four of them ruled in Kent alone. In fact, England then was very much like what Ireland was some centuries after—divided between kings and Druids, chieftains and priests; always at war with one another; carrying off each other's cattle and wives; burning, or selling, or ransoming their prisoners. One would have called it a barbarous life, and fit only for barbarians; but Christian men of this nineteenth century who don't live in woods, who don't paint their bodies with horrible colours to frighten their enemies, are just as barbarous, and on a much grander scale of savagery than these savage Celts. Therefore we will abstain from reflections. Of this Trinovant, which fantastic Celtic antiquaries in after ages called Troynovant, or New Troy, and fashioning a history to suit their invention, attributed the foundation of it to Æneas and the Trojans, we get only very scattered and unsatisfactory notices. We leave it, therefore, under that name, and follow it under its more modern name of London. Under that name it was not known to Cæsar; but it is mentioned by Tacitus, whose father-in-law, Julius Agricola, was the Roman governor here in the time of Domitian. As early as the middle of the first century—in the days of Nero—the historian speaks of London 'as a wealthy and important town for the multitude of its wares and traders.' After a short and sharp struggle with its conquerors, the town must have shot forward with wonderful rapidity. At Cæsar's landing it was no more than a barbarian enclosure in a thick wood defended by swamps;

the Thames overflowing its banks; the rivers and brooks standing in heavy pools all about the low grounds. A century after it had risen to so much importance as to be worthy the care and notice of the Roman. How it got the name of London, or Londinium, antiquarians are not agreed, and all their guesses are so wide of the mark it is not worth while to recount them. *Lin* and *Lhan* are common Celtic words, so is *Lun*, or *Lunum*, an enclosed space or town. So London means the town of *Lon*—whatever that is—probably some local feature or peculiarity, for it is not the name of any Celtic chief or king. Some think it means the 'city of ships;' that may be so; one conjecture is as near the truth as another. But whatever may be the origin of the name, you must dissever from it all the associations connected with the modern name of London. In appearance and extent, and in the appearance of all the surrounding country, it would be impossible to conceive a greater contrast than between the early and modern London. I have told you already that a dense forest of many miles in extent reached to the very walls of the old town, and covered it in on all sides, except on the east and the river quarters. Fleet Ditch, then a large river, protected it on the west. The Thames, not then so deep and so narrow as it is now, spread itself out into a broad expanse of waters, flooding all Lambeth and the country in the direction of Camberwell. Even now at very high tides the river occasionally overflows and buries under water the neighbourhood on the south side. Yet since then the bed of the river has been much deepened, and all the surrounding country raised several feet beyond the original level. The vast banks of the Thames, artificially constructed by the Romans, with great cost and labour, confined the river within a narrower channel, scoured by the ebbing and flowing of the tide; continually deepened by dredging and ballast-heaving. This early London, though built on the rising ground, did not reach to the water originally. It stood well away from it; though the river then rising higher than it does now, and the soil on which the city stands being at least twenty feet lower, brought up the river at high tide very near to the city walls. This explains a difficulty in the early descriptions of London. I mean the existence of fords not far from it; and the apparent ease with which the Danes and others seemed to cross from one side of the Thames to the other. The bed of the river was comparatively shallow to what it is now, and its waters, spreading themselves to a much wider extent on both banks, flowed up into arms and estuaries, such as at Fleet Ditch and Walbrook, which have now lost all traces almost of their primitive condition.

St. Paul's stood on an eminence outside the original city, on a sandhill caused by the wind and the tides, at a short distance, as I will presently explain, and apparently on a lower level than now. The heart of the city was the Old London Stone, or near it. The east side which by nature was less strong than any other, was fortified by the Romans by the Tower, which then stood outside the city, but soon rapidly joined it. The natives trading with the garrison, gathering round it for protection and commerce, would settle in the district, as they did in other cities, and in case of danger would make no difficulty of abandoning their huts and retiring into the city. The limits, therefore, of the original town, from west to east, would be on the further side of St. Paul's and this side of the Tower. Of course I do not mean the present Tower, but a fortress which stood on the same site. The northern line is not so clear; probably Lothbury and Bishopsgate Within remained for several ages in the same state. The temptation was to extend from east to west, not from south to north.

I have stated that the present St. Paul's stands outside

the old city. I will now say why. It was once thought that this was the site of a temple built in pagan times to the goddess Diana. 'Diana,' says Fuller, 'was most especially reverenced, Britain being then all a forest, where hunting was not the recreation but the calling, and venison not the dainties but the diet of the common people. There is a place near St. Paul's in London, called in old records 'Diana's Chamber,' where, in the days of King Edward I., thousands of the heads of oxen were digged up, whereat the ignorant wondered, whilst the learned well understood them to be the proper sacrifices to Diana, whose great temple was built thereabout. This rendereth their conceit not altogether unlikely, who will have London so called from *Llan-Dian*, which signifieth in British 'the temple of Diana.' And surely conjectures, if mannerly, observing their distance, and not impudently obtruding themselves for certainties, deserve, if not to be received, to be considered.' Thus Fuller. But, unfortunately for this conjecture, which was long a favourite with London antiquarians, when the foundations were dug for the present St. Paul's, by Sir Christopher Wren, no bullocks' heads, and no remains of such cattle, were found; but remains of far more interest than these. St. Paul's *Churchyard*, though greatly shorn of its original proportions, and though no longer used as a receptacle for the dead, still testifies by its name the older usages to which it was applied, from times long before Saxon or Roman set foot upon this island. This was the great burial-place of the forgotten dead. Who knows, as he treads the sounding pavement, on what dust below he is trampling; what kings' bones are mouldering there; what hearts are there gone, to ache no more, of chieftains who fought for rule against their neighbour chiefs; of priests who pondered over the mysteries of the sacred oak, or people that saw with wonder Cæsar's arms first glittering on the Thames! Here

Sir Christopher Wren found a semicircular chancel of Roman work, showing that the first church had been the work of Roman colonists. Here on the north side were innumerable remains of the dead from British and Roman times. Layer upon layer, there they lay; there they lie still, the successive generations which possessed the land. Back and back, from Stuarts, Tudors, Plantagenets, Normans, Saxons —still further back to Romans and Romanised Britons; layer upon layer, race upon race. Here were Saxons securely entombed between sarcophagi formed of great upright and horizontal flags, embedded in cavities lined with chalk stones. Here were Britons and Romans mixed, the ivory and boxwood pins which had fastened their shrouds still remaining, to tell what these dead bones once had been; and, lowest of all, eighteen feet below the surface, were fragments of Roman urns and British funeral remains, testifying to a still earlier age when Roman and Celt alike worshipped the gods of their own hands or their own imaginations; when wolves and foxes prowled around the grim enclosure, or hunger-starved, swept down from the neighbouring forest, to glut themselves on the remains of slaughtered victims or the fresh corpse. But the fact of the Romans not burying their dead within the city walls proper, and for various reasons introducing the same restrictions into the countries which they conquered, is a strong reason for supposing that the hill on which St. Paul's now stands was not enclosed within the walls of the original city.

With the exception, perhaps, of the Tower, this was the only structure which could be considered worthy of Roman renown. Amidst so many other indications of Roman occupation, the absence of any great ruins of columns, architraves, or splendid buildings, has often puzzled the antiquary. Roman pottery, pavements, remnants of all sorts are found in abundance. At the building of the New Exchange, all kinds of fragments—spur-leathers, bits of glass and pottery, decayed ironware, nails, knives, &c.—were discovered; indicating apparently that this had been the site of an old pond or pit, where the Romans or Romanised Celts had thrown away their useless lumber, just as a regiment of soldiers in barracks might do nów. But nothing has yet turned up which can fairly lead us to infer that Roman buildings of any splendour or magnitude existed in London. In an excavation made in Lombard Street in 1786, the soil was found divided into four strata : the uppermost, thirteen feet and a half, consisted of artificial earth ; then two feet of brick rubbish, apparently from buildings ; then three inches wood ashes, as if the town had been built of wood and destroyed by fire ; lastly and lowest Roman pavement. That points to this conclusion ; that, in the time of the Romans (at least in the early period of their occupation), the houses were universally built of wood ; and, as we find from different sources, and might expect, the town was more than once destroyed by fire. In fact, as late as the reign of King Stephen—that is, more than a thousand years after the Romans settled in London—the houses were for the most part made of wood and thatched with straw. Even then London, as I have said, was not closely built ; large patches of garden and park intervened in the densest neighbourhoods. In fact, with the exception of a few houses, here and there, of a better sort for the Roman officials, this original London was little more than a village of mud and plaster cottages one storey high; something like a Scotch or Irish shanty. The walls made of wattled osier, to be found in abundance by the Thames, were covered with whitewash, a favourite decoration in this island from time immemorial, of which we have not lost the taste even now. The roof, covered with boughs, easily brought from the neighbouring forest, and lined with turf or stubble (for *tiles*, as the word being Roman shows, were of later introduction), sheltered the predecessors of those merchant princes who would disdain to house their pigs even in the dwelling of the richest British merchant of those early days. When Christianity was introduced and churches built, they adhered to the same fashion. And as late as the tenth century, Hoel Dha, King of Wales, who made for himself a glorious palace to outstrip his predecessors in magnificence, constructed it of hurdle-work; but to difference and advance it above all other houses, the rods of which it was made were unbarked and the rind stripped off; 'which,' says my author, 'was then counted gay and glorious, as white-limed houses exceed those which are only roughcast.' Such was early London; like all great things—like all at least which are destined to prosper and continue long, sprung from very small and humble beginnings.

But though the Romans did not give their attention to grand buildings, they did that which was many times more valuable to a rising colony than temples, or churches, or palaces; the foundation of all civic prosperity, at least of all things material, without which all other advantages are useless: they constructed roads. And how well they did that we all are witnesses at this day. For there is not a man among us here who has not trodden the roads they made, and there is scarce a great highway in this kingdom we do not owe to the Romans. They cut through the great forests so that a man could travel from London to St. Albans, without losing his way and being devoured by the wolves and foxes. Nay, if he wanted, though that was not often, he could go to the Land's End. He might before just as well have tried to wade through the ocean, as lose himself in the interminable windings and thick underwood, or steer his course by the land floods and estuaries all along the banks of the Thames. Get a parish in England now-a-days to make a new road with all the modern means and appliances, or to take off the turnpikes—and see what they will say, if you want to know how much you owe to these Romans, who covered the island with a network of roads. 'Verily this was a wise and understanding people.' It was the foundation of national unity, and might have brought these early Britons into something more of unity and intercourse if there had not been radical defects in them which made them an easy conquest to the Romans first, to the Saxons afterwards. 'Rarely,' says Tacitus in his caustic fashion, 'will two or three of their towns meet together to avert a common misfortune. So whilst each one fights for his own interests, as a nation they are undone.' A wise reflection, as just and applicable now in the nineteenth as then in the first century.

One great effort the Britons made under Boadicea to expel the Romans and such of their compatriots as had made common cause with the Romans. It is the story of oppression sharpened to fury by religious fanaticism. They turned not merely on their conquerors, but on their own countrymen; and records now remain of the atrocities which were committed at that time. There was an indiscriminate massacre. Aged men were slain without mercy; beautiful women, says the historian, 'were hung up naked and impaled, their breasts cut off and sewed upon their mouths, as if they were eating their own flesh;' an emblem apparently of that treason to their common country of which they were supposed to be guilty by taking part with its common enemy the Roman. 'And all this was done,' continues the historian, 'in the midst of sacrifices and religious festivities, in other consecrated places, and especially in the grove of their God *Andate* (so they name Victory);' probably St. Paul's, or some Druidic fane in the surrounding forest.

After this we hear no more of insurrections. Julius Agricola does what he can to introduce Roman arts and refinements into the island, and it is during this and the subsequent period that Roman villas and baths, walls and altars were erected, and the various Roman remains which have been turned up, and are being turned up and discovered, in different parts of England. No doubt the introduction of Christianity so soon after the island was subjugated prevented the development of those grander buildings which Paganism erected, and the cultivation of those arts which had been consecrated to Pagan worship. In their abhorrence of all that savoured of that national idolatry which had so long enslaved the people, the early Christians set their faces, with as much zeal and as little discrimination as the Puritans of a later period, against all learning, arts, and buildings which could recall in the remotest degree the superstitions they had forsworn. And hence the general scantiness of all those memorials of grandeur and nobleness we expect to find in countries occupied at an earlier period by the Romans. Moreover there was nothing to detain the Romans in London. It did not take rank as a colony; as Tacitus says expressly. In that respect, Maldon or Colchester in Essex stood before it. It was not important as a military station, nor easily defended if attacked. The disturbances the Romans had to apprehend were from the north frontier towards Scotland, or in the north-west towards Wales. So of the twenty-nine legions which at the close of the second century constituted the standing army of the Roman Empire, three only (consisting in all of 6,000 men) were stationed in England. Of these, one legion was at Chester, one was at York, and the remainder in whole or in great part was stationed along the wall from the Tyne to the Solway. Left to itself, or under the inspection of inferior officers, London enjoyed uninterrupted repose and prosperity. The invaders had become the best of protectors and benefactors. In fact, it was this uninterrupted repose, and the needlessness of exercising themselves in war or providing for their own defence, which rendered the southern parts of the island an easy prey to the Saxons, and incapable of resisting these audacious but scanty marauders. Fortifications fell into ruins as century slipped away after century and no enemy appeared. Commerce went on without a check. Insecure and exposed; its fortifications, such as they were, dilapidated; its citizens unused to arms—we begin to hear at the end of the fourth century of a change in and about London. Roving bands of barbarians fill the wealthy citizens with terror and despair. Relief comes; but it is only a putting off of the evil day; no permanent remedy. Half a century more and the Saxons appear, and we have arrived at a new stage in the history of London. 'The south part of Britain,' says Bede, 'destitute of armed soldiers, of martial stores and of all its active youth, was wholly exposed to plunder, as being totally ignorant of the use of weapons.' The story here is a transcript of what takes place on a larger scale, at the same moment, throughout the vast fabric of the Roman Empire. Robber bands, swollen and led by runaway slaves, scour the fields; the inhabitants for protection are driven into the towns; all communication is cut off, agriculture is abandoned, famine and plagues ensue, and in the midst of these disorders the Anglo-Saxons manage to establish themselves in Kent, and spread themselves by degrees along the southern side of the Thames.

It might have been supposed that Anglo-Saxon London would have been more interesting to us, and more important than Roman London; as Anglo-Saxon institutions, and literature and language seem so much more akin to us than Roman. But it must be remembered that these people broke up into several kingdoms with their several capitals, all of which were more important than London and threw it into the shade. Thus Winchester, the capital of the West

Saxons, from whom came Alfred and the blood-royal of our kings, is of more dignity and consequence. So Chichester is the capital of the South Saxons; and Canterbury of the first settlers. Essex, of which London is the capital, is little more than an appanage to Kent; and when Christianity comes in, 150 years later, we find the King of Kent giving away London to its first Christian bishop Mellitus. 'In the year of our Lord 604,' says Bede, 'Augustine, archbishop of Britain, ordained two bishops, one named Mellitus, to preach to the province of the East Saxons, who are divided from Kent by the river Thames and border on the Eastern sea. Their metropolis is the city of London, which is situated on the bank of the aforesaid river, and is the mart of many nations, resorting to it by sea and land.' 'When the province received the word of truth by the preaching of Mellitus, King Ethelbert built the church of St. Paul in the city of London, where he and his successors should have their episcopal see.' Apparently, therefore, if these words of Bede are strictly correct, the older structure, of which Sir Christopher Wren discovered the remains, had fallen into ruins during the troubles of the two preceding centuries. Perhaps the materials, as were common with other Roman buildings, were carried away for other purposes. With this exception the Anglo-Saxons added nothing to the grandeur or magnificence of London. They could not build as the Romans builded; they could do little else than occupy what their predecessors had left, and admire but not imitate the magic arts of a people which could produce such marvellous things.

In fact, for the five centuries which succeeded, London made no improvement in material means of civilisation; probably it went back. The Anglo-Saxons were a barbarous people, with no arts and no knowledge, succeeding to the inheritance of those masters of the world who had rifled all its treasures and sciences. Coming also from their native forests, accustomed to a life of adventure, fond of the chase when not engaged in war, they could not endure the confinement of a city life. They spread themselves rather in the country than in the towns; they loved the oaks of England and its broad expanse of sky and land; and their very religious foundations, the abbeys and monasteries which they built and endowed, in every shire, bear testimony to their rural habits. You must seek them in the country, not in the narrow lanes and contracted quarters of the city. Every nook, road, hill and dale; every stream, well, freshet and runlet; brook and burn; bower and hamlet; oak, ash and beech, testify by their Anglo-Saxon names to the favourite haunts of our Anglo-Saxon forefathers: they tell of that undying love of the country which nothing can quench—no length of city life, no luxury, no riches—in the breasts of their descendants. As I have said before, London then was more like a straggling village with large gardens and open spaces of green meadow. And if there could have been a spot in the world to tempt the stranger to abandon the fields and settle in the town, it was London. Even now it is a glorious sight, in the early morning, to stand on one of its bridges, and gaze on its majestic river; even now, before the light has completely dawned, and the outline of church, palace, tower, and manufactory stands out sharply against the reddening sky, and the shadows fall dark and dense in massive contrast. But when the river ran clear as crystal; when the swans moved on its mirrored surface; when early birds carolled from the trees and copses on its banks; when the green hills of Surrey rose in one uninterrupted sweep of pleasant grass and dotted hawthorns on the southern side, far as the eye could reach, probably there was not a more enchanting sight; certainly none in any other city of equal size. But strong, yet apparently fruitless, were the efforts made to induce the Anglo-Saxon to settle in the town and apply to merchandise. 'Let the merchant who has made three voyages,' says the Anglo-Saxon law, 'be considered of the rank of thane;' that is, of lesser nobility: and this be it observed, is the law of a people who made no difficulty of going to sea, who had crossed the sea often enough some centuries before. So all the Anglo-Saxon literature, as it has descended to us, relates more to the country than the town. And even in the well-known ordinances made by the city of London, the fines are in oxen, cows, swine, and sheep; the offences are those of stealing the citizens' cattle— offences for which the neighbouring forest offered great facilities, but indicating a state of life very different from that which we associate with cities. These Anglo-Saxons would rather have been bee-keepers, shepherds, woodmen, neatherds, yes, and swineherds, in the green fields and beneath the shade of the broad oaks of the forest, than stand behind a counter or sell cloth at a booth in the town.

But what they did not do in these earlier times of their occupation—never would have done with their own goodwill at all—that they were compelled to do by the force of circumstances. Events which look only black and disastrous to careless readers of history, are big with consequences of the last importance to the conquerors of the land. First, strange to say, they are reckless and improvident; with all their love of a country life, they are like farmers' younger sons, fonder of the freedom and enjoyment than the hard work of the country. If they have land, they either do not know how, or have not the habits of self-control necessary to turn their land to a profitable account. It was all very well when there was plenty of fighting to be done; when there were battles to be fought against native Britons and Romans: it was not much worse when, for want of such enemies, these

Anglo-Saxons fought with one another—Kent against Wessex, or Wessex against Mercia. But when there was no more fighting to be done; when the kingdom was tolerably well settled under one royal line, then came the rub. Oh, this land! this grubbing up of weeds, this hedging and ditching, this planting and sowing and harvesting—this eternal round of the same duties in the same place—so very different from soldiering, so unlike the excitement of knocking a Roman or big Briton over the mazard, and rifling his money, to spend it next day in gambling, and then fill his Anglo-Saxon pockets again by a repetition of the same process! Oh, this land! it will not stick by him, by any means; nor by any means will he stick by the land. So you find in process of time the Anglo-Saxon smaller possessors, or the more improvident, gave up the land, and took service which seemed more attractive, but was more precarious, under some chief; fought his battles, did his bidding, received his wages; had the honour of being in his service (such as it was)—like Falconbridge in Shakespeare's 'King John:'—

> A foot of honour better than they were,
> But many a many foot of land the worse.

The poorer freemen, unprotected, the prey not unfrequently to these adventurous freebooters—they were nothing better—are compelled to follow the same example. And thus the land, and the insecurity of it, drove these men from a mode of life, to which life in the city can offer but one counterbalancing advantage, viz. its greater security. Then comes another scourge—the Danes, who overrun the country and drive the defenceless population into the towns as the only places of safety. We know it by the name of the Danish invasion; it was an invasion of all the idle, restless, martial spirits, who could not or would not find means of living in a settled state of society, headed by Danes. But not Danes only ; or so comparatively insignificant a body could not have set the whole nation at defiance, as these Danes did ; burning and plundering it in all directions.

Now this mention of the Danish invasion brings me back to London again ; for that invasion, as you know, has left its permanent mark here, in the name of St. Clement's Danes ; and in the Danish names of the two churches, St. Olave's and St. Magnus. And now, for the first time since the Anglo-Saxons have come in, we begin to hear something of what these Londoners have been doing, which shows they have not been all swept away by their Anglo-Saxon conquerors. They have contrived to build a wooden bridge across the Thames. Wood was cheap enough, the river much wider, the current less strong in consequence than it now is. Still, building a bridge across the Thames, though only a wooden one, is indicative of considerable mechanical skill. Men must have been good carpenters, joiners, smiths, builders in London to accomplish such a task. Nay, more ; these citizens must have had a good sort of government, and a considerable common stock of money, to be able and willing to undertake a work of such magnitude. Moreover, the work was not skimping work by any means ; it was a bridge of some pretensions, such as befitted Londoners to build. 'There was at that time '—i.e. A.D. 1008—says the old chronicler, 'a bridge erected over the river between the city and Southwark, so wide that if two carriages met they could pass each other. At the sides of the bridge, which looked upon the river, castles and ramparts were erected, with breastworks, to shelter those who manned them; and the bridge was sustained by piles fixed in the bed of the river.' This is the bridge that King Olave attacked in the year 1008 ; for which feat the Christian men of Southwark founded a church in honour of his name ; and his own pagan bard wrote a song in his praise : —

> Thou hast overthrown their bridges, oh, thou storm of the sons of Odin!
> Skilful, and foremost in battle!
> For thee was it happily reserved to possess the land of London's winding city.

But these invasions of the Danes, as I have stated before, are bringing London into importance. The citizens are valiant men; they fight like volunteers. It is no such easy matter for these pagan Danes. The Saxons crowd into London. The King holds in it his Wittenagemote. A fleet must be built to resist the general enemy. Everything—even misfortune itself—is paving the way to give to London not only a more important rank than it had before in the estimation of the Anglo-Saxon, but even above other cities; above even the royal city of Winchester. It is still the old town of hurdle-houses and whitewash; the streets were not so broad, probably, as the grand old bridge—so wide that 'if two carriages met they could pass each other.' There were no floors to the houses, and no flags to the streets; for on one stormy night the beams from Bow Church were carried by the wind, in the year 1091, 'and fell with such force, that several of the rafters, being about twenty-eight feet in length, pierced upwards of twenty feet into the ground'— a sort of spongy soil, penetrated by the ooze of the river, and kept constantly wet by the want of free circulation of air and the near enclosure of the forest.

What was going on in the old town these many years is hard to say; it is scarcely noticed by the chroniclers. We left it at the departure of the Romans, and under these masters it must have thriven. All evidence concurs in describing it, even in the middle of the first century, as wealthy and populous—the general resort of merchants. Tacitus testifies that, in the insurrection of Boadicea, 70,000 Roman citizens and others were massacred, belonging to Verulam and London. He was not a man to speak extravagantly.

We cannot suppose that this number constituted all the inhabitants of the two places, or one-half of them. But suppose only 20,000 survived in the old city, then came more than two centuries of uninterrupted repose and prosperity; fresh settlers, fresh merchants. We know how rapidly population increases under such circumstances, especially where the ordinary means of life—bread, beef, and mutton—are cheap and plentiful. A goat, in Anglo-Saxon times, was valued at 2*d*. or 4*d*. ; a sheep at 1*s*. ; a pig, 8*d*. ; an ox, 2*s*. 6*d*. ; a cow, 2*s*. ; a horse, 30*s*. Reckon the shilling then at thirty times or forty times its present value, beef and mutton must have been cheap and abundant ; and that is clear also from the great number of wild animals—boars, wolves, and foxes—found all over the island. So were fish, wild-fowl and game. As for corn, we find the celebrated Emperor Julian, on more than one occasion, exporting at one time as many as 800 vessels of corn from Britain, apparently from London, for the necessities of the Roman Empire ; this as late as the latter half of the fourth century. Then the name of *Augusta*, given to London by the Romans at this later period, the value they attached to the city, the visits they paid it to collect the means and men for quelling disturbances in the island, are so many indications of the importance and prosperity of London down to the time the Anglo-Saxons settled in the south. When *they* captured London we do not know. They settled in Essex, of which London was reckoned the chief town, in 527; that is, seventy years after Hengist and Horsa landed in Kent (I accept the account given by Bede, as perfectly consistent in itself and with the general history of the Roman Empire). Evidently the progress of these Anglo-Saxons is very slow, as it has ever been. How they obtained possession of London we do not know. Very inferior events are recorded, but not this, by the old annalist. When they got it, what did they do with it? Forty or fifty thousand people could not have run away; there was no motive for putting them to the sword. And against this supposition are these two facts: that London still existed as a metropolitan town, recognised as such by St. Augustine; less than seventy years after it is still a metropolis of Essex, and the seat of a bishop. We can only, therefore, infer that the population of London remained substantially the same; its masters were changed; its aristocracy, whether lay or clerical, drew off to the more Celtic and secure parts of the island; the great mass of the population—its traders and artisans—remained behind.

If so, then somewhat of the same scene must have been enacted here as we know was enacted by these Saxons in the rich and luxurious cities of Gaul a short time before. This Anglo-Saxon barbarian had come into a life of good things. He ate and enjoyed himself; he stretched his great lubberly limbs on beds, sofas, and chairs of the rich citizen and fine gentleman who had fled or been reduced to slavery; he smeared his long locks with fresh butter, and sang very noisy and uncouth songs about Woden and Walhalla, to the utter disgust of all educated Romans and Romanised Britons —such songs as you may hear now in a village alehouse in Essex and Sussex from their genuine descendants; Anglo-Saxon poetry and music, which Anglo-Saxon antiquarians believe to be the rudimentary state of the sublime and the beautiful. Well, we have most of us seen an Anglo-Saxon baby establish itself suddenly in a quiet household—an embryo giant, with its round chubby cheeks and fat arms. What a row it makes! how it bellows and fights until it is satisfied! what a ready and promising appetite it has! how all the hedge-sparrows of the family nest are laid under contribution to minister to its wants! That done, the said descendant of Odin is quiet enough; not cruel nor revengeful

—rather amusing and lively than otherwise. That is a type in duodecimo of a much larger invasion of the Anglo-Saxon in London and other towns in the fifth and sixth centuries. The Anglo-Saxon did not exterminate; he did not destroy. He was no dyspeptic, but a healthy feeder, and he assimilated the good things he found provided for him.